Be a Fodor's Correspondent

Your opinion matters. It matters to us. It matters to your fellow Fodor's travelers, too. And we'd like to hear it. In fact, we need to hear it.

When you share your experiences and opinions, you become an active member of the Fodor's community. That means we'll not only use your feedback to make our books better, but we'll publish your names and comments whenever possible. Throughout our guides, look for "Word of Mouth," excerpts of your unvarnished feedback.

Here's how you can help improve Fodor's for all of us.

Tell us when we're right. We rely on local writers to give you an insider's perspective. But our writers and staff editors—who are the best in the business—depend on you. Your positive feedback is a vote to renew our recommendations for the next edition.

Tell us when we're wrong. We're proud that we update most of our guides every year. But we're not perfect. Things change. Hotels cut services. Museums change hours. Charming cafés lose charm. If our writer didn't quite capture the essence of a place, tell us how you'd do it differently. If any of our descriptions are inaccurate or inadequate, we'll incorporate your changes in the next edition and will correct factual errors at fodors.com immediately.

Tell us what to include. You probably have had fantastic travel experiences that aren't yet in Fodor's. Why not share them with a community of like-minded travelers? Maybe you chanced upon a beach or bistro or B&B that you don't want to keep to yourself. Tell us why we should include it. And share your discoveries and experiences with everyone directly at fodors.com. Your input may lead us to add a new listing or highlight a place we cover with a "Highly Recommended" star or with our highest rating, "Fodor's Choice."

Give us your opinion instantly at our feedback center at www.fodors.com/feedback. You may also e-mail editors@fodors.com with the subject line "Las Vegas Editor." Or send your nominations, comments, and complaints by mail to Las Vegas Editor, Fodor's, 1745 Broadway, New York, NY 10019.

You and travelers like you are the heart of the Fodor's community. Make our community richer by sharing your experiences. Be a Fodor's correspondent.

Happy Traveling!

sher

CONTENTS

MAPS & PLANS

LAS VEGAS IN FOCUS

ABOUT
THIS BOOK

Sometimes you find terrific travel experiences and sometimes they just find you. But usually the burden is on you to select the right combination of experiences. That's where our ratings come in.

As travelers we've all discovered a place so wonderful that its worthiness is obvious. And sometimes that place is so experiential that superlatives don't do it justice: you just have to be there to know. These sights, properties, and experiences get our highest rating, **Fodor's Choice**, indicated by orange stars throughout this book.

Black stars highlight sights and properties we deem **Highly Recommended**, places that our writers, editors, and readers praise again and again for consistency and excellence.

By default, there's another category: any place we include in this book is by definition worth your time unless we say otherwise. And we will.

Disagree with any of our choices? Care to nominate a place or suggest that we rate one more highly? Visit our feedback center at www.fodors.com/feedback.

Hotel and restaurant price categories from ¢ to $$$$ are defined in the opening pages of each chapter. For attractions, we always give standard adult admission fees; reductions are usually available for children, students, and senior citizens. Want to pay with plastic? **AE, D, DC, MC, V** following restaurant and hotel listings indicate if American Express, Discover, Diners Club, MasterCard, and Visa are accepted.

Unless we state otherwise, restaurants are open for lunch and dinner daily. We mention dress only when there's a specific requirement and reservations only when they're essential or not accepted—it's always best to book ahead.

Hotels have private bath, phone, TV, and air-conditioning and operate on the European Plan (aka EP, meaning without meals), unless we specify that they use the Continental Plan (CP, with a continental breakfast), Breakfast Plan (BP, with a full breakfast), or Modified American Plan (MAP, with breakfast and dinner) or are all-inclusive (including all meals and most activities). We always list facilities but not whether you'll be charged an extra fee to

use them, so when pricing accommodations, find out what's included.

Many Listings
★	Fodor's Choice
★	Highly recommended
✉	Physical address
✛	Directions
⌂	Mailing address
☎	Telephone
🖶	Fax
⊕	On the Web
✍	E-mail
✆	Admission fee
☉	Open/closed times
Ⓜ	Metro stations
▭	Credit cards

Hotels & Restaurants
🏨	Hotel
⇖	Number of rooms
♿	Facilities
†◎†	Meal plans
✕	Restaurant
⌦	Reservations
⤢	Smoking
ⓆⓎ	BYOB
✕🏨	Hotel with restaurant that warrants a visit

Outdoors
🏌	Golf
⛺	Camping

Other
☞	Family-friendly
⇨	See also
✉	Branch address
☞	Take note

Experience
Las Vegas

Elvis driving the Strip

WORD OF MOUTH

"Imperial Palace was unexpected fun. Go to their Auto Museum—
it's a huge parking lot with collectible cars, most of them for
sale . . . The cheapest we saw was $17,000, the most expen-
sive $1,900,000. A car previously owned by Marilyn Monroe
was for sale, and the price tag said 'make an offer.'"

—FainaAgain

LAS VEGAS PLANNER

How's the Weather?

Vegas gets a bad rap for its brutally hot and dry summers, but the climate here is actually pretty wonderful most of the year, with an average of 300 days of sunshine annually. Even during the warmer months (June–September), it's entirely bearable.

The highs hover around 100°F with no humidity, and virtually every interior inch of this city is air-conditioned. Just drink lots of water, and we mean lots and lots.

The rest of the year, expect still more sun and only the occasional rainy days (the average annual rainfall is 4 inches) and wonderfully pleasant temps, with highs in the 70s and 80s in spring and fall, and in the upper 50s and 60s in winter.

Freezing temperatures are rare, but desert nights can get chilly between late fall and early spring, so bring a sweater or windbreaker for your evening strolls beneath the neon-bathed skies.

Getting Around

If you're exploring the Strip or Downtown, it's best just to park your car (it's free at most casinos) and walk. To get from one end of the Strip to the other, you might want to take a cab or the monorail. For other points in the city and beyond, use a car. Public bus transportation exists (on Citizens Area Transit, or CAT) but is geared more to locals than visitors. Both CAT buses and trolleys ply the Strip but can take forever in traffic—the fare on both is $2. Cabs are relatively expensive ($3.20 initial fare plus $2 per mile and $0.20 per 33 seconds) but can be very convenient and worthwhile, especially if a few of you are splitting a fare. A good rule of thumb is this: if you think you'll be operating beyond the Strip during your stay, consider a rental car. Otherwise, just plan on using cabs. Look at it this way: the few dollars you may save by renting a car rather than taking taxis is more than made up for in navigation and parking aggravation.

The Monorail runs from the MGM Grand to Harrah's before making a jog out to the Convention Center and terminating at the Sahara. Don't be fooled into thinking it's a sightseeing tour; the train runs along the ugly backsides of the resorts. It's a little pricy at $5 each way, but the ride makes sense on weekends when even the Strip's back streets are full of traffic.

GETTING ORIENTED

Detailed maps showing hotels and other sights appear on pages 43, 95, 97, and 98 in the Where to Stay & Play chapter. You'll also find floor plans for many casinos.

POPULATION OVERLOAD

More than 38 million people visit Las Vegas each year. That's about 65 times the U.S. Census Bureau's estimated population of Las Vegas for 2004.

The Vegas Strip: Seeing it is believing it.

Safety Tips

Few places in the world have tighter security than the casino resorts lining the Strip or clustered together downtown. Outside of these areas, Las Vegas has the same urban ills of any other big city, but on the whole, violent crime is extremely rare among tourists, and even scams and theft are no more likely here than at other major vacation destinations. Observe the same common-sense rituals you might in any city: stick to populated, well-lighted streets, don't wear flashy jewelry or wave around expensive handbags, keep valuables out of sight (and don't leave them in unattended cars), and be vigilant about what's going on around you.

Las Vegas Hours

Hoping for sushi at 4 in the morning, or looking to work out at a gym at midnight? Sounds like you're a night owl and that means Vegas is your kind of town. There are all kinds of businesses that run 24/7 in this city of sin, from supermarkets to bowling alleys . . . oh yeah, and they have casinos, too.

Attractions, such as museums and various casino amusements, tend to keep more typical business hours, but you can almost always find something to keep you entertained in this city no matter the day or the hour.

Reservations

Not many of the attractions in Vegas require reservations, but there are a handful of exceptions, including the popular gondola rides at the Venetian and the Haunted Vegas Tours. And don't think you're going to eat at Alex or Nobhill without a reservation. It's best to book that ahead of time too.

Most of the top golf courses in town require tee-time reservations, and at the best facilities in season (fall through spring), you should book as early as possible. When in doubt, ask the concierge of the hotel where you plan to stay.

Visitor Centers

The Las Vegas Convention and Visitors Authority (LVCVA) (702/892-0711, www.visitlasvegas.com) operates a visitor center at 3150 Paradise Road, open from 9 to 5. Stop by for brochures and advice on what to see and do in town.

The LVCVA also operates a reservation and information call center (877/847-4858), with operators on hand to book rooms and dispense advice daily 6 AM–9 PM PST.

LAS VEGAS IN FOCUS

Early Vegas

Though westward caravans were lured to the area by its verdant meadows and warm springs in the late 1820s, it was the San Pedro, Los Angeles & Salt Lake Railroad that made Las Vegas a locomotive watering stop, spurring the formation of a formal town charter in 1905. Over the next few decades, Las Vegas grew from an important rail hub and supply center to a dynamic leisure destination, thanks in part to the recreational opportunities presented by the construction of the Hoover Dam in the 1930s.

Gambling, Bugsy Siegel & the Fabulous Flamingo

Of course, it's gambling that put the city on the map, and it's gambling that's kept it there. Casinos and hotels began popping up almost immediately after the state legalized gaming (again) in 1931. It was mobster Bugsy Siegel who helped transform the once-humble gaming "industry" from sawdust into neon.

Siegel aimed to build and run the classiest resort-casino in the world, and he recruited Mob investors to back him. The Flamingo Hotel opened in 1946, millions of dollars over budget. It initially flopped making his partners unhappy and suspicious of embezzlement. Within six months, Siegel was rubbed out, but the Flamingo began to boom in earnest, as did the industry throughout Vegas.

Sin City Today

Since the days of Bugsy Siegel, Las Vegas has reinvented itself several times over. It's grown in population from 25,000 in 1950 to 125,000 in 1970 to nearly 600,000 today with no signs of slowing down. In terms of tourism growth, the numbers are staggering—between 1970

> **WHAT'S IN A NAME?**
>
> So how did mobster Bugsy Siegel come up with the name of his famed casino, the Flamingo? Supposedly he was inspired by the long legs of his showgirl girlfriend.

and 2005, the annual number of visits to Sin City grew from a respectable 6.7 million to 38.6 million. Bugsy Siegel and his cohorts wouldn't recognize the town today.

If you're a fan of gaming, Las Vegas surpassed *fabulous* long ago, and is now absolutely *stellar*. But what's truly wonderful about this city is that it's actually developed into an amazingly well-rounded destination. Today, Las Vegas is one of the most exciting dining cities in the world and the variety of dazzling, outlandish shows and super-exclusive nightclubs continues to increase. If the city hasn't exactly become a major cultural hub, there's still enough to see and do both on and off the Strip to keep you busy for days.

Visitors also sometimes forget that Las Vegas continues to grow not merely as a leisure destination but as a great place to live, with a generally low-cost but high standard of living. The more than 1.7 million people who live in Clark County work heavily in the gaming and tourism industries but also in construction, the military, retail, and high-tech industries. With a favorable climate, great proximity to the outdoors, and so many fascinating attractions, it's easy to see how Las Vegas and the surrounding area has grown from a mere railroad supply center to one of the most dynamic and important cities in North America in just a century.

Important Dates in Las Vegas History

1829–40s Western traders camp at the present site of Las Vegas, attracted by its springs and meadows

1864 Nevada is admitted into the Union as the 36th state

1905 The city of Las Vegas is formally laid out as a railroad hub (it's officially incorporated in 1911)

1931 Construction begins on Hoover Dam and gambling is legalized in the state of Nevada (as is a law greatly easing residency requirements for obtaining a divorce)

1932 The Apache opens downtown, becoming the city's first high-end gaming resort

1941 Thomas Hull, a successful California motor inn entrepreneur, builds El Rancho, the first casino on what would later become the Strip

1941 Frank Sinatra makes his feature film debut in *Las Vegas Nights*

1946 Bugsy Siegel opens his famed Flamingo casino resort

1956 Elvis Presley's Vegas debut, at the Frontier's Venus Room, opens to mixed reviews

1959 Sinatra and Dean Martin appear on a Las Vegas stage together for the first time at the Copa Room of the Sands. A year later they join forces with Sammy Davis Jr. and the rest of the Pack to film the consummate Rat Pack-in-Vegas movie, *Ocean's 11*

1966 The Roman-inspired Caesars Palace casino-resort opens on the Strip, setting a new standard for luxury and excess and becoming the city's first "theme" casino

1968 Howard Hughes buys his fifth (and last) casino from the Mafia, ending their total control of the city

1971 Hunter S. Thompson publishes *Fear and Loathing in Las Vegas: A Savage Journey to the Heart of the American Dream*, a semiautobiographical account of his sensational drug binge, during which he manages to cover a law enforcement narcotics convention for *Rolling Stone* and a motocross race for *Sports Illustrated*

1971 Hilton becomes the first major publicly traded hotel chain to operate a gaming resort in Las Vegas

1980 The 26-story MGM Grand Hotel and Casino (today's Bally's) catches fire with 5,000 guests and employees inside. Hundreds are injured and 87 die in the second-worst hotel accident in U.S. history

1992 Wolfgang Puck becomes the first major celebrity chef to open a Vegas restaurant, with his branch of Spago at the Forum Shops at Caesars Palace

1993 The Dunes hotel becomes the first major Vegas property to be imploded (on its site stands Bellagio)

2005 Wynn Las Vegas opens at the north end of the Strip, setting a new standard for over-the-top opulence and high prices

Updated by Swain Scheps

CITY ITINERARIES

Two Hours to Kill

For the most part, the Strip—with its gargantuan resorts and Herculean traffic snarls—should be avoided if you only have a couple of hours to burn, unless you head to **Mandalay Bay**. It's at the very south end of the Strip with easy access to the freeway when you're ready to head out. You can tour the **Shark Reef** in about 45 minutes and then spend the rest of your time shopping at **Mandalay Place,** lunching at trendy **Burger Bar,** or hitting the blackjack tables. You could also avoid the Strip entirely and head to the **Hard Rock Hotel and Casino** for some last-minute gambling. If you're hungry, head to **Pink Taco** or **Mr. Lucky's 24/7.** If you need to stay near the airport, drive five minutes east of McCarran to the wonderfully campy **Liberace Museum,** an amusing slice of quintessential Vegas kitsch where you can easily while away an hour or more.

The Vegas Virgin

Head straight for the heart of the Strip to take in all that glitz and glamour you've been itching to see. Walk across the miniaturized version of the Brooklyn Bridge at **New York–New York,** get all Francophiled at **Paris,** check out the dancing fountains in front of **Bellagio,** and do as the Romans would and take a stroll through **Caesars** (the Forum Shops have great lunch options, both simple and swanky). Ride a gondola at the **Venetian** and join the throngs of wide-eyed admirers at **Wynn Las Vegas.**

You'll want to go back to your hotel to freshen up before your night on the town. Then splurge on dinner at a true destination restaurant like **Joël Robuchon** at the MGM Grand or **Alex** at Wynn Las Vegas. Don't even think about turning in until you hit the nightlife scene. Our picks?

A burlesque show at **Ivan Kane's Forty Deuce,** or **Mix** atop THEhotel at Mandalay Bay for the sweeping view of the Strip. Then finish off with some gambling or a show—we love Cirque du Soleil's O.

The Sophisticate

Enjoy breakfast poolside at the **Verandah** restaurant in the tranquil, nongaming Four Seasons resort, on the property of Mandalay Bay. Continue on to the **Bathhouse Spa** inside the chic THEhotel, the boutique hotel at Mandalay Bay, where you can soak in an Asian green-tea bath. Take a cab to Bellagio and cruise the **Via Bellagio** for Prada, Armani, Chanel, and Tiffany & Co. At lunch nab a window seat at **Olives** for views of the dancing fountains and Lake Bellagio.

In the afternoon, take a breather and relax by the pool of your hotel, margarita in hand. Or, if you have nonstop energy, head to the Venetian's **Guggenheim Hermitage Museum,** which has exhibits from the Guggenheim Museum in New York and the State Hermitage Museum in St. Petersburg, Russia. Just be sure to give yourself enough time to get ready for dinner (try Hubert Keller's **Fleur de Lys,** or Michael Mina's **Nobhill**).

End the evening by attending **Love,** the Cirque du Soleil show. Or, as an alternative to a show, hit the nightclub scene, checking out either trendy **Tao** at the Venetian or **Pure** at Caesars Palace.

Bring the Kids

Though the casinos aren't the place for your kids, you can still find plenty of great family-oriented activities on the Strip. If your kids dig animals, check out the **Shark Reef** at Mandalay Bay, home to hammerhead, zebra, and bonnethead sharks. Next, head to **Gameworks,**

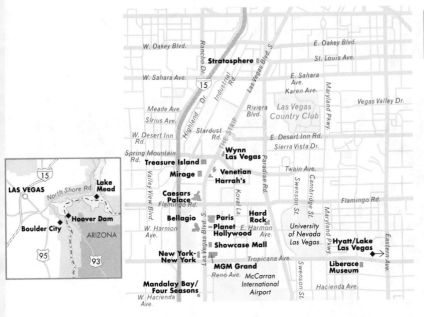

in the Showcase Mall (it's next to MGM Grand). It's a huge arcade and entertainment complex with tons of diversions for all ages. Break for lunch across the street in the lively Greenwich Village–theme food court at **New York–New York,** after which you might take a ride on **the Roller Coaster.** If you're up for an afternoon of thrills, continue north along the Strip to the **Stratosphere Tower.** Here, the Big Shot, X Scream, and Insanity–The Ride fly high above the Strip at 1,149 feet.

When you're ready for dinner, **Roxy's Diner** at the Stratosphere is a good choice. For a mellower but still enjoyable afternoon, head off to **Madame Tussaud's Wax Museum** at the Venetian. After posing next to Britney Spears and J-Lo look-alikes, go for a **gondola ride** on the Grand Canal through St. Mark's Square. Finish your evening by taking in one of the Strip sidewalk shows, either the **Bellagio** fountains or the exploding volcano at the **Mirage.**

Out for the Afternoon

Stunning desert scenery and outdoorsy diversions are much closer to the Strip than you might think. Make the 25-mi drive southeast of Vegas to **Boulder City,** stopping for a quick look at the handsome and historic **Boulder Dam Hotel.** Continue 8 mi to spectacular **Hoover Dam** for a tour and some great photo-ops of the Colorado River and Black Canyon. Next, it's a short drive to **Lake Mead,** where you can rent boats, take a cruise on the *Desert Princess* **paddle-wheeler,** or hike or sunbathe along the beach. On your way back to Vegas, detour to the glam **Las Vegas Lakes Resort,** where you can enjoy a dinner of sushi or mod Pan-Asian fare at the stellar **Japengo Restaurant.** (During hot summer days, plan your time at Lake Mead for the morning or perhaps very late afternoon.)

TOP LAS VEGAS ATTRACTIONS

Spectacular Spectaculars

(A) Will it be strange, cavorting Blue Men, or a sophisticated Cirque du Soleil acrobatic extravaganza? An afternoon comedy show, or Broadway light (90-minute cut-downs of the original New York theater productions)? A classic feather revue, or nouveau burlesque? Maybe you're just in the mood for a plain-old lounge show. Vegas has all the over-the-top razzle-dazzle you could ever hope for.

Gut-busting Buffets

(B) Buffets in Las Vegas—those tributes to extravagance and excess—are an event in and of themselves. There are still plenty of cheapies-but-goodies around, especially if you're willing to cast farther afield and explore some of the local casinos. But now that the city's become renowned as a gourmet food place, those ubiquitous buffets have followed suit. Loosen those belts, and get ready to pig out.

Rolling the Dice

(C) Never mind those buffets, swimming pools, spas, traffic jams, dancing girls (and boys, and water), wedding chapels, circus acts, and cavorting sea life. It's Vegas, baby, and you're here to gamble.

The Corner of Flamingo Road & the Strip

Casino-hopping is the best all-around way to explore this colorful, fanciful city, and the junction of Flamingo and Las Vegas Boulevard puts you right in the center of the action. Within a short walk are the Bellagio, with its dramatic fountains, gardens, and art museum; Paris, with its half-scale replica of the Eiffel Tower; and the Roman-theme Caesars Palace. It's an easy walk north to reach some of the Strip's other must-sees, including the Venetian and Wynn Las Vegas.

Siegfried & Roy's Secret Garden & Dolphin Habitat

(D) Of the handful of intriguing up-close animal encounters in Vegas, this lushly landscaped enclosure displays creatures you'll see in few places on the planet, from snow leopards to white tigers. Watching the bottle-nosed dolphins cavort about 2.5-million gallons of water is great fun, too.

The Stratosphere Thrill Rides

(E) If you're an adrenaline fiend, you can't miss the incredibly scary (and fun) rides perched atop the 112-floor Stratosphere Tower. The Big Shot fires you 160 feet up the Stratosphere needle, and both the X Scream and Insanity dangle you over the edge of the Stratosphere tower. These aren't for the faint of heart.

The Studio Walk at MGM Grand

(F) In a city that continues to dazzle foodies with its dozens of celebrity-helmed restaurants, this indoor promenade at MGM Grand has become arguably America's most impressive "Restaurant Row." Bring your appetite (and your charge cards) and eat your heart out at such culinary shrines as Joël Robuchon, Nobhill, Emeril's, Diego, and Shibuya—to name but a few.

Forum Shops at Caesars

(G) Opened in 1992, this chichi shopping and dining mall modeled after a Roman streetscape forever changed the retail and culinary scene in Vegas. In addition to stellar restaurants like BOA Prime Grill and Spago, this snazzy space contains dozens of fine stores, including Gucci, Fendi, Dolce & Gabbana, and Bulgari.

Legendary Nightlife

(H) Skyhigh bars. Burlesque. Wild dance clubs. Sophisticated lounges. Strip clubs. Beefy man shows. You can't go to Vegas and not at least check out the spectacle. So pick your scene, grab a martini, and join the 24-hour party.

Over-the-Top Pools

(I) The tanning booth is now a ubiquitous feature in the any-town strip mall, but it still can't compare with the old-fashioned poolside sun-soak—especially if that soak is in Las Vegas, land of toned bodies, cocktails, cabanas, swaying palms, man-made beaches, and swim-up blackjack.

Hoover Dam

(J) If you have time for just one trip outside of town, make it to this spectacular structure created during the 1930s—it's considered one of the seven wonders of the industrial world. Rising 726 feet above the Colorado River, the dam affords tremendous views, and tours into its interior are available. You can combine a trip here with a tour of the nearby body of water that the dam created, Lake Mead.

EDITOR'S PICKS

1. *Love,* Cirque du Soleil's new Beatles-inspired show

2. Fly-Away Indoor Skydiving

3. The Neon Museum

4. The Fountains of Bellagio

5. Eating at the Pink Taco

6. A weekend afternoon at the Hard Rock Pool

7. A ride on the Roller Coaster at New York–New York

8. An NFL Sunday at the Las Vegas Hilton sports book

GET TAKEN FOR A RIDE

You'd think the constant opportunity to win or lose enormous sums of money would be enough to make Las Vegas a thrill-seeker's nirvana, but there's oh-so-much more here to send your adrenal glands into spastic overdrive. During the spate of elaborately themed casino construction since the mid-'90s, a number of resorts along the Strip have developed wild-and-woolly rides and spellbinding try-yourself stunts. You really have to give special props to the twisted minds behind the Stratosphere's skyscraping rides, which were designed expressly to terrify people. And there's more—some arcades have excellent virtual rides that are just as fun as, say, driving a real stock car. If adventure's your game, these thrilling amusements are just your drug of choice. So strap on a safety belt, hold on tight, and read on for a sampling of Vegas's most exciting games and rides.

Adventuredome at Circus Circus. If the sun is blazing, the kids are antsy, and you need a place to while away a few hours, make for the big pink dome behind Circus Circus. The 5-acre amusement park has more than 20 rides and attractions for all age levels, including the world's largest indoor, double-loop roller coaster, a huge swinging pirate ship, a flume ride, bumper cars, several kiddie rides, a laser-tag room, a rock-climbing wall, and much more. Also check out the Inverter, which whips you upside down over and over. The Fun House Express, designed exclusively for Circus Circus, uses computer-generated images to portray a fast-paced roller-coaster ride through a spooky world called Clown Chaos. ⊠*Circus Circus, North Strip* ☎*702/794–3939 or 877/224–7287* ⊕*www.adventuredome. com* 🖃*$4–$7 per ride; all-day pass*

$22.95 ⊗*Sun.–Thurs. 10–8, Fri. and Sat. 10 AM–midnight (hrs are generally shorter late fall–early spring, check ahead for details).*

Circus Circus Carnival Midway. If you can't win the jackpot at the casino, try winning your sweetheart a teddy bear instead at this midway with more than 200 games. Here you can play old-time fair games like the dime toss, milk can, and bushel basket for the chance to win cuddly prizes. Every half hour from 11 AM to midnight, acrobats, high-wire walkers, jugglers, and trapeze artists perform free shows in the stands of the midway area. Get there at least 15 minutes in advance for a good spot to view the show. There are also clown-face painting and a state-of-the-art video arcade. ⊠*Circus Circus, North Strip* ☎*702/734–0410 or 800/634–3450* ⊕*www.circuscircus.com* 🖃*$3–$7, all-day wristband $24.95* ⊗*Daily 10 AM–midnight.*

Cyber Speedway at Sahara. Did you ever want to be a race-car driver? Well, here's your chance to get a taste of the action without having to risk your neck on a racecourse. First you get into a car about ⅞ the size of an authentic stock car. Then you buckle your seat belt and prepare for a ride that simulates the driving experience by moving your car on hydraulic bases. Meanwhile, you see the speedway rush past and under you on a 20-foot wraparound video screen. Each ride can feel different because you can customize your vehicle's horsepower, braking, transmission torque, suspension, and several other variables. ⊠*Sahara Las Vegas, North Strip* ☎*702/737–2111* ⊕*www. saharavegas.com* 🖃*$10, unlimited day pass (Speedway rides and roller coaster)*

$19.95 ⊙ *Sun.–Thurs. 10–9, Fri. and Sat. 10–midnight.*

Fantasy Faire Midway. The Midway is barely satisfactory for kids if you happen to already be at Excalibur, but if you're looking for the best arcade, head to GameWorks (⇨ *below*). The Midway is like a small medieval version of Chuck E. Cheese's, with skee-ball, old-fashioned horse-racing games, and a few high-tech video games, like the interactive Dance Dance USA. Check out **Merlin's Magic Motion Machine Film Rides** for a spin on a spooky roller coaster with Elvira, self-proclaimed Mistress of the Dark. There are a couple of other tame rides in this section, and you can try them all in about 10 minutes. ⊠ *The Excalibur, South Strip* ☎ *702/597–7084 or 800/937–7777* ⊕ *www.excaliburcasino.com* ◻ *$1–$2 arcade games; $4 per ride* ⊙ *Mon.–Thurs. 10 AM–11 PM, Fri.–Sun. 10 AM–midnight.*

★ **Fodor's Choice** **Flyaway Indoor Skydiving.** Here you can get the thrill of skydiving without leaving the ground. A vertical wind tunnel produces a powerful stream of air that lets you float, hover, and fly, simulating a real freefall experience. Airspeeds reach 120 mph. You can only make reservations with 10 or more people, but they close for private parties from time to time, so it's wise to call ahead under any circumstances. ⊠ *200 Convention Center Dr.* ☎ *702/731–4768 or 877/545–8093* ⊕ *www.vegasindoorskydiving.com* ◻ *$70* ⊙ *Daily, 10 AM; classes every ½ hr.*

★ **Fodor's Choice** **GameWorks.** Originally conceived by Steven Spielberg and the gaming gurus at Sega, GameWorks more than lives up to its hype—it's the biggest, most boisterous arcade in town. The multilevel arcade has more than 250 games, including Indy 500, Virtual Tennis, and House of the Dead 4. There are also several casual restaurants and 21-and-over bars with pool tables upstairs. ⊠ *3785 Las Vegas Blvd. S, next to MGM Grand, South Strip* ☎ *702/432–4263* ⊕ *www.gameworks.com* ◻ *Free entry, games cost $1–$2 each, $35 all-day pass* ⊙ *Sun.–Thurs. 10 AM–midnight, Fri. and Sat. 10 AM–2 AM.*

★ **Pharaoh's Pavilion at Luxor.** Inside the Luxor's pyramid is a gigantic atrium that houses a virtual treasure trove of attractions, including several scary 3-D motion-simulator rides in a giant stone temple; the city's largest IMAX theater; an authentic reproduction of King Tut's tomb, complete with gold sarcophagus and a small museum detailing the original discovery of the actual tomb by Howard Carter in 1922; a food court; and a two-story arcade. If you purchase the all-inclusive Passport to Adventure, you get access to all the attractions for a single price: $34.99. ⊠ *The Luxor, South Strip* ☎ *702/262–4000* ⊕ *www.luxor.com* ◻ *Attractions $5–$10, Passport to Adventure $34.99* ⊙ *Sun.–Thurs. 9 AM–11 PM, Fri. and Sat. 9 AM–midnight.*

★ **Fodor's Choice** **The Roller Coaster.** There are two reasons to ride the Coney Island–style New York–New York roller coaster: first, with a 144-foot dive and a 360-degree somersault, it's a real scream; and second, it whisks you around the amazing replica of the NYC skyline, giving you fabulous views of the Statue of Liberty, Chrysler building, and, at night, the Las Vegas lights—you climb to peak heights around 200 feet above the Strip. Get ready to go 67 mph over a dizzying succession of high-banked turns and cam-

elback hills, twirl through a "heartline twist" (like a jet doing a barrel roll), and finally rocket along a 540-degree spiral before pulling back into the station. ⊠*New York–New York, South Strip* ☎*702/740–6969* ⊕*www.nynyhotelcasino.com* ✆*$12.50* ⊘*Mon.–Thurs. 11–11, Fri. and Sat. 10 AM–midnight, Sun. 10 AM–11 PM, weather permitting.*

★ **Speed—The Ride at Sahara.** Launched from inside the NASCAR Cafe, the roller coaster uses magnetic technology to propel riders 25 feet down through an underground tunnel, around a loop, and in and around the massive Sahara marquee, accelerating from speeds of 35 mph to its fastest speed of 70 mph in two seconds. You stop at 224 feet above the Strip, then you do the entire path again—only backward. ⊠*2535 Las Vegas Blvd. S, North Strip* ☎*702/737–2111* ⊕*www.saharavegas.com* ✆*$10, unlimited day pass (roller coaster and Speedway rides) $19.95* ⊘*Mon.–Thurs. noon–10, Fri. and Sat. 11–midnight, Sun. 11–10.*

★ Fodor's Choice **Stratosphere Thrill Rides.** High above the Strip at the top of the Stratosphere Tower are three major thrill rides that will scare the bejeezus out of you, especially if you have even the slightest fear of heights. Don't even think about heading up here if you have serious vertigo. People have been known to get sick just watching these rides.

The **Big Shot** would be a monster ride on the ground, but starting from the 112th floor makes it twice as wild. Four riders are strapped into chairs on four sides of the needle, which rises from the Stratosphere's observation pod. With little warning, you're flung 160 feet up the needle, then dropped like a rock. The

WORD OF MOUTH

"The rides at Stratosphere—especially the X Scream—are insanely scary. A little tip for the feint of heart: wait to buy the ride tickets until you reach the top of the tower and are sure you want to do it. There's no refunds if you chicken out!" –SallyFin.

whole thing is over in less than a minute, but your knees will wobble for the rest of the day.

The **X Scream** tips passengers over the edge of the tower like a giant seesaw again and again. Sit in the very front so you'll get an unobstructed view of the Strip, straight down!

Another unobstructed view can be seen by dangling over the edge of the tower off the arm of **Insanity** (www.insanity-ride.com). The arm pivots and hangs you out 64 feet from the edge of the tower; then it spins you faster and faster, so you're lifted to a 70-degree angle by a centrifugal force that's the equivalent of 3 g-forces. ⊠*2000 Las Vegas Blvd. S, North Strip* ☎*702/380–7777 or 800/998–6937* ⊕*www.stratospherehotel.com* ✆*Tower $9.95, rides $8 each, unlimited rides and tower day pass $29.95* ⊘*Sun.–Thurs. 10 AM–1 AM, Fri. and Sat. 10 AM–2 AM.*

CHECK OUT THE RAZZLE-DAZZLE

Even the jaded, unflappable types among us can't resist the chance to oooh and aaah at a riotous visual spectacle. And Vegas exists to entertain us in ways that would make P. T. Barnum proud. There are the syncopated fountains outside Bellagio, the sensory-overloaded light shows at Fremont Street, and the nymphomaniacal sirens at Treasure Island.

Wherever you find resorts in this town, you'll find crowd-pleasing wonders. Here's a sampling of our favorites.

★ **Bellagio Conservatory.** The flowers, shrubs, trees, and other plants in the atrium are fresh and live, grown in Bellagio's 5-acre greenhouse. They change each season, and the lighted holiday displays in December and January are particularly dramatic. ⊠ *Bellagio, Center Strip* 🕾 *702/693–7111 or 888/744–7687* ⊕ *www.bellagio.com* 🔖 *Free* ⊙ *Daily 24 hrs.*

Festival Fountain & Fall of Atlantis shows at Caesars. If you already happen to be shopping or dining at the Forum, take a break to watch a goofy but entertaining laser-light show at the Festival Fountain, located next to the Cheesecake Factory. It features an animatronic discussion between Bacchus, Venus, Apollo, and Pluto. The Fall of Atlantis show, at the east end of the Forum Shops near the aquarium, uses lifelike animatronic figures to recount the myth of Atlantis. Both shows get crowded quickly, so make sure to get there early for the best spots, but don't go too far out of your way to watch either of these campy spectacles. ⊠ *Caesars Palace, Center Strip* 🕾 *702/733–7900 or 800/223–7277* ⊕ *www.caesarspalace. com* 🔖 *Free* ⊙ *Daily 10 –10, every hr on the hr.*

WORD OF MOUTH

"The Bellagio fountain show is as spectacular as expected. Watch it at least once during the day and once at night." —*caribtraveler.*

★ **Fountains of Bellagio.** Bellagio's signature outdoor water ballet, stretching across a lake in front of the hotel, was made instantly famous by an appearance in the 2001 remake of *Ocean's Eleven.* At the appointed time, more than 1,000 fountain nozzles, 4,500 lights, and 27 million gallons of water combine to dazzle audiences with dancing waters choreographed to music—the fountains shoot nearly 250 feet into the air. The best view is from the observation deck of the Eiffel Tower, directly across the street. Both the Paris and Planet Hollywood have restaurants with patios on the Strip that offer good views as well. ⊠ *Bellagio, Center Strip* 🕾 *702/693–7111 or 888/744–7687* ⊕ *www.bellagio.com* ⊙ *Weekdays 3–7 every ½ hr, 7–midnight every 15 mins; weekends noon–7 every ½ hr, 7–midnight every 15 mins.*

Fremont Street Experience. The light show's the thing downtown. Walk around Main Street after dark and you might find yourself slack-jawed along with the rest of the gawking tourists. Here's how the Experience breaks down by the numbers: the display is a little longer than the length of four football fields; consists of 12 million synchronized LED modules, including 180 strobes and eight robotic mirrors per block; and has 208 speakers that operate independently but combine for 550,000 watts of sound. Six-minute light shows are presented on

the hour after dark; it takes 31 computers and 100 gigabytes of memory to run the shows. What's all that mean? That all those lights are worth ogling. Beyond the Experience, the pedestrian mall is bland—you'll only want to bother with it as a means to ducking in and out of the casinos that line it. The mall is festooned with mediocre souvenir stands and a handful of mostly forgettable eateries. Live entertainment, ranging from mimes to rock bands, sometimes pull in crowds. ⊠*Fremont St. from Main to 4th Sts., Downtown* ☎*702/678–5600* ⊕*www. vegasexperience.com* 🎟*Free* ☉*Daily.*

Sirens of TI. This sexed-up, 20-minute-long free show includes a raunchy battle between the voluptuous Sirens and a band of renegade pirates ending with a Siren deejay scratching for the finale song-and-dance routine. It's more tacky than kitschy but worth a look-see, if only to watch the huge explosions. ⊠*Treasure Island Las Vegas (TI), Center Strip* ☎*702/894–7111 or 800/944–7444* ⊕*www.treasureislandlasvegas.com* 🎟*Free* ☉*Sun.–Thurs. 5:30–10 PM, Fri. and Sat. 5:30–11:30 PM, every 90 mins.*

Vegas Vic. The 50-foot-tall neon cowboy outside the Pioneer Club has been waving to Las Vegas visitors since 1947 (though, truth be told, he had a makeover and was replaced by a newer version in 1951). His neon sidekick, Vegas Vicki, went up across the street in 1980.

Volcano at Mirage. At some point while you're walking around the middle of the Strip, you're bound to see the Mirage Volcano erupt. The 54-foot fountain–volcano, on 3 water-covered acres, shoots flames and smoke 100 feet above the water below. Get there at least 10 minutes

BE DAZZLED

The beam of light atop the Luxor in Las Vegas is made up of 39 individual lamps. Each lamp costs $1,200 and lasts about 2,000 hours. The electric bill for the Luxor beam is $51 an hour, making the annual electric bill for the beam more than $400,000!

before the spewing starts for the best vantage point near the main drive entrance. ⊠*Mirage, Center Strip* ☎*702/791–7111 or 800/627–6667* ⊕*www.themirage. com* 🎟*Free* ☉*Daily from 7 PM, every 15 mins.*

TRAVEL THE WORLD

Yeah, yeah—we know you can't substitute a ride down the canals at the Venetian for a real trip to Venice, and the half-scale replica of the Eiffel Tower doesn't even come close to the real McCoy in Paris. But there's no denying the allure of having so many dramatic tributes to iconic attractions around the world all within the 702 area code. So go on, pose for a pic in front of the Sphinx or feel like an international high roller in the Monte Carlo casino—there's no other place we know of where you can spend your entire vacation with your tongue firmly planted in cheek.

Casino Hop the Strip

All right, globetrotters. Get ready to jet around the world without leaving the Strip. Take in Southeast Asia (Mandalay Bay), Egypt (Luxor), Manhattan (New York–New York), the French Riviera (Monte Carlo), Paris (ahem, at the Paris), Italy (Bellagio), Rome (Caesars Palace), Venice (The Venetian), and Greece (Greek Isles Casino).

Eiffel Tower Experience. Built exactly to a half-size scale, the Las Vegas version of the Parisian landmark rises above it all; three legs of the tower come right through the casino roof, resting heavily on its floor. The Eiffel Tower Restaurant is on the 11th floor and has its own elevator (which you need a reservation to board). To get all the way to the top, buy a ticket on the 10-person glass elevator that ascends to the tower's small observation deck (a caged catwalk) at the 460-foot level. Sure, the Stratosphere is taller, but the Eiffel Tower offers an incomparable view of the heart of Las Vegas. Plan on waiting in line. But once you're up there, you can stay on the observation deck as long as you want. After dark, watch for the dancing-

waters show at Bellagio, directly across the street. ⊠ *Paris Las Vegas, Center Strip* ☎ *702/946–7000 or 888/226–5687* ⊕ *www.paris-lv.com* 🎟 *$9* ⊙ *Daily 9:30 AM–12:30 AM weather permitting.*

Gondola Rides. Let a gondolier "o sole mio" you down Vegas's rendition of Venice's Canalozzo. We love this attraction because it's done so well—owner Sheldon Adelson was obsessed with getting the canals *just right*: he had them drained and painted three times before he was satisfied with the hue, and the colossal reproduction of St. Mark's Square at the end of the canal is authentic right down to the colors of the façades. The gondoliers who ply the waterway are professional entertainers and train for two weeks to maneuver the canals. It all makes for a rather entertaining way to while away an hour on the Strip. Outdoor gondola rides along the resort's exterior waterway are also available, weather permitting. A gondola carries up to four passengers. ⊠ *The Venetian, Center Strip* ☎ *702/733–5000 or 800/494–3556* ⊕ *www.venetian.com* 🎟 *$15 for indoor ride, $12.50 for outdoor ride* ⊙ *Sun.–Thurs. 10 AM–11 PM, Fri. and Sat. 10 AM–midnight.*

King Tut's Tomb. Inside the Pharaoh's Pavilion, this 20-minute self-guided walking tour is a re-creation of the archaeological site that uncovered stone chambers that housed statues of the gods, wooden boats, and vessels of food and drink for King Tut's passage to the underworld. ⊠ *The Luxor, South Strip* ☎ *702/262–4000* ⊕ *www.luxor.com* 🎟 *$9.99, includes audio tour* ⊙ *10 AM–11 PM.*

THE POOL SCENE

You, a lounge chair, and a tropical drink with an umbrella. Sound like paradise? Then plant yourself poolside in Sin City.

Las Vegas might just be America's coolest landlocked beach resort. Swimming pools can be just as over-the-top as the Strip sidewalk shows: fringed with lush landscaping and tricked out with wave machines, swim-up bars, ultraquiet misting machines, and wild water slides. Or they can be snazzy affairs—think private cabanas (satellite TV, Wi-Fi, and private misting machines), which range in price from about $40 a day for a basic one at the Stratosphere to $500 a day (on weekends) for one of the four cabanas at Mandalay Bay's topless beach club.

PLANNING YOUR TAN

Alas, unless you're a guest of the hotel, you're generally not allowed to use the pool facilities. If swimming and sunning are important to you, book your stay at a hotel with a great pool.

TOP PICKS

Flamingo Las Vegas

The Flamingo may have lost its luster, but don't overlook its pool—it's one of the most stunning and memorable around. Lose yourself in a tropical fantasyland where real penguins, swans, and pink flamingoes scamper about. Take a dip in Bugsy Siegel's original oval-shaped pool, or head to the Flamingo Pool's upper deck for swim-up blackjack (only 21-and-over allowed). Swim beneath dramatic stone grottoes and waterfalls fringed by greenery and towering palm trees in the lagoon pool (there's also a walkway allowing you to explore the grotto on foot). For the kids, there's a nice-size gated kiddie pool and a series of waterslides. The pool furniture is on the cheap side, but at the lagoon pool, you have the option of paying extra and upgrading to a double chaise lounge with pillows and a sunshade. The tan-and-white-striped cabanas have the standard amenities, but make reservations—with only about a dozen available, they go quickly.

PERKS WE LOVE: The romantic swim-through grottoes, ample supply of rafts and pool toys, separate kiddie pool, chaise lounge upgrades, the crazy wildlife. ⊠ Flamingo Las Vegas, 3555 Las Vegas Blvd. S, Center Strip ☎ 702/733-3111 ⊕ www.caesars.com/flamingo

Four Seasons Hotel Las Vegas

If the pool experience for you is more about serenity and special treatment than about seeing-and-being-seen and hobnobbing among the hoi polloi, this ultraprivate spread is for you. High-end, comfy chaise lounges are set up along a subtly landscaped (this isn't, like some competitors, a wild jungle-garden gone awry) pool deck with trellised arbors offering plenty of shade. Polite staff tend to your every need, from Evian spritzing to all the fresh ice water you need. There are no wacky water slides, no distracting rafts and inner tubes, no craziness whatsoever—just supreme calm. But here's the best part: if you do feel like letting your hair down, you're welcome to enjoy the fabulously raucous beach-pool extravaganza next door at Mandalay Bay. Yet, guests of Mandalay are not granted reciprocal privileges. Who knew such glamour and seclusion could be possible at a pool on the Strip?

PERKS WE LOVE: Fresh fruit at your fingertips, chilled towels, absolute exclusivity, solicitous attention, cucumber slices for your eyes. ⊠ Four Seasons Hotel Las Vegas, 3960 Las Vegas Blvd. S, South Strip ☎ 702/632-5000 ⊕ www.fourseasons.com

TOP PICKS

Hard Rock

No pool in town, save for the redesigned Palms, has a more happening scene than this one. The Hard Rock throws fabulous pool parties and bears an uncanny resemblance to that Polynesian beach hideaway you've always dreamed about. The Hard Rock has buckets of soft sand, both in the two pools and along its lushly landscaped beach. And lest you miss the pulse of the music while you're swimming laps, there's even a high-quality underwater sound system. Grab a colorful cocktail at Palapa Lounge, with its Indonesian vibe and tropical waterfalls. Feeling lucky? Hit the swim-up blackjack and craps bar. The cabanas are in keeping with the Polynesian vibe—they're gussied up to resemble Tahitian huts, with thatch roofs and rattan chairs. Predictably, the Hard Rock caters to a young-adult crowd of hipsters and bon vivants in their 20s and 30s. If you're outside this demographic, you may feel a bit like a fish out of water.

PERKS WE LOVE: Underwater music, four Jacuzzis (more than most properties), swim-up gaming, the Palapa Lounge.
✉ Hard Rock Hotel and Casino, 4455 Paradise Rd., Paradise Road
☎ 702/693-5000
⊕ www.hardrockhotel.com

Mandalay Bay

Pardon us if we sound like we're gushing, but we can't get over this place. Hands down, this is the mother of all Vegas pool scenes. Mandalay Bay's amazing pool experience includes an 11-acre beach spread with a huge wave pool (where else in town can you surf waves that rise as high as 6 feet?), a Euro-inspired topless pool with plush daybeds called the Moorea Beach club, a meandering river, and some of the cushiest cabanas in town. The beach is piled high with a couple thousand tons of California-imported golden sand, which feels just perfect between the toes. You can raft along the river, admiring the verdant foliage. After the sun sets, the beach becomes one of the city's hottest nightspots, attracting buffed and bronzed partyers for cocktails, music, and mingling. There are also two casual restaurants right by the beach. A huge soundstage overlooks the wave pool, hosting concerts by a wide range of rock and pop acts all summer long. The one complaint we have? It's relatively short on personal service and amenities.

PERKS WE LOVE: The comfy daybeds at Moorea Beach, sand—lots of it, the lazy river, the best outdoor concert venue on the Strip. ✉ Mandalay Bay Resort & Casino, 3950 Las Vegas Blvd. S, South Strip ☎ 702/632-7777
⊕ www.mandalaybay.com

HONORABLE MENTIONS

Loews Lake Las Vegas Resort

Granted the Loews is a schlep (17 miles) off the strip. But if the neon lights have started to drive you crazy, head here. This pool area is set along a glamorous, Moorish inspired terrace with awesome views of Lake Las Vegas. The pool area, like the casino-free hotel itself, is extremely family-friendly. The lower pool is great for kids with its shallower depth, 40-foot waterslide and rafts. The affordable cabanas here are simple, offering more privacy than crazy perks.

PERKS WE LOVE: Boat rentals on the lake, the white sand beach, Kids Camp poolside kids' programs, unbeatable mountain views and stargazing. ⊠ Loews Lake Las Vegas Resort, 101 Montelago Blvd., Henderson ☎ 702/567-6000 ⊕ www.loewshotels.com

Mirage

If you prefer a shaded, tropical spread, check out the verdant pool area at the classy Mirage. The two main pools are connected through a series of dramatic lagoons and waterfalls. The Mirage won't wow you with nonstop activities or goofy gimmicks—it's just a handsome, well-maintained pool that's ideal whether you're a serious aficionado or a toe-dipping dabbler. Lounge chairs are outfitted with comfy mesh sailcloth. The cabanas are chichi here, with teak chairs and high-end entertainment systems.

PERKS WE LOVE: Chaise lounge reservations, flat-screen TVs and BOSE Wave stereos in the cabanas, ample misting coverage, above-average chow in the poolside café and bar. ⊠ Mirage Hotel and Casino, 3400 Las Vegas Blvd. S, Center Strip ☎ 702/791-7111 ⊕ www.mirage.com

SWIM-UP BLACKJACK

Gamble? Or sun bathe? Don't decide between two vices—take your cards (and, at some places, your drink) for a dip at these resorts. After all, this is Sin City. The fading **Tropicana Resort and Casino** (⊠ 3801 Las Vegas Blvd. S, South Strip ☎ 702/739-2222 ⊕ www. tropicanalv.com) invented this quirky pastime and still offers it from late May to early September. Although the hotel is no great shakes overall, the pool area is quite handsome. The **Flamingo**

Las Vegas (⊠ 3555 Las Vegas Blvd. S, Center Strip ☎ 702/733-3111 ⊕ www.caesars.com/flamingo) is another old-school hotel offering this activity, although here it's poolside, rather than swim-up. The far snazzier **Hard Rock Hotel and Casino** (⊠ 4455 Paradise Rd., Paradise Road ☎ 702/693-5000 ⊕ www. hardrockhotel.com) has swim-up blackjack. **The Palms** (⊠ 4321 W. Flamingo Rd., West Side ☎ 702/942-7777 ⊕ www. palms.com) has poolside blackjack and massage.

ALSO WORTH NOTING

Green Valley Ranch Station Resort

The Palms
In 2006, the Hard Rock Hotel's archrival, the Palms, unveiled a spectacular $40 million makeover. Lounge poolside and enjoy music spun by top DJs, a hefty menu of cocktails, and slick decor. Our favorite feature is the Glass Bar, set cleverly under a glass-bottom pool deck. If you want to go all out, book one of the 27 cabanas or bungalows, which are outfitted with high-end sound systems, plasma TVs, and swank furnishings.

PERKS WE LOVE: Poolside massages, two-story bungalows, tasty nibbles from the pool café, colorful underwater lighting.

✉ The Palms, 4321 W. Flamingo Rd., West Side ☎ 702/942-7777 ⊕ www.palms.com

POOL PARTIES
Head to the festive beach at **Mandalay Bay** (✉ 3950 Las Vegas Blvd. S, South Strip ☎ 702/632-7777 ⊕ www.mandalaybay.com) to watch rockin' summer concerts—they've hosted such festive acts as the Go-Go's and the B-52's. **Hard Rock Hotel and Casino** (✉ 4455 Paradise Rd., Paradise Road ☎ 702/693-5000 ⊕ www.hardrockhotel.com) has become famous for Rehab, an all day Saturday and Sunday party that draws scads of good-looking scenesters. And here's a shocker: the lusty and busty **Hooters Casino Hotel** (✉ 115 E. Tropicana Ave., South Strip ☎ 702/739-9000) throws its share of raucous blowouts. Every weekend, there's a three-day party by the pool, where you're apt to find the 60-person hot tub abreast with revelers.

Vegas's perennial favorite with locals and savvy visitors, **Green Valley Ranch Station Resort** has a beautiful swimming complex with two infinity-edge pools, a glamorous and contemporary design, and comfy rattan chairs. The best of the Downtown pools, the **Golden Nugget Hotel and Casino** has a brand new pool area as of early 2007. The centerpiece is a waterslide that tunnels through the middle of the new 200,000 gallon aquarium before depositing riders into the redesigned pool. At the posh **Ritz-Carlton, Lake Las Vegas,** both the main pool and the adjoining lagoon with a private beach have views of desert mountains and Lake Las Vegas rather than the high-rises of the Strip—it's the one time we can say, without feeling clichéd, that we feel like we're in an exotic oasis in the desert. Another big plus here? The pool is open 24/7.

Green Valley Ranch Station Resort ✉ 2300 Paseo Verde Pkwy., Henderson ☎ 702/617-7777 ⊕ www.greenvalleyranchresort.com

Golden Nugget Hotel and Casino ✉ 129 E. Fremont St., Downtown ☎ 702/385-7111 ⊕ www.goldennugget.com

Ritz-Carlton, Lake Las Vegas ✉ 1610 Lake Las Vegas Pkwy., Henderson ☎ 702/567-4700 ⊕ www.ritzcarlton.com

TEE OFF

With an average of 315 days of sunshine a year and year-round access, Las Vegas's top sport is golf. The peak season is October through May. June through September only mad dogs and Englishmen are out in the noonday sun, and early-morning starting times are most heavily in demand. However, a number of the courses in Las Vegas offer reduced greens fees during the summer months, sometimes as much as 50% to 70% lower than peak-season fees.

Reservations for tee times can be made up to a week in advance (one or two days are sufficient at some courses, and a select few allow reservations up to three months in advance). Starting times for same-day play are possible, but you're given the first available time. Many of the big Strip resorts have a dedicated golf concierge who can advise you on a course that fits your tastes and, in some cases, get you access to private courses.

Best Courses

Bali Hai Golf Club. Inspired by the South Pacific, the 18-hole, 6,994-yard par-71 is dotted with palm trees, volcanic outcroppings, and small lagoons. The entrance is a mere 10-minute walk from Mandalay Bay. The clubhouse includes a pro shop and restaurant. Greens fees begin at $265 midweek, going up to $325 on weekends; ask about twilight specials that are $189 during the week and $229 on weekends. ⊠*5160 Las Vegas Blvd. S, South Strip* ☎*702/450–8170.*

Bear's Best Las Vegas. Replicas of the best 18 holes from Jack Nicklaus–designed courses in the Southwest and Mexico (such as the PGA West course in La Quinta, California, and Castle Pines in Colorado) are in one place at Bear's Best.

If the 7,229-yard par-72 course isn't tantalizing enough or if the greens fees are too steep, the clubhouse might be worth the drive to see all the Nicklaus memorabilia. A huge dining area doubles as a banquet hall, and an even bigger pavilion provides beautiful views of the mountains and the Strip. Greens fees are $195 during the week and $245 on weekends. ⊠*11111 W. Flamingo Rd., Summerlin* ☎*702/804–8500 or 866/385–8500* ⊕*www.bearsbest.com.*

The Falls Golf Club. This Tom Weiskopf–designed course opened in 2002 as the sister course to Reflection Bay, both centered around the Lake Las Vegas resort community. The Falls lives up to its name with elevation changes that grow more dramatic as you work your way through the course. The beautiful emerald fairways stand in stark contrast to the surrounding scrub desert and rocky crags, but water plays a factor in at least a third of the holes in this 18-hole, 7,250-yard par-72 course. Public greens fees start at $170 and, like the course's elevation, go up from there. ⊠*101 Via Vin Santo, Henderson* ☎*702/740–5258* ⊕*www.lakelasvegas.com.*

Las Vegas National Golf Club. Las Vegas's most historic course has five difficult par-3s and finishes with a killer 550-yard par-5 hole. During the 1996 Las Vegas Invitational, Tiger Woods played here on his way to claiming his first PGA Tour title, and Mickey Wright won two of her four LPGA Championships on this 6,815 yard par-71 course. Greens fees are $129 during the week and $159 on weekends. ⊠*1911 E. Desert Inn Rd., East Side* ☎*702/734–1796* ⊕*www.lasvegasnational.com.*

Paiute Golf Resort. You can play three Pete Dye–designed courses here: Wolf, Snow Mountain, and Sun Mountain. Snow Mountain fits most skill levels and has been ranked by *Golf Digest* as Las Vegas's best public-access course. Sun Mountain is a player-friendly course but is more challenging than Snow Mountain largely because of its difficult par-4s. Six of those holes measure longer than 400 yards, but the best is the par-4 fourth hole, which is 206 yards over water. Snow Mountain has wide fairways but also has its share of challenges, especially if you stray into the treacherous rough. Wolf, with its island hole at No. 15, is the toughest of the three and one of the most difficult in the area. Greens fees at 7,112-yard par-72 Snow Mountain and 7,146-yard par-72 Sun Mountain are $85 to $185, and Wolf is $105 to $215. ✉ *10325 Nu-Wav Kaiv Blvd., Northwest Las Vegas* ☎ *702/658–1400 or 800/711–2833* ⊕ *www.lvpaiutegolf.com.*

★ **Reflection Bay Golf Club.** Fifteen miles from the Strip and minutes from the Hyatt resort, the 7,261-yard par-72 Jack Nicklaus–designed Reflection Bay has a beautiful location fronting Lake Las Vegas, with 10 mi of lakefront beach. MiraLago Lakeside Mediterranean Café, in the elegant clubhouse, has a large patio overlooking the lake. Weekday greens fees are $275; $295 on weekends. Twilight rates are $160 weekdays and $180 weekends. Guests at Lake Las Vegas hotels pay about $60 less per round. ✉ *75 Monte-Lago Blvd., Henderson* ☎ *702/740–4653* ⊕ *www.lakelasvegas.com.*

Rhodes Ranch Golf Club. One of the better courses in the Las Vegas Valley, the 6,800-yard par-72 Rhodes Ranch course was designed by renowned architect Ted Robinson to provide enough challenges for any skill level—numerous water hazards, difficult bunkers, and less-than-even fairways. Greens fees are $130 Sunday through Thursday and $160 Friday and Saturday; twilight rates are $70 and $80, respectively. ✉ *20 Rhodes Ranch Pkwy., West Side* ☎ *702/740–4114 or 888/311–8337.*

Royal Links Golf Club. Similar to Bear's Best, this 7,029-yard par-72 course replicates the best of the British Open holes. You can play the Road Hole, from the famed St. Andrews, and the Postage Stamp, from Royal Troon. It's a rare chance to play links golf without having to cross an ocean, and the Las Vegas weather usually has far more sunshine and warmth. Also on-site is Stymie's Pub. Greens fees are $135 for weekday twilight, $155 for weekend twilight, $225 for weekdays, and $250 for weekends. ✉ *101 Via Vin Santo, Henderson* ☎ *702/740–5258 or 877/698–4653* ⊕ *www.waltersgolf.com.*

★ **The Wynn Golf Club.** You have to be a hotel guest to play award-winning course designer Tom Fazio's lavish urban golf course. The intimate arrangement incorporates the 37-foot Wynn waterfall feature on the 18th hole. Of the 18 holes along this challenging 7,042-yard par-70 course, 11 involve water hazards. The greens fee is $500. ✉ *Wynn Las Vegas, North Strip* ☎ *702/770–7100 or 877/321–9966* ⊕ *www.wynnlasvegas.com.*

HISTORY, VEGAS STYLE

Las Vegas celebrated its centennial in 2005, and although Sin City won't likely dethrone Philadelphia or Boston anytime soon in the category of historic attractions, this place does have a handful of genuinely engaging—if bizarre—diversions to please history buffs. There's a historic fort preserving the city's long-long-ago Mormon heritage and a museum dedicated to the region's slightly creepy history as a nuclear-test site. Other attractions trace the histories of everything from cocktails to neon signs. And you can be sure that most of the things you learn here in Vegas were never taught in the typical high school history class.

★ **Atomic Testing Museum.** Film footage and photographs of mushroom clouds; testimonials; and artifacts, including a deactivated bomb, twisted chunks of steel, and bomb-testing machinery, tell the story of the Nevada Test Site. Atmospheric, or above-ground, atomic testing took place in the southern Nevada desert, about 65 mi northwest of Las Vegas, from 1951 to 1962. During that time the Las Vegas Chamber of Commerce promoted the testing as an attraction, mostly to avoid losing wary visitors and their dollars. Publicity campaigns encouraged people to consider the mushroom clouds as entertainment to be watched and photographed. Atomic bomb postcards and souvenirs, and even the atomic cocktail (invented by a Vegas bartender), became extremely popular. After an explosion, Las Vegans would wait the seven minutes for the ensuing shock wave, which was known to break windows. Testing continued underground from 1962 until 1992, when the United States signed the Comprehensive Nuclear Test Ban Treaty with 71 other countries including France, Russia, China, and the United Kingdom. Narratives and exhibits at the Atomic Testing Museum describe the experiences of people who witnessed explosions and those who worked at the site. Of course, the aftereffects of radiation are not explored here. After your visit, you can browse the gift shop to see its Albert Einstein action figures and View-Master reels with 3-D images of atomic testing.

Group tours of the 1,375-square-mi Nevada Test Site—that's larger than the state of Rhode Island—take you onto the terrain for visits to test-site craters and observation points. To register for a tour, contact the Nevada office of the **National Nuclear Security Administration** (⌂ *Box 98518, Las Vegas 89193* ☎*702/295–0944* ⊕*www.nv.doe.gov*). ✉*755 E. Flamingo Rd., Desert Research Institute, East Side* ☎*702/794–5151* ⊕*www.atomictestingmuseum.org* ▣*$12* ☉*Mon.–Sat. 9–5, Sun. 1–5.*

Haunted Vegas Tours. As you ride through the streets of Las Vegas on this cheesy, 2½-hour tour, your guide, dressed as a mortician, tells the tales of Sin City's notorious murders, suicides, and ghosts (including Bugsy Siegel, Elvis, and Tupac Shakur). A 30-minute *Rocky Horror*–like sideshow, called Haunted Vegas, runs prior to the 21-stop tour. Because there's only one tour per night, reservations are suggested. ✉*Greek Isles Hotel, North Strip* ☎*702/737–5540* ⊕*www.hauntedvegastours.com* ▣*$48.25* ☉*Sat.–Thurs. 9* PM.

⟳ **Old Las Vegas Mormon Fort.** Southern Nevada's oldest historical site was built by Mormons in 1855 to give refuge to travelers along the Salt Lake–Los Angeles trail, many of whom were bound for the California goldfields. Left to Native

Americans after the gold rush, the adobe fort was later revitalized by a miner and his partners. In 1895 it was turned into a resort, and the city's first swimming pool was constructed by damming Las Vegas Creek. Today the restored fort contains more than half the original bricks. Antiques and artifacts help to re-create a turn-of-the-20th-century Mormon living room. ⊠ *500 E. Washington Ave., Las Vegas Blvd. N at Cashman Field, enter through parking lot B, Downtown* ☏ *702/486–3511* ⊕ *parks.nv.gov/olvmf. htm* 🎫 *$3* 🕙 *Mon.–Sat. 8–4:30.*

Lied Library. The special-collections department of this library of the University of Nevada–Las Vegas has the best collection of materials about Las Vegas and gambling that you can find anywhere. ⊠ *4505 Maryland Pkwy., University District* ☏ *702/895–2234* ⊕ *www.library. unlv.edu* 🎫 *Free* 🕙 *Mon., Wed., and Fri. 9–5, Tues. and Thurs. 9–9.*

Marjorie Barrick Museum of Natural History. Like the Lied Library, this museum is on the University of Nevada–Las Vegas campus. The museum has an excellent collection of objects that predate the arrival of Europeans in the American Southwest and throughout Mexico. There's also a live reptile exhibit featuring regional lizards and snakes. ⊠ *4505 Maryland Pkwy., University District* ☏ *702/895– 3381* ⊕ *http://hrc.nevada.edu/museum* 🎫 *Free* 🕙 *Weekdays 8–4:45, Sat. 10–2.*

Las Vegas Academy of International Studies, Performing and Visual Arts. This historic structure, the oldest permanent school building in Las Vegas, was built as a high school in 1930 for $350,000. It's a state historical landmark, the only example of 1930s art deco architecture in the city. ⊠ *315 S. 7th St., Downtown* ☏ *702/799–7800.*

Neon Museum. A giant neon horseman waves on the corner of Las Vegas Boulevard and Fremont Street. He's the first exhibit in the outdoor museum, a display of neon signs retired from various old Vegas landmarks. Others include the original Aladdin's lamp and the rider on horseback from the Hacienda Hotel. The signs can be seen along Fremont Street. Until the planned indoor venue opens, the Neon Museum has loaned some of its signs to the visitor center at the Old Fort (which requires an entrance fee). The Neon Museum also operates what they refer to as their "boneyard"—a 3-acre plot that houses all of the unrestored signs. Though it's not open to the public, Noble Gas-o-Philes might be able to visit by special appointment. ⊠ *731 S. 4th St., Downtown* ☏ *702/387–6366* ⊕ *www. neonmuseum.org* 🎫 *Free.*

🕙 **Nevada State Museum and Historical Society.** Regional history, from the time of the Spanish exploration to the building of Las Vegas after World War II, is the subject of this museum, which also covers the archaeology and anthropology of southern Nevada. It's near the lake in Lorenzi Park, an open space dotted with ponds and home to plants and animals native to the region. ⊠ *700 E. Twin Lakes Dr., 2 mi west of corner of Fremont and Main Sts., Downtown* ☏ *702/486–5205* 🎫 *$4* 🕙 *Daily 9–5.*

QUIRKY VEGAS

True, "quirky Las Vegas" almost sounds redundant, but even beyond this city's expected wackiness, you can find some wonderfully peculiar and offbeat attractions. The city has become something of a repository of odd collectibles—where else would you find the Liberace Museum or the unusual artifacts at Main Street Station? For more of the city's quirkiness besides the listings below, check out some of the tchotchke-filled pawn shops around town or simply people-watch at one of the many 24-hour coffee shops on or near the Strip.

Antique Collection at Main Street Station. Self-guided tours of the hotel's collection of antiques, artifacts, and collectibles include Louisa May Alcott's private railcar, a fireplace from Scotland's Prestwick Castle, lamps that graced the streets of 18th-century Brussels, the bronze doors and façade from the Kuwait Royal Bank, and beautiful statues, chandeliers, and woodwork from American mansions of long ago. There's even a piece of the Berlin Wall—in the men's room off the lobby. ⊠*200 N. Main St., Downtown* ☎*702/387–1896* ⊕*www.mainstreetcasino.com.*

Auto Collections at Imperial Palace. More than 250 antique, classic, and special-interest vehicles make up this collection. Because the vehicles are all for sale, the displays change from time to time, but among the cars, trucks, and motorcycles you might see one of the bugs from the movie *Herbie Fully Loaded,* a 1976 Cadillac Eldorado owned by Elvis Presley, or the world's largest Duesenberg collection, comprising 25 vehicles built between 1925 and 1937. The museum is on the fifth level of the hotel's parking garage (catch the elevator at the back of the casino). Coupons for free admis-

sion are available online and in some casinos. ⊠*Imperial Palace, Center Strip* ☎*702/731–3311* ⊕*www.imperialpalace.com* ⊠*$6.95* ⊙*Daily 9:30–9:30.*

Guardian Angel Cathedral. The Roman Catholic cathedral often has standing room only on Saturday afternoon, as visitors pray for luck—and sometimes drop casino chips into the collection cups during a special tourist mass. Periodically, a priest known as the "chip monk" collects the chips and takes them to the respective casinos to cash them in. Those staying on the south end of the Strip might find the **Shrine of the Most Holy Redeemer** (⊠*55 E. Reno Ave.* ☎*702/891–8600*) more convenient; it has three Saturday-afternoon and five Sunday masses. ⊠*302 Cathedral Way, North Strip* ☎*702/735–5241* ⊙*Weekdays mass 8 AM and 12:10 PM; Sat. mass 12:10 PM, vigil masses 2:30, 4, and 5:30; Sun. mass 8, 9:30, 11, 12:30, and 5.*

Jubilee! All Access Backstage Walking Tour. Admit it—you're just as mesmerized by all the sequins and fancy headpieces of a classic feather show as we are. On this tour, a real showgirl escorts you backstage to see firsthand the workings behind the curtains for this $50 million stage production. The hour-long tour shows you the mechanics of the stage, costumes, and dressing rooms. Visitors must be 13 years or older and should be able to move up and down several cases of stairs. ⊠*Bally's, Center Strip* ☎*702/946–4567* ⊕*www.ballyslv.com* ⊠*$15; $10 with purchase of show ticket* ⊙*Mon., Wed., and Sat. 11 AM.*

★ **Liberace Museum.** If you're out to find the kitschiest place in town, this is the jackpot: here you'll find costumes, cars,

photographs, even mannequins of the late entertainer. It's one of the most entertaining tributes you'll ever experience. The masterfully flamboyant pianist, who died in 1987 at age 67, opened the museum in 1979. And although it's set in a humdrum shopping center away from the Strip, it's worth the trip to admire "Mr. Showmanship's" trippy collectibles and memorabilia. In addition to Lee's collection of pianos (one of them was played by Chopin; another, a concert grand, was owned by George Gershwin), you can see his Czar Nicholas uniform and a blue-velvet cape styled after the coronation robes of King George V. Be sure to check out the gift shop—where else can you find Liberace soap, ashtrays, and candelabras? ⊠*1775 E. Tropicana Ave., East Side* ☎*702/798–5595* ⊕*www.liberace. org* 🎟*$12.50* ⊙*Tues.–Sat. 10–5, Sun. noon–4.*

★ **Madame Tussaud's Las Vegas.** Strike a pose with Simon Cowell (he's as irritable looking in wax as in person) or Muhammad Ali as you walk through the open showroom filled with uncanny celebrity wax portraits. Crowd pleasers include the figures of Tom Jones, Hugh Hefner, and Abe Lincoln. An interactive segment lets you play golf with Tiger Woods, shoot baskets with Shaquille O'Neill, play celebrity poker with Ben Affleck, dance with Britney Spears, or marry George Clooney. ⊠*The Venetian, Center Strip* ☎*702/862–7800* ⊕*www.mtvegas.com* 🎟*$24* ⊙*Sun.–Thurs. 10–9, Fri. and Sat. 10–10.*

Pinball Hall of Fame. In 2006 the Las Vegas Pinball Collectors Club opened 4,500 square feet in an unassuming shopping center that's filled to the brim with, you guessed it, pinball machines. More than 140 games from all eras are present, including the old woodrail models of the 1950s and modern games with fancy effects and complex play. Though this may sound more like an arcade than a museum, the local club is a nonprofit organization whose goal is to preserve this piece of Americana, and share the joy of the silver ball with as many folks as possible. Plus, your quarters get donated to the local Salvation Army. ⊠*3330 E. Tropicana Ave., East Side* ☎*No phone* ⊕*www.pinballmuseum.org* 🎟*Free entry, 25 or 50 cents per game* ⊙*Sun.–Thurs. 11–11, Fri. and Sat. 11* AM*–midnight.*

★ **Star Trek: The Experience.** Trekkies go nuts over the museum, which has a Star Trek timeline of future history, costumes and props, and video loops from the shows. During the 3-D motion simulator ride, the audience is kidnapped by the Klingons and beamed into the 24th century and onto the bridge of the Starship *Enterprise*; it's up to the crew to get everyone safely back to the 21st-century Hilton. The riveting BORG Invasion 4D uses a mix of live actors; dramatic visual, audio, and tactile special effects; and 3-D film to give visitors a sense of encountering a hostile BORG invasion. ⊠*Las Vegas Hilton, 3000 Paradise Rd., Paradise Road* ☎*702/732–5111 or 888/462–6535* ⊕*www.startrekexp.com* 🎟*$33.99 all-day pass* ⊙*Daily 11–11.*

WORKS OF ART

Wipe that look of disbelief off your face—for the past few years, real art has made its way to the neon city. World-renowned traveling art shows set up shop at the Bellagio Gallery of Fine Art and the Venetian's Guggenheim-Hermitage Museum. Uber-developer and noted art collector Steve Wynn has hung some of his more notable works in his namesake resort's public areas. And off-Strip is a burgeoning alternative gallery scene that's been brewing in a relatively neglected corner of Downtown—it's still fairly modest at this point, but the Downtown Arts District may just put Vegas on the international arts map before all is said and done.

Bellagio Gallery of Fine Art. Recent exhibits on view here have included *Ansel Adams: America,* and works by Picasso, Hopper, and Lichtenstein from the private collection of Steve Martin. ✉ *Bellagio, Center Strip* ☎ *702/693–7111 or 888/987–6667* ⊕ *www.bgfa.biz* 🎫 *$15 includes audio tour* ⊗ *Daily 9* AM–10 PM.

★ **Guggenheim-Hermitage Museum.** This museum showcases special exhibitions, most of them lasting a few months, as well as art pulled from three of the most revered permanent collections—the Guggenheim, in New York; the Hermitage, in St. Petersburg; and the Kunsthistorisches, in Vienna. Both exterior and interior walls of the museum are constructed of Cor-Ten steel, a material that has a softly rusted surface, and the visually striking façade can be seen from the Strip. ✉ *The Venetian, Center Strip* ☎ *702/414–2440* ⊕ *www.guggenheimlasvegas.org* 🎫 *$19.50 includes audio tour* ⊗ *Daily 9:30–8:30; last ticket sold at 7* PM.

Downtown Arts District. The emergence of the offbeat Downtown Arts District, an 18-block district bounded by South 7th, Main, Bonneville, and Charleston streets on downtown's eastern edge, continues to generate excitement in the city's arts community. With a number of funky, independent art galleries in its confines, the area, officially named in 1998, is a growing, thriving cultural hub—a sort of antithesis to the Strip. Trickling into the neighborhood's residences are Las Vegas's alternative artists, musicians, and writers. Each month the district hosts a "First Friday" gallery walk from 6 to 9 PM with gallery openings, street performers, and entertainment. It's an excellent time to come check out the still-nascent but steadily improving scene for yourself.

An intriguing concentration of antiques shops and galleries is found on East Charleston Boulevard and Casino Center Drive, anchored by the **Arts Factory** (✉ *101–109 E. Charleston Blvd., Downtown* ☎ *702/676–1111* ⊕ *www.theartsfactory.com* 🎫 *Free*). It houses several galleries, and hours vary, but they're generally Tuesday through Sunday, opening roughly from 10 to 6 (but often for shorter periods or by appointment). As part of the neighborhood's First Friday event, the Arts Factory hosts art openings and special events.

WALK ON THE WILD(LIFE) SIDE

Ever since the animal-training icons Siegfried and Roy began their white tiger magic acts at the Mirage in the 1960s, wild animals have been just one more part of the Vegas razzle-dazzle-'em campaign. And though the rest of Vegas isn't exactly child-appropriate, you can always bank on one of the following exhibits to enchant them.

Lion Habitat. This is as big a gamble as there is in Las Vegas. Nine times out of 10 when you walk through the see-through tunnel, you'll see the big cats snoozing above and below. But the habitat has acquired some younger, friskier kitties. The enclosure itself was designed to replicate the lions' natural habitat as closely as possible and has stone, trees and foliage, four waterfalls, and a pond. The lions don't actually live in Vegas. They're trucked in from animal trainer Keith Evans' 8½-acre ranch outside of town. ⊠ *MGM Grand, South Strip* ☎ *702/891–7776* ⊕ *www.mgmgrand. com* ⊠ *Free* ⊙ *Daily 11–10.*

★ **Shark Reef.** You start your journey through the mysterious realm of deep water at the ruins of an old temple. Here the heat and humidity may be uncomfortable for humans but it's quite nice for the golden crocodiles, endangered green sea turtles, water monitors, and tropical fish. Next, two glass tunnels lead you under the sea (or about 1.6 million gallons of it), where exotic tropical fish and other sea creatures swim all around you. Elsewhere a shallow touch pool gives you a chance to give a one-finger pet to small stingrays, small sharks, and starfish; and jellyfish swim a rhythmic dance in a specially designed environment. The tour saves the best for last—from the bowels of a sunken galleon, watch sharks swim below, above, and around the skeleton ship. ⊠ *Mandalay Bay, South Strip* ☎ *702/632–4555* ⊕ *www.mandalaybay. com* ⊠ *$15.95* ⊙ *Daily 10* AM*–11* PM*; last admission at 10.*

★ **Fodor's Choice** **Siegfried & Roy's Secret Garden & Dolphin Habitat.** The palm-shaded sanctuary has a collection of the planet's rarest and most exotic creatures, including white tigers and lions, a snow leopard, a panther, and an elephant. (No, the tiger that mauled Roy in 2003 is not on view.) At the Dolphin Habitat you can watch the Atlantic bottle-nosed dolphins swim around in a 2.5-million-gallon saltwater tank. Pass through the underwater observation station to the video room, where you can watch tapes of two dolphin births at the habitat. There's also a deluxe trainer-for-a-day program that gets you up-close and personal with the animals if you've got the time and $500 or so. ⊠ *The Mirage, Center Strip* ☎ *800/627–6667 or 702/792–7980* ⊕ *www.miragehabitat. com* ⊠ *$15* ⊙ *Secret Garden: May–Oct., daily 10–7; Nov.–Apr., weekdays 11–5:30, weekends 10–5:30; last admission half-hr before closing.*

★ ☺ **Wildlife Habitat at Flamingo.** Just next to the Flamingo's pool area, a flock of live Chilean flamingos, African penguins, swans, ducks, koi, goldfish, and turtles live on islands and in streams surrounded by sparkling waterfalls and lush foliage. You can watch as the penguins are fed a healthy diet of smelt, capelin, herring, and vitamins each day at 8:30 and 3. ⊠ *The Flamingo, Center Strip* ☎ *702/733–3111* ⊕ *www.flamingolv.com* ⊠ *Free* ⊙ *Daily 24 hrs.*

ALLEY OOP!

If Strip casinos have their shark tanks and roller coasters, off-Strip casinos have their, well, bowling alleys. Many of these are open 24/7, and they draw some serious crowds. At public alleys, it's a good idea to call ahead to make sure they're not booked up by local bowling leagues, which are all the rage in these parts.

Lucky Strike Lanes. By day the lanes are open to all, but after 9 PM it turns into a fusion of nightlife and bowling. Guests tired from hurling a ball can flop into comfy couches in the lounge, play the jukebox, or swirl cocktails under a neon-lit Vegas sign. ⊠ *Rio All-Suite Hotel & Casino, 3700 W. Flamingo Rd., West Side* ☎ *702/777–7999* ⊕ *www.luckystrikelv. com* ⊙ *Daily 11 AM–3 AM.*

Mahoney's Silver Nugget. Mahoney's has just 24 lanes and is the only one on our list that does not operate at all hours. But, they make up for it with new equipment, a pro shop, and a modern automatic scoring system. Their version of Cosmic Bowling, which includes fancy lights and a booming sound system, goes 8 PM–midnight on Friday and 7 PM–midnight on Saturday. Weekend days you can rent lanes by the hour, instead of paying per person per game. ⊠ *2140 Las Vegas Blvd. N, North Las Vegas* ☎ *702/320–2695* ⊙ *Sun.–Thurs. 9 AM–10 PM, Fri. and Sat. 9 AM–midnight.*

Orleans Hotel and Casino. The Orleans is in a working-class neighborhood, and its 70-lane bowling center sees lots of traffic, but its not-far-off-the-Strip location also makes it a popular spot for visitors. ⊠ *4500 W. Tropicana Rd., West Side* ☎ *702/365–7111.*

Sam's Town. With its 56 lanes and day-care center, this is the alley you'd choose for your bowling league if you lived in Las Vegas. But tourists like it too for the cocktail lounge, connecting casino, and weekend night "Extreme Bowling Experience" that's like bowling in a night club. The scoring system includes Spare Maker so rookies know where to aim. ⊠ *5111 Boulder Hwy., Las Vegas* ☎ *702/456–7777.*

Santa Fe Station Hotel and Casino. Santa Fe Station is a locals casino, but it's one of the area's most polished, and that's reflected in its bowling center. The 60-lane bowling facility features the top-of-the-line Brunswick electronic scoring system. ⊠ *4949 N. Rancho Dr., Rancho Strip* ☎ *702/658–4995.*

★ **Suncoast Hotel and Casino.** Reflecting its upscale Summerlin neighborhood, the bowling center at the Suncoast, with 64 lanes, is designed to provide every high-tech toy for bowlers. It's arguably the most attractive facility in town. ⊠ *9090 Alta Dr., Northwest Las Vegas* ☎ *702/636–7400.*

Texas Station Gambling Hall and Hotel. This 60-lane alley was the first to declare itself a nightclub hybrid by adding the "cosmic bowling" concept that's since been imitated at alleys all over town. It draws a youngish crowd, so if you like to party while you bowl, this is for you. Beginners like the "coach" feature on the scoring system that offers an aiming point for spare pickups. Thankfully the old hideous purple-and-blue carpeting was replaced in late 2006 with brand-new hideous purple-and-blue carpeting. ⊠ *2101 Texas Star La., Rancho Strip* ☎ *702/631–8128.*

FREE THINGS TO DO

Yes, Vegas brims with cash, glitz, and glamour, but that doesn't mean you can't find freebies or romp around the Strip and the downtown area without spending a dime.

Fremont Street Experience. The downtown casinos' answer to the spectacle of the Strip is the 90-foot-high arced canopy that covers the entire street. Every hour between sunset and midnight it comes alive as Viva Vision—an integrated video, graphics, and music show. Several different programs run each night at the top of the hour and contribute to a festive outside-in communal atmosphere that contrasts with the Strip's every-man-for-himself ethic. It's like a quarter-mile-long music video with a free neck-ache thrown in. But the price is right, and the kids will love it.

Watch a free show. You can easily spend $100 or more on even mediocre seats at a typical Vegas concert or big-name production, but several casinos offer fabulous, eye-catching extravaganzas that won't cost you a penny. There's the erupting volcano at the Mirage, which lights up after dark each night. At Treasure Island, watch the over-the-top *Sirens of TI.* And stand along the sidewalk by the lagoon at Bellagio to observe the graceful Fountains of Bellagio.

The New Old Downtown. The downtown casinos make no attempt to compete with the opulence of the Strip, but Fremont and connecting streets have a charm all their own. For cheapskate gamblers, browse through the Gamblers Bookstore and then take advantage of the free slot pulls and roulette spins offered at many of the downtown casinos. You can also view many of the Neon Museum's signs along

Fremont as well. Head over to the emerging Downtown Arts District for some free gallery tours and special events.

Lion Habitat at the MGM Grand. Of the handful of free animal spectaculars around town, don't miss walking through the tunnel at MGM Grand, where beautiful lions saunter around.

Cruising the Strip. You haven't done Vegas if you haven't been caught—either intentionally or unwittingly—in the slow-mo weekend-night crawl of traffic down the sexy midsection of Las Vegas Boulevard (aka the Strip). You can handle the experience like a been-there local, or you can play the delighted tourist: relaxed, windows down, your heart and mind ready to engage in silly banter with the carload of players in the convertible one lane over. We suggest the latter, at least once. Just be mindful of all the pedestrians, who can crowd the crosswalks like belligerent cattle and are just as dazed as you are by the cacophony.

Go Casino-hopping. Casino-hopping is a classic way to see Las Vegas resorts, with a little shopping, gambling, and noshing along the way—and, of course, it's always good fun simply to ogle passersby. Because nearly all the most intriguing properties are right on the Strip, you don't need to map out where to go; just pop into the casinos you want to see. Keep in mind that you want to wear comfortable shoes (no heels!) to cover the considerable distances between properties, and use those handy indoor walkways that connect many of the casinos along the Strip to save time and trouble.

TIE THE KNOT

Vegas wedding chapels: They're cute. They're white. They're flowers and neon and love ever after (or at least until tomorrow's hangover). They're also mighty quick, once you get that marriage license from the county. Will it be the historic Little Church of the West, Elvis's blessings at the Little White Wedding Chapel, or "until death do us part" in Klingon at Star Trek: The Experience? Perhaps you'll just spring for a drive-through wedding— on bicycles if you wish.

Have a no-frills civil ceremony at the **Clark County Marriage License Bureau** (✉ *201 Clark Ave., Downtown* ☎ *702/671–0600*). Appear with $55, some identification, and your beloved. It's open between 8 AM and midnight (as well as 24 hours on holidays). New Year's Eve and Valentine's Day are the most popular dates.

At the **Commissioner of Civil Marriages** (✉ *309 S. 3rd St., 1st fl., Downtown* ☎ *702/671–0600*), a surrogate-J.P. deputy commissioner will unite you in holy matrimony for $50 cash (exact change and a witness are required) until 10 PM any night of the week.

Best Chapels

★ **Little Church of the West.** Located on the South End of the strip, this cedar-and-redwood chapel is one of the city's most famous. The kitsch is kept in control here, and the setting borders on picturesque (it's even listed on the National Register of Historic Places—ah, Vegas). ✉ *4617 Las Vegas Blvd. S, South Strip* ☎ *702/739–7971 or 800/821–2452* ⊕ *www.littlechurchlv.com.*

Little White Wedding Chapel. Get hitched in a pink Cadillac while an Elvis impersonator croons. This is one of only two chapels that offer drive-through weddings

(the other is A Special Memory). Famous LWWC alums? Demi Moore and Bruce Willis, Michael Jordan, Britney Spears, and Frank Sinatra. Try the new Hawaiian theme, where the minister plays a ukulele and blows into a conch shell to close out the ceremony. ✉ *1301 Las Vegas Blvd. S, North Strip* ☎ *702/382–3546 or 800/545–8111* ⊕ *www.littlewhitechapel. com.*

Star Trek: The Experience. Ever dreamed of having a Klingon warrior bear witness to your nuptials? Who hasn't? You can put 45 guests on the bridge of the Starship *Enterprise* as a Starfleet Admiral officiates the ceremony. Afterward have a Borg assimilate into your wedding pictures with your new in-laws. ✉ *Las Vegas Hilton, North Strip* ☎ *702/697–8750 or 888/462–6535* ⊕ *www.startrekexp.com.*

Venetian Resort-Hotel-Casino. Say your vows in one of three chapels, on the Ponte al di Piazza, or on the canal itself in a gold-and-white gondola. The gondolier serenades and passersby applaud. ✉ *Center Strip* ☎ *702/414–4280 or 800/883–6423* ⊕ *www.venetianweddings.com.*

Viva Las Vegas Wedding Chapel. An endless variety of wedding themes and add-on shtick is available, ranging from elegant to casual to camp; say your vows in the presence of Elvis, the Blues Brothers, or Liberace. ✉ *1205 Las Vegas Blvd. S, North Strip* ☎ *702/384–0771 or 800/574–4450* ⊕ *www.vivalasvegasweddings.com.*

VEGAS & KIDS

Sin City's an adult playground, but there are a number of ways to keep kids occupied here. Any of the following destinations are sure to be a hit with the kids. Also, check out the Walk on the Wild(life) Side section for information on all the cool animals your kids can see, and the Day Trips chapter for everything from visiting a Wild West town to scrambling around in Red Rock.

CBS Television City. Screen potential new shows for parent company Viacom's networks, which also include Nickelodeon and MTV. A survey following the 45-minute previewed program lasts about 15 minutes, so you should expect to spend an hour total. ⊠ *MGM Grand, South Strip* ☎702/891–7776 ⊕*www.mgmgrand. com* ⛨*Free* ♥*Daily 8:30–10.*

Ethel M Chocolate Factory. That's M as in Mars (the bar not the planet). If your kids are the types who will want to breeze through the tour of the confectionary and get straight to the samples, the Ethel M is a good option. It's a self-guided tour, so if your youngsters start to get impatient, it's your own fault. There's a gift shop where you can buy more of the favorites you just tasted, plus an expansive cactus garden for botanically inclined families. ⊠*2 Cactus Garden Dr., Henderson* ☎702/458–8864 ⊕*www.ethelm.com* ⛨*Free* ♥*Daily 9:30–7.*

Las Vegas Natural History Museum. The museum has displays of mammals from the likes of Alaska and Africa and has rooms full of sharks (including live ones, swimming in a 3,000-gallon reef tank), birds, dinosaur fossils, and hands-on exhibits. Here kids can walk past a 35-foot-tall Tyrannosaurus rex that lowers its head and roars, see the ichthyosaur Shon-isaurus, Nevada's state fossil, and tour the Wild Nevada Gallery, where they can see, smell, and even touch Nevada wildlife. ⊠*900 Las Vegas Blvd. N, Downtown* ☎*702/384–3466* ⊕*www.lvnhm.org* ⛨*$7, $3 children 3–11* ♥*Daily 9–4.*

Lied Discovery Children's Museum. The Lied (pronounced *leed*) contains more than 100 hands-on exhibits covering the sciences, arts, and humanities, and it hosts several excellent traveling exhibits each year. Children can pilot a space shuttle, perform on stage, pretend-shop in a market, or stand in a giant bubble. ⊠*833 Las Vegas Blvd. N, Downtown* ☎*702/382–3445* ⊕*www.ldcm.org* ⛨*$8, $7 children 1–17* ♥*Tues.–Sat. 10–5, Sun. noon–5.*

Southern Nevada Zoological–Botanical Park. About a five-minute drive northwest of downtown, you'll find the last family of Barbary apes in the United States, along with chimpanzees, eagles, ostriches, emus, parrots, wallabies, flamingos, endangered cats (including tigers), and every species of venomous reptile native to southern Nevada—150 species in all. One exhibit features species native to Nevada such as mountain lions, coyotes, golden eagles, and deer; an underwater exhibit stars a 7-foot-long alligator named Elvis. The park has easy-view animal enclosures and a petting zoo with smaller animals. ⊠*1775 N. Rancho Dr., Rancho Strip* ☎*702/647–4685* ⊕*www.lasvegaszoo. org* ⛨*$7, $5 children 2–12* ♥*Daily 9–4:30.*

Where to Stay & Play

Paris Hotel

WORD OF MOUTH

"Not sure if it's full of 'glitz' but we like the Flamingo for its moderate rates and center-strip location. It's right in the middle of the action, so you can virtually walk anywhere . . . Request a newly renovated room and a view; most people are granted their requests."

—wanderluster

WHAT'S WHERE

GETTING ORIENTED

It's worth spending some time considering your needs and interests before choosing a hotel in Vegas, keeping in mind that factors such as size and property type can be every bit as important as cost and location. This chapter gives side-by-side reviews of both a property's hotel and casino, so you can easily figure out what will be the best fit for your visit. Almost all casino-hotels have a distinct personality and vibe; as you read the reviews, you'll be able to pick out which one will suit your needs.

1 The Strip: The more luxurious properties are at the south and center parts of the Strip. Bellagio, Bally's, Caesars Palace, and the Flamingo converge at the heart of the Strip, the intersection of Flamingo Road and Las Vegas Boulevard. Wynn Las Vegas and smaller, older hotels are north of Treasure Island.

2 Paradise Road: Parallel to the Strip, a short drive or 15-minute walk east, is mellower Paradise Road. There's less traffic and chaos and monorail service along one stretch. Hotel options include a mix of smaller, less interesting gaming resorts; some biggies, like Hard Rock; and some nongaming properties, including economical chain motels and upscale all-suites chain hotels.

3 The West Side: Due west of the Strip, on the other side of I–15, are the Palms, Rio, and the Orleans. The drawbacks? It's not a very glamorous section of town, the walk to the Strip is dull, and you'll be cabbing or driving to and from the Strip. But the views of the Strip from east-facing rooms are spectacular.

4 Downtown: Hotels are cheaper and favored by those with strictly adult pleasures: dice and drinks. They exist in the old Vegas tradition, when guests were expected to spend most of their hours in the casinos, not their rooms; consequently, rooms range from scuzzy to semi-pleasant. Stay here if you want to spend less than $50 per night.

5 The Burbs: Get away from it all at Lake Las Vegas to the southeast, near the suburb of Henderson, or the Summerlin section of Vegas to the west. Here you find sprawling, luxury full-service resorts with major golf and recreational facilities and spectacular natural settings. Or, stay at a locals casino on the Boulder or Rancho Strips.

The Flamingo Hotel

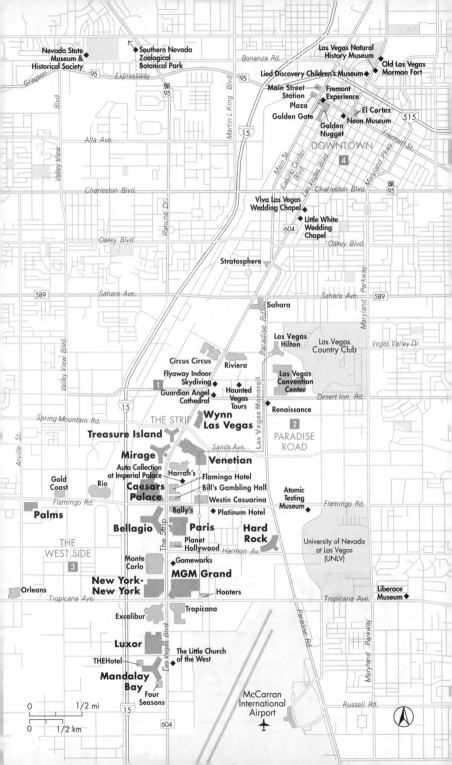

Nevada State Museum & Historical Society

Southern Nevada Zoological Botanical Park

Bonanza Rd.

Las Vegas Natural History Museum

Lied Discovery Children's Museum

Old Las Vegas Mormon Fort

Gragson

95

Expressway

Main Street Station

Fremont Experience

Plaza

Golden Gate

El Cortez

Neon Museum

515

Golden Nugget

Valley View Blvd.

BR 95

Alta Ave.

Martin L King Blvd.

15

DOWNTOWN

4

Main St.

Casino Center Blvd.

Rancho Dr.

Las Vegas Blvd.

Maryland Pkwy

Fremont St.

Charleston Blvd.

Charleston Blvd.

BR 95

Viva Las Vegas Wedding Chapel

Little White Wedding Chapel

Oakey Blvd.

604

Oakey Blvd.

Stratosphere

Sahara Ave.

589

Sahara Ave.

589

Sahara

Paradise Rd.

Las Vegas Hilton

Las Vegas Country Club

Vegas Valley Dr.

Circus Circus

Riviera

Las Vegas Convention Center

Flyaway Indoor Skydiving

Desert Inn Rd.

1

Guardian Angel Cathedral

Haunted Vegas Tours

Valley View Blvd.

THE STRIP

Wynn Las Vegas

Renaissance

2

Spring Mountain Rd.

Las Vegas Monorail

Arville St.

Treasure Island

PARADISE ROAD

Mirage

Sands Ave.

Auto Collection at Imperial Palace

Venetian

Gold Coast

Rio

Harrah's

Flamingo Hotel

Bill's Gambling Hall

Caesars Palace

Westin Casuarina

Atomic Testing Museum

Flamingo Rd.

Flamingo Rd.

Palms

Bally's

Platinum Hotel

Bellagio

Paris

Hard Rock

THE WEST SIDE

The Strip

Planet Hollywood

3

Harmon Av.

University of Nevada at Las Vegas (UNLV)

Monte Carlo

Gameworks

New York-New York

MGM Grand

Orleans

Tropicana Ave.

Hooters

Tropicana Ave.

Liberace Museum

Excalibur

Tropicana

The Little Church of the West

Luxor

Las Vegas Blvd.

THEHotel

Mandalay Bay

Four Seasons

McCarran International Airport

Paradise Rd.

Maryland Parkway

Russell Rd.

0   1/2 mi

0   1/2 km

15

604

WHERE TO STAY & PLAY PLANNER

Timing your Trip	The Lowdown on Rates

Timing your Trip

Though Las Vegas is home to most of the world's largest hotels, accommodations fill up fast around here, even when no major conventions or events are in town. When it's time for a big convention, it's not unusual for Las Vegas to sell out completely. Combine those with three-day weekends, holidays, large sporting events, and normally crowded weekends, and you can see why it's wise to make your lodging arrangements as far ahead of your visit as possible.

On the other hand, things change quickly here. If you arrive at the last minute without accommodations, you can almost always find a room somewhere in town—though the price might be double or triple what you would have paid with reservations.

If your original room is not to your liking, you can usually upgrade it around checkout time the next day.

The Lowdown on Rates

In general, rates for Las Vegas accommodations are lower than those in most other American resort and vacation cities, but the situation is a wacky one indeed, and as fancier new properties have opened in the past few years, rates have risen dramatically. There are about a hundred variables, depending on who's selling the rooms (reservations, marketing, casino, conventions, wholesalers, packagers), what rooms you're talking about (standard, deluxe, minisuites, standard suites, deluxe suites, high-roller suites, penthouses, bungalows), demand (weekday, weekend, holiday, conventions or sporting events in town), and management whim (bean-counter profit models, revenue-projection realities, etc.).

When business is slow, many hotels reduce rates on rooms in their least desirable sections, sometimes with a buffet breakfast or even a show included. Most "sales" occur from early December to mid-February and in July and August, the coldest and hottest times of the year, and you can often find rooms for 50% to 75% less midweek than on weekends. Members of casino slot clubs often get offers of discounted or even free rooms, and they can almost always reserve a room even when the rest of the hotel is "sold out."

WHAT IT COSTS

	¢	$	$$	$$$	$$$$
FOR 2 PEOPLE	under $60	$60–$130	$130–$200	$200–$270	over $270

All prices are for a standard double room, excluding 10% tax.

The lodgings we list are the cream of the crop in each price category. Properties are assigned price categories based on the range between their least and most expensive standard double rooms at high season (excluding holidays).

Assume that hotels operate on the European Plan (EP, with no meals) unless we specify that they use the Continental Plan (CP, with a continental breakfast), Modified American Plan (MAP, with breakfast and dinner), or the Full American Plan (FAP, with all meals).

Getting the Best Room

There's no surefire way to ensure that you always get the room that you want, when you want it, and for the lowest price possible. But here are a few tips for increasing your chances:

Book early. This town is almost always busy, so book as early as possible. Generally, if you book a room for $100 and later find out that the hotel is offering the same category of room for $60, the hotel will match the lower price, so keep checking back to see if the rates have dropped. Of course, this won't work if you prepay for a room on Expedia, Orbitz, Priceline, or some other online agency, so keep in mind that once you go this route, you either can't get out of the reservation, or you may have to pay a hefty cancellation fee.

Getting the room you want. Actual room assignments aren't determined at most Vegas hotels until the day before, or of, arrival. If you're hoping for a particular room (for example, a room with a view of the Strip), phone the hotel a day before you arrive and speak with somebody at the front desk. This is true whether you booked originally through the hotel or some other Web site. Don't be pushy or presumptuous. Just explain that although you realize the hotel can't guarantee a specific room, you'd appreciate it if they'd honor your preference.

Your second best bet. Simply check in as early as possible on the day of arrival—even if no rooms are yet available, you're likely to get first preference on the type of room you're seeking when it opens up.

What about upgrades? It's virtually never inappropriate to request a nicer room than the one you've booked. At the same time, it's virtually always inappropriate to expect that you'll receive the upgrade. The front-desk clerk has all the power and discretion when it comes to upgrades and is unlikely to help you out if you act pushy or haughty. Gracious humility, smiles, and warmth go a long way.

Do I tip for an upgrade? It's not customary to tip hotel clerks for upgrades, especially at nicer properties. If you wave some cash around discreetly, it might not hurt, but it won't necessarily help either.

Getting bumped. Hotels do overbook, and this happens more often in Las Vegas than in other cities. If you know you're arriving late, especially on a weekend, call the hotel and let them know. At busy times, this is imperative—the late arrivals are the ones who are bumped.

What's Next

Steve Wynn's follow-up to Wynn Las Vegas, a $1.74 billion project aptly called Encore, is slated to open at the end of 2008. The neighboring Venetian, run by Wynn's archrival, Sheldon Adelson, had a head start on its 3,020-room, $1.8 billion Palazzo addition, which opened in late 2007. Other major hotel-casino projects on tap for the coming years include W Las Vegas (2009) with a Fred Segal boutique among other hot shops; the Trump International Hotel (2008), which will be near the Fashion Show Mall; Echelon Place Resort (2010) will replace the Stardust; a Charlie Palmer boutique hotel (mid-2008); and the South Beach–inspired Fontainebleau (2009), just to name a few.

Additionally, the massive MGM Mirage closed the Boardwalk casino to clear the way for a $7 multibillion-dollar leviathan, tentatively known as Project CityCenter. Parts of it are scheduled to open by 2009 on the land between Monte Carlo and Bellagio resorts, and will include a Mandarin Oriental Hotel. The Grand Hyatt expects to unveil the fabulous new, $1.8 billion, 3,000-room condo and hotel project called Cosmopolitan Resort in 2008. Station Casinos is opening Aliante Station Resort and Casino in late 2008. There are several more big developments on the way for 2010 and beyond, so stayed tuned.

2

WHERE TO STAY & PLAY PLANNER

Tips for a Good Trip

Stay near where you want to play. If you want to gamble downtown, book a room off the Strip. If you think you're going to spend most of your time at Hard Rock, look into staying there or somewhere else on Paradise Road.

Huge megaresorts can feel like cities within cities and be noisy, chaotic, and challenging to navigate. Avoid trekking all over your hotel by asking for a room near an elevator.

Book a room at one of the smaller, lower-key casino resorts a few miles from the Strip—these can be relaxing places to stay, and you can always take trips to the Strip to gamble and have fun.

If you're not much of a gambler go with a nongaming property (the Ritz-Carlton, the Platinum, the Renaissance Las Vegas) or one with a relatively small or unobtrusive casino (the Westin).

MGM Grand's Lion Habitat

Save vs. Splurge

Whether you're rollin' high or down on your luck, Vegas has a place for you. Check out the following steals and splurges.

SAVE

El Cortez. The vintage El has 1940s-style rooms at 1940s prices. It's a dive, but you can't beat these rates. From $29.

Main Street Station. You can find cheaper rooms downtown, but these tasteful and spacious digs might be the nicest you can find in the city for under $100. From $50.

The Orleans Hotel. If you don't mind the location a bit west of the Strip, the surprisingly charming Orleans offers bright, clean, affordable rooms with plenty of elbow room. From $50.

SPLURGE

The Palms. The 2,900-square-foot Real World Suite at the Palms, made famous on MTV, has three bedrooms, a pool table, and ample room to throw a party for a few dozen pals. From $7,500 per night.

Ritz-Carlton, Lake Las Vegas. The palatial Ritz-Carlton suite occupies the top-center section of the Pontevecchio and has a formal dining room, kitchen, and extra-large balconies overlooking Lake Las Vegas. You could angle for trout from your suite. From $5,000 per night.

MGM Grand. If money is truly no object, consider the largest of the 29 villas inside the super-exclusive 300,000-square-foot Mansion at MGM Grand, which is modeled after an 18th-century Tuscan villa. $5,000–$15,000 per night.

Hard Rock Hotel. The 5,000-square-foot Penthouse Suite crash pad comes with its own bowling alley, a pool table, and a six-person hot tub flanked by massive plasma-screen TVs. Free! (If you spend $50,000 on food and drinks.)

2

BELLAGIO LAS VEGAS

Rooms
★★★★☆
Dining
★★★★☆
Sightseeing
★★★★☆
Shopping
★★★★☆
Nightlife
★★★☆☆

Bellagio opened in 1998 as the city's premier luxury resort, and it remains a top getaway despite the considerable competition from upscale properties. It's still impressive more for its refined elegance than for gimmicks, although hipsters and minimalist-minded travelers may find the gilt and glitter here too much to stomach. The selection of restaurants is top-tier, comparable to MGM, Mandalay Bay, and Wynn. Then, of course, there's the Bellagio fountain show: more than 1,000 fountains erupt in a choreographed water ballet across the man-made Bellagio lake. Walking into the lobby of Bellagio, you're confronted with a fantastic and colorful glass sculpture called Fiori di Como, by famed artist Dale Chihuly.

Updated
by Andrew
Collins
and Mike
Weatherford

An indoor botanical conservatory, two wedding chapels, and the Spa Tower complete the extravagant picture. One potentially off-putting aspect of Bellagio is that the casino dominates the property, and it's hard to avoid when getting from one section of the resort to another. That being said, rooms in the Spa Tower are farthest from the gaming action. *Parents take note: no one under 18 is allowed on the property unless they are staying at the hotel, and even then, Bellagio is generally an adult-oriented option.*

THE ROOMS

$$–$$$$
Fodor'sChoice
★

This is a hard place to land good deals, although it never hurts to check the hotel's Web site for specials: rates average $250 to $300 much of the year, but during slower weeks you can usually snag a room for around $170 to $180 (competitive in comparison with other high-end Strip properties). If it's pampering you're after, stay in the Spa

BELLAGIO AT A GLANCE

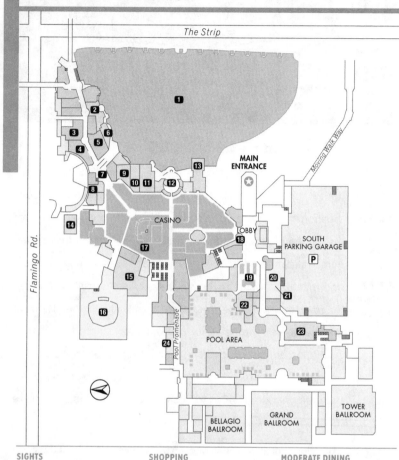

Yes, the fountains dance, but can they do the hustle?

THE CASINO

The casino proper is roomy, luxurious, and filled with a big-money international elite surrounded by gawking tourists. Under its hushed orange canopies you can easily spot a high roller betting $5,000 a hand as if it were pennies. But don't worry; there are games throughout the floor for the more average budget. Low-denomination slots are tucked in the back corners for low rollers (if you can find them) and excellent blackjack games are offered for mid- to high-level players.

The casino's epicenter remains its now-famous poker room, which rose to national notoriety as a key element of the TV poker fad. The race and sports book are super high-tech; each seductive leather seat is equipped with its own TV monitor. Things are a bit crowded with gawkers in the conservatory on the south end.

CAESARS PALACE

Rooms
★★★★☆
Dining
★★★☆☆
Sightseeing
★★★☆☆
Shopping
★★★★☆
Nightlife
★★★★☆

The opulent entrance, fountains, Roman statuary, bas-reliefs, and roaming centurions all add up to the iconic, over-the-top Las Vegas hotel. Here you can get your picture taken with Caesar, Cleopatra, and the centurion guard; find the full-size reproduction of Michelangelo's *David*; amble along Roman streetscapes in the Forum Shops to see the robotic Fall of Atlantis show; or scout for Elton John merchandise (he'll be performing numerous concerts throughout the year at Caesars).

Overall, Caesars has the best shopping of any Vegas casino resort, with more than 160 stores at the Forum and Appian Way Shops. An outdoor plaza and live entertainment area on top of an underground parking garage at the south end is geared to pedestrians at the Flamingo Road intersection. If you're a pedestrian coming in from the Mirage, to the north, a moving sidewalk whisks you over the swirl of traffic.

THE ROOMS

$$–$$$$
★

Caesars was one of the first properties in town to create rooms so lavish that guests might actually want to spend time in them; although plenty of competitors have sprung up over the years, this expansive property with a kitschy yet sumptuous Roman theme has continued to expand and upgrade. For typically $30 to $50 more per night, you can book a Spa Deluxe Room, which has marble-and-brass bathrooms with oversize whirlpool tubs. A variety of fancier and more expensive suites are also offered, some with parlors, wet bars, and marble rotunda entryways. The expansive and opulent Augustus tower added nearly 1,000 suites in 2005, all with soaring 9-foot ceilings and a minimum of 650 square feet of space. On the tower's second floor, famed French chef Guy Savoy opened his first restaurant outside Paris. The lavish

CAESARS PALACE AT A GLANCE

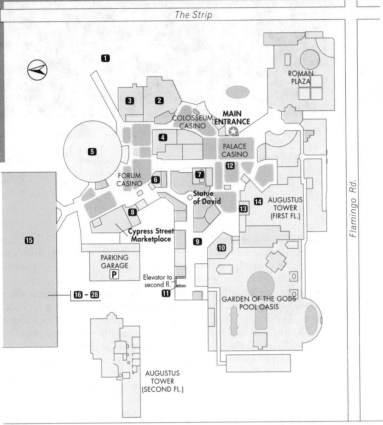

SIGHTS

Neil Leiffer Gallery **14**

SPAS

Qua Baths & Spa **11**

SHOWS

Colosseum at Caesars Palace,
Arts Center **5**

Elton John in The Red Piano,
Theater **5**

NIGHTLIFE

Cleopatra's Barge, Lounge **7**

PURE, Dance Club **2**

Pussycat Dolls Lounge,
Burlesque Show **3**

Shadow, Piano Bar/Lounge **6**

The Sports Book, Bar **12**

SHOPPING

Appian Way at Caesars, Mall **9**

Burberry,
Men and Women's clothing **27**

Fendi, Accessories **20**

Forum Shops at Caesars, Mall .. **15**

Gucci, Women's Clothing **19**

Harry Winston, Jewelry **18**

Hugo Boss, Men's Clothing **25**

Louis Vuitton,
Luggage & Accessories **24**

Nike Town, Sporting Goods **17**

Versace Jeans Couture,
Men and Women's Clothing **26**

West of Santa Fe,
Household Items/Furniture **16**

EXPENSIVE DINING

BOA Steakhouse, Eclectic **21**

Bradley Ogden, Contemporary ...**8**

Mesa Grill, Southwestern **4**

Sushi Roku, Japanese **28**

MODERATE DINING

808,Pacific Rim **13**

Chinois, Pan-Asian **22**

Spago Las Vegas,
Contemporary **23**

"C'mon 7! Mama needs a new pair of Manolo's."

Garden of the Gods Pool Oasis—a complex of Roman-style gardens, baths, and fitness areas anchored by the Neptune lap pool—is one of the better pool spots in town. ⊠*3570 Las Vegas Blvd. S, Center Strip, 89109* ☎*702/731–7110 or 877/427–7243* ⊕*www.caesarspalace.com* ⤵*1,834 rooms, 1,504 suites* ⊟*AE, D, DC, MC, V.*

THE CASINO

Caesars is the never-ending casino and, in recent years, one in constant transition. Two sprawling wings used to change character from one end of the property to the other, but a gradual remodeling brought most of the casino space into alignment with the faux–ancient Roman theme of the adjacent Forum Shops mall. Some of the original south casino, however, retains its 1966 intimacy, with a low ceiling and high stakes. The newer Olympic Casino wing, with its high ceiling, soaring marble columns, graceful rooftop arches, and lower limits, embraces the middle market with 5¢ and 25¢ slots. The gradual influence of Harrah's Entertainment had a positive influence on the casino's video-poker pay schedules, and Caesars ran counter to the prevailing tides when it opened a live keno lounge with hip decor and plasma TV screens to reinvent the sleepy game.

The end of the original Caesars is marked by Cleopatra's Barge, one of the last remnants from the old days, a one-of-a-kind lounge floating in an indoor pool. The Forum Casino, adjacent to the mall, was remodeled to service the Colosseum concert venue where Celine Dion performed. The gaming floor is now augmented with the Cypress Street Marketplace, a "fast casual" food court that sells dishes such as pizza and Asian noodles. The huge race and sports book was one of the first outrageously big ones and is still something to see. Wear your walking shoes and prepare to get lost in this Roman empire.

2

HARD ROCK HOTEL & CASINO

Rooms
★★★☆☆

Dining
★★★☆☆

Sightseeing
★★★★☆

Shopping
★☆☆☆☆

Nightlife
★★★★☆

The Hard Rock doesn't try to be cool—it just is—and it is the cool-without-trying who hang out here. A vast collection of rock-and-roll memorabilia fills the property, from a Kurt Cobain guitar to a Britney Spears outfit. Navigating the Hard Rock is simple: it's completely circular. On the inside of the circle is the small but accommodating gaming floor, and on the outside, shops and restaurants, which rank among the best of any off-Strip casino. An ambitious plan to expand the casino, build a new showroom, and add condos to the mix was suddenly tabled by Hard Rock Chairman Peter Morton's spring 2006 decision to sell the property to Morgan Hotel Group for a rockin' $770 million. He couldn't completely let go however—as part of the agreement Morton will keep some memorabilia, including a Jimi Hendrix Flying V guitar.

THE ROOMS

$$–$$$$
★

It's impossible to forget you're in the Hard Rock, no matter where you go in this rock-fixated joint: even the hall carpeting is decorated with musical notes. The rooms are large, with sleek furnishings, Bose CD-stereos, and flat-screen plasma TVs that show continuous music videos on one channel. Some beds have leather headboards, bathrooms have stainless-steel sinks, and the double French doors that serve as floor-to-ceiling windows actually open. The Hard Rock's pool area—a tropical beach–inspired oasis with a floating bar, private cabanas, and

HARD ROCK HOTEL & CASINO AT A GLANCE

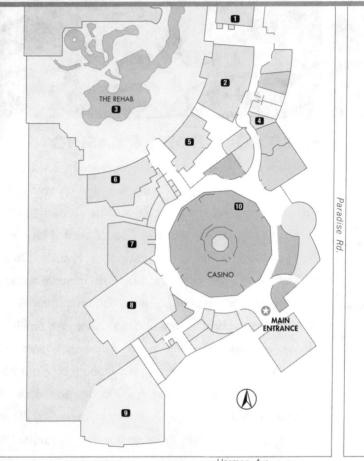

THE REHAB

CASINO

MAIN ENTRANCE

Paradise Rd.

Harmon Ave.

SIGHTS
Hard Rock Pool **3**
SHOWS
The Joint, *Arts Center* **8**
NIGHTLIFE
Body English, *Dance Clubs* **9**
Cuba Libre, *Lounge* **4**
Viva Las Vegas **10**

EXPENSIVE DINING
A.J.'s Steakhouse, *Steakhouse* **1**
Nobu, *Japanese* **5**
MODERATE DINING
Simon Kitchen & Bar, *American* ..**6**
INEXPENSIVE DINING
Mr. Lucky's 24/7,
American-Casual **7**
Pink Taco, *Mexican* **2**

Where money is god—but Clapton is, too.

poolside blackjack—is a favorite filming location for MTV and popular TV shows. Very crowded (but fun) public areas offer plenty of opportunities for people-watching. It's possible to score reasonable rates here on weeknights—the Hard Rock has definitely lost a bit of its arrogance, thanks to all those competing hipster-infested hotels in town, and works harder to please guests. The Rock Spa is one of the coolest places in town to get a massage. ✉*4455 Paradise Rd., Paradise Road, 89109* ☎*702/693–5000 or 800/473–7625* ⊕*www.hardrockhotel.com* ⬑*583 rooms, 64 suites* ▭*AE, D, DC, MC, V.*

THE CASINO

Slots have guitar-neck handles, blackjack layouts are customized with rock-related art, craps tables are adorned with Grateful Dead lyrics, and the rock music plays nonstop. The machines not only look good, but the player's club is surprisingly generous with bonus programs that are more like a locals-oriented casino than a tourist trap. There's a fun pickup bar in the middle that's designed for eyeballing the miniskirts walking by. Though you have to look for the tables with the best rules, it's usually a lively place to play, and the young and good-looking dealers often have as much fun as the players.

Because of the extremely modest original construction of the Hard Rock, the small sports book was made into a separate area closed off from the main casino—with its own bar, this self-contained environment is a haven from the craziness outside. Head out to the pool for swim-up blackjack tables.

LUXOR RESORT & CASINO

Rooms
★★★☆☆

Dining
★★☆☆☆

Sightseeing
★★★★☆

Shopping
★★☆☆☆

Nightlife
★★☆☆☆

Welcome to the land of the Egyptians—Vegas style. This modern world wonder is topped with a xenon light beam that burns brighter than any other in the world and can be seen from anywhere in the valley at night; for that matter, it's even visible from space. The exterior is made with 13 acres of black glass. Inside is the world's largest atrium— you get the full impact of the space from the second floor (also known as the Attractions Level for its two-level arcade with interactive race cars, small motion simulators, and state-of-the-art video games). Though this used to be a semi-cheesy, totally Egyptian-theme resort, it's now following the strategy of the vaguely pirate-theme TI–Treasure Island: the theme elements have been toned down to turn the focus from Kitsch Egyptian to the somewhat spruced-up restaurant and nightlife offerings (like the Fantasy topless show and the new nightclub LAX Las Vegas). Still, this is chiefly a place to stay, not play.

A tram connects Luxor with its sister casinos, Mandalay Bay (far more elegant but pricier) and Excalibur (far less elegant, despite a makeover in 2006, and only slightly less expensive). Mandalay Place, a high-end shopping mall with a few good restaurants, also connects Luxor to Mandalay Bay.

LUXOR AT A GLANCE

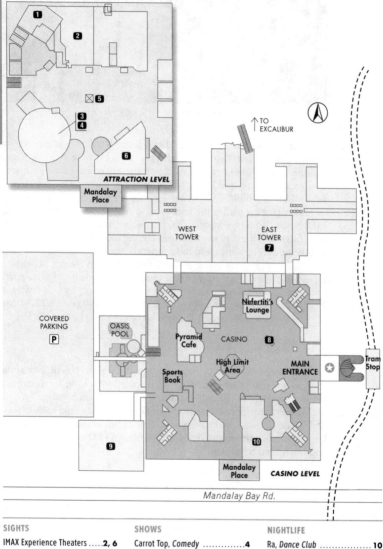

ATTRACTION LEVEL

↑ TO EXCALIBUR

Mandalay Place

WEST TOWER

EAST TOWER

COVERED PARKING

OASIS POOL

Pyramid Cafe

CASINO

Nefertiti's Lounge

High Limit Area

Sports Book

MAIN ENTRANCE

Tram Stop

Mandalay Place

CASINO LEVEL

Mandalay Bay Rd.

SIGHTS

IMAX Experience Theaters **2, 6**
King Tut Museum **1**
Pharoah's Pavilion **5**

SHOWS

Carrot Top, *Comedy* **4**
Criss Angel's Mindfreak,
Theater **9**
Fantasy, *Theater* **3**

NIGHTLIFE

Ra, *Dance Club* **10**

SHOPPING

Dandera's Bath & Body,
Bath Products **7**
Luxor Outlet Store, *Gifts* **8**

Where to get your pharoah on.

THE ROOMS

$-$$$$ ★   Four "inclinators" (elevators) travel the 39-degree incline of the pyramid to the guest rooms; "hallways" overlook the world's largest atrium. Rooms are large and maintain the Egyptian motif, with scarabs, palms, ankhs, and hieroglyphic design elements. One wall slopes because of the building's design—it's an interesting effect, but kind of annoying as it makes the room feel cramped. We prefer the identical 22-story towers next door: they're newer and have brighter rooms with large windows, many of them offering nice views of the pyramid. Bathrooms are spacious and have separate showers and tubs. Furnishings and design carry out a subtly Middle Eastern theme; artwork is Egyptian inspired. Spa suites in the pyramid have plenty of extra space and deep whirlpool tubs with brilliant views of the skyline. ⊠3900 Las Vegas Blvd. S, South Strip, 89119 ☎702/262–4000 or 888/777–0188 ◄₄4,040 rooms, 364 suites ⊕www.luxor.com ⊟AE, D, MC, V.

THE CASINO

Luxor's casino is not only huge, it's also square, so it will take some time to get your bearings. (Orient yourself by looking for periphery landmarks such as the coffee shop, sports book, and lounge.) You'll find surprisingly fresh air and a muted noise level as a solid middle-class and black-clad-chic crowd gawk at this eighth wonder of the world. On weekends, minimums are usually around $15, but during the week you might find $5 tables.

MANDALAY BAY RESORT & CASINO, WITH THEHOTEL & FOUR SEASONS

Rooms
★★★★☆
Dining
★★★★☆
Sightseeing
★★★★☆
Shopping
★★★☆☆
Nightlife
★★★★☆

Mandalay is an ancient inland temple city in Burma (Myanmar), which has no bay. And although the real Mandalay is in Southeast Asia, the hotel-casino is decked out like a South Seas beach resort, complete with the scent of coconut oil drifting through the casino and pagodas and gardens rising out of the vast casino floor. We like Mandalay because unlike other properties, such as Excalibur or Paris, it has wide-open spaces and broad, pleasant walkways.

We love the selection of trendy restaurants, the distinctive and offbeat upscale shops, and the dramatic Shark Reef aquarium and rollicking House of Blues music club and restaurant. The pool area, put simply, rocks—there's a lagoon with a huge wave pool (8-foot waves, roughest waters on the Strip), a ¾-mi-long "lazy river" pool, and a man-made beach. Then, there's the presence of a Four Seasons hotel and the glamorous all-suites THEhotel property. It all contributes to the property's cool-without-trying-too-hard vibe.

THE ROOMS

Mandalay Resort has three distinct hotel options: the main hotel tower; the independently operated Four Seasons; and THEhotel, an entirely separate all-suites property in its own massive tower.

$–$$$$
★

🏨 **Mandalay Bay.** The main hotel is the more affordable and less fabulous lodging component of Mandalay Bay, but it's still a first-rate property with cavernous rooms. Prices still do run pretty high. Bathrooms have understated, elegant stone floors and counters as well as deep soaking tubs with separate showers. The breezy, low-key decor is luxurious without being overbearing. ✉ *3950 Las Vegas Blvd. S, South Strip,*

MANDALAY BAY AT A GLANCE

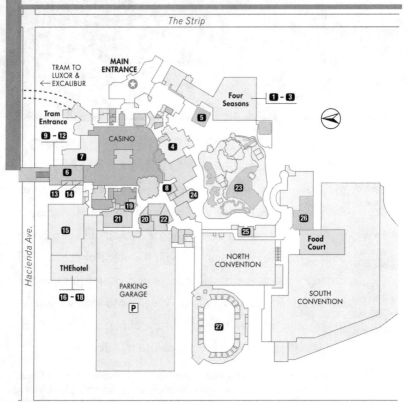

89119 ☎702/632–7777 or 877/632–7700 ⊕*www.mandalaybay.com* ⇨*3,215 rooms, 1,100 suites* ▤*AE, D, DC, MC, V.*

$$–$$$$
Fodor'sChoice
★

📺 **THEhotel at Mandalay Bay.** If James Bond were staying on the Strip, something tells us he'd book a suite here. Elaborate wet bars, giant 42-inch plasma TVs, plush carpeting, dark wooden desks, floor-to-ceiling windows, mirrored wardrobes at the foot of the most comfortable beds we've ever tried, and even a bowl of fake cherries on the coffee tables all add up to the perfect bachelor pad. The property is connected to the rest of Mandalay Bay but also has its own lobby and check-in, stellar full-service spa and fitness center, swank coffee bar, see-and-be-seen lounge, and respectable 24-hour restaurant (they turn out a commendable lobster salad). It's all unquestionably high end, but rates are surprisingly competitive with other leading hotels. Be sure to ask for a room above the fifth floor or so; otherwise, those floor-to-ceiling windows will be wasted on views of the rooftop ventilation system. ✉*3950 Las Vegas Blvd. S, South Strip, 89119* ☎*877/632–7800* ⊕*www.thehotelatmandalaybay.com* ▤*AE, D, DC, MC, V.*

$$$$
Fodor'sChoice
★
☾

📺 **Four Seasons Hotel.** If peace and quiet's what you're after, this is your spot. The hotel is on the top floors of the main hotel tower at Mandalay Bay, cushioned from the general casino ruckus. You have your own check-in, express elevators, pool, a fantastic health club and spa, recreation area, private parking, and posh restaurants, including the acclaimed Charlie Palmer Steakhouse—in short, you can avoid the gambling scene altogether, if you so choose. If you do feel that urge to join the Vegas madness, all of Mandalay Bay resort's offerings are available to you as well. We love the marble bathrooms with deep soaking tubs and separate showers as well as the fabulous views—floor-to-ceiling windows look over the Strip or the Las Vegas Valley (you'll pay a good bit more for a Strip vista). Afternoon tea, served daily in the Verandah lounge, is a lavish array of delicious savories and sweets. The pampering policy here even extends to the smallest guests: every child will find a stuffed animal and milk and cookies on arrival. ✉*3960 Las Vegas Blvd. S, South Strip, 89109* ☎*702/632–5000* ⊕*www.fourseasons.com* ⇨*338 rooms, 86 suites* ▤*AE, D, DC, MC, V.*

THE CASINO

Drool at the hordes of fabulous beautiful people and millionaires crowding the tables of this very hip and luxurious high-roller casino, which feels more casual and lively than pretentious counterparts such as Bellagio or the Venetian. The huge sports book is one of the Strip's top hangouts for enthusiasts, but is set off from the main traffic flow. The comp program links Mandalay with other MGM Mirage properties. For a break from the action, sit amid the virtual vegetation, rock waterfalls, and lily pond of the Coral Reef Lounge, one of the largest lounges in town.

MGM GRAND HOTEL & CASINO

Rooms
★★★☆☆

Dining
★★★★☆

Sightseeing
★★★☆☆

Shopping
★★☆☆☆

Nightlife
★★★★☆

A regal, bronze rendering of the roaring MGM lion mascot fronts the four emerald-green, fortresslike towers of the MGM Grand, one of the largest hotels in the world (it's so big that simply entering the parking garage gives you the feeling of being inside a giant ant farm). The self-proclaimed "City of Entertainment" is loosely based on Oz, though it comes off as having a bit of an identity crisis because it tries just a little too hard to be something for everyone.

Tony bars, trendy nightclubs, a stunning roster of knockout restaurants, and the impressive Grand Garden Arena—which hosts big-name music concerts and championship boxing matches—attract well-heeled and expense-account travelers as well as conventioneers from the adjacent convention center. When it comes to dining, MGM ranks among the city's top casino-resorts, with eateries run by such noted chefs as Emeril Lagasse, Joël Robuchon, and Michael Mina. Kids enjoy the lion habitat on the casino's west perimeter; there's also a complete day-care facility for the kids. There's a fairly short corridor of shops between the hotel and garage for the Strip monorail.

THE ROOMS

$–$$$$

Rooms in these four 30-story towers come in nine varieties. Standard rooms have soothing, earth-tone color schemes and are reasonably large. Further up the line, the various types of suites are more stylish and striking, and offer all sorts of fun perks: the 650-square-foot Bungalow suites are fitted with black-and-white Italian-marble bathrooms; slightly larger Celebrity Spa suites add whirlpool tubs with separate showers; and corner Premiere suites (950 square feet!) come with four-person dining areas and two TVs. At the very high end, two-story Terrace suites have 14-foot vaulted ceilings, and the 1,500-square-foot

MGM GRAND AT A GLANCE

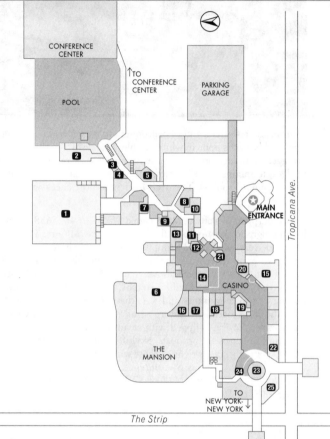

Sometimes you have to laugh to keep from crying.

Marquee suites offer a pair of bedrooms and master baths with gigantic mirrored hot tubs done in white marble. Few resorts in the world have a bigger or bolder pool and sunbathing area—a maze of pedestrian bridges, fountains, river courses, and waterfalls lends a tropical air to these popular grounds. The MGM offers airport check-in from 9 AM to 11 PM.

The superposh **Skylofts at MGM Grand** (☎877/646–5638, www.sky-loftsmgmgrand.com) occupy the hotel's top two floors. The magnificent two-story lofts have 24-foot floor-to-ceiling windows and come in one-, two-, and three-bedroom configurations. Skylofts perks include airport transfers via Mercedes Maybach 62 limos, separate check-in, butler service, Bang & Olufsen stereos, Sony HDTVs, and preferred seating at top restaurants and *KÀ* (the Cirque du Soleil show). Perhaps the most decadent feature of all is the "Immersion Chamber" bathrooms; they're equipped with steam rooms, infinity-edge Jacuzzi tubs, and Bulgari bath products. Skylofts, with rates starting at nearly $1,000 per night, ranks right up there with any hotel experience offered in Vegas. ♺*4,204 rooms, 802 suites* ✉*3799 Las Vegas Blvd. S, South Strip, 89109* ☎*702/891–1111 or 877/880–0880* ⊕*www.mgmgrand. com* ⊟*AE, D, DC, MC, V.*

THE CASINO

The biggest of the Las Vegas casinos, the MGM has a staggering amount of gaming space, which includes 3,500 slot machines and 165 table games with high minimums (blackjack and roulette mostly start at $10; you might find a $5 table in the afternoon if you look hard enough). The Strip entrance is slot heavy and at night takes on a fun atmosphere, with videos and music geared to the lines outside the Studio 54 club.

A separate high-roller casino falls in the middle of the long hike to "restaurant row," the Grand Garden arena, and massive sports book (remodeled after the opening of Wynn Las Vegas to stay competitive). You also find symmetrical rows of table games on this end, including poor-odds novelties such as Casino War. It's another good hike from the parking garage to the Casino. However, those in a wheelchair will appreciate the spacious aisles and well-spaced slot machines.

2

MIRAGE HOTEL AND CASINO

Rooms
★★★☆☆
Dining
★★★☆☆
Sightseeing
★★★☆☆
Shopping
★☆☆☆☆
Nightlife
★★★☆☆

The Mirage rang in the modern era of Las Vegas, but then started to look a little too "1989" thanks to modern evolutionary trends. So MGM Mirage gave the casino and restaurants an end-to-end makeover, all timed to the mid-2006 opening of Cirque du Soleil's Beatles-theme show. Even the campy exploding volcano (it erupts every 15 minutes from 7 PM until midnight, shooting fire high into the air) received some souped-up special effects. The design still stems from the glass dome inside the resort's front entrance, one that covers a lush rain forest with palm trees, cascading waterfalls, meandering lagoons, and exotic tropical flora.

They cut into the foliage a bit on the casino side to create an atmospheric lounge that's part of the popular Chicago-based eatery Japonais, one of a handful of excellent restaurants that have opened here since 2005, vastly improving the dining scene. A huge aquarium buzzing with leopard sharks, puffer fish, and about 90 other species makes for a stunning backdrop to the front desk. There is also a new lobby bar for those who want to contemplate the fish over a cold one.

The Mirage's tropical design scheme was partly inspired by the Siegfried & Roy show and their "Jungle Palace" home; though, after Roy Horn's near-fatal tiger bite in 2003 the show was replaced by Cirque, the hotel kept the outdoor Secret Garden of Siegfried & Roy animal and dolphin attraction, as well as the white-tiger display near the south exit on the Caesars Palace side. However, the duo's gift shop at the north end of the property was sacrificed to build part of Jet, a multiroom nightclub that commands weekend lines extending a hundred yards or so down the hallway. If your feet are tired, there's a complimentary slow-moving tram to Treasure Island next door.

MIRAGE AT A GLANCE

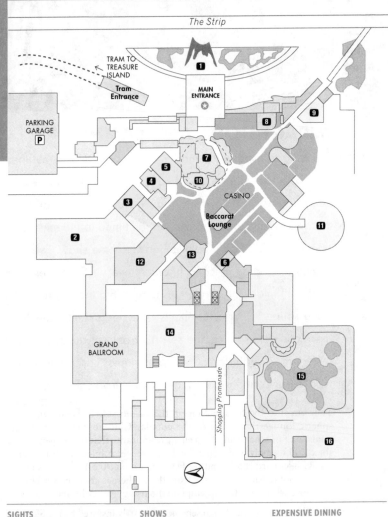

"You're cute and all, but don't ever split 5s and ruin my blackjack again."

THE ROOMS

$–$$$$ 🛏 Immaculate, upscale but not outlandishly priced rooms are done with an elegant South Seas theme and botanical prints; they all have antiquey-looking custom-made desks and marble entryways, and suites are decked in imported silks and hand-loomed carpets. Bathrooms have marble accents and sumptuous appointments but tend toward the small side. Rooms with incredible views of the Strip and the volcano cost a bit more, but you can sometimes get a free upgrade if you request one at check-in. Several upscale restaurants, including STACK and Japonais, have helped give the Mirage an impressive slate of both high-end and casual eateries. ✉*3400 Las Vegas Blvd. S, Center Strip, 89109* ☎*702/791–7111 or 800/627–6667* ⊕*www.themirage.com* 🛏*2,763 rooms, 281 suites* ▤*AE, D, DC, MC, V.*

THE CASINO

The casino has high minimums (such as $500 slots and a plush private pit where the minimum bet is $1,000), ionospheric maximums, and an overall atmosphere of sophisticated fun. The property's makeover got rid of the pretentious trappings in the High Limit Lounge and Baccarat Lounge, opting for a cool modern look with blue backlighting behind the service bars. The poker room is huge and bustling, more about volume and energy than the subdued, high-limit atmosphere at the Bellagio.

The focal point of the casino is the lush tropical garden that leads into the main area. Where else in town can you sit at a slot machine and breathe in fresh air and second-hand smoke? But the Polynesian theme overall has been toned down, with some of the new restaurants opening out to the casino to provide more visual interest. The hip STACK restaurant, for instance, took its design motif from Red Rock Canyon. A new lounge, Revolution, carries the Beatles theme of the *Love* show into a mini-nightclub for pre- and postshow gatherings. The race and sports book at the south end is full of giant screens that resemble NASA's mission control. The overall effect is exceptionally energizing.

NEW YORK–NEW YORK HOTEL & CASINO

Rooms
★★★☆☆
Dining
★★★☆☆
Sightseeing
★★★★☆
Shopping
★☆☆☆☆
Nightlife
★★★★☆

Vegas takes on Manhattan in this fantasy version of Gotham City. The mini-Manhattan skyline is one of our favorite parts of the Strip—there are third-size to half-size re-creations of all the biggies: the Empire State Building, the Statue of Liberty, the Chrysler, Seagram, and CBS buildings, the New York Public Library, Grand Central Terminal, and the Brooklyn Bridge. A wrought-iron fence near the model of a New York fireboat has items donated by people from all over the world in a tribute to the victims of 9/11. Looping around it all is the Manhattan Express roller coaster.

The Big Apple flavor continues inside: walk through an art deco lobby, play virtual reality games at an arcade reminiscent of Coney Island, chow down at a surprisingly good food court patterned after Greenwich Village, and all the while keep your eye out for details such as names on mailboxes and brownstone apartment façades with air-conditioners in the windows.

THE ROOMS

$–$$$$

Rooms in this sprawling compound are quite a bit larger than the typically tiny hotel rooms in the *real* Gotham. Beyond all the legroom, they're not particularly fancy, but the hotel has made some improvements in recent years. Bedspreads are busy, however, lighting is too bold, and furniture is somewhat utilitarian (although attractive art deco–inspired armoires are a nice touch). Also, the trek from the front desk to some of the towers can feel longer than the New York City Marathon, and the Manhattan Express roller coaster that loops around the hotel can be obnoxiously loud if your room is near the

NEW YORK-NEW YORK AT A GLANCE

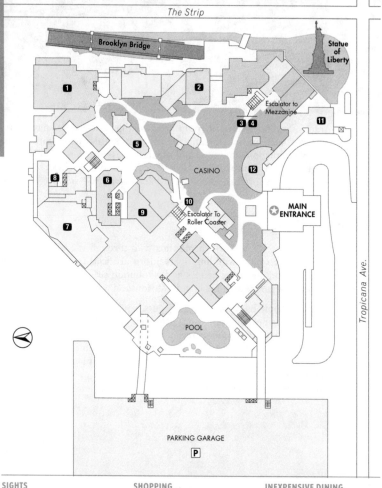

The Strip

Brooklyn Bridge

Statue of Liberty

❶

❷

Escalator to Mezzanine

❸ ❹

❺

CASINO

❻

❽

⓮

❾

❿

Escalator To Roller Coaster

MAIN ENTRANCE

❼

Tropicana Ave.

POOL

PARKING GARAGE
P

No matter how much you lose here, it probably pales compared with what you'd have spent on vacation in the real New York.

tracks. Several grades of room are available, and as you pay more, you get such plush amenities as separate sitting areas with sofas, marble bathroom counters, and separate glass showers. ✉*3790 Las Vegas Blvd. S, South Strip, 89109* ☎*702/740–6969 or 888/693–6763* ⊕*www.nynyhotelcasino.com* ⬎*1,920 rooms, 104 suites* ▭*AE, D, DC, MC, V.*

THE CASINO

The intricate New York theme runs wild through the Central Park–esque casino pit. Twinkling lights adorn artificial trees on the main casino floor, and faux hedges and a fountain set off Gaming on the Green, a separate area for high-limit slots and table games.

The Big Apple Bar almost literally puts bands on a pedestal, towering over the casino floor, and the sports book has a fun synergy with the adjacent ESPN Zone theme restaurant. We think it's all worth a look-see, but we'd recommend you gamble elsewhere: table game limits are high, and the rules aren't tempting for discerning players. Space limitations make the casino floor, particularly the pit area, crowded and cramped—just like its namesake.

2

THE PALMS

Rooms
★★★★☆
Dining
★★★☆☆
Sightseeing
★☆☆☆☆
Shopping
★☆☆☆☆
Nightlife
★★★★☆

Striated shadows across the ceiling bring to mind palm fronds in this contempo California–style hot spot. The charismatic Maloof brothers, who also own pro basketball's Sacramento Kings, opened the city's first true luxury boutique hotel in 2001. Fame came quickly, as one of its posh suites provided the setting for MTV's *The Real World: Las Vegas* (Britney Spears stayed in that very suite during the weekend of her quickly annulled first marriage in January 2004, further heightening the intrigue surrounding the Palms). The hotel still attracts both the glitterati and a younger, cool crowd that keeps the public places—lounges, clubs, and restaurants—hopping every weekend night.

The three-story spa has an aromatherapy bar, massages, wraps, and facials; and Alizé, the 50th-floor restaurant helmed by famed local restaurateur André Rochat, offers one of the most memorable and romantic dining experiences in the city. There are plenty of ways to have a blast here, from sipping cocktails in the open-air Ghost Bar, a snazzy rooftop lounge on the hotel's 50th floor, to catching a flick in the movie theater, which is outfitted with high-back rocker love seats and wall-to-wall curved screens.

The Maloofs aren't about to slow down any time soon. They added the first new Playboy Club in 25 years here in 2006, a new 600-room condo-hotel and spa opened in 2007, and several more themed "mega-suites" were added to the 40-story Fantasy Tower. The Palms might have always taken second place to Hard Rock as the best place to revel (at least in our book), but now that Hard Rock's future is less secure, the Palms looks like it's poised to assume top party dog.

THE PALMS AT A GLANCE

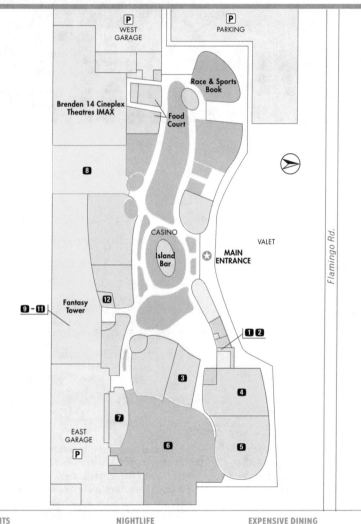

2

Astrophysics is a common topic of hilarity at the Palms.

THE ROOMS

$–$$$$ Rooms are large, opulent, and modern, with some unusual ameni-
★   ties for Las Vegas—such as beds with ultrafirm mattresses, duvets, cof-
feemakers, and Davies Gate bath products—and most provide a good
view of the city. The incredible, sleek pool, completely redone in 2006,
is surrounded by cabanas with TVs and hammocks, patches of grass
and sand, three bars, and a concert venue. The Fantasy Tower that
opened in 2006 added another 225 rooms and two "Party Floors" that
include a suite with a hardwood basketball court and a nearby record-
ing studio for bands or pop stars who want to mix business with plea-
sure. ⌂*4321 W. Flamingo Rd., West Side, 89103* ☎*702/942–7777
or 866/942–7777* ⊕*www.palms.com* ↻*605 rooms, 52 suites* ▤*AE,
D, DC, MC, V.*

THE CASINO

The Palms opened with a bold plan to be two casinos in one. By day
it's a locals' casino on the west end (the one near the food court, sports
book, and movie theaters). Come nighttime, there's a hip casino that
serves as serious competition for the Hard Rock Hotel (thanks to the
nightclubs on the east end of the property). That duality is still evident,
though the influence of the hip side is clearly taking over. Retirees at
the slots coexist with young suits wearing cell-phone headsets, eyeing
cocktail waitresses in shiny black vinyl high-heeled boots and short-
short skirts.

The Palms is clean and well ventilated, with slot sections sprinkled
comfortably along its wood floors, low lighting, and giant fans that
hang low from the ceiling and pass the time in a slow, easy spin. The
collective effect is a nice flow from the tattoo joint at one end to the
food court at the other. The Palms does take big bets but the table-game
rules are average. The slots and video-poker machines, however, are
hands down the best among any of the featured casinos in this chapter;
you have to venture far from the Strip to far less sexy gambling halls
to find coin games that compete. Look for swim-up blackjack, which
is played in the poolside lounge. Or, head upstairs to gamble in the
Playboy Club, which offers blackjack tables in a retro-cool setting with
crystal chandeliers and bunny-eared dealers.

PARIS LAS VEGAS

Rooms
★★★☆☆

Dining
★★★☆☆

Sightseeing
★★★★☆

Shopping
★★☆☆☆

Nightlife
★★☆☆☆

This homage to the City of Lights aims to conjure up all the charm of the French capital. Paris Las Vegas isn't quite as glamorous as the Strip's other Euro-metropolis-theme wonder, the Venetian, but it's still good fun. Outside are replicas of the Arc de Triomphe, the Paris Opera House, the Hôtel de Ville, and the Louvre, along with an *Around the World in Eighty Days* balloon marquee. Inside, everything is decked out in Gallic regalia, including village façades with arched windows, fake trees, and three massive legs of the 50-story Eiffel Tower replica jutting through the roof and resting on the Monet-style floral carpet. Fountains and statues are everywhere. There's even a cobblestone walkway to Bally's, with a mime on the loose and kiosks selling French pastries.

THE ROOMS

$–$$$$ 🖼 Midpriced among the Center Strip's high-profile resorts, Paris actually offers more elegant digs—even in its standard units, which have marble baths with separate tubs and showers—than some of its pricier and more talked-about competitors, although some find the heavy-handed decor a little busy. Every room has custom-designed furniture with Franco-inspired decorative elements and artwork, and east-facing rooms overlook the magnificent fountains and lagoon across the street at Bellagio. Otherwise, your room may overlook the pleasant pool area. Suites add more space, of course, plus considerably more dashing red, beige, and gold furniture and rich fabrics. The fabulous

PARIS LAS VEGAS AT A GLANCE

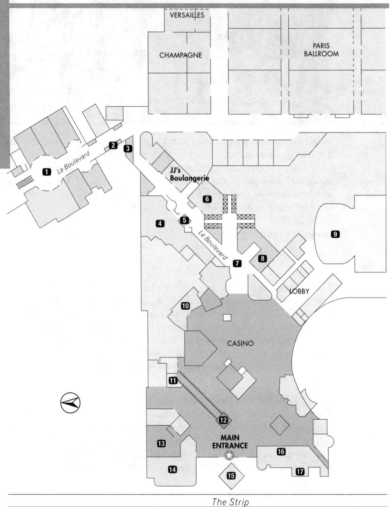

The Strip

Some people come for the topless statues.

buffet serves dishes from five French regions. The other dining options are mostly quite good, a couple of them excellent, although none is truly a showstopper, save perhaps for Mon Ami Gabi bistro. A massive octagonal pool sits in the shadows of the ersatz Eiffel Tower, on the hotel rooftop—it could use a little more shade, but it's surrounded by neatly tended gardens. ✉ *3655 Las Vegas Blvd. S, Center Strip, 89109* ☎ *702/739–4111 or 877/796–2096* ⊕ *www.paris-lv.com* ➘ *2,621 rooms, 295 suites* ▤ *AE, D, DC, MC, V.*

THE CASINO

The spacious and whimsical dazzler of a casino may make you forget that you won't find many breaks here. The main casino floor conveys a dreamlike feeling, which you enter under an artificial pastoral blue sky dotted with white clouds (future historians might note the '90s-era of Vegas architecture as the "domed ceiling painted blue with fake clouds" period). The attention to French detail, down to fancy floral wash basins in the Provençal-style bathrooms, adds up to a charming yet classy casino.

Amid all this Parisian charm, take note that game rules are poor for the player. Roulette is slightly more prominent here than at other casinos; perhaps it's in keeping with the theme. Be sure to check out the dozen LeRoy Neiman paintings that grace the walls of the high-roller pit. An increasingly rare live music lounge, Le Cabaret, can be seen and heard in the larger casino. As all the dealers say, *bonne chance*!

TREASURE ISLAND LAS VEGAS (TI)

Rooms
★★★☆☆

Dining
★★★☆☆

Sightseeing
★★★☆☆

Shopping
★☆☆☆☆

Nightlife
★★★☆☆

The jury is still out on Treasure Island's decision to pursue a trendy, younger crowd by nicknaming itself TI, but most signs suggest this rebranding of sorts is a fairly solid success. Gone are the distinctive skull-and-crossbones outdoor sign and the indoor pirate theme. Fronting the resort is a huge body of water—called Siren's Cove instead of Buccaneer Bay—that is the crux of the new TI. Instead of pirates and sailors duking it out, sexy sirens lure pirates into the cove in a kitschy show with pop music.

We think the best assets of TI are *Mystère*, a Cirque du Soleil show, and the popular nightclub–burlesque bar Tangerine. It's a decent choice if you're looking for a party vibe in the middle of the Strip. But TI has also added a handful of excellent restaurants in recent years, making it much more of a destination among foodies. A short, free tram ride connects to the Mirage next door.

THE ROOMS

$–$$$$ TI's rooms received a significant makeover in the mid-2000s and are now contemporary and inviting, with soft hues, marble bathrooms, and floor-to-ceiling windows. Several cavernous suite types are available, some outfitted with Bose CD-stereos and all with whirlpool tubs. The pool area is very pleasant, and at night you can have drinks at the Kahunaville tropical nightclub. ⊠ *3300 Las Vegas Blvd. S, Center Strip, 89109* ☎ *702/894–7111 or 800/944–7444* ⊕ *www.treasureislandlasvegas.com* ⊅ *2,665 rooms, 220 suites* ⊟ *AE, D, DC, MC, V.*

TREASURE ISLAND AT A GLANCE

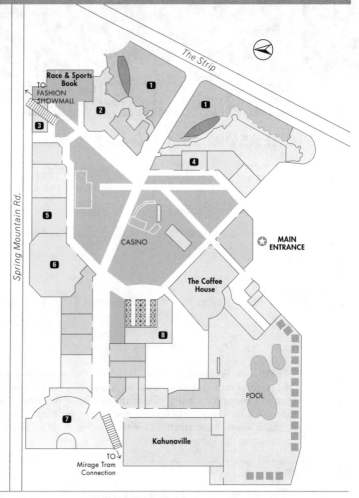

2

The Sirens of TI give new meaning to "pirate's booty" nightly at 7pm.

THE CASINO

Medium budgets can go either direction here: on one side of an aisle is a full-view pastry kitchen, part of the impressive Dishes buffet; across that aisle is a bank of 2-cent machines. Nickel progressives stand opposite the Isla Tequila bar's banks of obscure labels. Basically, now that the pirate theme is toned down, the somewhat cramped casino here is upscale and attractive but oddly generic.

As with most MGM Mirage properties, expect $15 table minimums on a Saturday night, but try tables during the week for lower minimums. Race- and sports-betting fans find an oasis in the black leather chairs and desks with individual TV screens found north of the main traffic flow in the sports book. The ferocious crowds from the *Sirens of TI* show create traffic-flow problems each time one of the performances ends (look for a pedestrian bridge to the Fashion Show Mall at the north end for a faster escape).

VENETIAN RESORT HOTEL CASINO

Rooms
★★★★☆
Dining
★★★★☆
Sightseeing
★★★★☆
Shopping
★★★☆☆
Nightlife
★★★☆☆

This theme hotel re-creates Italy's most romantic city with meticulous reproductions of Venetian landmarks. From the Strip you enter through the Doge's Palace, set on a walkway over a large lagoon. Inside, Renaissance characters roam the public areas, singing opera, performing mime, jesting, even kissing hands. Walking from the hotel lobby into the casino is one of the great experiences in Las Vegas: overhead, reproductions of famous frescoes, highlighted by 24-karat-gold frames, adorn the ceiling; underfoot, the geometric design of the flat marble floor provides an Escher-like optical illusion of climbing stairs.

The Venetian is renowned for having many of the city's leading high-end restaurants and shops, and some of the amenities here are downright breathtaking: the Guggenheim Hermitage Museum shows rotating exhibits from the Guggenheim and Hermitage collections; the Canyon Ranch Spa Club offers the same lavish treatments as the spa resort's main campuses in Arizona and Massachusetts; and Grand Canal Shoppes has noted boutiques such as Burberry, Jimmy Choo, and Sephora. A nice range of hip restaurants and bars has helped up the trend factor here in recent years. Rest assured, you won't run out of things to see and do at this lavish hotel.

THE ROOMS

$$–$$$$
Fodor's Choice
★

Some of the Strip's largest and plushest suites are found at this elegant, gilded resort that's a hit with foodies, shoppers, and high rollers. It's all about glitz and wow effect here, which makes it a popular property if you're celebrating a special occasion or looking for the

VENETIAN AT A GLANCE

2

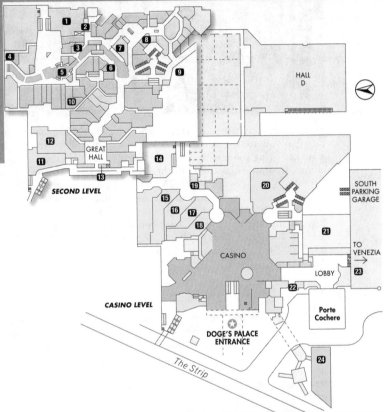

At the Canal Shoppes you won't find anything for a song, but you will hear singing gondoliers serenading the shoppers.

quintessential over-the-top Vegas experience. The 700-plus-square-foot guest quarters, richly adorned in a modified Venetian style, have a sunken living room with dining table and convertible sofa, walk-in closets, separate shower and tub, three telephones (including one in the bathroom), and 27- or 36-inch TVs. The even posher Venezia Tower has a concierge floor, private entrance, fountains, and gargantuan suites with mosaic walls, vaulted ceilings, and carved marble accents. Service here, at one time a bit uneven, has improved markedly in recent years. ✉3355 Las Vegas Blvd. S, Center Strip, 89109 ☎702/414–1000 or 888/883–6423 ⊕www.venetian.com 📠4,027 suites ▭AE, D, DC, MC, V.

THE CASINO

The underwhelming gaming area almost seems like an afterthought compared to the more interesting peripheral elements of the Venetian. You almost get the idea the gaming is there only because people expect it to be. Still, players can benefit from the casino's "boutique" status—in terms of its individual ownership, not sprawling acreage—for treatment of repeat customers and high rollers. The blackjack tables in particular have very good odds for high-level players; it's hard to find a single-deck game, but the double-deck games come with the once-standard, but now rare payoffs and rules.

There's an open lounge with live music at one end of the casino and a food court not too far from that. A high-limit slot area is nestled into a subdued corner, and the player's club employs an ultrahigh-tech tracking system that enables you to comp yourself using your slot club points at any machine in the casino. The Venetian kept up with the poker craze by adding a room with more than two dozen tables in 2006.

2

WYNN LAS VEGAS

Rooms
★★★★☆

Dining
★★★★☆

Sightseeing
★★★☆☆

Shopping
★★★★☆

Nightlife
★★★☆☆

In a city that keeps raising the bar for sheer luxury, the Wynn—monolithic in both name and appearance—takes a new, more discreet turn for the tasteful. With this mammoth resort, Steve Wynn, the high-profile developer of the Mirage, Treasure Island, and Bellagio, shirked the campy, theme-park trend he brought on in the '90s for a new one: haute Las Vegas. At $2.7 billion, this was the most expensive hotel project ever undertaken, but you won't find any sign of that in the form of a public spectacle. There's no volcano or dancing-waters, and the man-made "mountain" with a short multimedia show at night is concealed from the Strip, on view mainly to restaurant and nightclub patrons.

What's all the fuss about? First, there's the Madison Avenue lineup of boutiques: Chanel, Manolo Blahnik, Gaultier, de la Renta. Then, there's the assemblage of talented chefs, including New York's Daniel Boulud, legendary Japanese chef Takashi Yagahashi, and France's most renowned pastry chef, Frédéric Robert. There's a Ferrari car dealership, a theater-in-the-round showroom, an exclusive championship golf course (retained from the Desert Inn days), a poolside cabana-style casino (play blackjack while you swim!), and a sybaritic spa offering everything from sake-and-rice body treatments to feng shui–inspired "good luck rituals." It's a best-of-everything list under one roof—a playground for jet-setters, high rollers, or anyone who wants to feel like one.

Some naysayers think Wynn looks like "Bellagio Version 1.5," thanks to the blatant similarities in design (the deep red color scheme notwithstanding). But we're not sure that's a downfall, and Wynn does feel a

WYNN AT A GLANCE

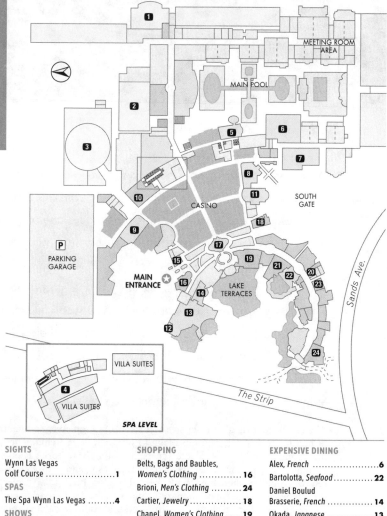

A rose by another name: the Wynn once again raises the bar for elegance.

bit more sleek and streamlined, a Bellagio for the 21st century. Construction has begun on Wynn's adjacent encore project, named—what else?—Encore, slated to open late in 2008.

THE ROOMS

$$$–$$$$
Fodor$Choice
★

Decked out with replicas of pieces from Steve Wynn's acclaimed art collection, the princely rooms, averaging a whopping 650 square feet, offer spectacular views through wall-to-wall floor-to-ceiling windows. Rest your head at night on custom pillow-top beds with 320-thread-count linens, and stay plugged into the world with cordless phones—bedside drapery and climate controls are another nice touch. The superposh Tower Suites Parlor and Salon units have use of a separate pool and lanai and have such opulent amenities as granite wet bars, separate powder rooms, 42-inch flat-screen TVs, and walk-in closets. Even relatively minor touches, such as richly appointed armchairs with ottomans and giant, fluffy Turkish towels, speak to the sheer sumptuousness of this place. ⊠ *3131 Las Vegas Blvd. S, Center Strip, 89109* ☎ *702/770–7100 or 888/320–9966* ⊕ *www.wynnlasvegas.com* ⤶ *2,359 rooms, 357 suites* ▤ *AE, D, DC, MC, V*

THE CASINO

The bad news–good news on the Wynn casino depends on how much money you come with. You'll see $500-minimum blackjack tables on the regular casino floor, not just inside the high-rollers casino (which is adjacent to a casino lounge). If you can pony up the cash for tables with a $100 buy-in or higher, though, you'll have some of the best rules possible. During the day or early evening, you can find $15 tables, but they're dealt from a shoe or automatic card shuffler. Lest you dismiss Wynn Las Vegas as completely snooty, rest assured that a healthy number of one-cent slots are out in a prominent area, not shuffled off to some remote corner. It may also surprise you that the coin games have some of the best pay schedules in town, and the Red Card player's club has generous sign-up bonuses. The multilevel poker room unfolds near the exotic car dealership, and there's a nice bar area next to the sports book, where plush chairs line the individual viewing cubicles augmenting the usual big-screen TVs.

SPAAAAH

Ah, Vegas. Sin City caters to your every indulgence, and over-the-top luxury day spas are no exception. So go ahead, book that hour-long massage and whatever else your heart desires. Need an excuse for all that pampering? Just remember, you could be spending that money at the tables.

The big Strip hotels offer the poshest pampering in luxury spas and the latest in trendy treatments from around the globe. Expect to be smeared with exotic Balinese spices, swished in a watsu pool, or submerged in a bath enriched with Black Moor mud, all in splashy, stylish spa facilities.

To indulge in these royal treatments, expect to pay anywhere from $20 to $50 to use the fitness facilities, take the waters, and enjoy lavish spa amenities such as lounging areas, whirlpools, steam rooms, saunas, and an array of personal care products in the shower areas. However, most waive the daily facility fee if you purchase treatments, classes, or personal training sessions.

Although most spas are open to the public, many, such as Bellagio or Wynn Las Vegas, reserve certain days of the week for the hotel's guests. Some only allow you in if you book a treatment, some don't. Make sure to ask about the spa's policy and usage fees before visiting or while making an appointment.

SPA SAVVY

SPA NAME	Body Treatments	Facials	Sun Rescue/ Hydrating	Treatments for Two	Non-guest Spa Facility Day Pass	Sauna	Steam Room
Aquae Sulis	$65–$185	$65–$250	yes	no	$45	yes	yes
THE Bathhouse	$75–$250	$75–$190	yes	no	$35	yes	yes
Canyon Ranch Spa Club	$140–$420	$140–$255	yes	yes	$35	yes	yes
Elemis Spa	$100–$480	$120–$230	yes	yes	$35	yes	yes
Four Seasons Spa	$85–$320	$140–$215	yes	yes	Free with a service	yes	yes
MGM Grand Spa	$75–$310	$65–$370	yes	yes	$25	yes	yes
Nurture Spa	$70–$220	$75–$190	no	no	$25	yes	yes
Palms Spa	$65–$140	$75–$220	yes	yes	$25	yes	yes
Spa Bellagio	$85–$350	$85–$285	yes	yes	$25	yes	yes
Qua Baths & Spa	$100–$300	$180–$325	yes	yes	$35	yes	yes
Spa Mandalay	$70–$235	$70–$170	yes	no	$30	yes	yes
Spa Vita di Lago	$45–$220	$95–$255	yes	yes	$40	yes	yes
The Spa Wynn Las Vegas	$175–$320	$120–$460	yes	yes	$25	yes	yes

(left) Spa, Planet Hollywood Resort & Casino, (above) Spa Bellagio

SPAAAAH

2

TOP SPOTS

The Spa, Wynn Las Vegas

■ TIP→ Many spas offer special treatment for bachelorette parties or couples; just ask and a secret party room may open up for you.

The Spa Wynn Las Vegas

Designed according to Feng Shui principles, and set away from the bells and jangles of the Strip, the Spa exudes an elegant Zen calm while remaining very cozy. There's a fireplace and flat screen TV in the lounge areas, and the hot and cool plunge area is naturally lit, lush with thriving palms and orchids.

Treatments, such as the Fresh Sake Body Treatment, are Asian-inspired. The Good Luck Ritual is based on the Five Elements of Feng Shui, and includes a massage with Thai herbs, an ultra-moisturizing hand therapy, and a wild lime botanical scalp treatment. For the ultimate in combating the drying desert clime, try La Mer The Facial, which lathers Créme de la Mer over the face and décolletage.

BODY TREATMENTS. **Massage:** Swedish, aromatherapy, deep tissue, couples massage, pregnancy massage, reflexology. **Exfoliation:** body polish, salt glow, sugar polish, waxing.

BEAUTY TREATMENTS. Anti-aging treatments, hair cutting, facials, manicure, pedicure, waxing, hot-lather shaves for men.

PRICES. Body Treatments: $175–$320. Facials: $120–$460. Manicure/Pedicure: $30–$95. Waxing: $35–$100.

Canyon Ranch Spa Club at the Venetian

Vegas's largest spa—one of the best day spas in the country—is this outpost of Tucson's famed Canyon Ranch in the Venetian. The extensive treatment menu here covers any desire, including Tibetan Bowl Healing and an Ayurvedic herbal rejuvenating treatment. The unusual Rasul Ceremony is a Middle Eastern treatment of herbal steam and medicinal mud in a tiled steam chamber—we think it's perfect for couples.

Weekend warriors love the health club, the Strip's largest, with its 40-foot climbing wall and frequent fitness and yoga classes. The nutrition, wellness, and exercise physiology departments also offer free lectures, Lifetime Nutrition Consultation, and acupuncture. An adjoining café serves healthy cuisine and smoothies.

BODY TREATMENTS. **Massage:** Swedish, aromatherapy, stone, couples massage, Ashiatsu, deep tissue, pregnancy massage, ayurvedic rejuvenation, hydromassage, reflexology. **Exfoliation:** body polish, salt glow, sugar polish, Vichy shower, waxing.

BEAUTY TREATMENTS. Anti-aging treatments, facials, manicure, pedicure, hair cutting, waxing, hair extensions, make-up.

PRICES. Body Treatments: $140–$420. Facials: $140–$255. Manicure/Pedicure: $15–$145. Waxing: $30–$110.

Canyon Ranch Spa Club

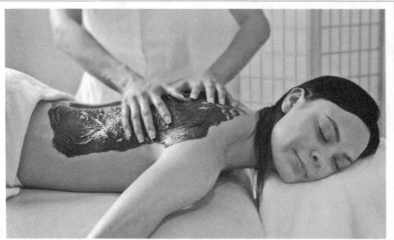

Spa Bellagio

Spa Bellagio

Besides the calming reflecting pools and the Reflexology Pebble Walk, this swank Zen sanctuary has treatments such as Thai yoga massage and Gem Therapy. The 6,000-square-foot fitness center has a gorgeous view of the Mediterranean gardens and the pool. There's even a candlelit meditation room with fountain walls.

If Vegas over-indulging and the dry climate have gotten to you, try the Thalasso Therapy Session for seaweed and water-based detoxifying and hydrating treatment. Spa Bellagio offers Watsu, an aquatic massage using Zen Shiatsu techniques that takes place in a warm pool while floating.

Spa services are exclusive to Bellagio guests, and the fitness area is only open to other MGM Mirage guests Monday through Thursday.

BODY TREATMENTS. **Massage:** Swedish, aromatherapy, stone, couples massage, Watsu, Ashiatsu, Thai yoga, deep tissue, pregnancy massage, Jamu, Indian head massage, reflexology. **Exfoliation:** body polish, salt glow, sugar polish, coconut scrub Vichy shower, Moor Mud, seaweed, gold, coffee, waxing.

BEAUTY TREATMENTS. Anti-aging treatments, facials, manicure, pedicure, hair cutting, waxing, hot-lather shaves for men.

PRICES. Body Treatments: $85–$350. Facials: $85–$285. Manicure/Pedicure: $25–$140. Waxing: $25–$100.

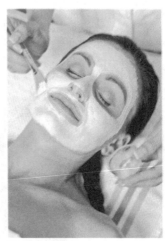

Spa Bellagio

TOP SPOTS

Spa Vita Di Lago

Spa Vita Di Lago

Luxurious treatments at this Tuscan villa in the Ritz-Carlton resort on Lake Las Vegas reflect Mediterranean and desert influences. Some treatment rooms open onto a terrace facing the lake, giving this spa an Italian feel. You can order a meal alfresco in the private, formal Mediterranean garden or enjoy a very un-Vegas activity—stargazing on the spa's patio.

Cool off the desert heat with a Mesquite Tree Renewal body polish or a Moisture Drench Facial. Along with the sauna and whirlpool are a cool plunge pool, wellness and herbal consultations, and free yoga and fitness classes in a sun-splashed studio. Outdoor activities include kayaking, guided hikes, and mountain biking along lake and mountain trails.

Open to the public, the spa is worth a day trip off the Strip, and the Ritz Carlton service is excellent.

BODY TREATMENTS. **Massage:** Swedish, aromatherapy, stone, couples massage, deep tissue, pregnancy massage, reflexology. **Exfoliation:** body polish, waxing.

BEAUTY TREATMENTS. Anti-aging treatments, facials, hair cutting, manicure, pedicure, waxing.

PRICES. Body Treatments: $45–$220. Facials: $95–$255. Manicure/Pedicure: $40–$105. Waxing: $30–$100.

Elemis Spa at Planet Hollywood

Authentic Middle Eastern furnishings, hanging lanterns, textiles, and art decorate this medina-like Moroccan fantasy. The changing area has a huge hydrotherapy pool surrounded by tall Moroccan vases, and you may await your treatment sipping mint tea in the opulent Moorish Retreat.

Top-quality spa treatments outshine even these rich surroundings. Try the Well-Being massage or the Balinese Hot Spice Ritual, a deep-tissue massage after an Exotic Lime and Ginger Salt Glow. The Hawaiian Wave Four Hand Massage consists of two massage therapists giving a very heavenly tandem massage.

Open to the public.

BODY TREATMENTS. **Massage:** aromatherapy, couples, deep tissue, pregnancy massage, reflexology. **Exfoliation:** body polish, salt glow. **Wraps/Baths:** herbal wrap, mud wrap, seaweed wrap. **Other:** hot tubs, sauna, steam room.

BEAUTY TREATMENTS. Anti-aging treatments, facials, manicure, pedicure, waxing.

PRICES. Body Treatments: $100–$480. Facials: $120–$230. Manicure/Pedicure: $25–$140. Waxing: $30–$175.

Spa Vita Di Lago

HONORABLE MENTIONS

MGM Grand Spa

Though this well-managed spa lacks the stunning architecture of other Strip spas, it makes up for it with accommodating attendants and a serene, Feng Shui–designed atmosphere.

The Ritual Experiences menu offers creative treatments from around the world, including the Turkish Hammam Tradition, the Icelandic Fire and Ice Experience, and a Japanese Yuzu Ritual massage.

Too adventurous? Detox your hangover with the Morning After Arabica, an exfoliating scrub with coffee, Dead Sea salts, and peppermint and rosemary oils.

Spa services are available to nonguests Monday through Thursday only.

BODY TREATMENTS. **Massage:** Swedish, aromatherapy, deep tissue, pregnancy massage, shiatsu, stone, reflexology, ayurvedic treatments. **Exfoliation:** sugar and coffee scrubs. **Wraps/Baths:** herbal wrap, mud wrap, seaweed wrap.

BEAUTY TREATMENTS. Anti-aging treatments, hair cutting, facials, manicure, pedicure.

PRICES. Body Treatments: $75–$310. Facials: $65–$370. Manicure/Pedicure: $45–$110.

MGM Grand Spa

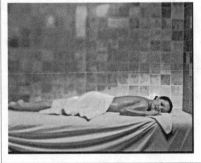

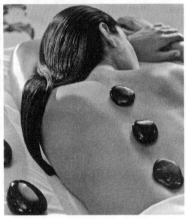

Spa Mandalay

Spa Mandalay

Modeled after a Turkish-style bath, the hot, warm, and cold plunges are surrounded by marble, fountains, and plenty of places to lounge. In what must be a first in Las Vegas, the Spa offers yoga on the beach (of the Mandalay Bay wave pool) mornings at 7 (confirm with the staff).

Try the Ayurvedic Elemental Balancing massage, based on the principals of Ayurveda, a 5,000-year-old healing tradition from India. The spa offers the only Hot Stone Pedicure in town.

BODY TREATMENTS. **Massage:** aromatherapy, Swedish, deep tissue, pregnancy massage, shiatsu, stone, reflexology. **Exfoliation:** herbal, mud, sugar and salt scrubs. **Wraps/Baths:** herbal wrap, aromatherapy wrap. **Other:** hot, warm, cool plunges, sauna, steam room.

BEAUTY TREATMENTS. Anti-aging treatments, hair cutting, facials, manicure, pedicure.

PRICES. Body Treatments: $70–$235. Facials: $70–$170. Manicure/Pedicure: $35–$135.

Four Seasons

Tiny by local standards, this spa offers the very best in service. Decorated in the rich décor of Bali, the traditional Balinese and Javanese body treatments have unusual details rarely seen in Vegas. For example, your path from massage room to bath area during the Bali Spice Ritual is strewn with rose petals, and the meditative Jamu Massage is offered with a choice of exotic oils made of island fruits, spices, or flowers.

Four Seasons

The spa is open to the public if you indulge in a spa service. You also have access to Mandalay Bay's larger spa and Mandalay Beach.

BODY TREATMENTS. **Massage:** Swedish, aromatherapy, deep tissue, couples, Thai herbal, pregnancy massage, stone, reflexology. **Exfoliation:** body polish, herbal and salt glows. **Wraps/Baths:** herbal wrap, mud wrap, seaweed wrap.

PRICES. Body Treatments: $85–$320. Facials: $140–$215. Waxing: $35–$45.

GLOSSARY

acupuncture. Painless Chinese medicine during which needles are inserted into key spots on the body to restore the flow of *qi* and allow the body to heal itself.

aromatherapy. Massage and other treatments using plant-derived essential oils intended to relax the skin's connective tissues and stimulate the flow of lymph fluid.

Ayurveda. An Indian philosophy that uses oils, massage, herbs, and diet and lifestyle modification to restore perfect balance to a body.

body brushing. Dry brushing of the skin to remove dead cells and stimulate circulation.

body polish. Use of scrubs, loofahs, and other exfoliants to remove dead skin cells.

hot-stone massage. Massage using smooth stones heated in water and applied to the skin with pressure or strokes or simply rested on the body.

hydrotherapy. Underwater massage, alternating hot and cold showers, and other water-oriented treatments.

reflexology. Massage of the pressure points on the feet, hands, and ears.

reiki. A Japanese healing method involving universal life energy, the laying on of hands, and mental and spiritual balancing. It's intended to relieve acute emotional and physical conditions. Also called radiance technique.

salt glow. Rubbing the body with coarse salt to remove dead skin.

shiatsu. Japanese massage that uses pressure applied with fingers, hands, elbows, and feet.

shirodhara. Ayurvedic massage in which warm herbalized oil is trickled onto the center of the forehead, then gently rubbed into the hair and scalp.

sports massage. A deep-tissue massage to relieve muscle tension and residual pain from workouts.

Swedish massage. Stroking, kneading, and tapping to relax muscles. It was devised at the University of Stockholm in the 19th century by Per Henrik Ling.

Swiss shower. A multijet bath that alternates hot and cold water, often used after mud wraps and other body treatments.

Temazcal. Maya meditation in a sauna heated with volcanic rocks.

Thai massage. Deep-tissue massage and passive stretching to ease stiff, tense, or short muscles.

thalassotherapy. Water-based treatments that incorporate seawater, seaweed, and algae.

Vichy shower. Treatment in which a person lies on a cushioned, waterproof mat and is showered by overhead water jets.

Watsu. A blend of shiatsu and deep-tissue massage with gentle stretches—all conducted in a warm pool.

HIGHLY RECOMMENDED HOTELS

ON THE STRIP

$–$$$$ **Bally's Las Vegas.** We don't make a special sightseeing stop at Bally's—it has a cool façade, but you can see that from the sidewalk—but we think this is an underrated choice for a Strip stay. Large, tasteful rooms have great views and prices are reasonable, although it's about time this tried-and-true option received a makeover. If you like sports betting, check out the lively sports book—it's detached from the main casino and feels more like an upscale sports bar. Bally's is connected to Paris Las Vegas via a small shopping mall. It's one of the few Strip properties with tennis courts. ⊠*3645 Las Vegas Blvd. S, Center Strip, 89109* ☎*702/967–4111, 800/634–3434, or 888/742–9248* ⊕*www.ballyslv.com* ⇆*2,567 rooms, 265 suites* ☰*AE, D, DC, MC, V.*

$–$$$$ **Excalibur Hotel and Casino.** The giant Lego-like castle is still a popular pick for families—child-oriented attractions are in the basement arcade and on the second floor above the casino—but a makeover means it's starting to look more grown-up. The immense casino floor has lower table minimums than neighbors Luxor and Mandalay Bay, and the restaurants generally serve food more fit for an indentured servant than a king. The pool area was completely redesigned in 2007. ⊠*3850 Las Vegas Blvd. S, South Strip, 89119* ☎*702/733–3111 or 877/750–5464* ⊕*www.flamingolv.com* ⇆*4,008 rooms* ☰*AE, D, DC, MC, V.*

$–$$$$ **Flamingo Las Vegas.** You can't think Vegas without thinking Bugsy Siegel. And yes, this is his ill-fated foray into Vegas real estate. But though it's massive, pink, and smack dab in the middle of the Strip, it's bland. Thankfully, the property is in the midst of a major room renovation, the first phase of which was completed early in 2007, with the rest to follow eventually. In the meantime, the elaborately landscaped complex of four pools is still one of the best and the newly redone rooms (called Flamingo Go rooms, and running about $50 to $100 more per night than standard rooms), with MP3 docking stations, 42-inch flat-screen TVs, and a futuristic look, are downright stylish. Gamble elsewhere—the casino's too plain-Jane. ⊠*3555 Las Vegas Blvd. S, Center Strip, 89109* ☎*702/733–3111 or 888/308–8899* ⊕*www.flamingolv.com* ⇆*3,545 rooms, 233 suites* ☰*AE, D, DC, MC, V.*

$–$$$$ **Monte Carlo Resort and Casino.** The Strip could use more places like ★ this: it's handsome but not ostentatious, and they haven't skimped on ⚙ the rooms, which are outfitted with elegant cherrywood furnishings. If you have kids, it's a good alternative to Excalibur: family-friendly perks include a kiddie pool and a mini-"water park." There's a decent selection of restaurants (among them, Andre's) and the casino is so orderly you can follow a carpeted "road" from one end to the other. The pool was handsomely renovated in 2006. ⊠*3770 Las Vegas Blvd. S, South Strip, 89109* ☎*702/730–7777 or 888/529–4828* ⊕*www.montecarlo.com* ⇆*2,743 rooms, 259 suites* ☰*AE, D, DC, MC, V.*

$–$$$$ **Planet Hollywood Resort & Casino.** Planet Hollywood teamed with Starwood Hotels (Sheraton, W Hotels, Westin, etc.) to take over the Aladdin back in 2004 and has been remodeling the casino and planning a name change ever since—finally, a new lobby and other Planet Hollywood–theme changes were unveiled in 2007, and the makeover should be complete by 2008 (be aware that ongoing construction can be noisy and inconvenient in the meantime). The underwhelming casino still needs more work than the rooms, which are large and pleasant—if unspectacular—and are geared to business travelers (cordless dual-line phones, marble bathrooms). A makeover of the Desert Passage mall is toning down its North African vibe and will get a new name: Miracle Mile. It's expected all these changes will fix the confusing casino, mall, and parking design. All things considered, the hotel is a bit pricier than several better competitors on the Strip. ✉ *3667 Las Vegas Blvd. S, Center Strip, 89109* ☎ *702/785–5555 or 877/333–9474* ⊕ *www.aladdincasino.com* ⤴ *2,344 rooms, 223 suites* ▤ *AE, D, DC, MC, V.*

¢–$$$ ▥ **Tropicana Resort and Casino.** Enjoy the 5-acre pool and swim-up
  ⊛   blackjack while you still can—this Strip original has been sold to a new owner. Though the property will be kept intact and given an overhaul, it has long been rumored for the wrecking ball, so this reprieve could prove temporary. Rooms vary in size, depending on the age of the tower or wing. The confusing casino speaks to piecemeal additions but, at least until the place is reborn, carries an almost-quaint but also rather tired '70s-style nostalgia. Tropicana is known for hosting interesting traveling museum exhibitions, such as Titanic and Bodies. ✉ *3801 Las Vegas Blvd. S, South Strip, 89109* ☎ *702/739–2222 or 888/826–8767* ⊕ *www.tropicanalv.com* ⤴ *1,680 rooms, 198 suites* ▤ *AE, D, DC, MC, V.*

$–$$ ▥ **Hooters Hotel and Casino.** Tacky and Vegas go together, so Hooters ("Delightfully tacky" . . . you know the rest) and Vegas make a natural marriage. This blown-out Hooters restaurant has female dealers in those orange-and-white outfits (perhaps to distract you from the horrible table rules?) and the first of many beer taps is about 6 feet inside the front door. The compact rooms have a tropical vibe and such sophomoric touches as "no knockers" do-not-disturb signs. ✉ *115 E. Tropicana Ave., South Strip, 89109* ☎ *702/736–1120 or 866/584–0087* ⊕ *www.hcbvegas.com* ⤴ *696 rooms* ▤ *AE, D, DC, MC, V.*

OFF THE STRIP

NEAR THE STRIP

$–$$$$ ▥ **Las Vegas Hilton.** They can't bring back Elvis, but the Hilton is trying to regain its former prominence. The hotel woos delegates from the connected Convention Center with convenient, spacious, but uninteresting rooms. There's a lively lounge called Tempo, regular concerts by Barry Manilow, and an only–in–Las Vegas *Star Trek*–theme casino. A gigantic sports book seems like it could field every bet in the galaxy. ✉ *3000 Paradise Rd., Paradise Road, 89109* ☎ *702/732–5111 or 800/732–7117* ⊕ *www.lvhilton.com* ⤴ *2,833 rooms, 124 suites* ▤ *AE, D, DC, MC, V.*

$–$$$$ ▥ **Rio All-Suite Hotel & Casino.** Rio, Brazil, is party-central, and so is
  ★   this sprawling resort. The standard so-called suites don't actually have

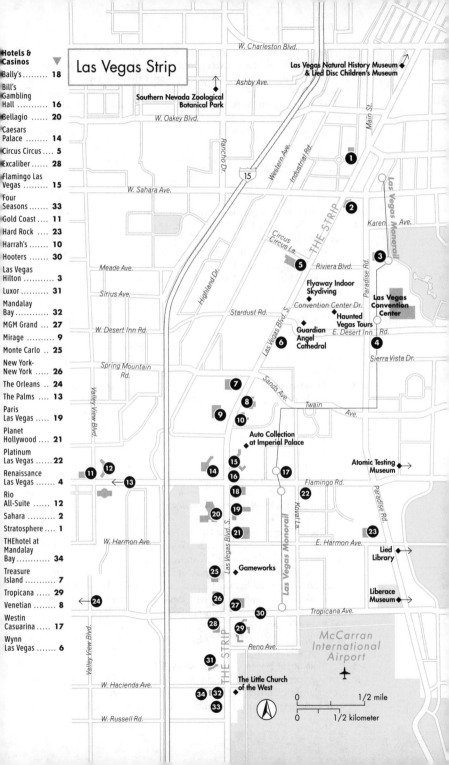

Las Vegas Strip

W. Charleston Blvd.

Las Vegas Natural History Museum & Lied Disc Children's Museum ◆

Ashby Ave.

Southern Nevada Zoological Botanical Park

W. Oakey Blvd.

Main St.

Rancho Dr.

Western Ave.

Industrial Rd.

15

❶

THE STRIP

Las Vegas Monorail

W. Sahara Ave.

❷

Karen Ave.

Circus Circus La.

Paradise Rd.

❸

Riviera Blvd.

❺

Flyaway Indoor Skydiving ◆

Las Vegas Convention Center

Meade Ave.

Sirius Ave.

Highland Dr.

Convention Center Dr.

Stardust Rd.

Haunted Vegas Tours ◆

E. Desert Inn Rd.

W. Desert Inn Rd.

Guardian Angel Cathedral ◆

❻

❹

Sierra Vista Dr.

Spring Mountain Rd.

Las Vegas Blvd. S.

❼

Sands Ave.

Valley View Blvd.

❽

Twain Ave.

❾

❿

Auto Collection at Imperial Palace ◆

Atomic Testing Museum →

❶❺

❷❹

❶❶

❶❷

❶❹

❶❻

❶❼

Flamingo Rd.

❷❷

❶❸

Kovival La.

❶❽

Paradise Rd.

❶❾

❷❸

❷❶

E. Harmon Ave.

W. Harmon Ave.

Las Vegas Blvd. S.

❷❿

Lied Library ◆

W. Harmon Ave.

Gameworks ◆

❷❺

Liberace Museum ◆

Las Vegas Monorail

❷❻

❷❼

❸❿

Tropicana Ave.

❷❹

Valley View Blvd.

❷❽

❷❾

McCarran International Airport ✈

THE STRIP

Reno Ave.

❸❶

W. Hacienda Ave.

The Little Church of the West ◆

❸❹ ❸❷

❸❸

W. Russell Rd.

0 _____ 1/2 mile

0 _____ 1/2 kilometer

separate bedrooms, but they're spacious (at least 600 square feet) and contained within two towers (one rising to 20 stories, the other to 41 floors). But there are higher-end units that are twice the size and have double whirlpool tubs, wet bars, and other cushy touches. The chief attraction is Masquerade Village, with shops and Mardi Gras floats circling from a ceiling track. "Bevertainers" periodically stop their drink-slinging to break into song or dance. Approach games with caution—the casino edge is one of Vegas's worst. Rio has some of the best buffet dining, as well as several good and reasonably priced à la carte restaurants, in town. ⊠ *3700 W. Flamingo Rd., West Side, 89103* ☎ *702/777–7777 or 866/746–7671* ⊕ *www.playrio.com* ⇄ *2,548 suites* ☰ *AE, D, DC, MC, V.*

$$–$$$$ ★   🏨 **Platinum Las Vegas Hotel.** This swank, nongaming, condo hotel has quickly become a fashionable hideaway for Vegas regulars who prefer top-notch amenities but still wish to be close to the action. The all-suites hotel has huge rooms, starting at 900 square feet, and all have 42-inch plasma TVs, living rooms with convertible sofas, lavishly appointed kitchens with stainless-steel appliances, whirlpool tubs, and MP3 radios; the top units also have fireplaces. Views from most of the upper floors take in the Strip, and additional perks include a first-rate restaurant, complimentary valet parking, and an amazing spa. All told, you get the style and substance of one of the city's top resorts with highly personalized service. ⊠ *211 E. Flamingo Rd., Paradise Road, 89169* ☎ *702/365–5000 or 877/211–9211* ⊕ *www.theplatinumhotel. com* ⇄ *255 suites* ☰ *AE, D, DC, MC, V.*

$$–$$$$ Fodor'sChoice ★   🏨 **Renaissance Las Vegas Hotel.** With a "mere" 548 rooms, this hip, beautifully decorated, Rat Pack–inspired hotel feels downright intimate—in fact, rooms with two beds feel a bit cramped, but given their stylish look, they're just dandy. Bathrooms are diminutive, too, but do come with separate tubs and glass shower stalls. It's otherwise supremely inviting and classy, without a casino but with everything to suit a business traveler's needs, including the superb ENVY Steakhouse. About the only drawback among the amenities is the small pool. ⊠ *3400 Paradise Rd., Paradise Road, 89109* ☎ *702/733–6533 or 800/750–0980* ⊕ *www.renaissance-lasvegas.com* ⇄ *518 rooms, 30 suites* ☰ *AE, D, DC, MC, V.*

DOWNTOWN

$–$$$$ 🏨 **Golden Nugget Hotel and Casino.** New owners took over the Golden Nugget in 2003 and again in 2005; since that time, the place has continued to rank as downtown's leading property, although it doesn't have quite the flair it did back when Steve Wynn operated it. Among its neighbors, the hotel has the biggest and best pool. The well-kept rooms are modern and comfortable, with desks, high-speed Internet, armoires, and marble bathrooms. Casino policies are inconsistent, but a popular permanent poker room is likely to last. ⊠ *129 E. Fremont St., Downtown, 89101* ☎ *702/385–7111 or 800/634–3454* ⊕ *www.goldennugget.com* ⇄ *1,805 rooms, 102 suites* ☰ *AE, D, DC, MC, V.*

¢–$ ★   🏨 **Main Street Station Casino, Brewery & Hotel.** It's worth a visit to this pint-size property for the aesthetics alone. Originally built by the owner of Orlando's Church Street Station, it's full of stained glass, marble, and antiques, including a Pullman railroad car. The rooms are less

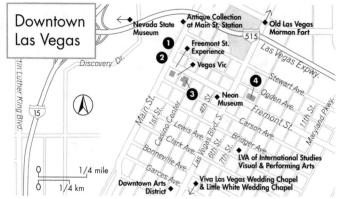

expensive than the Golden Nugget but arguably as nice and available at rock-bottom prices much of the time. ⊠*200 N. Main St., Downtown, 89101* ☎*702/387–1896 or 800/713–8933* ⊕*www.mainstreetcasino. com* ⬧*392 rooms, 14 suites* ⊟*AE, DC, MC, V.*

WORTH THE DRIVE

$$–$$$$ 🏨 **Green Valley Ranch Resort, Casino & Spa.** The Discovery Channel show
Fodor's Choice *American Casino* popularized this low-key, refined place beloved by the
★ high-end crowd, who nonetheless prefers style over bustle (the Strip is a 20-minute drive away). Vineyards and a pool–outdoor nightclub with distant views of the Strip make it oh-so-sophisticated. Spacious rooms have cherrywood furniture, plush chairs, and beds with down comforters. There's a slew of both fine and casual restaurants and shops. ⊠*2300 Paseo Verde Pkwy., Henderson, 89052* ☎*702/617–7777 or 866/617–1777* ⊕*www.greenvalleyranchresort.com* ⬧*400 rooms, 90 suites* ⊟*AE, D, DC, MC, V.*

$$–$$$$ 🏨 **JW Marriott Las Vegas Resort, Spa & Golf.** If you have a penchant for
Fodor's Choice pampering and personal service, and especially if your plans include
★ golfing or hiking, choose this stunner in the Summerlin section of far west Las Vegas. This sterling resort overlooks two golf courses, and Red Rock Canyon is a few miles away. Enormous (starting at 560 square feet) rooms have marble bathrooms with separate whirlpool tubs and raindrop showers. The small, low-key casino is popular with locals. We like the live music lounge and a small but elegant sports book. The Aquae Sulis Spa, at 40,000 square feet, is one of the biggest and best in town, and there's a giant pool, too, which underwent a major renovation in early 2007. ⊠*221 N. Rampart Blvd., Summerlin, 89145* ☎*702/869–8777 or 877/869–8777* ⊕*www.jwmarriottlv.com* ⬧*463 rooms, 78 suites* ⊟*AE, D, DC, MC, V.*

$$$–$$$$ 🏨 **Loews Lake Las Vegas Resort.** Part of the Hyatt chain before Loews
🌙 took over late in 2006, this lavish resort on the shores of Lake Las Vegas has plush, richly appointed rooms; arched windows offer sweeping views of the glittering lake and desert. There's even a small beach where soft, white sand is trucked in every summer. The meager casino seems like

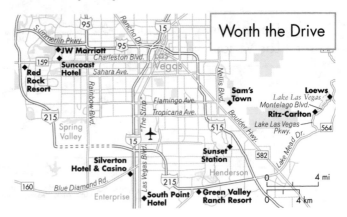

it was added to appease guests who expect to find one in a Nevada hotel. ✉ *101 Montelago Blvd., Henderson, 89011* ☎ *702/567–6000 or 866/768–6658* ⊕ *www.loewshotels.com* ⤶ *450 rooms, 46 suites* ▭*AE, D, DC, MC, V.*

$$–$$$$ 🏨 **Red Rock Casino Resort Spa.** Opened in 2006 on the western edge of
★   Las Vegas suburbia, near Red Rock canyon, is this swanky golden-age Vegas throwback—there are crystal chandeliers throughout (an interesting contrast to earthy sandstone walls and teak-marble floors), a large pool area, a 16-screen movie theater, a vast selection of excellent restaurants (some with outdoor patios), and rooms with floor-to-ceiling glass windows and 42-inch TVs. An early 2007 expansion added another 450 rooms. The sports book has its own VIP area and three video walls that can combine into one huge screen. ✉ *11011 W. Charleston Blvd., Summerlin, 89011* ⤶ *805 rooms, 45 suites* ☎ *702/797–7777 or 866/767–7773* ⊕ *www.redrocklasvegas.com* ▭*AE, D, DC, MC, V.*

$$–$$$$ 🏨 **Ritz-Carlton, Lake Las Vegas.** The Mediterranean-style Ritz is all about
Fodor'sChoice   rest, playing outdoors, and wandering around the MonteLago Village
★   retail center. Large rooms soothe with soft gold, honey, and cream tones and huge, cushy pillows and Frette linens atop feather beds. Plush slippers and robes are provided in the bathrooms. Club Level rooms and suites bump it up a notch with a location on the Pontevecchio, which spans Lake Las Vegas. ✉ *1610 Lake Las Vegas Pkwy., Henderson, 89011* ☎ *702/567–4700 or 800/241–3333* ⊕ *www.ritzcarlton. com* ⤶ *314 rooms, 35 suites* ▭*AE, D, DC, MC, V.*

$–$$ 🏨 **Silverton Hotel & Casino.** Don't overlook this Rocky Mountain lodge–theme hotel, a 10-minute drive south of the Strip. What to look for: a huge Bass Pro Shop; the Mermaid Lounge, with its gigantic salt-water aquarium with 4,000 fish; and the down-home yet trendy Shady Grove Lounge, complete with a bowling alley and 12 huge plasma-screen TVs airing sporting events. Rooms are done with timber-beam ceilings, mounted deer heads, and comfy pillowtop beds with high-quality linens. The hotel is away from the Vegas hubbub but just off I–15, making it a convenient option. ✉ *3333 Blue Diamond Rd., South Las Vegas, 89139* ☎ *702/263–7777 or 866/946–4373* ⊕ *www.silvertoncasino. com* ⤶ *288 rooms, 12 suites* ▭*AE, D, DC, MC, V.*

ALSO RECOMMENDED

MODERATE

ON THE STRIP

Harrah's Las Vegas Casino & Hotel (☎702/369–5000 or 800/214–9110 ⊕*www.harrahs.com*), done in a Mardi Gras theme, is within easy walking distance of such popular resorts as Caesars Palace, the Mirage, and the Venetian. Rooms are modest, and dealers are friendly. **Bill's Gamblin' Hall & Saloon** (☎702/737–2100 or 866/BILLS-45 ⊕*www.billslasvegas.com*), the former Barbary Coast, which was bought and renamed by Harrah's early in 2007, is small but well situated, and loyalists like the unusually good restaurants while low-rollers rave about the drink prices at the lively central bar. Table minimums are usually lower than the big-boy casinos next door. Stay at **Sahara Hotel and Casino** (☎702/737–2111 or 866/382–8884 ⊕*www.saharavegas.com*) only if you nail down an amazingly good deal (rates can be among the lowest of major casinos in this part of town), or if there aren't many vacancies elsewhere on the Strip. Rooms show their age, but a monorail stop makes them a convenient "dormitory" for visiting more exciting attractions. In March 2007, the dreary property was sold to investors who plan to completely redesign it, developing it into a much snazzier resort—stay tuned.

NEAR THE STRIP

Westin Casuarina Hotel and Spa (☎702/836–5900 or 888/625–5144 ⊕*www.westin.com*), is a good choice for business travelers: the attractive, warmly furnished rooms have high-speed Internet, 27-inch TVs, spacious marble bathrooms, and spare, contemporary furnishings.

INEXPENSIVE

ON THE STRIP

Stratosphere Casino Hotel and Tower (☎702/380–7777 or 888/212–0093 ⊕*www.stratospherehotel.com*) has the tallest observation tower west of the Mississippi—it's topped off with thrill rides and a revolving restaurant. Pleasant rooms rent for low rates (because of the too-far-north location), drawing a younger, budget-minded crowd. It's a good choice if you have a car, but a bit of a haul from the rest of the Strip properties without one. Families flock to the free circus acts on the arcade level of **Circus Circus** (☎702/734–0410 or 877/224–7287 ⊕*www.circuscircus.com*) and the Adventuredome, an indoor theme park. But we must warn you—the casino (low-ceiling and claustrophobic) and rooms (garishly decorated) are pretty scary. Strictly for budget-minded families.

NEAR THE STRIP

Locals come to the sprawling **Orleans Hotel and Casino** (☎702/365–7111 or 800/675–3267 ⊕*www.orleanscasino.com*) for the headline entertainment, movie theaters, hockey games, and player-friendly casino odds. The rooms feel perfectly livable and comfy, if not spectacular. It's a terrific deal.

DOWNTOWN

Looking for the original Vegas? The **El Cortez Hotel** (☎702/385–5200 or 800/634–6703 ⊕www.elcortezhotelcasino.com) still has its 1940s façade and oft-photographed neon sign. The casino has low minimums and plenty of old-Vegas characters. Rooms are tiny and cell-like but cost less than a good bottle of wine.   The faded casino in the **Plaza Hotel and Casino** (☎702/386–2110 or 800/634–6575 ⊕www.plazahotelcasino.com) offers great, old-fashioned table game rules. Rooms in the newer tower are nicer than those in the original, but don't expect the finest.

LOCALS' CASINOS

Locals' casinos are a good bet if you're a seasoned gambler and looking for the best gaming odds, or if you want a hotel that's more family-oriented. Keep in mind that most of these properties aren't on the Strip (they're usually a 10- to 30-minute drive), so you'll definitely need a car to get around. **Sam's Town Hotel and Gambling Hall** (☎702/456–7777 or 800/634–6371 ⊕www.samstownlv.com) has an indoor park with animatronic howling wolves, restaurants, and a waterfall under a greenhouse-style glass atrium. It's an excellent value, especially on weekdays, and the rooms are surprisingly pleasant given the low rates. **Santa Fe Station Hotel and Casino** (☎702/658–4900 or 866/767–7770 ⊕http:// santafe.stationcasinos.com) is a classy and relatively compact joint in fast-growing northwest Las Vegas with lots of sandstone columns, half walls, and a movie multiplex. The **South Point Hotel and Casino** (☎702/796–7111 or 866/796–7111 ⊕www.southpointcasino.com), formerly the South Coast Hotel and Casino, has movie theaters, a huge sports book, an Equestrian and Events Center designed to draw world-class horse shows, and capacious rooms with 42-inch plasma TVs and mp3 player plug-ins. The **Suncoast Hotel and Casino** (☎702/636–7111 or 877/677–7111 ⊕www.suncoastcasino.com) is a luxurious, glass-sheathed mid-rise with spacious (550-square-foot) sun-filled rooms with floor-to-ceiling windows. Service is more hands-on and personal than at comparable Strip properties, and guests enjoy an excellent selection of restaurants plus free shuttle service to the Strip. The Spanish-Mediterranean themed **Sunset Station Hotel and Casino** (☎702/547–7777 or 888/SUNSET–9 ⊕www.sunsetstation.com) is almost always packed with local players or those attending the attached movie theater or outdoor concerts in the summer. Check out the funky circular Gaudi Bar (designed in homage to the artist).

HOTELS AT A GLANCE

HOTEL NAME	Cost	Rooms	Restaurants	Pools	Health Club	Spa	Lounge	Casino	Showroom	Nightclub	Shopping (LV)	Other (LV)	Location
AmeriSuites	$89–$299	202		1	yes	yes	3		3			kitchens	Las Vegas
Bally's Las Vegas	$79–$359	2832	12	1	yes	yes	3	yes			yes		Center Strip
Bill's Gamblin' Hall	$59–$210	198	3				2	yes	1			salon	Center Strip
★ Bellagio Las Vegas	$169–$799	3933	17	6	yes	yes	1	yes	1	1	yes		Center Strip
Budget Suites of America	$239 per week	639		1	yes							kitchens	Las Vegas
★ Caesars Palace	$140–$450	3338	12	3	yes	yes	4	yes	1	2	yes		Center Strip
Circus Circus	$65–$249	3774	8	3				yes			yes		North Strip
Doubletree Club Hotel	$99–$209	190		1	yes								Las Vegas
El Cortez Hotel	$29–$99	409	4				2	yes				salon	Downtown
Embassy Suites	$139–$329	220	1	1	yes		1						Las Vegas
Embassy Suites	$139–$449	288	1										Las Vegas
Excalibur Hotel	$51–$379	4008	6	2	yes	yes	3	yes	1		yes		South Strip
Flamingo Las Vegas	$80–$320	3642	8	3	yes	yes	3	yes	1		yes	salon	Center Strip
★ Four Seasons	$345–$5,000	424	2	1	yes	yes	1				yes		South Strip
Golden Nugget	$79–$279	1907	6	1	yes	yes	4	yes	1			salon	Downtown
★ Green Valley Ranch	$129–$379	490	17	4	yes	yes	3	yes			yes	salon	Henderson
★ Hard Rock Hotel	$159–$329	647	6	1	yes	yes		yes		1	yes	salon	Paradise Road
Harrah's Las Vegas	$85–$250	2677	10	1	yes	yes	3	yes	1	1	yes	salon	Center Strip
Hooters Hotel and Casino	$69–$199	696	6	1		yes	5	yes					South Strip
★ JW Marriott Las Vegas	$179–$329	541	9	1	yes	yes	4	yes			yes	salon	Summerlin
Las Vegas Hilton	$126–$316	2957	15	1	yes	yes	8	yes	1	1		salon	Paradise Road
Loews Lake Las Vegas Resort	$199–$479	496	4	2	yes	yes	2	yes		1		salon	Henderson
★ Luxor	$69–$650	4404	8	1	yes	yes	5	yes	1	1	yes	salon	South Strip
★ Main Street Station	$40–$120	406	3				1	yes					Downtown
★ Mandalay Bay	$110–$600	4315	23	4	yes	yes		yes	1	1	yes		South Strip
MGM Grand	$89–$499	5006	19	5	yes	yes	6	yes	1	1	yes	salon	South Strip
Mirage	$109–$599	3044	14	2	yes	yes		yes	1	1	yes	salon	Center Strip

Hotel	Rates	Rooms	Restaurants	Pools	Health Club	Spa	Lounge	Casino	Showroom	Nightclub	Shopping (LV)	Other (LV)	Location
★ Monte Carlo	$70–$450	3002	10	1	yes	yes	2	yes	1		yes		South Strip
Motel 6	$47–$220	607		1									Las Vegas
New York–New York	$89–$449	2024	8	1	yes	yes	4	yes	1	1	yes	salon	South Strip
Orleans Hotel and Casino	$49–$118	1886	14	1	yes	yes	4	yes	1			salon	West Side
★ The Palms	$119–$529	657	8	1	yes	yes	4	yes		1	yes	salon	West Side
Paris Las Vegas	$99–$439	2916	10	1	yes	yes	4	yes	1	1	yes		Center Strip
Planet Hollywood	$99–$429	2567	22	2	yes	yes	4	yes	1	1	yes		Center Strip
★ Platinum Las Vegas	$190–$370	255		1	yes	yes	1						Paradise Road
Plaza Hotel	$49–$139	1037	5	1	yes		1	yes	1			salon	Downtown
★ Red Rock Casino, Resort and Spa	$149–$389	850	2	1	yes	yes	4	yes	1	1		salon	West Las Vegas
★ Renaissance Las Vegas	$169–$429	548	1	1	yes		1						Paradise Road
Residence Inn Las Vegas	$175–$499	192		1	yes		2					kitchens	Las Vegas
★ Rio All-Suite	$80–$340	2548	20	5	yes	yes	2	yes		1	yes	salon	West Side
★ Ritz-Carlton	$179–$399	349	2		yes	yes	1					salon	Henderson
Sahara Hotel and Casino	$49–$149	1700	6	1			2	yes				salon	North Strip
Sam's Town	$49–$249	646	8	1			1	yes					Boulder Strip
Santa Fe Station	$44–$179	200	4					yes	yes				Rancho Strip
Silverton Hotel & Casino	$80–$160	300	4		yes		1	yes	1				Las Vegas
South Point	$59–$159	1350	6	1	yes	yes	3	yes					South Strip
Stratosphere	$59–$109	2444	6	1	yes	yes	1	yes	1		yes	salon	North Strip
Suncoast	$59–$179	442	3	1	yes		1	yes	yes				Summerlin
Sunset Station	$79–$169	457	10	1	yes			yes					Henderson
★ THEhotel at Mandalay Bay	$160–$650	1117	1	1	yes	yes				1			South Strip
Treasure Island Las Vegas (TI)	$99–$499	2885	11	1	yes	yes	4	yes		1	yes	salon	Center Strip
Tropicana Resort	$46–$220	1878	7	3	yes	yes	2	yes	1			salon	South Strip
★ Venetian	$179–$899	4027	17	3	yes	yes	4	yes	1	1	yes		Center Strip
Westin Casuarina	$135–$199	826	2		yes	yes		yes	1	1			Paradise Road

Gamble

Paris Hotel

WORD OF MOUTH

"Learn to play basic strategy blackjack (look it up online or check out a book at the library on blackjack). It's very easy to learn and it actually gives you some of the best odds of any game in a casino."

—Bubba

By Swain
Scheps

YOU'VE COME A LONG WAY to see the spectacle, stroll the strip, and commune with Elvis. But we know what you really want: to hit the tables.

We're here to tell you that you don't need to be a gambling expert or know a secret handshake to sit and play. All you need are the basics supplied below. Really. And as long as you're realistic about your chances of winning (slim), your chances of having a great time are excellent. Roll up your sleeves and pull up a chair—it's gambling time.

THE BASICS

CASINO STRATEGY

There's nothing wrong with dreaming of three sevens clicking into place in slow-motion on the slot machine reels or imagining yourself holding a ridiculous oversize check, grinning madly as flashbulbs pop. But you shouldn't have the stated goal of returning home with fatter pockets than when you left—Las Vegas was built on illusions like that. The purpose of any visit should simply be to have fun—gamble as a pastime, as an intellectual challenge, as an enjoyable activity with friends or family. (Notice the phrase "to win money" appeared nowhere in the previous sentence.)

The best casino strategy we can offer is found at the intersection of Smart and Fun streets. No, that's not the address of the newest megacasino! What we mean is that you should learn enough about the games to prevent giving away your money by either playing out-of-control or making stupid bets. That's the smart part. The fun part? Entertainment is what Las Vegas is all about, and that includes the casinos and sports books and poker rooms. With so many games to play, there's one out there for just about everyone. Play games that make you smile and those that make you forget about life's dreary hours. If that means you're not making the absolute best bet in the casino, then so be it.

If you bring reasonable expectations to the casino, have fun playing your game(s), and know and respect your financial limits, you're bound to have a successful trip, with or without the oversize check photo-op. That's your basic casino strategy. Read on to find out more about the smart parts of playing the games.

THE HOUSE ADVANTAGE

Casinos make money a penny at a time. Think of a coin-flip game paying you $1 on heads and taking $1 on tails. Over time, you'd win about as much as you'd lose. But a *casino*-hosted coin-flip game would only pay $0.98 on heads while still taking your buck on tails.

That two cents is the "house advantage." It might not seem like much, but if enough people play, the casino earns millions; it's a mathematical certainty. Your $1,000 win streak is being covered by some poor

How Not to Go Broke

Decide before leaving on your vacation how much money you'll spend on gambling. This is your gambling bankroll—try not to go over it. Gambling newbies are shocked at how quickly the chips can disappear at the table in just a short time. Even though the house advantage is small in any given game, those 2% and 3% pinpricks can quickly turn into a bankroll hemorrhage as you play hand after hand of your favorite game. Whether you can

afford to lose $200 or $2,000 per day, place bets that fit your bankroll, and when you reach your daily limit, stop playing. Period. Don't even think about hitting up the credit-card cash withdrawal machines—not only are the surcharges and interest rates sky-high, you will be gambling with money you don't even have, which can have devastating consequences.

sap one table over who just lost $1,001. If a casino underpays on wins and overcharges on losses, then they're always taking a little more than they give.

So how does the house advantage affect you? Not all games have the same house advantage. Some take your money quickly. Others allow you to flounder in financial limbo for a while before putting you out of your misery. Knowing the house advantage is the first step to choosing the best game for you.

LUCK VERSUS THE EDGE

There's a lot of talk about luck inside a casino. Good luck, rotten luck, dumb luck. There's hot streaks, hot dice, cold tables, icy cards. There are even overdue numbers and jinxed dealers.

Let's get real. Lady Luck turned in her magic wand years ago and now lives in a small cabin outside of Reno, so gamblers shouldn't count on her help at the tables. But don't worry—you won't even miss her. We think it's a comfort to know that the games are not beholden to mysterious powers. Gambling is a knowable world, with quantifiable and predictable outcomes. Casinos take advantage of the games' predictability and as a player, you can do almost the same thing. You may not make money in the long run, but you can maximize your "edge"—that is to say, you can use time-tested strategies for cutting the house advantage to an absolute minimum.

Lucky streaks, good or bad, are nothing more than swings of the statistical pendulum; they have nothing to do with how you put your pants on in the morning, or your broken mirror, or that lost four-leaf clover. But using proper strategy—placing the correct bets of the proper size at the right time—can help you maximize your edge and give you the very best chance to win.

THE GOOD BETS

OK, we've given you the lecture about gambling for fun instead of for profit. But there's no sense in throwing your money away.

■ Here are the games you can actually beat under the right circumstances: Poker, Sports Betting, Horse Racing, Video Poker.

■ Study up and play just right, and you'll lose money very slowly with these games: Baccarat (Bank), Blackjack, Craps (Pass/Don't Pass, Come/Don't Come), Pai Gow Poker, Single-Zero Roulette, some slot machines.

■ Games you should never play because of the terrible odds: Keno, Double-Zero Roulette, Big Six (Wheel of Fortune).

If you didn't see your favorite in there, it's because the odds are no good. But hey, if playing double-zero roulette brings you immeasurable joy, then more power to you. At least your decline into bankruptcy will be with a smile on your face.

BETTER BETTOR ETIQUETTE

Dealers are certainly available to answer your questions, but learn the basics first. Ask about beginner's classes.

Understand the betting limit plaques before you sit down; they show the minimum bet per hand and explain gaming rules for that table.

Buy chips at the tables, but remember that the dealers can't take cash directly from your hand.

Don't expect dealers to give you more than 20 minimum bets at a time. If you hand over three $100 bills, they aren't going to give you 60 red ($5) chips; they'll give you 20 $5 chips and 8 $25 chips. Ask for change as needed.

COMPS, CLUBS & COUPONS

These days, everyone has a loyalty program and Vegas is no exception. Nearly every establishment has a frequent gambler club they use to identify and reward gamblers who spend a lot of time (and money) on their property. And while that fabled comps system is still in place, gamblers are usually required to belong to the frequent gambler club to even get a whiff of freebies. Our advice? Sign up right away.

Some clubs publish exactly how much you have to play to qualify for rewards, but casino personnel still has the freedom to hand out perks to good gamblers. Tell the nearest casino suit in your pit that you're interested in show tickets or a buffet voucher; ask them what you need to do to get what you want. The system favors friendly extroverts.

Casino clubs aren't for everybody. If you don't want casinos tracking your every move and bombarding you with junk mail, but you still want the freebies, ask about hotel "funbooks" (free coupon books for hotel guests) when you check in to your hotel. Most big casinos offer them to hotel guests; some offer them to gamblers as an entry-level comp. Funbooks are just books of coupons with various freebies and discounts. There are sometimes free plays or double-winnings coupons for the tables or slots that can extend your bankroll. The best funbooks can be found at the less glamorous places like Casino Royale.

CASINO RULES

You'll notice a bunch of strange rituals being carried out as suited big shots count chips, speak in arcane code, and sign endless triplicate forms. The dealers have their odd tics and hand gestures that in any other environment would prompt a call to the local asylum. But the unique nature of the casino business requires rules to keep operations safe and in compliance with regulatory agencies.

Gamblers have a part to play in all these directives, too. Here's what you need to know:

■ Carry your ID with you and keep it in a handy pocket. Dealers are instructed to strictly enforce the gambling age minimum, which is 21 years old everywhere in Nevada.

■ No kids are allowed in gaming areas unless they are passing through.

■ Casinos forbid anything that distracts gamblers at the tables, like phones or Blackberries. Put 'em on vibrate and in your pocket. If you must take a call, walk away from the table.

■ In sports and race books, any device that permits two-way communication will get you escorted to the door by a security guard.

■ Smoke-free areas are everywhere now, so ask before you fire up.

THE GAMES

BEST FOR BEGINNERS

The whole gambling scene can seem intimidating for the first-timer. And for a while it was—rude dealers tolerated rude players (particularly those who thought it possible to "jinx the deck" or "take the bust card" at blackjack), sending newbies running to the machines. But casinos now cater to the novice a bit more in the hopes that they'll be back again and again, which makes this the perfect time for you to pony up to that roulette wheel. Here's what you need to know to get started:

BEST BEGINNER CLASSES

If you're headed to Vegas with more table gaming ambition than actual experience, you'll find free lessons widely available. The format varies; most of the big resorts have live lessons at scheduled times on the casino floor (just ask any dealer). Some resorts have a dedicated in-house TV channel that constantly replays classes on the most popular games. If you're stuck at your great-aunt's house out in Henderson (the one who doesn't even have basic cable) and need a venue for lessons, we like Excalibur. Every weekday the casino offers roulette lessons at 11 AM, blackjack at 11:30 AM, and craps at noon. If you're downtown, the Golden Nugget has lessons every weekday for the most popular games: 3-card poker at 10 AM, Pai Gow at 10:30 AM, craps and Texas Hold'em at 11 AM, roulette at 11:30 AM, and blackjack at noon. For video-poker strategy, Bob Dancer, coauthor of the *Las Vegas Review-Journal*'s column "The Player's Edge," often holds free classes at local casinos like the Fiesta Henderson and the Silverton. Look in the "Neon" section of the Friday edition of the *Review-Journal* to see if Dancer is holding court when you're in town.

BEST DEALERS

Dealers on the Strip keep the games moving fast and aren't prone to mistakes, but they often don't go in for a lot of small talk. Many beginners feel more comfortable at tables that are social and lively. For that, try the folksy atmospheres of the locals' casinos off the Strip and away from downtown like Gold Coast or Sunset Station. Vegas is about fun, so consider the Imperial Palace, and Harrah's if you want a light-hearted atmosphere with some musical accompaniment while you play. For sheer brainpower, Golden Nugget, Treasure Island, and Mirage have the most knowledgeable floor crews; watch and learn. There are ways to get the kind of dealer you want. Before you choose a table and sit down, observe the demeanor of the dealer and the players and pick the milieu that suits your gambling style. Here's a helpful tip if you're looking to chat with your dealer: many casinos display their employees' hometowns on their nametags. Locate a dealer from a familiar or interesting city and strike up some friendly banter. And above all other rules-of-thumb to adhere to while gambling: if you don't like the vibe your dealer is giving out, pick up your remaining chips and leave immediately. Beating a disagreeable dealer is not nearly as gratifying as losing to that same jerk is miserable. Never play for revenge.

EASIEST GAMES & WHERE TO PLAY THEM

Roulette is considered the easiest table game, but it's also one with a high house advantage (craps is the hardest, blackjack somewhere in the middle). That advantage can be cut by finding a "single-zero" wheel—as opposed to those that have a second green niche, the 00, or double-zero—but they are rare and often balance the improved odds with higher minimums. Since you're playing a "house" game, play it at a fun place such as the Hard Rock or Sunset Station.

If you're too intimidated to even walk up to a table, you can play keno while you eat in a coffee shop. You just mark numbers with a crayon, give them to the keno runner with a buck or two, and watch a board to see if your numbers come up.

Bingo is also a fun Vegas casino game. It's played in specialized parlors with a crowd of people sitting at tables in a large room listening for their lucky numbers. The people you run into are often casino personnel, dealers, cocktail waitresses, and even show girls and entertainers who like bingo's humble aesthetic after a long day filled with glitz.

Slot machines are the easiest mechanical games—put the money in (or bet the credits) and pull the handle (or push the button).

3

BACCARAT

Baccarat (pronounced bah-kah-rah) is a classic casino card game played with an aristocratic feel at a patient rhythm. It's not an American favorite, but it's popular around the world in varied forms. There's something quite *continental* about Baccarat; it's easy enough to play but it retains an air of mystery, like a single raised eyebrow.

PLAYING THE GAME

Up to 15 players can squeeze into a Baccarat table, but the game is played out with just two hands, known as the Player hand and the Bank hand. Before play starts, you place your bet on one of three possible outcomes: that the Player hand will win, that the Bank hand will win, or that play will result in a Tie. One player each game helps the dealers distribute the cards. When it's your turn, you can either accept the responsibility of representing the Bank (in which case you must place a Bank bet), or you can pass the shoe on to the next player in line.

The dealers, with an assist from the Bank player holding the shoe, start the game by dealing two two-card hands face down. The player hand is traditionally placed in front of the gambler with the largest Player bet, who then turns them over and slides them back to the dealer. The player holding the shoe does the same with the Bank hand. These rituals are only for ceremony. Everyone at the table is tied to these two hands, regardless of how they're dealt and who gets to turn them over.

With both hands exposed, the dealer announces the value of each hand to the table. Depending on the value of the hands, a complicated system of card-drawing begins where an extra card can be added to each of the two hands. The Player hand is the first to act; depending on the value of the two hands it will either stand as it was dealt or the dealers will add a third card to the original two. Then the Bank hand is played out according to the rules. The casino makes the drawing rules available to every bettor at the table in the form of a small printed card. Whether you understand them or not doesn't really matter—the game is played out completely by the casino dealers. In spite of the confusing drawing rules, Baccarat is a simple game for gamblers: no decisions are required beyond which side to bet on.

After the drawing is complete, the dealer announces the final score and declares one side the winner. The winning hand is the one that

comes closest to 9 without going over. Baccarat hands are calculated by adding all the card values together. But Baccarat math is a little weird: face cards are equal to zero and any amount over 9 trips the odometer and the first digit gets ignored. (If the cards total 14, it's really only a 4.)

STRATEGY

There's no strategy in Baccarat; the game is carried out according to preset rules. Nevertheless, players enjoy watching the game go back and forth between Bank bet wins and Player bet wins. Like Roulette players tracking Red versus Black wins, Baccarat players look for some hidden pattern that will help them place their bets.

The Bank bet has slightly better than even money odds. Always avoid a Tie bet because it has an excessive house advantage.

MINI-BACCARAT

A more accessible version of Baccarat is called Mini-Baccarat. If you have a taste for Baccarat but can do without the high minimums, the glacial pace, and the odd Monaco-wannabe rituals, look for a Mini-Bac table. They're in the main pit of any casino, with the other common table games. Mini-Bac follows the same rules as its blue-blooded cousin, but the table minimums are low and the single dealer dispenses with the ceremony and cranks out the hands.

Baccarat on a budget: Harrah's and the Golden Nugget have tables with reasonable minimums.

To get on the cover of National Enquirer: The Mirage's high-limit games consistently attract sports superstars and the Hollywood elite.

WHERE TO PLAY

Baccarat Table

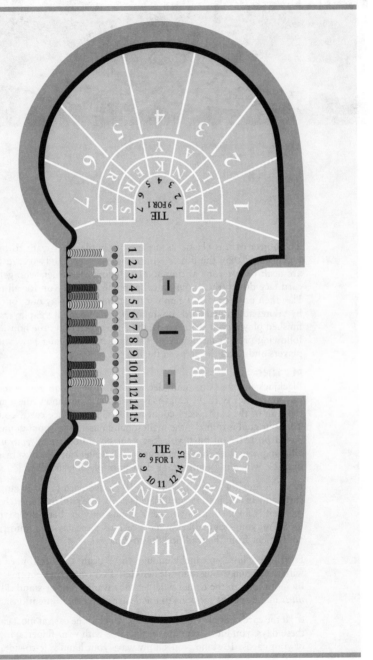

BLACKJACK

Blackjack, a.k.a. "21," anchors virtually every casino in America. It's the most popular table game because it's easy to learn, fun to play, and has excellent odds.

The object of this classic card game is simple. You want to build a higher hand than the dealer without going over 21. Two-card hands are dealt to everyone at the table, including the dealer, who gets one card face down (the "hole" card) and one card face up for all to see. Play then proceeds from gambler to gambler. You play out your hand by taking additional cards or standing pat. When all the players have finished playing out their hands, the dealer then plays the house hand following preset rules. Once that's complete, the dealer pays winning players and rakes the chips of the losers.

PLAYING THE GAME

Blackjack involves one main decision: to add cards to your hand—to *hit*—or to stick with the hand as is—to *stand*. The hand value is simply the sum of the cards; aces count as 1 or 11, and face cards count as 10. Your goal is to make the highest hand possible without going over 21—a *bust*. If you bust, you lose your bet automatically, no matter what happens with the dealer's cards. The dealer can also bust by going over 21, which is an important element of playing strategy.

If you're dealt a combination of a 10-valued card (a 10 or any face card) and an ace, it's a *natural* blackjack. You're paid immediately after the deal is finished, plus you get a bonus on your bet—the payout is 6-to-5 on your original bet in most casinos these days, an unfortunate adjustment from the traditional 3-to-2 payout.

For those who aren't lucky enough to be dealt a natural, play starts with the person sitting to the dealer's left. Everyone plays out their hand by motioning to the dealer whether they want to hit or stand. Players *must* make specific motions to the dealer about their intentions:

- If the cards have been dealt face up, which is the case at most casinos these days, you hit by tapping on the table with your finger(s) in front of your cards. To stand, you simply wave your hand side-to-side.

■ If the cards have been dealt face down, pick them up and hold them with one hand. To hit, you "scratch" on the table with the corner of your cards. To stand, you slide the cards under your chips.

■ As long as your hand is less than 21, you can continue hitting and taking cards. When you're satisfied with your hand, you stand. At that point the dealer then turns to the next player in line and repeats the same hit/stand process. Once everyone's had a chance to add to their hand, the dealer reveals the hidden card and plays out the hand according to the following rules:

■ Dealer shows 16 or less: hit

■ Dealer shows 17 or more: stand

Once the dealer's hand is complete, the bets are either paid (if the player's hand is higher than the dealer's) or raked (if the dealer's hand is higher than the player's). If the dealer has busted, the players remaining in the hand win their bets. In the event a player's hand value is equal to that of the dealer, it's a *push* (the dealer will knock on the table in front of the bet); the bet is neither paid nor raked.

DOUBLING-DOWN

Who doesn't remember this rule from *Swingers*—you always double-down on an 11. But what exactly does that mean, and do you only double-down on an 11 and nothing else? Basically, all it means is that you double your bet and receive only a single card in lieu of the normal hit/stand sequence. If your first two cards total 9, 10, or 11, it can be a very good strategy to put more money in play—10-cards are so common that adding one to a 9, 10, or 11 would create a very strong hand.

Casino rules vary on which hands you can double-down on, but the rules are usually printed on the game table felt.

SPLITTING

If you want to put more money on the table, splitting is a good way to do it. If your first two cards are of equal value, you can split them apart and form two separate hands, then play each hand out separately as if it were a brand-new hand. When you want to split, push a stack of chips equal to your original bet into the betting circle, and tell the dealer your intentions.

INSURANCE Don't ever make this bet. When the dealer's up card is an ace, she'll ask if anyone wants to buy Insurance. If the dealer makes blackjack, the Insurance bet pays off at 2 to 1 odds; if she doesn't, the Insurance bet is lost. Experts consider this a bad bet. Always pass on it.

AT A GLANCE

Format: Single-dealer card game played with up to 7 players

Goal: Players compete against the dealer for highest hand without going over 21

Pays: Even-money on regular winning bets, 3 to 2 if player receives 21 on first 2 cards

House Advantage: 1.5%

Best Bet: Play blackjack with basic strategy. Avoid 6-to-5 blackjack games

Worst Bet: Insurance side bet, games with limited Split/Double-Down rules

Blackjack Table

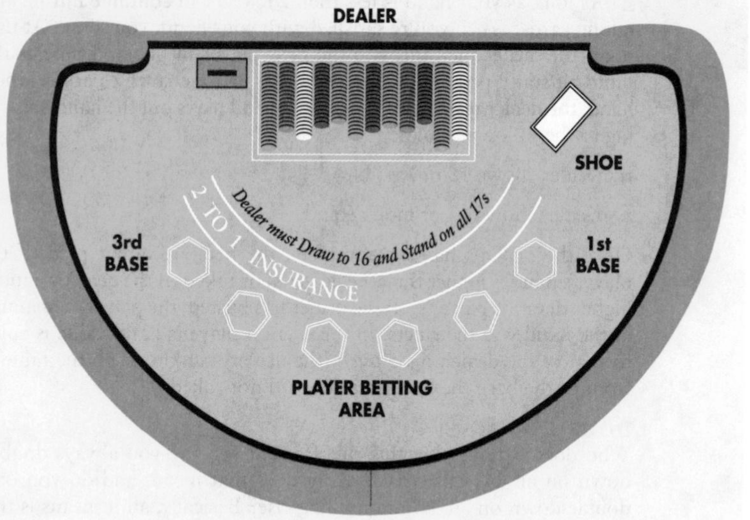

DEALER

Dealer must Draw to 16 and Stand on all 17's

2 TO 1

INSURANCE

SHOE

3rd
BASE

1st
BASE

PLAYER BETTING
AREA

STRATEGY

While it's easy to learn, blackjack has varying layers of complexity that can be taken on and conquered depending on your interest level.

The key to all blackjack strategy is the *Ten Assumption*. Because there are so many 10-valued cards in blackjack (16 per deck in play), the Ten Assumption says that the cards you *don't* see are assumed to be tens. All the decisions you make are based on the idea that should you choose to hit, the card will be a 10. Obviously, the card doesn't always turn out to be a 10, but, because the probability is so high, the Ten Assumption has to always be on your mind.

Bad hands—hands unlikely to produce a win—are known as *bust hands*. If your hand value is between 12 and 16, you have a bust hand. The reason has to do with a combination of dealer's drawing rules and the Ten Assumption. Remember that dealers have to keep hitting until they reach a value of 17 or higher. If your hand is 16 or lower, your hand isn't high enough to beat the dealer, but at the same time, because of the Ten Assumption, you know that a 10-card lurks nearby in the deck. If you hit, there's a strong chance that you'll get a 10, and if you do, you'll bust. There's no good option.

Basic strategy, then, involves looking at the dealer's up card, and acting under the assumption that the hole card is a 10. If the dealer shows a 9, she or he likely has 19. If the dealer shows a 4, she or he likely has a 14. You then act accordingly, standing pat or hitting depending on the dealer's hand. Mathematicians calculated all the odds based on this basic strategy long ago. Without listing out every single possible scenario, here's what basic strategy dictates you do, given the dealer shows the following up card:

- Ace, 10, 9, 8, 7—you assume the dealer has a made hand (i.e., will not need to draw). If your hand is 17 or higher, stand. If your hand is 16 or lower, you should hit.

- 2, 3, 4, 5, 6—you assume that the dealer has a bust hand. Because the dealer must continue to draw if his hand is below 17, the Ten Assumption works in your favor, and there's no need to take any risks. You should stand unless there's no risk of busting.

There are some special player hands that require different actions:

- Your hand is 11 (such as a 7 and a 4). Because of the Ten Assumption, adding a 10 to this hand would create a 21, the best possible hand. Double-Down.

- If the player's hand is 8, 8 or A, A, it's better to split your cards.

- Player's hand is either 4, 4; 5, 5; or two 10-valued cards. Never split these hands.

Most casinos offer basic strategy crib cards in the gift shop. They have a full blackjack play grid that tells you exactly what to do under every possible scenario. There's nothing illegal about pulling out a strategy card while you're playing; it's a great way to learn the game.

SPANISH 21   Spanish 21 is a blackjack variation that uses a modified deck (no 10s). Wacky rules allow players to do common blackjack things at strange times—you can surrender at anytime or double-down on any number of cards. Plus, hands like 6-7-8 and 7-7-7 pay automatic bonuses. The house edge is low with perfect play, but blackjack basic strategy doesn't work. Find a specialty book and study up.

WHERE
TO PLAY

For the most fun: Hard Rock Hotel—the dealers are in your corner; Harrah's—no grouches allowed in the "party pit;" and Imperial Palace—dealers occasionally serenade players mid-hand.

For tournaments: The Palms provides some fun twists to an old game.

On a tight schedule: Luxor, where you can reserve table seats ahead of time. Of course, you have to buy-in with a certain amount of money, and bet according to the table minimums.

To learn the game: Slots–A–Fun (✉ *2890 Las Vegas Blvd. S, Downtown* ☎ *800/354–1232*) has low-limit tables that help the learning curve.

Chart KEY
H—Hit
S—Stand
D—Double Down
SP—Split

BLACKJACK BASIC STRATEGY CHART

Your Hand	\multicolumn{10}{Dealer's Up Card}
	2	3	4	5	6	7	8	9	10	A
5–8	H	H	H	H	H	H	H	H	H	H
9	D	D	D	D	D	H	H	H	H	H
10	D	D	D	D	D	D	D	D	H	H
11	D	D	D	D	D	D	D	D	D	D
12	H	H	S	S	S	H	H	H	H	H
13	S	S	S	S	S	H	H	H	H	H
14	S	S	S	S	S	H	H	H	H	H
15	S	S	S	S	S	H	H	H	H	H
16	S	S	S	S	S	H	H	H	H	H
17	S	S	S	S	S	S	S	S	S	S
18	S	S	S	S	S	S	S	S	S	S
19	S	S	S	S	S	S	S	S	S	S
20	S	S	S	S	S	S	S	S	S	S
21	S	S	S	S	S	S	S	S	S	S
A,2	H	H	D	D	D	H	H	H	H	H
A,3	H	H	D	D	D	H	H	H	H	H
A,4	H	H	D	D	D	H	H	H	H	H
A,5	H	H	D	D	D	H	H	H	H	H
A,6	D	D	D	D	D	H	H	H	H	H
A,7	S	D	D	D	D	S	S	H	H	H
A,8	S	S	S	S	S	S	S	S	S	S
A,9	S	S	S	S	S	S	S	S	S	S
A,A	SP	SP	SP	SP	SP	SP	SP	SP	SP	SP
2,2	H	SP	SP	SP	SP	SP	H	H	H	H
3,3	H	H	SP	SP	SP	SP	H	H	H	H
4,4	H	H	H	D	D	H	H	H	H	H
5,5	D	D	D	D	D	D	D	D	D	H
6,6	SP	SP	SP	SP	SP	H	H	H	H	H
7,7	SP	SP	SP	SP	SP	SP	H	H	H	H
8,8	SP	SP	SP	SP	SP	SP	SP	SP	SP	SP
9,9	SP	SP	SP	SP	SP	S	SP	SP	S	S
10,10	S	S	S	S	S	S	S	S	S	S

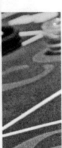

3

CRAPS

Even if you've never played this game, you may have heard the roar of a delighted crowd of players from across the casino floor. Up to 12 players crowd around a sunken felt table that's surrounded by a padded wall. Craps is a dice game; the dice shooter tosses two dice to the opposite end of the table, over (and sometimes through) the chip stacks of players' bets. The main layout is duplicated on the right and left sides of the table, although the middle section (the proposition area) is common to both wings of the craps table.

BASIC RULES

Playing craps looks intimidating, but it's actually not as mind-boggling as it appears. To play, just step up to the table wherever you can find an open space. You can start betting casino chips immediately, but you have to wait your turn to be the shooter. If you don't want to roll the bones (a.k.a. dice), motion your refusal to the stickman, and he'll skip you.

Playing craps is fairly straightforward; it's betting on it that's complicated. The basic concepts are as follows: if the first roll turns up a 7 or 11, that's called a "natural"—an automatic win. If a 2, 3, or 12 comes up on the first throw (called the "come-out roll"), that's termed "crapping out"—an automatic lose. Rolling a 4, 5, 6, 8, 9, or 10 on a first roll is known as hitting a "point": the bet stays on the table as the shooter continues rolling the dice until that number comes up again to win. If a 7 turns up before the number does, the shooter's "sevened out," or lost.

But "winning" and "losing" rolls of the dice are entirely relative in this game, because there are two ways you can bet at craps: "for" the

Craps Table

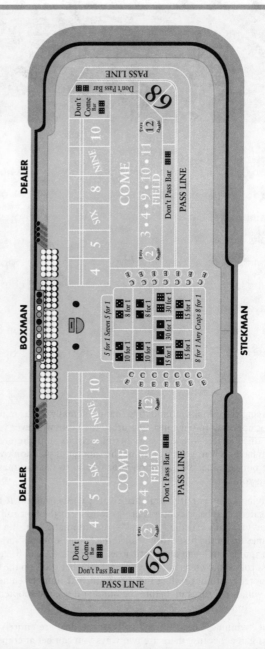

shooter (also called right way bets) or "against" the shooter (or wrong way bets). Betting for means that the shooter will "make his point" (win). Betting against means that the shooter will "seven out" (lose). (Either way, you're actually betting against the house, which books all wagers.) If you're betting *for* on the come-out, you place your chips on the layout's "pass line" before the come-out roll. If a 7 or 11 is rolled, you win even money. If a 2, 3, or 12 (craps) is rolled, you lose your bet. If you're betting *against* on the come-out, you place your chips in the "don't pass" space on the table. A 7 or 11 loses; a 2 or 3 wins (a 12 is a push). With the other numbers,

AT A GLANCE

Format: Dice game played around a specialized elongated table

Goal: Players bet that certain numbers or sequences of numbers will be rolled

Pays: Even money on Pass/Don't Pass, Come/Don't Come, various for other bets

House Advantage: 1.8%

Best Bet: Don't pass with full odds

Worst Bet: Field bet, any proposition bet

the *for* bettors are hoping the shooter hits his point before sevening out, while the *against* bettors hope just the opposite. (Note that the 7 is good during the come-out roll, but bad during a point roll.) A shooter must have either a Pass Line or Don't Pass bet on the table in order to roll the dice, although wrong way bettors often prefer not to shoot for the simple reason that they win by sevening out, and the rules of the game dictate that a player who sevens out must pass the dice.

OTHER BETS

In addition to Pass and Don't Pass bets, you can also make the following important wagers at craps:

Come/Don't Come Place a Come bet before any point roll. Think of a Come bet as being just like its own little private Pass Line bet. Regardless of what is happening with the rest of the table and the rest of the bets, the Come bet follows the main sequence with two phases of rolls just like a Pass Line bet. The first roll after placing the Come bet adheres to come out roll rules for the Come bet only, winning on 7 or 11, losing on 2, 3, or 12, and passing to the point phase for any other number. What's confusing is that one single roll of the dice may mean a loss for your Pass Line bet and a win for the Come bet.

Odds This is an important bet for holding the casino edge to a minimum. After your Pass Line or Come bet has moved into the point phase, you're allowed to "back," or add on to it, with Odds. An Odds bet wins or loses along with the Pass or Come bet it's attached to, so your rooting interest in the dice doesn't change. If your Pass Line bet needs a 10 to win, so does the Odds bet behind it. The advantage of an Odds bet? Instead of paying even money for wins like the base Pass Line and Come bets, the house pays off an Odds bet at true odds: your reward is exactly equal to your risk, a rarity in a casino wager.

SAMPLE BETTING SEQUENCE

Here's a sample sequence of bets, starting with a new shooter coming out. You begin by placing a $10 bet on the Pass Line:

Roll 1. Come out: shooter throws an 11, a winner for the Pass Line. The dealer pays you $10. Since no point is established, the dice are still in the come out phase.

Roll 2. Come out: shooter throws a 2—craps. Dealer takes your $10 Pass Line chip, which you replace to keep playing.

Roll 3. Come out: shooter throws a 4—a point. The dice now move to phase two. Your Pass Line bet will win if another 4 is thrown and lose if a 7 is thrown. Nothing else affects it. You place a $10 Come bet.

Roll 4. Shooter throws a 12—craps. Your Pass Line bet is unaffected because it's in the point roll phase. But your Come loses because the come out rules apply to it. You place another $10 Come bet.

Roll 5. Shooter throws a 9. Your Pass Line bet is unaffected. Your Come bet moves to the 9 square. That bet now enters the point roll phase: for it to win, the 9 must come before the 7. You're now rooting for two numbers, 4 and 9.

Roll 6. Shooter throws a 12—craps. But both of your bets are in phase two, no worries.

Roll 7. Shooter throws a 9. Your Come bet is a winner.

Roll 8. Shooter throws a 7. Your Pass Line bet loses.

Odds on the 6 and 8 pay off at 6 to 5, on the 5 and 9 at 3 to 2, and on the 4 and 10 at 2 to 1. Casinos have different rules for what multiple of your original bet you can use to back your wager; it can be single, double, triple, or up to 100-times odds (depending on the house rules). Generally speaking, the higher Odds you're allowed, the better. Placing an Odds bet is as simple as placing extra chips behind your Pass Line bet after a point has been established. For Come bets, you place your chips in the come area and ask the dealer for an Odds bet on top of your Come bet. Wrong way bettors can back their Don't Pass and Don't Come bets with Odds as well, but the payouts are inverted: 6 and 8 pay at 5 to 6, 5 and 9 pay 2 to 3, and 4 and 10 pay at 1 to 2.

■TIP➔If you're worried your Odds chips will be mistaken for another bet when you make an Odds bet on your Come bet, just place the chips right on the line between the Come area and the Field area. Dealers are trained to scan the table for in-between chips. When they spot it, they'll shoot you a quizzical look, so just tell them what you want.

PLACE

If you want to bet on a number directly, without going through the come out phase, you can make a Place bet. You can make a Place bet any time, although most bettors wait until the shooter has established a point before making Place bets. To make the bet, just drop your chips on the layout in front of you and tell the dealer which number to "place" your bet on. The dealer puts your chips on the number; if it's rolled before a 7 comes up, you win; otherwise, you lose. The 6 and 8 pay 7 to 6, the 5 and 9 pay 7 to 5, and the 4 and 10 pay 9 to 5. The Place bets on 6 or 8 have a decent (under 2%) house edge, but the others are expensive in that regard. On the other hand, unlike Pass Line or Come bets, you can take your Place bets back if you lose your nerve. Just get the dealer's attention before the next roll and tell him you want to take your place bet(s) down.

STRATEGY

The bets listed above are the only bets worth playing, although they are by no means the only bets on the craps layout. Money flies around the tables at an alarming rate as people place Proposition bets (hard ways and the like) and Field bets, but don't fall for any of them. The best odds in the house come from betting the Pass Line and Come bets and taking maximum odds.

Craps is a game that can decimate your bankroll if you go on a cold streak, so be careful. With all the odds bets and side plays and simultaneous number betting going on, it's easy to have 8 to 12 times the minimum bet riding on one throw of the dice, even though you never intended to bet so aggressively.

You may encounter books or Web sites that offer craps betting systems, which usually consist of a predetermined sequence of bets to make at the craps table. Unlike betting systems for other games, craps systems can actually be quite useful in terms of managing your money. For example, there are systems out there that dictate that you have a certain number of Come bet points active at any given time during a roll. The systems are designed to help you ride the hot streaks and avoid the cold streaks. No system will help you overcome the house advantage, but craps is a game where your emotions can get the best of you, so sometimes having any system is better than nothing.

WHERE TO PLAY

For the highest odds: Main Street Station downtown offers up to 20-times odds and several $5 tables. On the strip, Casino Royale has relative bargains in a prime location.

For fresh air: Try the table at Slots–A–Fun downtown where you're almost standing on Fremont Street when you roll the dice.

For the best dealers: The crews at Treasure Island or Mirage will help you learn and keep your bets on track.

KENO

Keno is bingo's sophisticated cousin, which isn't saying much. In standard casino keno, players select numbers (or *spots*) on a game card. The card is then matched up with a set of randomly drawn numbers to determine whether any of the selected numbers match up with any of the drawn numbers.

Keno is a game of convenience. Gamblers can play keno even as they do other things because you can buy tickets well in advance. Keno seems to follow gamblers around: keno runners roam back rooms of the casino restaurants, keno results boards appear in places throughout the hotel, and there's even sometimes a channel on the TV that shows real-time keno drawing results all day and all night.

BASIC RULES

Before the game begins, you "X" out anywhere from one to 15 numbers between 1 and 80 on a keno game sheet, then turn in your card at the keno counter, pay your wager, and are given an official game ticket in return. When the game begins, 20 numbers are randomly selected, one every few seconds. Players can sit and watch the drama unfold, checking off matched spots as they appear, or they can come back later to have their ticket checked for winners.

Keno pays off according to three variables: the amount of your wager, how many spots you selected, and the number of your spots that matched the randomly drawn numbers. If you're lucky enough to match 15 out of 15, the payout on a $1 bet can be in the hundreds of thousands of dollars.

SPOTS PICKED	SAMPLE KENO PAYOFFS (FOR A BET OF $1)									
	SPOTS MATCHED									
	1	2	3	4	5	6	7	8	9	10
1	$3									
2		$12								
3		$1	$42							
4		$1	$4	$112						
5			$2	$20	$480					
6			$1	$4	$88	$1,480				
7				$2	$24	$360	$5,000			
8					$9	$92	$1,480	$18,000		
9					$4	$44	$300	$4,000	$20,000	
10						$2	$20	$132	$960	$3,800	$25,000

STRATEGY

Keno is a classic numbers game where luck is the only factor in winning and losing. The numbers drawn by the casino are completely random. And every game is an independent even, with each number being just as likely to be one of the 20 selected in one game as it is in another game. So as tempting as it may be, it is fruitless to seek statistical patterns in the numbers being drawn. There's no such thing as an "overdue" number in keno.

For the superstitious, keno can be a fun game of birthdate, age, and other lucky-number picking. For everyone else, it is a game of relaxation and quiet contemplation. The best keno strategy is to bring a good book with you to the keno lounge, sink into a chair, sip a cold beverage, and relax amid the beehive of activity surrounding you.

WHERE TO PLAY

While you watch the big game: At Four Queens Hotel & Casino (✉*202 Fremont St., Downtown* ☎*702/385–4011 or 800/634–6045* ⊕*www.fourqueens.com*), the keno room is right next to the sports book.

For the people-watching: Play the red and gold games in the small open lounge right in the middle of the Caesars Palace Colosseum pit. You'll be an island amid a stream of well-dressed and nicely coiffed guests moving to and fro.

AT A GLANCE

Format: Number-picking game. Players buy game tickets from central counter or dedicated runners

Goal: Players select up to 15 numbers (sometimes more) between 1 and 80 to be matched with a randomly selected set of 20 numbers

Pays: From even money up to hundreds of thousands of dollars, depending on the number of spots you selected and the number that matched

House Advantage: Stratospherically high–over 20%, depending on payout schedule

POKER

People can't seem to get enough of poker. The best players in the world are recognizable celebrities and poker's on TV more than hockey is! But if you've played the game, then none of that will surprise you since you know how much fun it can be. No matter what the variation is, the game offers an intellectual challenge to suit any size brain. It's as complex as you want it to be. And it has an egalitarian quality that beginners love; sometimes the cards just fall right for learning players and they take home the big pot, or the tournament trophy.

BASIC RULES

In poker you can win one of two ways: by betting more than anyone else is willing to bet, or by having the best hand out of those players remaining in the game after the final round of betting. The twist is that some or all of each player's hand is hidden from view, so you can only speculate on other players' hand values.

The variations played in casinos—7-card stud, Texas Hold'em, Omaha, and a smattering of others like Razz and Pineapple—all rely on creating the best five-card hand from a deal that originates from a single standard deck of 52 cards. Five-card hands are valued in order of their statistical rarity:

- **Straight Flush:** Cards of the same suit in consecutive rank
- **Four of a Kind:** Four cards of the same rank
- **Full House:** Three cards of one rank and two of another
- **Flush:** Five cards of the same suit, regardless of rank

■ **Straight:** Five cards in consecutive rank

■ **Three of a Kind:** Three cards of the same rank and two other non-matching cards

■ **Two Pair:** Two cards of one rank, and two cards of another, with a fifth nonmatching card

■ **Pair:** Two cards of one rank, and three other nonmatching cards

■ **High Card:** Any five cards that don't fit into one of the above categories

Aces are usually considered the highest ranked card, although they can act as the low end of a 5-high straight (Ace, 2, 3, 4, 5), which is beaten by a 6-high straight (2, 3, 4, 5, 6). The suits are all equal in poker; identical flushes or pairs of the same rank split the pot.

AT A GLANCE

Format: Multiplayer card game, dealt by house dealer

Goal: Bet your opponents out of the game, and, failing that, have the highest five-card poker hand in the final showdown

Pays: Varies; each hand's pot goes to winner or winners

House Advantage: None. The house rakes a small percentage of each pot but there is no built-in house advantage over the player

Best Bet: Tournaments are a great way to stretch your poker dollar, even for novices

Worst Bet: Underestimating your competition. Granny's probably a Great White

The game starts when cards are dealt to all players at the table, who then put money into a central pot in sequence during a set number of betting rounds. At any time, players can decide their hand is not strong enough to win and *fold,* which means they no longer participate in the hand. Any money they've already bet stays in the pot. As players take turns betting, they must match, or *call,* the highest amount bet from an individual player to stay in the game. Players can also *raise,* which means that they are calling the highest bet and making the minimum bet higher. The betting round continues until everyone who wishes to stay in the game has contributed an equal amount to the pot.

Once the betting rounds are over there's a showdown where the cards are revealed. In most games the highest hand wins, although there are common variations in casinos where the pot is split between the high hand and the low hand.

RULES FOR THE MOST POPULAR VARIATIONS

TEXAS HOLD'EM RULES

Hold'em is the most popular form of poker. Each player (up to 10 can play one game) is dealt two cards face-down, followed by a betting round. Then five community cards are dealt on the table in three groups, each followed by a betting round. First is a group of three cards (the *flop*), and then there are two more rounds of one card each (the *turn* and the *river*). You can use any combination of the seven cards to create your best five-card hand.

Position is very important in Hold'em. The deal rotates around the table, and with it, the blinds (minimum opening bets). Depending on house rules, one or two players must automatically bet blinds in the first round. To stay in and see the flop, the other players must match or raise the blind bet, ensuring no player advances to the important second round for free, and adding some heft to the pot to boot. Because players must match the blind bet to stay in, the later position in the betting rounds is more advantageous—those players can raise, call, or fold depending on what they've seen the other players do.

OMAHA RULES
Omaha is very similar to Texas Hold'em except that the players are each initially dealt four down cards, with the caveat that they can only use two of the four in their final hand.

7-CARD STUD RULES
Poker players who have been away from the game may be more comfortable with this classic. In 7-card Stud there are no community cards; you're dealt your own set of seven cards, which are distributed in rounds: an initial batch of three (two down, one up); three single up-card deals plus betting rounds; and a final down-card deal followed by a betting round. By the showdown, every player remaining in the game has three down cards and four up cards from which to make his best five-card hand.

STRATEGY

If you're a beginner, focus on learning how to play the game at tables with low betting minimums before you invest any serious bankroll. The old adage "if you aren't sure who the sucker is at the table, it's you" is never more true than at a Las Vegas poker table. There are indeed sharks in the water. Online poker is a valuable tool for players who are trying to learn the game prior to a Vegas trip, but don't be fooled—the style of play is very different between the two formats. Playing online ignores a lot of the subtleties of playing live, including the all-important *tells,* outward quirks that reveal the contents of your hand to experienced players.

Although bluffing and big showdowns are part and parcel of the TV poker phenomenon, casino poker success comes with a steady, conservative approach. The most important thing to learn is how to calculate pot odds. You compare the amount of money in the pot—your potential win—with the relative odds of improving your hand sufficiently enough to win. If the pot is big enough, it's worth it to stay in the game and continue betting even if only one single card could help your hand.

There are no shortcuts to poker strategy. Each variation of the game has its nuances. Part of learning the game is understanding how good your hand has to be, on average, to win a pot. And it's only through repetition and study that you can make this second nature.

POPULAR POKER VARIATIONS

CARIBBEAN STUD

Caribbean Stud is played against a dealer on a blackjack-size table. The basic goal is to beat the dealer, but the fun part of the game is that you get paid better odds for having high-end poker hands like straights and flushes. Each player places an initial ante bet to start the game. The dealer then deals five-card hands to every player followed by one hand for the house, of which a single card is turned up. The players then look at their five cards and evaluate whether to remain in the game, in which case they place an additional bet. They also have the option to fold, in which case they lose their ante.

If your hand is better than the dealer's, your ante bet pays off at even money, no matter what. But in order for your main bet to pay off, the dealer's hand must have a minimum value of Ace-King high. Anything less (for example, the dealer has Ace-Queen and three other non-paired cards) means the dealer doesn't *qualify*. When that happens, all players receive even money on their original bet only. When the dealer does qualify, the house hand is compared with each player's hand. If the player's hand is a superior poker hand, the ante is paid off at even money and the bet is paid off according to a payout chart that awards more to better hands. If the dealer's hand is superior, the dealer wins the ante and the bet. Most tables also offer a hard-to-resist $1 side bet for a progressive jackpot that offers abominable odds.

CARIBBEAN STUD PROGRESSIVE JACKPOT PAYOUT SCHEDULE		
Hand	**Dollar Jackpot**	**Odds Against**
Flush	$50	508 to 1
Full House	$75	693 to 1
Four of a Kind	$100	4,164 to 1
Straight Flush	10% of progressive jackpot	64,973 to 1
Royal Flush	100%of progressive jackpot	649,740 to 1

LET IT RIDE

Let It Ride is another table game that uses poker hands to determine winning bets. Play starts with each player at the table making three bets of equal size. The dealer then deals each player three cards, plus two face-down community cards. In the first round, you review your cards and decide whether to stay in the game (basic strategy says you'd better be on your way to at least a straight to stick around). If you want out, you can take back one of the three bets and exit the game. If, on the other hand, you think your three cards have the makings of a good poker hand, you let it ride. The dealer then turns over one of the two community cards. Here's another bail-out opportunity—you can take back a bet or let it ride. If you're still "riding," the final community card is flipped and all bets are paid according to a payout table.

PAI GOW POKER

In Pai Gow Poker, you're dealt seven cards from which you make one five-card and one two-card poker hand. There's a joker in the mix, which can be used as an ace or a wild card to complete a straight, flush, or straight flush. You play against the dealer, who also makes two hands from seven cards.

HAND	PAYOUT
Pair of Tens or Better	**1 to 1**
Two Pairs	2 to 1
Three of a Kind	3 to 1
Straight	5 to 1
Flush	8 to 1
Full House	11 to 1
Four of a Kind	50 to 1
Straight Flush	200 to 1
Royal Flush	1,000 to 1

If both of your hands are beat by the dealer's hands, you lose. If you lose one and win one, you push. If you win both hands, you win even money on your bet, minus a 5% commission to the casino. If the pace of blackjack has you feeling a little light in your wallet, this is a good game to sit down to for a while. Odds are that you'll push more often than you'll win or lose, so you can usually get some good table time in without cleaning out your pockets—granted that you bet conservatively.

THREE-CARD POKER

Three-Card Poker is now more popular than Let It Ride and Caribbean Stud combined and can be found in virtually any Las Vegas casino. Like Caribbean Stud, the players compete against a dealer with an ante (the initial bet) followed by an equal bet if they like their hand after the cards are dealt. The dealer qualifies with a Queen-high. In Three-Card Poker, the player is only dealt—you guessed it—three cards, which makes for some poker-hand twists (a straight actually beats a flush in three-card poker). A bonus table is in play, awarding jackpots to big hands. There's also a bonus bet called Pair Plus that pays a bonus on any pair or better player hand.

WHERE TO PLAY

To learn Pai Gow: The Flamingo, where they offer "Mini-Pai Gow"—a slightly less complicated version of the full game.

If you like watching beautiful people as much as you like getting a Straight Flush: The Palms.

Where the big boys play: The Rio, the regular home of the World Series of Poker finals, and Bellagio, the jewel in the poker-room crown on the Strip.

Best all-around poker room: The Caesars Palace poker room is huge, well-run, and offers a great variety of games and stakes.

3

ROULETTE

Anyone can play roulette—it's an easy way to cut your teeth on the whole table-game experience if you're too nervous to saunter up to a poker table. Basically, roulette is an enjoyable number-picking game played at a leisurely, South-of-France pace. You select and bet on numbers or a color (red or black), watch as the dealer drops a ball on a spinning wheel, and cross your fingers that the ball will land on the right space. It really doesn't get more straightforward than this.

BASIC RULES

The wheel is divided into red and black slots numbered 1 through 36 along with two green slots labeled 0 and 00 (zero and double-zero). The dealer (or croupier) drops a little white ball onto the spinning wheel, and as it loses momentum, it falls onto a series of randomizing obstacles until it settles into one of the numbered slots. You place your bet on a layout filled with numbers; the main area has 3 columns of 12 rows each, which cover numbers 1 through 36. There are also spaces for betting on 0, 00, and groups of numbers; the colors red or black; odd or even numbers; and low and high numbers. You can even place a "dozen" bet—a bet on a third of the numbers at a time—by covering one of the columns or four of the rows.

Unlike other games, when you buy into roulette you're issued specialty chips that are usually valued at $1 (or less in the lower-limit games). Each player at the table has his own color of chips so everyone knows whose money belongs to whom. You can bet on the same numbers as other players—just put your chips on top of theirs. You can keep placing bets until the croupier calls "no more bets" and waves his or her arm over the layout. ■TIP→**You can usually tip the cocktail wait-**

resses with roulette chips if that's all you have.

You have to meet the table minimums when you're betting. Table minimums are different for the inside bets and outside bets. If the table minimum is $5, you must bet $5 *per bet* on outside bets. Inside bets only need to add up to the minimum (even if outside bets have been placed). That means you can bet 5 $1 chips, instead of $5 per bet.

Once the betting is halted and the ball lands in its spot on the wheel, the croupier places a marker on the winning number. All the losing chip areas, inside and outside, are raked, and the croupier pays out each winning bet. Don't grab your chips until the marker's lifted (we know it's tempting, but trust us, it's not worth the death look the dealer will give you).

Payouts in roulette can be quite dramatic with inside bets. Here are the payouts for every bet on the table:

STRATEGY

Roulette is as simple a game as you'll find in the casino. The only complexity is in learning exactly where to place bets to cover the numbers you like. The odds, though, aren't good. The casino keeps over 5% of the total amount wagered on American roulette.

Though the odds make this game one to avoid, we think it's too much fun to give up playing. The best plan, if you're going to get serious about playing this game, is to seek out the handful of single-zero wheels in Las Vegas—most of them are Downtown, and the few that are on the Strip reside behind the velvet ropes of the high-limit areas. Without the dreaded double-zero, your odds improve to a respectable 2.5% house advantage.

WHERE TO PLAY

For single-zero games: Monte Carlo has a table running every night during the week and all day on Saturday and Sunday.

To watch the ball bounce all night: Golden Nugget has great croupiers who will hold your spot while you run to the 24-hour Starbucks in the North Tower for a jolt of gambling gasoline.

Roulette Table

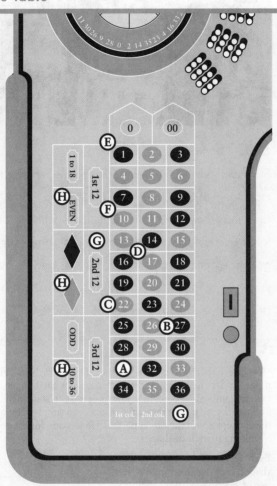

	Bet	Payoff
A	Single number	35 to 1
B	Two numbers	17 to 1
C	Three numbers	11 to 1
D	Four numbers	8 to 1
E	Five numbers	6 to 1
F	Six numbers	5 to 1
G	12 numbers (column)	2 to 1
G	1st 12, 2nd 12, 3rd 12	2 to 1
H	1-18 or 19-36	1 to 1
H	Odd or Even	1 to 1
H	Red or black	1 to 1

SLOTS

Slot machines are the lifeblood of Vegas, earning the casinos mountains of cash. Remember, there's a reason why there are what seems like zillions of slot machines compared to table games—the odds are worse. But some gamblers can't get enough of the one-armed bandits, and if you're one of them (a gambler, not a bandit), set yourself a budget and pray for those three 7s to line up.

BASIC RULES

Slots are basically the same as they've always been. Players insert money, start the game, and watch to see what happens. Instead of inserting individual coins, it's now quite easy to slide in bills. Instead of pulling an arm to start the game, players can simply press a button. But the concept is still the same: players are looking for the reels to match a winning pattern of shapes.

Each reel may have a few dozen shapes, creating an enormous number of possible patterns. The payout varies depending on how rare the pattern is. Prizes range from merely returning the bettor's initial stake, all the way up to multimillion dollar *progressive* prizes. These enormous jackpots are available by linking slot machines together across a pit, a casino, or even across many casinos.

UNSPOKEN RULE

Be aware that veteran slot players can be territorial about their machines and they may even play several at one time. If there's any doubt about whether a machine is currently "occupied" or not, politely ask before you sit down. If in doubt, casino slots personnel can direct you to open machines.

STRATEGY

All slot machines, including every mechanical reel game, are run by on-board computers. The machine's computer brain generates a new random number thousands of times a second, which then determines where each reel will come to rest.

Although the casino can set the payout odds that determine the percentage an individual machine will retain for the house over the long term, the individual spins are random events. That means that even if the jackpot reel pattern appears and pays a huge amount to the winner, the jackpot is equally likely to appear the very next spin. Each spin is an individual trial—an independent event. This means that there is no such thing as an overdue machine, or a machine that's "tapped out." If someone just walked away after losing their whole bankroll to a particular machine, you're just as likely to win the jackpot on that machine on your first pull. Of course, be prepared for some dirty looks if that happens.

> **AT A GLANCE**
>
> **Format:** Coin and bill operated electronic/mechanical machines
>
> **Goal:** Line up winning symbols on machine's reels
>
> **Pays:** Varies by machine and casino
>
> **House Advantage:** Varies widely; Strip average is close to 5%
>
> **Best Bet:** Playing "loose" machines close to the change booth or coffee shop
>
> **Worst Bet:** Playing "tight" machines at noncasino locations (e.g., the airport or service stations)

Slot payout ranges vary between 70% and 98%. Of course, the information on which slot machines in the casinos are the *loosest,* meaning which ones pay out the most, is hard to obtain. Some casinos advertise that their machines pay out at a certain rate, but that usually only refers to certain machines within the property. Play games you enjoy playing, but never lose sight of the fact that payout percentage will usually determine how much money you escape with.

■ TIP→ **Always insert your players club card. The promotions offered to slots players are often quite lucrative, especially the sign-up bonuses.**

To get the most out of every spin, it's a good idea to play the maximum coins with every play. If that means stepping down to a lower denomination machine (e.g., from dollars to quarters) so you can afford it, then do it. Many slot machines require maximum "participation" from players in order to be eligible for the full jackpot or progressive. If you're going to play at all, play for the big payouts.

WHERE TO PLAY

For sheer volume and variety of machines: MGM Grand on the Strip, the Orleans off the Strip.

For penny slots: Bring your copper to Palace Station (✉*2411 W. Sahara Ave., West Side* ☎*702/ 367–2411 or 800/634–3101* ⊕*www. palacestation.com*) and Sam's Town.

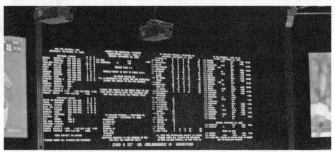

SPORTS BETTING

In Nevada—and only Nevada—you can legally bet on sporting events. The betting takes place in specialized places called sports books, large rooms, or small areas of casinos with an array of TVs for you to watch the games you've bet on. You can try your luck on all the major team sports in America, plus a few individual sports, and you can place a wide variety of wagers—from betting on the outcome of a single game, to betting who will win next year's championship.

Sports books make money by taking a small percentage of the total amount bet on both sides of a game. The goal of a sports book is to get even amounts of money bet on both sides of a game. That way, they take their cut regardless of who actually wins the game. Sports books will try to entice as many people to bet on an underdog as on a favorite.

BASIC RULES

Most basic bets in a sports book are called 11-to-10 bets. That means for every $11 you risk (or *lay*), you win a profit of $10.

POINT SPREADS

In a point spread listed game, one team is usually the favorite (denoted with a negative number), and one is the underdog (with a positive number). Consider this point spread listing:

Steelers

Cowboys -6.5

The sports books have determined that the public believes the Cowboys are more likely to win the game. To lure bettors to the Steelers, the casino will take away 6½ points from the Cowboys' final score when the game is over and it's time to evaluate which bet won. In essence, this evens out the two teams, making them equally attractive to gamblers. Sports bettors will say that the spread on this game is "the Cowboys minus 6½" or "the Steelers plus 6½."

The Cowboys have to win by greater than the point spread to win the bet. If you bet on the Steelers, you want the Cowboys to win by less than the spread or lose the game outright.

OVER/UNDER

Here you're betting on whether the *combined* final score of the game will be either over or under a designated total. The total is determined by the sports book and usually appears in the point spread listing like this:

Giants 42.5

Eagles -7

The negative number is the point spread, and it has no effect on over/under bets. The other number, 42.5, is the total for this game. Bettors are welcome to bet on the point spread, the over/under, or both. Over/under bettors would try to predict whether the *combined* score of the Giants and Eagles would be higher or lower than the total (in this case, 42.5). If the Giants won 24–20, the combined score would be 44, so the over bets win and the under bets lose. An over/under bettor wouldn't care who won the game, as long as either lots of points were scored (over bettors) or few points were scored (under bettors).

AT A GLANCE

Format: Wagering against the house at a dedicated betting counter

Goal: Correctly predict the outcome of sporting events

Pays: Varies by type of bet and casino. Standard is $10 won for every $11 bet

House Advantage: 4.55% on 11-to-10 bets, varies with other types of bets

Best Bet: NCAA basketball; NFL over/unders

Worst Bet: Proposition bets; Futures bets

TEASER BETTING ODDS			
Number of Teams	6 Points	6 ½ Ponts	7 Points
2	Even	10–11	1–12
3	9–5	8–5	3–2
4	3–1	5–2	2–1
5	9–2	4–1	7–2
6	7–1	6–1	5–1

■TIP→ Sports books sometimes use a half-point in totals and point spreads because they eliminate the possibility of ties.

MONEY LINES

Bets listed as money lines have no scoring handicap attached to them (such as a point spread). The bet wins or loses with the team's actual win or loss. Sports books use money lines to entice you to bet on underdogs by increasing the payout in the event the team wins. And they discourage bettors from taking the better team by reducing the payout if they win. Let's take a look at an example:

Astros +150

Cubs -170

The two numbers represent money lines. The underdog has a positive number and the favorite has a negative number. For underdogs, the amount shown is the amount you'd win on a $100 bet. In this case, if the underdog Astros won and you bet $100, you'd win $150. On the other hand, the Cubs money line represents the amount you have to risk to win $100. Because the Cubs are more likely to win, the sports book asks a bettor to pony up a lot more dough up front—to win $100, you'd have to bet $170.

Note: you don't *have* to bet $100-plus at a time. The money line just represents the proportions of amount risked to amount won (and vice versa). Most casinos require a $5 or $10 minimum bet.

PARLAYS

A parlay bet is a combination bet where you need two or more events to win in order for your bet to win. A parlay is the equivalent of betting on one game, then taking the proceeds and betting it all on a second game. Parlays can be fun in that you can place bets on a mixture of sports, as well as both point spread and over/under bets.

Standard parlay payouts are:

PARLAY BETTING ODDS		
Number of Teams	Payout Odds	True Odds
2	13–5	3–1
3	6–1	7–1
4	10–1	15–1
5	20–1	31–1
6	35–1	63–1
7	50–1	127–1
8	100–1	225–1
9	200–1	511–1
10	400–1	1023–1

If you get all wins plus a tie on your parlay, don't worry. It still pays, just at the next lowest level of odds. For example, if you bet a 4-team parlay and three of the bets beat the spread but the final game tied against the spread, you'd be paid 6-to-1 as if it were a 3-teamer. If you get a win and a tie on a 2-team parlay it pays as if it were a straight 11-to-10 bet.

STRATEGY

Sports betting is harder than it looks. Just because you're a fan of a game doesn't mean you can win. The best tips for smart sports betting are:

■ Pick teams and stick with them. Don't try to learn the habits of the entire league. Find a niche—a conference or a few teams—and become an expert.

■ Look for motivations. Pro sports have achieved remarkable parity that makes any team capable of beating any other. Bet on the team with more on the line, or against the team with nothing to gain by playing hard.

■ Be realistic. Sporting events include incalculable random events, so even the best sports bettors are thrilled to win 60% of their 11-to-10 bets.

■ Avoid exotic bets. Casinos let you bet on almost anything; don't take them up on it. Stick with the bets listed in this chapter.

■ Beware of hype. It's often wrong. Do your own homework and draw your own conclusions. The sports media has a way of making certain teams look utterly unbeatable. No team is. Ever.

■ Become an NCAA hoops fan. With so many teams in play on Winter Saturdays, it's easy for odds-makers to get a point spread wrong.

■ Take a pass. Remember that a losing bet not placed is a win.

WHERE TO PLAY

For all-around fanatics: Mandalay Bay's sports book is as spacious as a blimp hangar, has comfortable seating, and a nearby snack bar.

To kick it NORAD-style: The Las Vegas Hilton, home of the original megabook, doesn't have all that pupil-constricting lighting found in the newer places. We like its dark setting because if you're doing something besides watching, you shouldn't even be in here.

To watch the big game with your buddies: The South Point has a few hundred seats in their race and sports book with all the amenities you need just a 10-minute cab ride from the South end of the strip. There's no need to fight for a seat for the privilege of watching the main event at a big-name casino.

VIDEO POKER

With the rise in popularity of poker, more people than ever understand the order of the hands and the basic strategies involved. Now a generation of formerly slot-bound gamblers who wouldn't dare buy in at a table game have swollen the ranks of the video-poker players, and the casinos have responded in kind by expanding the number and selection of their machines. So pony on up if you're not ready for the bluffing and betting of real poker and hone your skills against the computer.

BASIC RULES

Video poker is unlike regular poker in that your only goal is to achieve certain hands. Like we said before, you don't have to worry about other players, so you're not going to deal with bluffing or real betting. In almost every variation of video poker, your sole objective is to create the best five-card hand by either keeping or discarding cards. You may keep or throw away as many cards as you like by activating the appropriate button underneath every card. After selecting the card(s) you want to hold or discard, press on "deal/draw." The cards you didn't want to hold are replaced with new cards. If the new hand contains a winning combination, you get paid. It's that simple.

"Jacks or Better," "Jokers Wild," and "Deuces Wild" machines are commonly identified as the optimal game formats to play for folks looking to win money.

STRATEGY

The number one element of any video-poker strategy is finding the right machines. That's because even though two machines may be identical in the game or games they offer, slight variations in the payoff table make one far more advantageous to play than the other.

Video-poker machines are commonly identified by certain amounts in their pay tables. The single-coin payouts for the full house and the flush are the identifying characteristics to seek out prior to dropping coins in the machine. What does all this mean? Put simply, what you want are 9/6 machines (that is "nine six" machines, not "nine sixths" machines) rather than 8/5 machines; they pay out 9 coins to 1 on a full house and 6 coins to 1 on a flush.

3

Certain video-poker games are actually listed as positive advantage games, meaning the potential exists for players to win money over the long term (unlike just about every other game in the casino). This is possible because that payout level assumes a player wins the straight flush, the rarest, and highest-paying, video-poker hand. Without the straight flush, the casino enjoys an advantage of several percentage points. You actually play with that disadvantage for hours on end, waiting for an occasional bankroll windfall from 4-of-a-kind or a straight flush. The time—and bankroll—that may be necessary to invest before hitting the straight flush can be prohibitive, so don't count on paying for your kid's college with video-poker proceeds.

WHERE TO PLAY

For the most full-payout machines: The Gold Coast (✉ *400 W. Flamingo Rd., West Side* ☎ *702/367–7111 or 800/331–5334* ⊕ *www.goldcoast-casino.com*) has an abundance of 9/6 machines, as does the Red Rock Casino, Resort and Spa.

For high-end video poker: The Wynn has blue-collar gaming in a glamorous atmosphere.

For low-end video poker: Four Queens and the Orleans both have a great array of full-pay nickel machines.

■ TIP→Want the best deals, promotions, and events? Read what the locals read: The **Las Vegas Advisor** (⊕ *lasvegasadvisor.com*) and **Gaming Today** (⊕ *gamingtoday.com*) are two publications that keep the rest of the world up to speed on Las Vegas comings and goings. Read them on the Internet before you leave home.

Las Vegas Lingo

Before you gamble, learn some key words in the local language.

Bankroll. The amount of cash an individual has to gamble with.

Black chip. $100 casino chip.

Buy-in. The amount of cash with which a player enters a game.

Cage. The casino cashier station; exchange your chips for cash here.

Chase. Increasing the size of your bet during a losing streak. (See also Press)

Check. A.K.A. a casino chip.

Color Up. To exchange a stack of lower denomination chips for fewer high-denomination chips.

Comp. A gift from the casino of a complimentary drink, room, dinner, or show; a freebie.

Cut. A ritual splitting of a deck or cards performed after shuffling.

Eye-in-the-sky. The overhead video surveillance system and its human monitors in a casino.

Floorman. Casino employee who oversees operations at several adjacent table games in a pit. Floormen typically report to the pit boss.

Full-pay video poker. A video-poker game that, if you know strategy, gives you an edge over the casino.

Green chip. $25 casino chip.

High roller. A casino customer who plays with significant bankroll.

Hold. The house profit from all the wagers; what the casino wins.

House. Another name for the casino.

Low roller. A typical tourist making 25¢ slot-machine bets or $1 and $3 table-game bets.

Marker. A casino IOU. Players sign markers and get chips at the tables; they then pay off the markers with chips or cash.

Money Plays. A term used by a player requesting to bet with cash instead of chips. .

Pit. A group of tables forming a closed circle on the floor. The pit bosses and dealers stand in the middle and serve the customers, who sit on the outside. Visitors can't walk into the middle of the pit.

Pit boss. The senior casino employee who supervises the gaming tables.

Players Club card. A card with a magnetic stripe on it used to track a gambler's activities in a casino, rate them, and get them comps.

Press. To increase the size of a bet, especially during a win streak. (See also Chase)

Push. A tie bet, where you neither win nor lose.

Rating. Tracking a gambler's average bet, length of time played, and net loss. Getting rated helps you get comps.

Red chip. $5 casino chip, usually red.

Shoe. A small box in a table game from which cards are dealt.

Sports book. The casino area for sports betting.

Table games. All games of chance such as blackjack and craps played against the casino.

Toke. A tip (short for token).

Where to Eat

Tuna at Fusia, Luxor

WORD OF MOUTH

Try Lotus of Siam. It's as good as any of the Thai food you'll get in Bangkok.

—Bisbee

WHERE TO EAT PLANNER

Raves & Faves

Best Burger Selection: Who knew a simple hamburger could be so much fun? The create-your-own Burger Bar is perfect for those who enjoy their beef with a bit of a twist.

Best Hidden Jewel: You wouldn't guess from Marrakech's boxy exterior that this red-velveted Middle Eastern restaurant is one of the coziest and most romantic rooms in town.

Best View: Though drink and entrée prices are just as sky-high, at Mix the view of the Strip's glittery lights is spectacular.

Best Casino for Dining: The glamorous Wynn has set the new standard for culinary greatness with its selection of dazzling restaurants, most of them helmed by chefs who are less famous than Emeril, Wolfgang, and others, but arguably more talented.

Emeril's (MGM) chef Jean Paul Labadie.

How to Use This Chapter

This chapter divides Las Vegas restaurants by location (the Strip, Downtown, Paradise Road, Greater Las Vegas). Within each section, the restaurants are grouped first by type of cuisine and then by price range.

Tips, Taxes & Tipping

When planning your dining-out excursions in Las Vegas, try to hit at least one or two places off-Strip. You may find that prices are lower—and food quality sometimes just as high—as in the places that cater to tourists. The pace is usually more relaxed, too, and you can often leave your car just steps from the door.

While you're on the Strip, keep your eyes peeled for the legendary bargains; not all Las Vegas establishments have gone highbrow. You can still find a 99-cent half-pound hot dog at Slots–A–Fun, for instance. Some casino food courts offer high-quality deli-style food instead of the usual fast fare. And don't miss the crepes window at Paris.

Unless otherwise noted, the restaurants listed in this guide are open daily for lunch and dinner.

A tip of 15%–20% is common. In some circumstances you might want to slip the maître d' $5 or $10 for a special table.

What It Costs

¢	$	$$	$$$	$$$$
under $10	$10–$20	$20–$30	$30–$40	over $40

Prices are per person for a main course at dinner.

Updated
by Andrew
Collins

LAS VEGAS HAS—HOWEVER IMPROBABLY—BECOME AMERICA'S hottest restaurant market. Each new megaresort brings its own multiple dining options, with celebrity chefs adding clones of famous signature restaurants and newborn establishments to the mix. And while bargain buffets and coffee shops still abound, the arrival of the superchefs has left its mark on the steak houses and buffets—many of the latter of which have gone upscale. Away from the Strip, the unprecedented population growth in the city's suburbs has brought with it a separate and continuous wave of new restaurants, both familiar chains and independent spots opened by local and nationally based entrepreneurs.

DINE VEGAS STYLE

Joining a few gourmet pioneers such as Hugo's Cellar and André's, and spurred on by Wolfgang Puck, who tested the desert waters with Spago in 1992, a flood of newer restaurants and ever-more-prominent chefs have radically changed the experience of eating in Las Vegas. Status-conscious hotel-casinos now compete for star chefs and create lavish, built-to-order dining rooms for well-known tenants. These new establishments rival the upscale restaurants of the country's dining capitals in quality and service.

The restaurant explosion has been partially geared to satisfying high rollers, who are fed for free as a reward for their often-astronomical bets at the blackjack and baccarat tables, but the city's new reputation as a culinary capital is also drawing attention from those who simply enjoy outstanding food. Las Vegas's tendency to do everything to an extreme creates the possibility that too many spectacular restaurants will starve each other, but there's no sign of that yet. Although Sin City's reputation as being recession-proof may be a bit overstated, the city knows how to continually reinvent itself to ensure the 40 million or so visitors—many of them with fat expense accounts—keep on coming.

Even low rollers with thin wallets have plenty of dining options in Las Vegas. Despite the influx of upscale restaurants, you can still find a complete steak dinner for only $4.95 (Ellis Island), a 99¢ shrimp cocktail (Golden Gate), and $2.99 steak-and-eggs breakfast specials (Arizona Charlie's). And of course, the ever-popular buffet is found in nearly every casino in town.

Crowds at the hotels, long lines at the buffets, and the jangling noise of slot machines prompt some to seek refuge away from the casinos. Venture into the residential areas for a steadily increasing variety of restaurants that suit most pocketbooks. Rosemary's, André's, Lotus Thai, and other off-Strip dining rooms satisfy the craving for a civilized meal. Mid-price family eateries (such as Memphis Championship Barbecue, India Oven, Doña Maria, and Billy Bob's Steak House) offer reliable quality at reasonable prices.

THE STRIP

AMERICAN

$$$$ ✕ **Aureole.** Celebrity chef Charlie Palmer re-created his famed New
★ York restaurant for Mandalay Bay. He and designer Adam Tihany added a few playful, Las Vegas–style twists: a four-story wine tower, for example, holds 10,000 bottles that are reached by "wine fairies" who are hoisted up and down via a system of electronically activated pulleys. Seasonal specialties on the fixed-price menu might include French onion soup with foie gras, truffles, and Sonoma squab topped with seared foie gras and served in a preserved-cherry jus. For dessert try innovative offerings like citrus-scented cheesecake with huckleberry compote or crème brûlée ice cream with maple–brown sugar sauce. ✉Mandalay Bay Resort & Casino, 3950 Las Vegas Blvd. S, South Strip ☎702/632–7401 ⌂Reservations essential ▤AE, D, DC, MC, V ⊙No lunch.

$$$$ ✕ **Nobhill.** San Francisco cuisine is the star at Michael Mina's hand-
Fodor'sChoice some, understated brasserie with clean lines and polished-wood floors.
★ The menu's emphasis is on seasonal regional favorites such as a duet of sturgeon (caviar as well as the smoked fish, served with poached quince and vanilla oil), lobster potpie (containing a huge 2-pound Maine lobster and swimming in rich brandy cream), and steak with seared foie gras and a pinot noir reduction. There are no weak spots in Mina's repertoire. A selection of five flavors of mashed potatoes, such as lobster, curry, or basil, is included with dinner, and you can bet the sourdough bread's the real deal. ✉MGM Grand Hotel and Casino, 3799 Las Vegas Blvd. S, South Strip ☎702/891–7337 ▤AE, D, DC, MC, V ⊙No lunch.

$$$$ ✕ **Picasso.** This restaurant, adorned with the artist's original works,
★ raised the city's dining scene a notch when it opened. Although it's still much adored, some believe it may be resting a bit on its laurels, and that chef Julian Serrano doesn't change his menu often enough. The artful, innovative cuisine is based on French classics but also has strong Spanish influences. Appetizers on the seasonal menu might include warm quail salad with sautéed artichokes and pine nuts or poached oysters with osetra caviar and vermouth sauce. Sautéed medallions of fallow deer, roasted milk-fed veal chop, or roasted almond–and–honey crusted pigeon might appear as entrée choices. Dinners are prix fixe, with four- or five-course menus. ✉Bellagio Las Vegas, 3600 Las Vegas Blvd. S, Center Strip ☎702/693–8105 ⌂Reservations essential ▤AE, D, DC, MC, V ⊙Closed Tues. No lunch.

$$$–$$$$ ✕ **Bradley Ogden.** San Francisco culinary wizard Bradley Ogden brought his magic touch to Vegas with this sleek, modern room at Caesars. What's the key to Ogden's brilliant flavors? He uses only fresh ingredients (many of them organic) from small farms. Try the osetra caviar with a blue-corn pancake to start, followed by slow-roasted Muscovy duck with endive, purple artichokes, polenta, and rhubarb. Save room for the divine passion fruit and chocolate cake. Go formal in the main dining room, flanked by a fireplace and waterfall, or take it down a notch on the patio or in the lounge. ✉Caesars Palace, 3570

Las Vegas Blvd. S, Center Strip ☎702/731–7731 ▭*AE, D, DC, MC, V* ⊘*No lunch.*

$$$–$$$$ ✕ **Tableau.** Cloistered away from the busier parts of the Wynn, this restaurant overlooks a serene pool and garden off the gleaming Tower Suites lobby. Tableau serves three anything-but-square meals a day. A highlight is the fabulous brunch, where you might try Maine lobster salad with baby beets and winter citrus, or huckleberry-ricotta pancakes. The Dungeness crab club sandwich with smoked bacon makes a memorable lunch option, while at dinner you can feast on pancetta-wrapped monkfish with horseradish-whipped potatoes, or roasted Colorado rack of lamb with chestnut flan, lamb sausage, and potato gratin. Tableau also offers an extraordinary vegetarian tasting menu, which might feature ricotta ravioli with black truffle–and–fennel sauce, or caramelized onion–and–feta tart with watercress salad. ⊠ *Wynn Las Vegas, 3131 Las Vegas Blvd. S, North Strip* ☎702/248–3463 ▭*AE, D, DC, MC, V.*

$$–$$$$ ✕ **FIX.** The ceiling, constructed almost entirely of Costa Rican Padouk
★ wood, curves like a breaking wave at this upscale comfort-food restaurant. A-list celebrities frequent this spot, and for good reason: all your favorite childhood foods are prepared with a twist for your grown-up taste buds. Take the mac-and-cheese side dish, for example—it's croquettes and a cheese sauce for dipping. Craving carbs? Indulge in lobster mashed potatoes. Entrées include a delicious lobster with prosciutto, gnocchi, and truffle cream, and sea bass with baby shrimp in a lobster broth. Banana doughnuts served with two dipping sauces are a perfect ending. The kitchen serves until midnight most evenings, and until 2 ⊦ Friday and Saturday. ⊠*Bellagio Las Vegas, 3600 Las Vegas Blvd. S, Center Strip* ☎702/693–7111 ▭*AE, D, DC, MC, V* ⊘*No Lunch.*

$$–$$$$ ✕ **Red Square.** Theatrical designs, including a long bar made of ice and soaring coffered ceilings, temper an upscale menu at this Soviet-chic place, where a massive, headless Lenin statue guards the entrance. For starters, swill a martini made from one of the 100 varieties of vodka and graze on caviar, crab-stuffed portobello mushrooms, or tuna and smoked salmon tartare. Settle into chicken Kiev, lobster and black-truffle fettuccine, or Roquefort-crusted filet mignon for dinner before finishing with the warm chocolate cake or crème brûlée. You can check out the walk-in vodka freezer, in which frequent patrons can rent their own space, if you splurge on an expensive bottle. There's better food at Mandalay Bay, but few restaurants measure up when it comes to panache. ⊠*Mandalay Bay Resort & Casino, 3950 Las Vegas Blvd. S, South Strip* ☎702/632–7777 ⌧*Reservations essential* ▭*AE, D, DC, MC, V* ⊘*No lunch.*

$$–$$$$ ✕ **STACK.** Curving strips of exotic wood form the "stacked" walls of
★ this beautiful restaurant that opened inside Mirage in 2006, evidence of the resort's aim to ratchet up its dining reputation by several notches. The vibe closely resembles Fix at Bellagio, another late-night restaurant created by the white-hot Light Group, the force behind such chic nightspots as Jet and Caramel Lounge. Start with the crunchy tuna tacos with mango-wasabi sauce or the miso black cod before tuck-

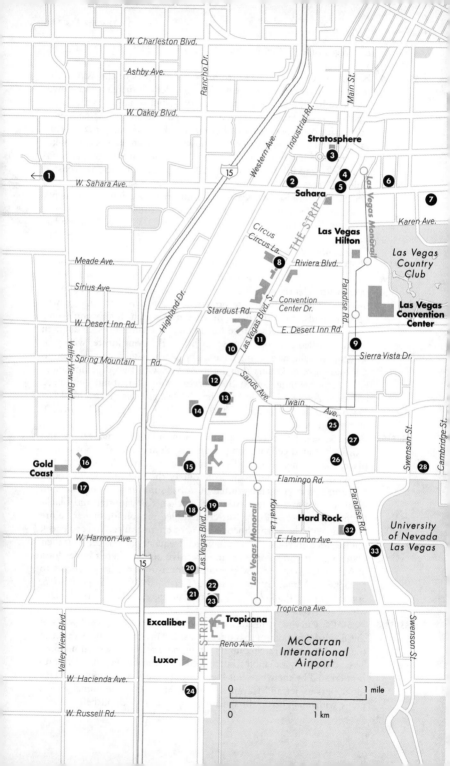

W. Charleston Blvd.

Ashby Ave.

W. Oakey Blvd.

Rancho Dr.

Industrial Rd.

Western Ave.

Main St.

Stratosphere ③

① ← W. Sahara Ave.

② ④
⑤
Sahara

⑥

⑦

Karen Ave.

Las Vegas Monorail

THE STRIP

Circus La.
Circus La.

Las Vegas
Hilton

Las Vegas
Country
Club

⑧ Riviera Blvd.

Las Vegas Blvd. S.

Highland Dr.

Stardust Rd.

Convention
Center Dr.

Paradise Rd.

Las Vegas
Convention
Center

Meade Ave.

Sirius Ave.

W. Desert Inn Rd.

E. Desert Inn Rd.

Spring Mountain Rd.

⑩

⑪

⑨

Sierra Vista Dr.

Valley View Blvd.

Sands Ave.

⑫

⑬

Twain Ave.

⑭

㉕

㉗

Gold
Coast

⑯

⑮

㉖

Swenson St.

Cambridge St.

⑰

Flamingo Rd.

㉘

⑱ ⑲

Koval La.

Hard Rock

University
of Nevada
Las Vegas

W. Harmon Ave.

Las Vegas Blvd. S.

Las Vegas Monorail

E. Harmon Ave.

㉜

⑳

㉝

15

㉑

㉒
㉓

Tropicana Ave.

Swenson St.

Excaliber

Tropicana

McCarran
International
Airport

Valley View Blvd.

THE STRIP

Reno Ave.

Luxor ▶

W. Hacienda Ave.

㉔

0   1 mile

0   1 km

W. Russell Rd.

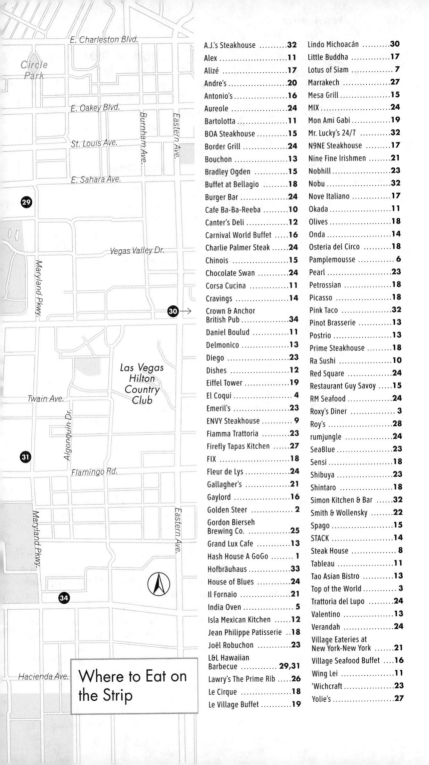

Where to Eat on the Strip

ing into the lamb shank with lentils and watercress or the bone-in 24-ounce cowboy steak. There's an extensive selection of martinis, single-malt scotches, and cognacs. It's open until 2 AM on weekends, 11 the rest of the week. ⊠ *Mirage Hotel and Casino, 3400 Las Vegas Blvd. S, Center Strip* ☎ *702/693–8300* ⊟ *AE, D, DC, MC, V.*

BRUNCH SPOTS TO AVOID

We've suggested lots of great buffets. Here are a few to avoid:

Buffet at the Golden Nugget

MGM Grand Buffet

Circus Circus

$–$$$$ ✕ **Postrio.** This elegant Wolfgang Puck import from San Francisco has an informal and less pricey "outdoor" café along the Venetian's retail promenade as well as a slightly dressier dining room; the latter is trimmed in rich burgundy and accented with strips of Gaudí-esque stained glass. The ubiquitous Puck pizzas are here, but so are some excellent salads and pastas. Dinner emphasizes steaks and seafood, including mesquite-grilled *côte de boeuf* with horseradish mashed potatoes and green-peppercorn sauce. ⊠ *Venetian Resort-Hotel-Casino, 3355 Las Vegas Blvd. S, Center Strip* ☎ *702/796–1110* ⊟ *AE, D, DC, MC, V* ⊗ *No lunch in Dining Room.*

$–$$$$ ✕ **Spago Las Vegas.** His fellow chefs stood by in wonder when Wolf-
★ gang Puck opened this branch of his famous Beverly Hills eatery in the culinary wasteland that was Las Vegas in 1992, but Spago Las Vegas has become a fixture in this ever-fickle city, and it remains consistently superb. The less expensive Café, which overlooks the busy Forum Shops at Caesars, is great for people-watching; inside, the dinner-only Dining Room is more intimate. Both menus are classic Puck. In the Café, sample white-bean cassoulet with chicken sausage and whole-grain mustard. Top picks in the Dining Room include porcini mushroom ravioli with Muscovy duck confit and white-truffle foam, and coriander-crusted yellowfin tuna with a lemongrass, coconut, and sea urchin sauce. ⊠ *Forum Shops at Caesars, 3500 Las Vegas Blvd. S, Center Strip* ☎ *702/369–6300* ⊟ *AE, D, DC, MC, V.*

$$–$$$ ✕ **Verandah.** Informal, peaceful, and refined, this beautifully decorated
★ though somewhat overlooked gem at the Four Seasons offers the perfect antidote to the noisier and flashier restaurants elsewhere at Mandalay Bay. It's easy to carry on a conversation outside on the tropically landscaped terrace or inside the dining room with its muted colors and candlelit tables. Service here rivals any in town, and the presentation and quality of the innovative dishes leaves nothing to be desired, especially considering the comparatively reasonable prices. You might start with the smoked salmon–and–potato galette with celery-root rémoulade and lemon essence, followed by mushroom-truffle gnocchi with broad beans or pistachio-crusted New Zealand snapper with roasted corn, pearl pasta, and citrus sauce. Many of Mandalay Bay's best restaurants don't serve breakfast or lunch—Verandah does an admirable job with both. ⊠ *Four Seasons Hotel, 3960 Las Vegas Blvd. S, South Strip* ☎ *702/632–5000* ⊟ *AE, D, DC, MC, V.*

Continued on page 153

BEST BUFFETS

Despite Vegas's hoity-toity culinary makeover, there's nothing we like more than the city's famous and fabulous buffets that continue to rake in the masses. Why? Because who doesn't love that uniquely American obsession—unlimited gorging for one set price?

Buffets originated in the late 1940s as an attention-grabbing loss leader that would attract hungry gamblers to the casinos (and keep them there). Now the buffet concept has grown into an important tradition at virtually every resort. Bargain-hunters will still find plenty of economical deals, but the top buffets typically charge upwards of $25, or even $40, per person at dinner. Hey, there are lobster tails, Kobe beef, and unlimited champagne at some of these spreads—you get what you pay for. With that in mind, here's a look at some of the best buffet bangs for the buck, from the chichi Buffet at Bellagio to the value-packed Feast Around the World.

TOP PICKS

The Buffet at Bellagio

Step into the regal dining room, tricked out with opulent chandeliers and elegant artwork, and any hesitation that a buffet could be gourmet enough to deserve Bellagio's hefty price tag vanishes. Even the most discerning foodie should find something to like among urbane cuisine like venison chops, apple-smoked sturgeon, and (especially) elaborate pastries.

Some say the Buffet is overrated and overcrowded, but don't be put off by the naysayers—if you skip items that you could easily get at any Vegas buffet (such as pizzas and pastas), you'll do well here. The staff does a first-rate job tending to everybody's needs.

If you want to try to avoid the dinner lines, show up right when dinner starts (4 PM Monday–Thursday, 4:30 PM Friday–Sunday). You might be eating earlier than normal, but the trade-off is worth it.

BEST DISHES: Eggs Benedict, crab omelets (with real lump crab meat), Kobe beef, Chilean sea bass, baby squid, crab legs, sushi, smoked Scottish salmon, tandoori game hen, steamed clams, the salad bar.

PRICES: Breakfast $15, champagne brunch $29, lunch $20, dinner $28–$36.

☎ 702/693-7111 ⊕ www.bellagio. com ⊟ AE, D, DC, MC, V.

Le Village Buffet/Paris

Let other buffets touch on international foods—Paris Las Vegas owns the world's foremost cuisine, and Francophiles unite jubilantly here to sample Vegas's take on French fare. The verdict? Okay, this isn't going to beat out Joël Robuchon's Left Bank L'Atelier, but in terms of buffets and other similarly priced Strip dining, the food here is mouthwatering.

The cooking stations are themed to the regions of France, such as Burgundy, Normandy, Alsace, and Brittany (head here for the delicious dessert crepes). Raclette (a dish of melted aged cheese) and the towering pile of snow-crab clusters are always popular, and there's a particularly impressive spread of cheeses (naturally).

Drop by Le Flambé station for bananas Foster to top off your meal. The dining room, fashioned after a quaint French village, is a kick: stone walls and floors lend a charming feel, if not one that's especially conducive to quiet conversation, and the flattering, soft lighting is a rarity among Vegas buffet restaurants.

BEST DISHES: Chicken chasseur (sautéed in a brown sauce), roasted duck, bouillabaisse, veal marengo (in olive oil with tomatoes, onions, olives, garlic, and white wine), smoked-salmon salad, raclette, braised lamb, chocolate mousse, made-to-order crepes, Belgian waffles, French bread pudding.

PRICES: Breakfast $13, champagne brunch $25, lunch $18, dinner $25.

☎ 702/946-7000 ⊕ www. parislasvegas.com ⊟ AE, D, DC, MC, V.

TOP PICKS

Cravings/Mirage

A chic reinterpretation of the usual Vegas buffet, Cravings was designed in bold colors by noted designer Adam Tihany (who designed Bouchon, Aureole, and Spago, among many others). Aesthetically, it's the anti-buffet—the futuristic back-lighted glass walls, dramatic geometric patterns, and low-slung chairs and tables give it the feel of a mod cafeteria from the next century. The brash lighting can be headache-inducing, but otherwise this is a fun, stylish place to nosh. You can even watch cooking shows on the several flat-screen TVs.

Thirteen separate cooking stations freshly prepare all types of eats, including all-American barbecue, wood-fired pizza, Chinese entrées, Mexican dishes, and even sushi. Many selections are made to order, and the Asian items consistently draw top praise. The mouthwatering dessert section with hand-scooped Italian ice cream, coffee gelato, and chocolate mousse with raspberry puree may entice you to skip the main course.

BEST DISHES: Dim sum, peel-and-eat shrimp, prime rib, bruschetta, fried chicken, chipotle-mashed potatoes, Asian noodles, wonton duck soup, macaroons, croissant pudding.

PRICES: Breakfast $13, champagne brunch $21, lunch $18, dinner $24.

☎ 702/791-7223 ⊕ www.mirage.com ☰ AE, D, DC, MC, V.

Village Seafood Buffet/Rio

For lovers of all creatures from the water, the notion of an all-you-can-eat seafood buffet sounds almost too amazing to be true. And, well, it is. This nautical-theme dinner buffet at the Rio isn't the seafood nirvana that you'll find at pricey restaurants like Mandalay Bay's RM Seafood or the MGM Grand's Seablue. But hey, it's still impressive. In keeping with the around-the-world theme of Rio's standard buffet (Carnival World), the Village Seafood spread ventures, to Mexico (with seafood fajitas), Italy (try the cioppino), China (delicious kung pao scallops), and elsewhere. The relatively steep price still rewards you with plenty of value—just think what you'd pay a la carte for heaping platters of sushi, lobster, raw shellfish, and the like. Skip the baked or fried fish fare (flounder, cod, salmon), as it doesn't always hold up as well as the shellfish and raw-bar items, although there are exceptions. Fear not if you despise fish and you're just going along to placate a seafood lover—there's plenty of chicken and beef, including delicious barbecue beef ribs.

BEST DISHES: Oysters Rockefeller (above), seafood cannelloni, broiled swordfish, lobster tail, peel-and-eat shrimp, seafood gumbo, snow-crab legs, clams and oysters on the half-shell, chocolate cheesecake.

PRICES: Dinner $35 (no lunch).

☎ 702/777-7777 ⊕ www.playrio.com ☰ AE, D, DC, MC, V.

4

BEST BUFFETS

HONORABLE MENTIONS

Dishes/Treasure Island

The layout here looks a lot different from other buffets. Six live-action stations with marble and stainless-steel counters are arranged like individual restaurants along a street, and the dining room is divided into a number of small sections with tables and booths. The pricier "Swanky Dishes" Friday-and Saturday-night dinners include a number of high-ticket items.

BEST DISHES: North Carolina–style barbecue pork, barbecue brisket, dry-rub ribs, lobster ravioli, ricotta tortellini, chile rolls, Chinese chicken salad, house-made doughnuts, cotton candy.

PRICES: Breakfast $12, lunch $15, dinner $20, Swanky Dishes buffet $26.

☎ 702/894-7111 ⊕ www.treasureisland.com ▤ AE, D, DC, MC, V.

Carnival World Buffet/Rio

Carnival World might have been among our top picks, given its excellent desserts and loyal following, but this international spread occasionally misses the mark on food quality. It's still a winner, but considering the steep prices, there's room for improvement. It serves dozens of Mexican, Italian, Chinese, Japanese, American, and other ethnic specialties under one large and colorful roof. Don't miss the dessert area: it's one of the best and biggest, with more than 70 varieties of homemade pies, cakes, and pastries, plus nine flavors of gelato.

BEST DISHES: Burgers and fries, fish-and-chips.

PRICES: Breakfast $14, champagne brunch $24, lunch $17, dinner $24.

☎ 702/777-7777 ⊕ www.playrio.com ▤ AE, D, DC, MC, V.

CHAMPAGNE BRUNCH

Virtually every buffet mentioned here offers an elaborate champagne brunch, usually on Saturday and Sunday mornings. But there are also a few regular restaurants that offer special weekend brunch spreads. Here are the ones you shouldn't miss.

At Mandalay Bay, tap your toes at the wonderful gospel brunch served at the **House of Blues** (☎ 702/632-7600 ⊕ www.hob.com), where you feast on terrific soul food. Out at stunning Lake Las Vegas, the **Ritz-Carlton** (☎ 702/567- 4700 ⊕ www.ritzcarlton.com) presents one of the most lavish brunches at the Medici Café and Terrace—there's lobster-scrambled eggs and chocolate-chip pancakes. For sheer over-the-top opulence, don't miss the weekly **Bally's Sterling Brunch** (☎ 702/967-7999 ⊕ www.ballylasvegas. com), a swanky affair set inside the casino's handsome steak restaurant.

Celebrity Chefs A–Z

CLOSE UP

Hoping to catch a glimpse of a celebrity while in Vegas? Next time you're seated in a fine restaurant, don't limit your star search to the dining room. Keep your eyes trained on the kitchen, and you may see a chef whose celebrity rivals that of any Hollywood star's saunter through those swinging doors.

Here's a partial list of some of the hottest chefs with restaurants on the Strip.

Mario Batali B&B Ristorante, Venetian

Daniel Boulud Daniel Boulud Brasserie, Wynn Las Vegas

Bobby Flay Mesa Grill, Caesars Palace

Hubert Keller Fleur de Lys, Mandalay Bay

Thomas Keller Bouchon, Venetian

Emeril Lagasse Emeril's, MGM Grand

Grant MacPherson Executive Chef, Wynn Las Vegas

Michael Mina Seablue and Nobhill, MGM Grand

Bradley Odgen Bradley Odgen's, Caesars Palace

Wolfgang Puck Spago, Caesars Palace; Trattoria del Lupo, Mandalay Bay; Wolfgang Puck Bar & Grill, MGM Grand.

Joël Robuchon Joël Robuchon at the Mansion, MGM Grand

Guy Savoy Guy Savoy, Caesars Palace

Julian Serrano Picasso, Bellagio

Jean-Georges Vongerichten PRIME Steakhouse, Bellagio

$–$$$ ✕ **Pinot Brasserie.** James Beard Foundation Award–winning chef Joachim Splichal and his wife and partner Christine have duplicated their acclaimed Los Angeles Pinot restaurant—an urban-casual bistro with unpretentious Franco-Californian cuisine. The storefront façade, imported from France, allows passersby to glimpse diners at their tables and cooks at work. Seafood is king here, and selections include oysters on the half shell (imported from wherever they are the freshest), scallop tartare, chilled lobster, and Atlantic salmon with horseradish-potato gratin. At lunch, don't miss the apricot brandy–glazed pulled pork sandwich with garlic fries. Pinot serves very good breakfasts, too. ✉ *Venetian Resort-Hotel-Casino, 3355 Las Vegas Blvd. S, Center Strip* ☎ *702/735–8888* ▭ *AE, D, DC, MC, V.*

$–$$ ✕ **Grand Lux Cafe.** The Venetian's 24-hour operation is no diner or coffee shop. A member of the same family as the Cheesecake Factory, Grand Lux is an attractive, expansive space in contemporary colors. The menu's all over the place, including such items as Asian nachos, Madeira chicken, and Mongolian steak. And whatever you do, be sure to leave room for the strawberry shortcake or a slice of cheesecake or key lime pie. ✉ *Venetian Resort-Hotel-Casino, 3355 Las Vegas Blvd. S, Center Strip* ☎ *702/414–3888* ▭ *AE, D, DC, MC, V.*

$–$$ ✕ **Nine Fine Irishmen.** Irish craftspeople and materials were used to construct this authentic-feeling pub and restaurant inside the New York–New York. Live bands and Irish dancers perform as patrons down draught Guinness, Harp Lager, or Killian's Red. Soda bread and classic, hearty Irish fare fills the menu. Main courses include crab-stuffed salmon, Irish sausage, and corned beef and cabbage. Finish off with a black-and-tan cake consisting of dark-, milk-, and white-chocolate filling. ⊠*New York–New York Hotel and Casino, 3790 Las Vegas Blvd. S, South Strip* ☎702/740–6969 ⊟*AE, D, MC, V.*

¢–$$ ✕ **Burger Bar.** You build your own burger at this fun joint with marble
Fodor'sChoice   tables and wood-panel walls. First, start with your meat; selections
★   include Colorado lamb, Black Angus beef, and Kobe beef, just to name a few (there are also a few vegetarian alternatives). Then pile on the toppings, like prosciutto, pan-seared foie gras, fried egg, sliced zucchini, smoked salmon, or grilled lobster. Desserts continue the burger theme with choices such as the peanut butter–and–jelly burger (a warm doughnut with peanut butter mousse and raspberry jelly). The Bar is in Mandalay Place, the small shopping center between Luxor and Mandalay. ⊠*Mandalay Bay Resort & Casino, 3950 Las Vegas Blvd. S, South Strip* ☎702/632–9364 ⊟*AE, D, DC, MC, V.*

¢–$ ✕ **Roxy's Diner.** At this playful replica of a 1950s-era diner, you can dig
☺   into mammoth hot-fudge sundaes, sizable burgers, fried catfish, old-fashioned thick milk shakes, po'boy sandwiches, blue plate specials that include meat loaf and roast turkey breast, and other inexpensive American classics. Most items, with the rib-eye steak a worthwhile exception, cost less than $10. ⊠*Stratosphere Casino Hotel and Tower, 2000 Las Vegas Blvd. S, North Strip* ☎702/380–7777 ⊟*AE, D, DC, MC, V.*

¢–$ ✕ **'Wichcraft.** Skip the drab fast-food court at MGM and grab a bite at this futuristic space with marble-top café tables, vibrant lime-green walls, and blond-wood floors. The creative sandwiches include Sicilian tuna with fennel, black olives, and lemon juice on a baguette, and meat loaf with bacon, cheddar, and tomato relish on a roll. It's a great option for breakfast, too—try a roll stuffed with a fried egg, bacon, blue cheese, and greens. Although it's possible to make this an early dinner option, keep in mind that it closes at 6 on weekdays, 8 on Friday and Saturday. ⊠*MGM Grand Hotel and Casino, 3799 Las Vegas Blvd. S, South Strip* ☎702/891–3166 ♜*Reservations not accepted* ⊟*AE, D, DC, MC, V.*

CAFÉS

¢   ✕ **Chocolate Swan.** Break from shopping in glitzy Mandalay Place for a sweet snack at this old-fashioned-looking pastry and ice-cream shop. The specialties here are many, including chocolate pecan pie, cappuccino torte, candied ginger dipped in dark chocolate, and classic hot fudge sundaes made with frozen custard. Peet's Coffee and Tea is served, too. ⊠*Mandalay Place, 3930 Las Vegas Blvd. S, South Strip* ☎702/632–9366 ⊟*AE, D, DC, MC, V* ☉*No lunch.*

¢   ✕ **Jean Philippe Patisserie.** You can always order a fresh fruit smoothie at
Fodor'sChoice   this Wonka-esque sweet shop at Bellagio, but why would you commit a
★   healthy act like that? This artful homage to chocolate has so many decadently devilish desserts, including cakes, cookies, gelato, hand-dipped chocolate candies, and particularly memorable crepes (try the one filled with mango, coconut, passion fruit, and pineapple sorbets). Café tables are set around a gorgeous circular bar, or you can dine in the airy

foyer of Bellagio Tower, where the patisserie is located. ⊠*Bellagio Las Vegas, 3600 Las Vegas Blvd. S, Center Strip* ☎702/693–1111 ▭*AE, D, DC, MC, V.*

CAJUN–CREOLE

\$\$–\$\$\$\$ ✕ **Emeril's New Orleans Fish House.** Enter this boisterous spot, chef Emeril Lagasse's first Las Vegas restaurant (and one of the city's earlier celeb-helmed eateries), under an arch of water spouting from a wrought-iron fish. Creative dishes, like fried creole-marinated calamari, Hudson Valley foie gras on a peach tart, and Louisiana cedar-plank campfire steak, are exquisitely prepared. A sommelier will guide you through the selection of some 2,000 wine bottles in the wine tower. Finish with a slice of banana cream pie. ⊠*MGM Grand Hotel and Casino, 3799 Las Vegas Blvd. S, South Strip* ☎702/891–7374 ♤*Reservations essential* ▭*AE, D, DC, MC, V.*

CARIBBEAN

\$–\$\$\$ ✕ **Rumjungle.** This Mandalay Bay establishment is so hugely popular as a dance club that some locals are surprised to learn it even serves food in the evening hours. That's not exactly how it was intended. The intensely themed interior—all waterfalls and fiery displays—was designed with the Brazilian *rodizio* (fire pit) in mind; a popular choice is the prix-fixe dinner of pork, lamb, chicken, fish, and vegetables served on skewers. Individual entrées include many Caribbean-theme dishes, such as Cuban sandwiches, garlic-lime chicken, and oven-roasted lobster with curried mashed potatoes. ⊠*Mandalay Bay Resort & Casino, 3950 Las Vegas Blvd. S, South Strip* ☎702/632–7777 ▭*AE, D, DC, MC, V.*

CHINESE

\$\$–\$\$\$\$ ✕ **Pearl.** This restaurant in the MGM Grand Studio Walk might appear a bit gimmicky at first, with its high-tech decor that includes a digital menu scrolling down a video monitor at the entrance. But sample the consistently delicious modern Chinese cuisine and you'll have little trouble understanding why Pearl has become a favorite among the Strip's many Asian restaurants. Feast on such bold starters as shark fin–and–Dungeness crab spring rolls and Shanghai-style eel before moving on to wok-fried spiny lobster, macadamia Kung Pao chicken, or fire-roasted Mongolian beef. ⊠*MGM Grand Hotel and Casino, 3799 Las Vegas Blvd. S, South Strip* ☎702/891–7380 ▭*AE, D, DC, MC, V* ☾*No lunch.*

\$\$–\$\$\$\$ ✕ **Wing Lei.** This restaurant in the Wynn has all the panache of an
★   Asian royal palace. It's named for its talented chef, who presents contemporary French-inspired Chinese cuisine that blends the Cantonese, Shanghai, and Szechwan traditions. The decadent five-course Peking duck dinner for two is one of the restaurant's true showstoppers, but don't overlook the stir-fried minced squab, prawns with walnuts and a honey-peach sauce, or orange beef with ginger, scallion, bok choy, and a tangerine-peel sauce. And be sure to order a side of the tantalizing abalone fried rice. The service is informative and resolutely cheerful. ⊠*Wynn Las Vegas, 3131 Las Vegas Blvd. S, North Strip* ☎702/248–3463 ▭*AE, D, DC, MC, V.*

CONTINENTAL

$$$$ ✕ **Fleur de Lys.** The first thing you notice entering this Hubert Keller
★ space is the massive leaf-shape frame filled with thousands of fresh-cut roses that adorns the towering sandstone wall. The natural, earthy design scheme tempers the soaring ceilings and white-clothed tables, and four private curtained cabanas are available by reservation (no minimum spending amount required). As at the namesake original in San Francisco, the menu here is divided into three-, four-, and five-course prix-fixe meals featuring fish, poultry, or game. Especially tasty are the Colorado lamb loin and sweetbreads with spiced honey and caramelized cumin seed sauce, and the hazelnut-crusted salmon with leeks, duck confit, and black truffle vinaigrette. ⊠*Mandalay Bay Resort & Casino, 3950 Las Vegas Blvd. S, South Strip* ☎702/632–9400 ▤*AE, D, DC, MC, V* ⊘*No lunch.*

$$$–$$$$ ✕ **MIX.** Look out over Las Vegas from Chef Alain Ducasse's 64th-floor perch atop THEhotel at Mandalay Bay. Stylish and sexy diners seated at small tables or in egg-shape pods tuck into French-influenced fare, such as bluefin tuna tartare and bison tenderloin au poivre. A 24-foot-tall Murano blown-glass chandelier made up of some 15,000 hand-blown spheres never fails to amaze newcomers. An attentive staff can help you navigate through the more than 1,300 nightly wine options, but don't overlook the list of eye-catching cocktails (such as the "peara-dise," with gin, apricot brandy, triple sec, and pear puree). Portions are on the small side, but remember you're also paying for the view, which may just be the best of any Vegas restaurant; every seat in the house has great sightlines through the floor-to-ceiling windows. ⊠*Mandalay Bay Resort & Casino, 3950 Las Vegas Blvd. S, South Strip* ☎702/632–9500 ▤*AE, D, DC, MC, V* ⊘*No lunch.*

$$$–$$$$ ✕ **Top of the World.** The Stratosphere was among the first in Vegas to offer dining with a view at this strikingly romantic landmark restaurant. Rounded, floor-to-ceiling windows at this airy eatery near the top of the tall tower give 360-degree views of the Vegas Valley. The entire dining room revolves once every 80 minutes. The fare here is standard Continental with a few twists: lobster ravioli, Kurobuta pork with an apple-apricot compote, and Kobe beef with lentil risotto. But remember, you're paying primarily for the view—were this restaurant at street level, you probably wouldn't be reading about it in this book. The place also has a stationary cocktail lounge for casual sipping. ⊠*Stratosphere Casino Hotel and Tower, 2000 Las Vegas Blvd. S, North Strip* ☎702/380–7711 ⚖*Reservations essential* ▤*AE, D, DC, MC, V.*

DELI

¢–$ ✕ **Canter's Delicatessen.** You'll find this noisy, crowded, but festive version of the 1930s Los Angeles institution next to the Sports and Race Book in Treasure Island. A stainless-steel counter and dining tables make for a clean, almost futuristic look. Dive into huge sourdough rye sandwiches packed with corned beef, pastrami, and other deli meats and cheeses, or try a bowl of the restaurant's famous barley-bean soup. The New York–style cheesecake is another signature dish. ⊠*Treasure Island Hotel, 3300 Las Vegas Blvd. S, North Strip* ☎702/894–6390 ⚖*Reservations not accepted* ▤*AE, D, DC, MC, V.*

Great Snacking

With so many sumptuous, celebrity-packed restaurants popping up in Vegas these days, it's sometimes easy to forget about all the terrific holes-in-the-wall and take-out counters around town serving tasty treats for those on the go. Here's a round-up of favorites:

Ethel's Chocolate Lounge. Inside the Fashion Show Mall, as well as other locations around town, this home-grown purveyor of top-notch chocolates serves exquisite hot cocoa, espresso drinks, fine-crafted chocolate bars, and other sweets in a cushy café with comfy sofas. ⊠ *Fashion Show Mall, 3200 Las Vegas Blvd. S, South Strip* ☎ *702/796–6662.*

Fatburger. Billing itself immodestly "the Last Great Hamburger Stand," this fast-food joint across from Monte Carlo (with about a dozen locales elsewhere around town) cooks up toothsome charbroiled burgers, hefty chili dogs, and crispy "fat fries."

⊠ *3763 Las Vegas Blvd. S, South Strip* ☎ *702/736–4733.*

Luv-it Frozen Custard. Pull up to this tiny take-out stand at the north end of the Strip, on the edge of downtown, to sample unbelievably delicious, velvety smooth frozen custard. The flavors change daily, and sundaes are a popular offering—try the "Jimmies Scotch Treat," with butterscotch sauce, jimmies, sliced bananas, and a maraschino cherry. It's been goin' strong since 1973. ⊠ *505 E. Oakey Blvd., North Strip* ☎ *702/384–6452.*

Pink's Hot Dogs. A Hollywood legend since 1939, Pink's now has a branch inside the Planet Hollywood Hotel. It's here that you can nosh on what some believe is the world's best chili dog, or opt for the massive Poli-Bacon Burrito (a Polish hot dog slathered in bacon, cheese, chili, and onions). It's all happily bad for you. ⊠ *Planet Hollywood Resort & Casino, 3667 Las Vegas Blvd. S, Center Strip* ☎ *702/785–5555.*

ECLECTIC

$$–$$$$
Fodor'sChoice
★

✕ **Sensi.** It's no easy feat coming up with a truly original restaurant in Vegas that offers more than just a gimmicky theme or celebrity-chef pedigree. Sensi, a casual but upscale spot that's secluded from Bellagio's noisy gaming areas, succeeds on all counts. Chef Martin Heierling, who's highly respected in culinary circles, presents a menu that's divided into four distinct culinary realms: Asian dishes, Italian fare, raw and seafood specialties, and grilled meat. Specialties include chicken tikka prepared in an authentic tandoori oven, ahi tuna ceviche, and wood-fired focaccia topped with Vacherin cheese and black truffles. Quench your thirst with a glass of housemade ginger ale. If you have a couple of friends with you, try the showy dessert sampler, which offers a taste of several sugary creations. The dining room, with its sandstone and glass walls and flowing waterfalls, is as dramatic as the food. ⊠ *Bellagio Las Vegas, 3600 Las Vegas Blvd. S, Center Strip* ☎ *702/693–8800* ⊟ *AE, D, DC, MC, V.*

¢
✕ **Village Eateries at New York–New York.** Just about every big casino on the Strip has an inexpensive food court, but most feature bland, fast-food chain restaurants. New York–New York stands out from the pack on several fronts. There are numerous dining options in this

faux–Greenwich Village setting where the resort's wild roller coaster whizzes overhead. You can nosh on pizza, clam rolls, bratwurst, cheese steaks, fish-and-chips, ice cream, and plenty of other treats. ⊠ *New York–New York Hotel and Casino, 3790 Las Vegas Blvd. S, South Strip* ☎702/740–6969 ⚔*Reservations not accepted* ⊟*AE, D, DC, MC, V.*

FRENCH

$$$$
Fodor'sChoice
★

✕ **Alex.** Super chef Alessandro Stratta serves his high-end French Riviera cuisine to the well-heeled at this drop-dead-gorgeous dining room, reached via a grand staircase. Stratta's four-course prix-fixe menu ($145) and seasonal tasting menu ($325, with wine pairings) are not for the meek of wallet, but the artfully presented food here absolutely delivers. Specialties include foie gras ravioli in a truffle bouillon with duck confit salad and wild turbot with salsifis (an herb whose edible root has an oysterlike taste), black truffles, almonds, and a red wine sauce. Dessert tends toward the fanciful, including a wonderful chocolate-banana malt with caramel–and–macadamia brittle ice cream. This is one Vegas restaurant you might want to dress your best for—jackets aren't required but are suggested. ⊠ *Wynn Las Vegas, 3131 Las Vegas Blvd. S, North Strip* ☎702/248–3463 ⚔*Reservations essential* ⊟*AE, D, DC, MC, V* ☉*Closed Mon. No lunch.*

$$$$

✕ **Joël Robuchon at the Mansion/L'Atelier.** Arguably the biggest name in contemporary French cuisine, chef Joël Robuchon came out of retirement to open two massively hyped (and some say criminally overpriced) side-by-side restaurants at the MGM Grand in 2005. L'Atelier, less formal though still highly refined, offers à la carte entrées plus a long list of small "tasting" portions (such as crispy langoustine fritters with basil pesto, and free-range quail stuffed with foie gras) that let you create your own fantasy meal. But it's the Mansion that has every foodie in Vegas buzzing. For the ultimate gastronomical rush, you can spring $360 for the full tasting menu; less expensive versions with fewer courses are also available. The cuisine changes daily and includes such rarefied creations as panfried sea bass with lemongrass foam and stewed baby leeks. This is one impressive operation, but a number of stellar restaurants in town deliver a similar caliber of service and food at half the price. ⊠ *MGM Grand Hotel and Casino, 3799 Las Vegas Blvd. S, South Strip* ☎702/891–7925 ⚔*Reservations essential* ⊟*AE, D, DC, MC, V.*

$$$$
Fodor'sChoice
★

✕ **Le Cirque.** This sumptuous restaurant, a branch of the New York City landmark, is one of the city's best. The mahogany-lined room is all the more opulent for its size: in a city of mega-everything, Le Cirque seats only 80 under its drooping silk-tent ceiling. Even with a view of the hotel's lake and its mesmerizing fountain show, you'll only have eyes for your plate when your server presents dishes such as the roasted venison loin, braised rabbit in Riesling, or grilled monkfish tournedos. The wine cellar contains about 1,000 premium selections representing every wine-producing region of the world. Although men aren't required to wear a jacket and tie, most do. ⊠ *Bellagio Las Vegas, 3600 Las Vegas Blvd. S, Center Strip* ☎702/693–8100 ⚔*Reservations essential* ⊟*AE, D, DC, MC, V* ☉*No lunch.*

$$$$ ✕ **Restaurant Guy Savoy.** The most recent American celebrity-chef addition to the strip is this ultraswank dining room on the second floor of the Augustus Tower at Caesars Palace. Here three-Michelin-star winner Guy Savoy introduces Vegas gourmands to his richly masterful creations, such as artichoke–black truffle soup, butter-roasted veal sweetbreads, and roast duck with citrus-scented turnips. Prices creep into the upper stratosphere, but the restaurant has earned high marks from all and not just for its stellar modern French cuisine. The selections from the Savoy's 15,000-bottle wine cellar along with its intimate setting—the restaurant opens to a terrace with clear views of the Strip—only add to its appeal. ✉*Caesars Palace, 3570 Las Vegas Blvd. S, Center Strip* ☎*702/731-7731* ▣*AE, D, DC, MC, V* ⊘*No lunch.*

$$$–$$$$ ✕ **André's French Restaurant.** This second location of André's French Res-
★ taurant serves food that's as excellent as that at the downtown original but in a more spectacular room packed with lavish Louis XVI furnishings. Specialties here include filet mignon tartare prepared tableside with potato pancakes and arugula salad, and seared venison loin with crème fraîche polenta, Napa cabbage, Granny Smith apples, and bing cherry chutney. A clubby cigar bar has an amazing selection of ports. (⇨*André's French Restaurant in Downtown.*) ✉*Monte Carlo Resort and Casino, 3770 Las Vegas Blvd. S, South Strip* ☎*702/798-7151* ♧*Reservations essential* ▣*AE, DC, MC, V* ⊘*No lunch.*

$$–$$$$ ✕ **Daniel Boulud Brasserie.** Chefs Daniel Boulud and Philippe Rispoli have dreamed up a sophisticated yet accessible menu at this snazzy spot, which has an open kitchen, a bustling dining room, and patio seating overlooking Wynn's man-made lake. You could make a memorable meal by ordering three or four of the superb starters, such as tuna tartare, roasted beet salad, pumpkin soup with spiced-apple compote, or escargots. The crispy duck confit stands out among the entrées, as does the incredibly rich DB burger stuffed with braised short ribs, black truffle, and foie gras. ✉*Wynn Las Vegas, 3131 Las Vegas Blvd. S, North Strip* ☎*702/248-3463* ▣*AE, D, DC, MC, V* ⊘*No lunch.*

$$–$$$$ ✕ **Eiffel Tower Restaurant.** The must-do restaurant of Paris Las Vegas is a
★ room with a view, all right—it's about a third of the way up the hotel's half-scale Eiffel Tower replica, with views from all four glassed-in sides (request a Strip view when booking for the biggest wow factor—it overlooks the fountains at Bellagio, across the street). But patrons are often pleasantly surprised that the food here measures up to the setting. The French-accented menu includes appetizers of cold smoked salmon, sea scallops, and Russian caviar. On the entrée list, you find Atlantic salmon in pinot noir sauce, lobster thermidor, roasted rack of lamb Provençal, and filet mignon in mushroom sauté. ✉*Paris Las Vegas, 3655 Las Vegas Blvd. S, Center Strip* ☎*702/948-6937* ♧*Reservations essential* ▣*AE, D, DC, MC, V.*

$–$$$ ✕ **Bouchon.** Ask leading chefs to name their idol, and more than a few will cite French Laundry chef Thomas Keller, who opened this stunning, capacious French bistro and oyster bar in the Venezia Tower at the Venetian. Soaring Palladian windows, antique lighting, and painted tile lend a sophisticated take on French country design, but the service often fails to live up to the standards you'd expect. Bouchon's folded brown-paper menu opens to reveal classics like steak frites, braised pork with cabbage fondue, and mussels with white wine. Finish with profiteroles, a lemon tart, or crème caramel. Bouchon does turn out a memorable breakfast, where you might try bread pudding–style French toast or a smoked-salmon baguette. The restaurant began serving lunch in 2007. ⊠ *Venetian Resort-Hotel-Casino, 3355 Las Vegas Blvd. S, Center Strip* ☎ *702/414–6200* ▤ *AE, D, DC, MC, V.*

$–$$$ ✕ **Mon Ami Gabi.** This French-inspired steak house that first earned
★ acclaim in Chicago has became much beloved here in Vegas. It's the rare restaurant with sidewalk dining on the Strip—enjoy the views of nearby casinos and the parade of curious passersby. For those who prefer a less lively environment, a glassed-in conservatory just off the street conveys an outdoor feel, and still-quieter dining rooms are inside, adorned with chandeliers dramatically suspended three stories above. The specialty of the house is steak frites, offered four ways: classic, au poivre, bordelaise, and Roquefort. The skate with garlic fries and caper-lemon butter is also excellent. This place is a favorite for Sunday brunch. ⊠ *Paris Las Vegas, 3655 Las Vegas Blvd. S, Center Strip* ☎ *702/944–4224* ▤ *AE, D, DC, MC, V.*

ITALIAN

$$–$$$$ ✕ **Corsa Cucina.** In this intimate space with red leather chairs, white
★ napery, an open kitchen, and a long, swanky bar, fans of Italian cooking encounter a menu that mixes the traditional with the innovative. It's one of the few Wynn restaurants that, while still upscale, won't cost you a king's ransom, yet a dinner here rivals just about any fine Italian restaurant on the Strip. There's a long list of chilled and hot appetizers, from red snapper carpaccio to fried artichokes with lemon-caper sauce. Specialties include seared roasted monkfish in parchment with artichokes, fingerling potatoes, and tomato-lemon confit; braised rabbit with sweet English peas and handmade pappardelle pasta; and goat's-milk-ricotta ravioli with brown butter, walnuts, sage, and balsamic syrup. ⊠ *Wynn Las Vegas, 3131 Las Vegas Blvd. S, North Strip* ☎ *702/248–3463* ▤ *AE, D, DC, MC, V* ⊙ *No lunch Mon. and Tues.*

$$–$$$$ ✕ **Fiamma Trattoria.** A beautiful, postmodern space with a split-level
★ dining room that's done in rich chocolate, copper, and tan tones, this trattoria sits along MGM's booming restaurant row, the Studio Walkway. Chef Michael White, whose Fiamma restaurant in New York City has earned tremendous acclaim, turns out relatively simple, deftly seasoned Italian fare, such as citrus-grilled octopus with a chunky green-olive sauce, and rosemary-grilled prawns with charred-tomato vinaigrette. Among the mains, consider gnocchi with Maine lobster ragu, or olive oil–roasted Alaskan halibut with braised artichokes and basil pesto. It's a very good value as the city's fine Italian restaurants go. ⊠ *MGM Grand Hotel and Casino, 3799 Las Vegas Blvd. S, South Strip* ☎ *702/891–7600* ⌕ *Reservations not accepted* ▤ *AE, D, DC, MC, V* ⊙ *No lunch.*

$$–$$$$ ✕ **Onda.** You enter this restaurant through a piano bar opening onto the casino. Beyond the lounge, with its arched, stained-glass ceiling and marble floor, is the restaurant, tucked behind one-way glass. The

Cheap Eats

Blueberry Hill: A local minichain that feels a bit like Denny's but serves far superior food, including hearty Mexican specialties, fruit-topped pancakes and waffles, and a number of "diet delight"–type platters, Blueberry Hill has a few locales within a short drive of the Strip (some are open 24 hours). ✉ *4434 Las Vegas Blvd. N, The Strip* ☎ *702/643–9600* ✉ *1280 S. Decatur Blvd., West Side* ☎ *702/877–8867* ✉ *1723 E. Charleston Blvd., East Side* ☎ *702/382–3330* ✉ *1505 E. Flamingo Rd., University District* ☎ *702/696–9666* ✉ *3790 E. Flamingo Rd., East Side* ☎ *702/433–9999.*

Capriotti's Sandwich Shop: This East Coast transplant serves giant subs, including a Philly-style cheese steak, a pastrami sandwich, and a divine creation called the Bobbie, which is pretty much Thanksgiving dinner on a bun. ✉ *322 W. Sahara, The Strip* ☎ *702/474–0229* ✉ *4747 S. Maryland Pkwy., University District* ☎ *702/736–6166* ✉ *1146 Sunset Rd., Henderson* ☎ *702/558–9111* ✉ *11155 S. Eastern Ave., Henderson* ☎ *702/257–3354* ✉ *3981 E. Sun-*

set Rd., East Side ☎ *702/898–4904* ✉ *8450 W. Sahara Ave., West Side* ☎ *702/562–0440* ✉ *3830 E. Flamingo Rd., East Side* ☎ *702/454–2430* ✉ *4983 W. Flamingo Rd., West Side* ☎ *702/222–3331* ✉ *4825 S. Fort Apache, South Las Vegas* ☎ *702/873–4682* ✉ *1200 Town Center Dr., Summerlin* ☎ *702/304–8001.*

In 'N' Out: The simple menu of fresh burgers, just-cut french fries, and milk shakes makes this affordable West Coast fast-food joint a cult favorite. ✉ *2900 W. Sahara Ave., West Side* ✉ *4705 S. Maryland Pkwy., University District* ✉ *4888 Dean Martin Dr./Industrial Rd., West Side* ✉ *1051 W. Sunset Rd., Henderson* ✉ *51 N. Nellis Blvd., North Las Vegas* ✉ *1960 Rock Springs Dr., North Las Vegas* ☎ *800/786–1000.*

Jason's Deli: Soups, sandwiches—including hero-style muffulettas and po'boys—and salads star on Jason's extensive menu. ✉ *3910 S. Maryland Pkwy., East Side* ☎ *702/893–9799* ✉ *1000 S. Rampart Blvd., Northwest Las Vegas* ☎ *702/967–9008* ✉ *1281 Warm Springs Rd., Henderson* ☎ *702/898–0474.*

menu offers seafood choices such as garlic-crusted sea bass and lobster Milanese as well as traditional pasta dishes such as lasagna, fettuccine Alfredo, and angel-hair pasta with shrimp, garlic, white wine, tomatoes, and bread crumbs. House specials include baked eggplant stuffed with ricotta cheese, and veal picatta with a lemon-shallot butter sauce. ✉ *Mirage Hotel and Casino, 3400 Las Vegas Blvd. S, Center Strip* ☎ *702/791–7111* ▤ *AE, D, DC, MC, V* ⊘ *No lunch.*

$$–$$$$ ✗ **Osteria del Circo.** With its expansive view of the lake, this is one of Bellagio's prime dining spots. The colorful Circo sports velveteen harlequin-pattern seats and whimsically decorated chandeliers, and serves home-style Tuscan food. Among the appetizers are house-cured beef with an arugula, Parmesan, and lemon vinaigrette, and seared scallops over cauliflower and crispy pancetta. The homemade pastas include ravioli with spinach and sheep's milk ricotta in a butter-sage sauce. Caviar of various types is offered by the ounce for dinner, and the extensive wine cellar has selections from every wine-producing region of the world. It's the casual sister restaurant of next-door Le Cirque. ⊠*Bellagio Las Vegas, 3600 Las Vegas Blvd. S, Center Strip* ☎*702/693–8150* ▤*AE, D, DC, MC, V* ⊘*No lunch.*

$$–$$$$ ✕ **Valentino.** The Grill, the busy front room of this dual contemporary Italian eatery on the Venetian's busy "restaurant row," has a casual, urban vibe. Choose either appetizer or entrée portions of pasta, or heartier fare such as three-meat lasagna, a rosemary-infused veal steak, or shrimp-and-calamari skewers. In the opulent Dining Room, you choose almost any appetizer and entrée for about $50 (a few high-end items have supplemental fees). Among the former, try the horseradish-flavored crostini with flageolet beans and goat cheese mousse. Excellent main courses include lamb T-bone steak with rhubarb sauce and sautéed sunchokes. The wine list has an astounding 24,000 bottles. ⊠*Venetian Resort-Hotel-Casino, 3355 Las Vegas Blvd. S, Center Strip* ☎*702/414–3000* ▤*AE, D, DC, MC, V.*

$–$$$ ✕ **Il Fornaio.** Cross the Central Park footbridge inside the wonderfully quirky New York–New York Hotel and Casino, and you come to Il Fornaio, a cheery and bright Italian café. You can dine "outdoors" beneath old-fashioned street lamps, on a terrace by the meandering lagoon, or at a table inside. Cooks in an exhibition kitchen prepare fresh fish, wood-oven pizzas, spinach linguine with shrimp, and gnocchi with sausage, onions, mushrooms, tomato cream sauce, and Parmesan. Very good breads (including delicious ciabatta) are baked twice daily, and you can buy loaves to go. For breakfast, choose from French toast, a selection of omelets, and cholesterol-free eggs. ⊠*New York–New York Hotel and Casino, 3790 Las Vegas Blvd. S, South Strip* ☎*702/740–6403* ▤*AE, MC, V.*

$–$$$ ✕ **Trattoria del Lupo.** Wolfgang Puck's first Italian eatery is in a rustic-looking dining room with a bar and wine room, an exhibition pizza and antipasto station, and a lovely terrace with a wrought-iron fence. Imaginative traditional and contemporary dishes include orange-and-rosemary-preserved salt cod with lobster broth; linguine with spinach, eggplant, cipollini onions, and roasted garlic; and seared yellowfin tuna with fava beans and oyster mushrooms. There are also delectable pizzas. It's not the most spectacular restaurant in Mandalay Bay, but it's reliable and affordable. For dessert, try the tiramisu cappuccino. ⊠*Mandalay Bay Resort & Casino, 3950 Las Vegas Blvd. S, South Strip* ☎*702/740–5522* ▤*AE, D, DC, MC, V.*

JAPANESE

$$$–$$$$ ✕ **Shintaro.** Less-heralded than some of the city's flashier Asian restaurants, this place off the gaming floor at Bellagio serves outstanding California-influenced Pacific Rim cuisine, including a huge selection of sushi dishes and numerous teppanyaki specialties such as Kobe beef, Maine lobster, and diver sea scallops. Diners convene at marble-top tables in a dining room made serene by stone floors and soft lighting and views of Lake Bellagio. There's an excellent selection of sake and Japanese beers. ⊠*Bellagio Las Vegas, 3600 Las Vegas Blvd. S, Center Strip* ☎*702/693–8255* ▤*AE, D, DC, MC, V* ⊘*No lunch.*

$$–$$$$ ✕ **Okada.** At the helm in this kitchen is James Beard Award–winning
★   chef Takashi Yagihashi, a standout in both Japanese and contempo-
rary French cuisine. The attractively designed restaurant, like most
of the others at Wynn, is set away from the din of the casino. There
are sake and sushi bars, as well as *robatayaki* (marinated skewers of
meat, poultry, and seafood) and teppanyaki grills. A floating pagoda
table has views of the lagoon, and many tables overlook the serene
gardens. Yagihashi uses plenty of French flair in his specialties, which
include baked sweet-sake black cod. For starters, take a caviar-tasting
tour or try the red miso bouillabaisse. ⊠ *Wynn Las Vegas, 3131 Las
Vegas Blvd. S, North Strip* ☎702/248–3463 ▤*AE, D, DC, MC, V*
⊘*No lunch.*

$$–$$$$ ✕ **Shibuya.** This hot spot along MGM's Studio Walk has skyrocketed
★   in popularity, as much for the finely prepared Japanese dishes as for
the dazzling decor. Items such as the Mifune roll (with soft-shell crab,
tobiko caviar, scallion, daikon, and spicy mayo) have made it the Strip's
top sushi destination. A massive purple video screen showing images of
swimming fish shines out over the varnished-wood tables in this dash-
ing space. Not-to-be-missed sushi alternatives are oysters with green-
apple ponzu sauce, braised short ribs with seared foie gras, and diver
scallops teppanyaki. Lemon-verbena cake with green-tea foam and ice-
wine sorbet ranks among the top desserts. The restaurant claims the
best selection of sake in North America. ⊠*MGM Grand Hotel and
Casino, 3799 Las Vegas Blvd. S, South Strip* ☎702/891–1111 ▤*AE,
D, DC, MC, V* ⊘*No lunch.*

¢–$ ✕ **Ra Sushi.** Take a break from shopping at the Fashion Show Mall
and stop into this dimly lit restaurant and lounge that's part of a growing chain. Try the Gojira roll, with shrimp tempura, crab mix, cream
cheese, and cucumber, or the Crazy Monkey roll, which is stuffed with
smoked salmon, mango, and cream cheese and topped with avocado,
red tempura bits, cashews, and a mango-sauce drizzle. Heartier fare
includes seared albacore or apple teriyaki salmon (a marinated grilled
fillet topped with sautéed-Fuji-apple glaze and served with wasabi
mashed potatoes). Late-night noshers like that it's open until midnight
(and the bar keeps serving cocktails until 2 AM). ⊠*Fashion Show Mall,
3200 Las Vegas Blvd. S, North Strip* ☎702/696–0008 ▤*AE, D, DC,
MC, V.*

MEDITERRANEAN

$$–$$$ ✕ **Olives.** Chef-owner Todd English has incorporated the best features
of his Boston-area Olives and Figs restaurants in his Las Vegas eatery, which received a snazzy makeover in 2006. The patio overlooking
Bellagio's spectacular lake is perfect for alfresco dining, and the dining
room has great views of the lake as well as the open kitchen. Among the
highlights are appetizers of beef carpaccio on crispy Roquefort polenta,
portobello *picatta*, and venison bruschetta. Entrées include crispy-skin
duck breast on pumpkin *agrodolce* (with a sweet-sour pumpkin sauce)
and a signature butternut-squash *tortelli*. The chocolate falling cake is
tantalizing. ⊠*Bellagio Las Vegas, 3600 Las Vegas Blvd. S, Center Strip*
☎702/693–8181 ▤*AE, D, DC, MC, V.*

Save vs. Splurge

Whether you're rollin' high or down on your luck, Vegas has good eats in your price range. Check out the following steals and splurges:

SAVE

Golden Gate. The 99¢ shrimp cocktail. ☎800/426–1906.

Siena Cafe, at the Suncoast Casino. The $1.95 breakfast or the $2.95 steak-and-eggs graveyard special. Available midnight to 9 am. ☎877/677–7111.

Ristorante Dei Fiori, at the San Remo. The $5.95 prime rib dinner, including potato and vegetables. Available 24 hours daily. ☎800/851–1703.

Marilyn's Café, at the Tuscany. The 99¢ breakfast with two eggs, two pancakes, and potatoes and gravy. Available from 11 pm to 7 am. ☎800/851–1703.

SPLURGE

Burger Bar, at Mandalay Bay. Go for the $60 Rossini Burger, made with Kobe beef and topped with foie gras, black truffles, and a Madeira sauce. ☎702/632–9364.

Prime Steakhouse, at Bellagio. A shot of Chivas Regal 1953 Royal Salute runs $1,050 here. The bottle is one of only 255 produced to celebrate the coronation of Queen Elizabeth. ☎877/234–6358.

Isla, at Treasure Island. The $99 Goddess Elixir margarita is made from five-year-aged Herradura Selección Suprema tequila, Grand Marnier, 100-year-old Anniversary Cointreau, and fresh citrus syrup. ☎702/894–7111.

MEXICAN

$$–$$$ ✕ **Diego.** This isn't your typical Americanized Mexican food, but rather authentic regional cooking served in a whimsically decorated space decked with hammered-tin mirrors, bright red walls, and a well-dressed crowd. Sink into the *arroz a la tumbada,* a brothy Mexican paella of white rice studded with shrimp, scallops, mussels, calamari, and roasted tomatoes, or opt for the *carne asada de la tapatia,* a beef rib eye marinated in red chili adobo, then grilled over a wood fire and topped with black beans and a salsa made with tequila, roasted cactus, and onion. Roll-'em-yourself soft tacos of garlic-lime-marinated skirt steak or chicken are also exceptional. Diego serves only 100% blue agave tequilas and mescals and offers more than 90 varieties of the stuff to choose from. Our favorite menu pick? The frozen-fruit margarita on a stick. There's a handy to-go window to grab a bite on the run. ✉MGM *Grand Hotel and Casino, 3799 Las Vegas Blvd. S, South Strip* ☎702/891–3200 ☰AE, D, DC, MC, V ☾No lunch.

$–$$$ ✕ **Isla Mexican Kitchen & Tequila Bar.** The spotlight's on tequila at this loud (close to the slots), brashly decorated nouveau Mexican place. A circulating Tequila Goddess teaches you all the specifics of the liquor and offers recommendations on tequila-based specialty drinks. But before you start on the Mexican cucumber martini or blackberry mojito, place your order and try chef Richard Sandoval's crispy red snapper, chicken breast with corn dumplings, or Mexican meatballs with chipotle tomato sauce. The guacamole is done table-side on a roving cart. ⊠*Treasure Island Las Vegas (TI), 3300 Las Vegas Blvd. S, North Strip* ☎702/894–7349 ⊟*AE, D, DC, MC, V* ☾*No Lunch*.

PAN-ASIAN

$$–$$$ ✕ **Tao Asian Bistro.** Yet another of the Strip's see-and-be-seen night-
★ clubs that's sometimes overlooked as a dining option, Tao offers all the panache of the Manhattan original, including a dark and seductive dining room filled with candles and Buddha statues (including one that's 20 feet tall and seated above a carp-filled pool). The expertly prepared Asian fare includes sushi and sashimi (consider the spicy lobster roll with black caviar) as well as chilled sake-infused shrimp with sesame-crusted beefsteak tomatoes, corn-and-crab soup, miso-glazed Chilean sea bass with wok vegetables, and wasabi-crusted filet mignon with tempura of onion rings. Stick around after your meal for cocktails and dancing. ⊠*Venetian Resort-Hotel-Casino, 3355 Las Vegas Blvd. S, Center Strip* ☎702/796–8338 ⋞*Reservations essential* ⊟*AE, D, DC, MC, V.*

$–$$$ ✕ **Chinois.** Here's yet another offering in the ubiquitous Wolfgang Puck–Las Vegas restaurant collection—this one is Puck gone Pacific Rim and is a branch of the noted restaurant in Santa Monica. The menu changes daily, but there's a good balance of classic Chinese dishes and more innovative offerings. Although several substantial entrées—such as Cantonese duck with hoisin–passion fruit sauce—are always featured, the emphasis is on smaller and simpler plates, including spicy rice noodles with peanuts, chicken, and shrimp; sweet curried beef *satay* (small cubes of meat on a skewer); and a tartare trio for starters. And there's plenty of sushi. A sophisticated crowd frequents the OPM lounge upstairs, hobnobbing to the beat of hip hop, salsa, or Top 40 tunes. ⊠*The Forum Shops at Caesars, 3500 Las Vegas Blvd. S, Center Strip* ☎702/737–9700 ⊟*AE, D, DC, MC, V.*

RUSSIAN

$–$$$ ✕ **Petrossian.** This elegant bar with dark-wood paneling and a baby grand piano sits just off Bellagio's lobby, near the famous Dale Chihuly glass ceiling. It's open for cocktails 24/7, but the best time to visit is during the lavish afternoon tea, held daily from 2 to 5. You might sample foie gras terrine, fine cheeses, smoked salmon, and several different kinds of caviar. Light food and caviar are also available from noon to midnight (and until 1 AM Friday and Saturday). ⊠*Bellagio Las Vegas, 3600 Las Vegas Blvd. S, Center Strip* ☎702/693–8484 ⋞*Reservations essential* ⊟*AE, D, DC, MC, V.*

SEAFOOD

$$$–$$$$ ✕ **RM Seafood and Rbar Café.** This bilevel space at Mandalay Place was
★ opened in 2005 by one of the culinary world's leading proponents of the sustainable seafood movement. Rick Moonen refuses to serve Chilean sea bass and other overfished species. Fear not—you'll find plenty of delicious treats from the sea. On the upper level, the more formal restaurant, with its sleek mahogany decor, feels a bit like a luxury yacht. Here you might dine on Nantucket Bay scallop carpaccio, or farm-raised abalone with sea-urchin butter. On the more casual lower level, at the Rbar Café, you'll find a bustling raw bar with oysters from

throughout North America and simpler treats like New England clam chowder, lobster rolls, and jumbo lump crab cakes. ⊠*Mandalay Bay Resort & Casino, 3950 Las Vegas Blvd. S, South Strip* ☎*702/632–9300* ⊟*AE, D, DC, MC, V* ⊗*No lunch.*

$$$–$$$$ ✕ **SeaBlue.** Faux-brick floors, a shimmering water wall, a tank swarming with hundreds of colorful fish, and trancy music welcome you into Michael Mina's dynamic, über-hip restaurant specializing in simple but sensational seafood. The emphasis is on wood-grilled dishes, and the fish is flown in from all over the world—pink dorade from Senegal, striped bass from Nantucket, barramundi from Australia. You might start off with the chestnut-and-chorizo soup with spiny lobster and garlic foam, or the fried lobster corndogs served with wholegrain mustard. Moroccan-style tagines are a specialty here—consider the one with North Sea cod, cannellini beans, duck confit, and black truffles. There's an inspired list of desserts, including a chocolate-chambord baba cake. ⊠*MGM Grand Hotel and Casino, 3799 Las Vegas Blvd. S, South Strip* ☎*702/891–3486* ⊟*AE, D, DC, MC, V* ⊗*No lunch.*

$$–$$$$ ✕ **Bartolotta.** The best lunch choice among the Wynn's many restau-
★   rants specializes in Italian seafood (and makes for a superb meal at dinner, too). Set along the resort's chic shopping promenade, it has a curving bar on the upper level, from which a staircase leads down to a dining room and patio. Chef Paul Bartolotta has his fish (sea bream and purple snapper, for example) flown in daily from the best markets in Europe. You might start with the warm seafood salad before graduating to a main dish of sautéed Mediterranean turbot in a white wine broth with leeks and clams. ⊠*Wynn Las Vegas, 3131 Las Vegas Blvd. S, North Strip* ☎*702/248–3463* ⊟*AE, D, DC, MC, V* ⊗*No lunch.*

SOUTHWESTERN

$$–$$$$ ✕ **Mesa Grill.** Playful splashes of bright green, blue, red, and yellow offset the swanky curved banquettes and earth tones at American Iron Chef and grill-meister Bobby Flay's first restaurant outside New York City. The menu's decidedly Southwestern but with plenty of contemporary twists, with choices like blue-corn-crusted red snapper with a salsa of cherry tomatoes, green olives, capers, and fiery serrano chiles; and ancho chile–cumin–rubbed rabbit with butternut squash–wild mushroom risotto and pan juices. Some tables have views of the casino sports book. There's an impressive weekend brunch. ⊠*Caesars Palace, 3570 Las Vegas Blvd. S, Center Strip* ☎*702/731–7731* ⊟*AE, D, DC, MC, V.*

$–$$$ ✕ **Border Grill.** The popular cooking personalities from the Food Net-
Fodor's Choice   work, Mary Sue Milliken and Susan Feniger, have earned plenty of
★   kudos at their Las Vegas location at Mandalay Bay. Appetizers include green-corn tamales, ceviche, and plantain empanadas; for lunch try the turkey tostada or grilled skirt steak; and for dinner the sautéed rock shrimp, stacked enchilada, or chicken *chilaquiles* (corn tortilla strips sautéed with vegetables and cheese). Oaxacan mocha cake and key lime pie are among the desserts. You'd be hard-pressed to find a tastier margarita in town, with the pomegranate version particularly delicious. ⊠*Mandalay Bay Resort & Casino, 3950 Las Vegas Blvd. S, South Strip* ☎*702/632–7394* ⊟*AE, D, DC, MC, V.*

4

SPANISH

$–$$ ✗ **Cafe Ba-Ba-Reeba.** Enjoy the tastes of Spain at this Vegas branch of the Chicago favorite, tucked in the Fashion Show Mall. Dine inside among the murals of bullfighters and conquistadors or pick a quieter table on the large outside patio whose wall of green ivy separates you from the bustling Strip. Nosh on plates of tapas, both hot and cold, such as marinated artichokes, braised-lamb couscous, beef empanadas, marinated Manchego cheese, and gazpacho. The lobster paella is a house specialty. Cool off with the peach or berry sangria, and try the lush white-chocolate soup for dessert. ⊠ *Fashion Show Mall, 3200 Las Vegas Blvd. S, North Strip* ☎ *702/258–1211* ☰ *AE, D, DC, MC, V.*

STEAK

$$$$ ✗ **Delmonico Steakhouse.** Hammy showbiz chef Emeril Lagasse gives the ★ New Orleans touch to this big city–style steak house at the Venetian. Enter through 12-foot oak doors; you'll find a subdued modern interior that creates a feeling of calm, and friendly but professional staff members who set you at ease. Consider the classic steak tartare with Dijon emulsion or the panfried oysters with shrimp, mushrooms, and spinach pasta for starters, and such entrées as grilled rack of lamb with parsnip potatoes and port wine–cherry reduction, or the tender bone-in rib steak. Don't miss the apple–and–cheddar cheese bread pudding for dessert. ⊠ *Venetian Resort-Hotel-Casino, 3355 Las Vegas Blvd. S, Center Strip* ☎ *702/733–5000* ⚞ *Reservations essential* ☰ *AE, D, DC, MC, V.*

$$–$$$$ ✗ **BOA Steakhouse.** This bold space brightened with massive red lan- ★ terns overlooks the immense atrium of the Forum Shops at Caesars— the tables up front offer the best people-watching, but it's quieter and more secluded in back, where you can cozy up in a plush leather booth. Choose from the long list of meats, such as bone-in Kansas City filet mignon or free-range veal chop, and then match your selection with any number of rubs, sauces, and mustards (blue cheese, chimichurri, or horseradish, to name a few). Surf-and-turf is taken to new levels here with the Australian lobster tail, Kobe filet mignon, and Hudson Valley foie gras. It's not easy to save room for dessert, but if you can pull that off, order the chocolate mousse parfait with snicker doodle cookies. The service is outstanding from the moment you set foot inside. ⊠ *Forum Shops at Caesars, 3500 Las Vegas Blvd. S, Center Strip* ☎ *702/733–7373* ☰ *AE, D, DC, MC, V.*

$$–$$$$ ✗ **Charlie Palmer Steak.** The whole idea of putting a Four Seasons hotel inside Mandalay Bay was to have a quiet enclave "hidden" within a busy hotel-casino complex. Charlie Palmer got the idea right away. Although his Aureole at Mandalay Bay can be something of a scene, the nearby steak house is easygoing and understated—it's also a comparative bargain in a city of ultra-pricey steak joints. The mahogany-panel room off the Four Seasons lobby serves only Black Angus that's been dry-aged for 21 days. There's commendable seafood, too, such as oven-roasted day-boat halibut and stuffed Maine lobster. Among the several first-rate desserts, try the warm banana bundt cake absolutely swimming in butterscotch sauce and topped with vanilla ice cream and caramelized bananas. The lounge welcomes the revival of the cigar and presents live entertainment on weekends. ⊠*Four Seasons Hotel, 3960 Las Vegas Blvd. S, South Strip* ☎*702/632–5120* ⚒*Reservations essential* ▭*AE, D, DC, MC, V* ⊗*No lunch.*

\$\$–\$\$\$\$ ✕ **Gallagher's.** This credible remake of the famed 1927 Manhattan original offers an old-school carnivores' experience inside the cleverly decorated New York–New York Casino. The walls of this convivial tavern are lined with black-and-white photos of sports stars, actors, and politicos, and the hardwood floors and tray ceilings transport guests directly to Gotham. You can admire the aged steaks in a big cooler visible from the cobblestone promenade near the entrance. The menu is refreshingly simple: pick your main dish (Colorado lamb chop, center-cut filet mignon, and so on) and then one of the four sauces (Béarnaise, brandied peppercorn, caramelized shallot, and beaujolais) to accompany it. ⊠*New York–New York Hotel and Casino, 3790 Las Vegas Blvd. S, South Strip* ☎*702/740–6450* ▭*AE, D, DC, MC, V* ⊗*No lunch.*

\$\$–\$\$\$\$ ✕ **Prime Steakhouse.** Even among celebrity chefs, Jean-Georges Vongerich-
★   ten has established a "can't touch this" reputation. Prime—with its gorgeous view of the fountains—has become a place to see and be seen at Bellagio. In a velvet-draped gold, burgundy, and blue room that recalls a Prohibition-era speakeasy, choice cuts of beef are presented with mustards and sauces, from the classic Béarnaise to the more adventurous kumquat-pineapple chutney. You can also try signature Vongerichten dishes, such as crab spring rolls with tamarind sauce and tuna au poivre with wasabi mashed potatoes and steamed bok choy. Men are asked, but not required, to wear jackets. ⊠*Bellagio Las Vegas, 3600 Las Vegas Blvd. S, Center Strip* ☎*702/693–8484* ⚒*Reservations essential* ▭*AE, D, DC, MC, V* ⊗*No lunch.*

\$\$–\$\$\$\$ ✕ **Smith & Wollensky.** The legendary New York restaurant has been replicated on the Strip, where it's a Las Vegas oddity: a stand-alone restaurant. With hardwood floors and no plush surfaces to soak up the ricocheting sound, it's a raucous place, but that's part of the fun. For steak, try the big Brooklyn porterhouse for two or the "Old Butcher Style" filet mignon. Other specialties include Maryland crab cakes, classic Dover sole, mustard-crusted tuna, lamb chops, and the famed crackling pork shank with firecracker applesauce. Wollensky's Grill, a lively, more casual gathering spot that's open well past midnight, serves the same menu, as well as sandwiches and pizzas. ⊠*3767 Las Vegas Blvd. S, South Strip* ☎*702/862–4100* ▭*AE, DC, MC, V.*

\$\$–\$\$\$\$ ✕ **Steak House.** Believe it or not, many local residents think this steak house set within the craziness of Circus Circus is among the best. It's totally unlike the rest of Circus Circus; wood paneling and antique brass furnishings adorn a dark, quiet room reminiscent of 1890s San Francisco. A ton of beef—aged 21 days—is displayed in a glassed-in area at one side; the cooking takes place over an open-hearth mesquite grill. Steaks, chops, chicken, and seafood make up the menu, and all entrées are accompanied by soup or salad, fresh bread, and a giant baked potato. There's also a champagne Sunday brunch. ⊠*Circus Circus, 2880 Las Vegas Blvd. S, North Strip* ☎*702/794–3767* ⚒*Reservations essential* ▭*AE, D, DC, MC, V* ⊗*No lunch.*

Las Vegas Downtown Where to Eat

DOWNTOWN

AMERICAN-CASUAL

¢–$$ ✕ **Carson Street Cafe.** The Golden Nugget is one of the only notable casino hotels downtown, and its Carson Street Cafe is one of the neighborhood's more reliable options, especially late at night (it's open 24/7). The restaurant has a stylish Southern plantation feel and plays host to downtown's movers and shakers during weekday breakfast and lunch hours. Among the breakfast selections are eggs Benedict and the Vegas Experience—banana bread with walnut-cinnamon cream cheese, bananas, kiwi, and strawberries. Old familiars on the lunch and dinner menus include rainbow trout, Southern fried chicken, and slabs of baby back ribs. ⊠*Golden Nugget Hotel and Casino, 129 E. Fremont St., Downtown* ☎*702/385–7111* ☲*AE, D, DC, MC, V.*

CHINESE

$–$$$ ✕ **Lillie's Noodle House.** Even as the number of high-profile Chinese restaurants has increased dramatically on the Strip, this longtime Downtown institution (formerly known as Lillie Langtry's) continues to draw crowds with its excellent, reasonably priced food. In an effort to stay current, the dining room was remade in contemporary style in 2006. The Cantonese dishes include old familiars such as moo goo gai pan

Room with a View

Bombastic, curious, and gaudy, the Las Vegas Strip has one of the most dramatic and recognizable skylines in the world. One memorable way to take in the incredible views is to dine at one of the city's sky-scraping restaurants. Keep in mind that the best views are often had from settings off the Strip, rather than right in the middle of it. You'll probably need to make a reservation early at these literally high-profile dining rooms.

Alizé. A fine French restaurant set high atop the Palms Casino, Alizé lies far enough west of the Strip to offer amazing views of the skyline. André Rochat, of André's French Restaurant fame, runs this remarkable eatery. ⊠ *The Palms, 4321 W. Flamingo Rd., West Side* ☎ *702/951–7000.*

Eiffel Tower Restaurant. Sheer height isn't everything. This restaurant atop a half-scale replica of the Eiffel Tower rises 11 stories—nothing special in this town. But this beautifully decorated dining room with its

glassed-in walls sits in the middle of the Strip, offering great views of Bellagio, Caesars Palace, and several other landmarks. ⊠ *Paris Las Vegas, 3655 Las Vegas Blvd. S, Center Strip* ☎ *702/948–6937.*

MIX. You can enjoy the remarkable contemporary French cuisine of world-renowned chef Alain Ducasse in this ultrahip restaurant on the 64th floor of THEhotel at Mandalay Bay. The floor-to-ceiling windows afford unobstructed views all the way up the Strip. ⊠ *Mandalay Bay Resort & Casino, 3950 Las Vegas Blvd. S, South Strip* ☎ *702/632–9500.*

Top of the World. The name here says it all. Although Top of the World serves only passable Continental cuisine, the revolving dining room sits some 800 feet above the Strip, offering positively mesmerizing views. ⊠ *Stratosphere Hotel Tower and Casino, 2000 Las Vegas Blvd. S, North Strip* ☎ *702/380–7711.*

and moo shu pork, plus spicier choices such as Szechuan shrimp. The black-pepper steak is a must for charcoal aficionados, and the lemon chicken is a classic. But if you'd rather, you can always go with a 22-ounce porterhouse or a 28-ounce rib eye. Don't miss the dragon-eye fruit for dessert. It's open until midnight on weekdays, and an hour later on weekends. ⊠ *Golden Nugget Hotel and Casino, 129 E. Fremont St., Downtown* ☎ *702/385–7111* ⊟ *AE, D, DC, MC, V* ⊗ *No lunch.*

CONTINENTAL

$$$–$$$$ ✕ **Hugo's Cellar.** Every woman receives a red rose at this romantic downtown favorite. Hugo's has been popular with Las Vegas locals since it opened in 1976. The staff is attentive and the narrow, brick-lined room has deep, comfortable booths. Offbeat touches include a hot rock appetizer (you cook marinated meats right at your table on a granite slab that is heated to 500°F) and a salad cart (you design your own salad tableside). Entrées vary from beef fillet stuffed with crab meat and wrapped in bacon to Indonesian-spiced rack of lamb. ⊠ *Four Queens Hotel and Casino, 202 Fremont St., Downtown* ☎ *702/385–4011* ⊟ *AE, D, DC, MC, V* ⊗ *No lunch.*

FRENCH

$$–$$$$ ✕ **André's French Restaurant.** Cynics predicted an early demise for André
★ Rochat's venture when he opened a classic French restaurant in an ivy-
covered 1930s-era home blocks from the bright lights of downtown's
famous Glitter Gulch. That was in 1980, and Las Vegans and visiting
conventioneers are still savoring his Duo of Colorado Lamb (consisting
of mustard-crusted rack of lamb and braised-lamb-shoulder ravioli with
chestnut puree), fillet of beef in green-peppercorn and cognac cream
sauce, and tantalizing soufflés. You also find more updated creations;
selections change daily. ⊠ *401 S. 6th St., Downtown* ☏ *702/385–5016*
⚭ *Reservations essential* ⊟ *AE, DC, MC, V* ⊙ *No lunch.*

MEXICAN

¢–$ ✕ **Doña Maria.** You forget you're in Las Vegas after a few minutes in
★ this relaxed and unpretentious cantina. Stop in on a Wednesday night
and you might see a crowd gathered for the *fútbol* game on satellite-
provided Mexican TV. All of the combinations and specials are good,
but the best play here is to order the enchilada-style tamale (with red or
green sauce), for which Doña Maria is justly renowned. You also won't
go wrong with the *queso fundido con chorizo* (melted cheese with sau-
sage). ⊠ *910 Las Vegas Blvd. S, Downtown* ☏ *702/382–6538* ⊠ *3250
N. Tenaya Way, Summerlin* ☏ *702/656–1600* ⊟ *AE, D, DC, MC, V.*

STEAK

$–$$$$ ✕ **Pullman Grille.** It may be close to one end of downtown Las Vegas's
Glitter Gulch, but Main Street Station is a quiet island of Victorian
elegance, magnified in the Pullman Grille. There's even a Pullman car
right in the restaurant; you can retreat to it for a cigar and a port after
dinner if you'd like. Dinner leans heavily to steaks, but other choices
include salmon, swordfish, and succulent lamb chops. ⊠ *Main Street
Station, 200 N. Main St., Downtown* ☏ *702/387–1896* ⊟ *AE, D, DC,
MC, V* ⊙ *Closed Mon. and Tues. No lunch.*

PARADISE ROAD

AMERICAN

$$–$$$$ ✕ **Lawry's The Prime Rib.** In a city famous for low-price prime-rib specials, Lawry's is a refined, art deco–style palace dedicated to the pur-
suit of excellence in the guise of slow-roasted, aged rib roasts. The
dining room, with hardwood floors and plush banquettes, is staffed
by waitresses in 1930s-style uniforms and by white-clad carvers, who
roll gleaming domed silvery carts up to your table. Atlantic lobster
tails and a daily fresh-fish entrée are quite good, too. The constant line
of fancy cars outside the front door attests to Lawry's popularity with
movers and shakers. ⊠ *4043 Howard Hughes Pkwy., Paradise Road*
☏ *702/893–2223* ⊟ *AE, MC, V* ⊙ *No lunch.*

$$–$$$$ ✕ **Simon Kitchen & Bar.** The Hard Rock masses and requisite celebrity
★ crowd flock to this cool-looking space for chef Kerry Simon's sophis-
ticated comfort food. Favorites include tandoori salmon, meat loaf,
bone-in rib-eye cowboy steak, and double-cut Colorado lamb chops.
He also does some more unusual dishes, including pumpkin soup, ahi

tuna wood-roasted pizza with cilantro and wasabi, and the colossal crab cake, which is served with papaya slaw. Desserts are playful; how about a bowl of cotton candy, or maybe a peanut-butter-and-jelly ice-cream sandwich crafted from a pair of cookies, hot fudge, and Concord grape jelly? ⊠*Hard Rock Hotel and Casino, 4455 Paradise Rd., Paradise Road* ☎*702/693–4440* ☐*AE, D, DC, MC, V* ⊗*Closed Tues. and Wed. No lunch.*

AMERICAN–CASUAL

$–$$ ✕ **Gordon Biersch Brewing Co.** The Palo Alto import is popular with both singles and the power-lunch crowd. Glassed-off brewing kettles are the design centerpiece as well as the main attraction at the square center bar, which offers specialty brews such as Marzen and Hefeweizen. The menu offers up some fairly creative appetizers, including tamarind-marinated chicken skewers and crispy artichoke hearts tossed with Parmesan. Entrées include blackened mahimahi sandwich, wood-oven pizzas, pan-seared ahi tuna, and old-fashioned meatloaf with brown gravy. ⊠*3987 Paradise Rd., Paradise Road* ☎*702/312–5247* ☐*AE, D, DC, MC, V.*

¢–$ ✕ **Mr. Lucky's 24/7.** The hippest casino coffee shop in Las Vegas is
★   inside the Hard Rock Hotel, overlooking the gaming area. Light-wood floors and vintage rock-and-roll posters highlight this bubbly, circular café. You can have a vegetable omelet, pizza, or pasta; more filling options include steak, grilled salmon, and baby back ribs. The garlic mashed potatoes are superb. Insiders ask about the off-the-menu steak special: an 8-ounce New York steak, three grilled shrimp, baked potato, and salad for $7.77. As the name implies, this place is open 24/7. ⊠*Hard Rock Hotel and Casino, 4455 Paradise Rd., Paradise Road* ☎*702/693–5000* ⚠*Reservations not accepted* ☐*AE, D, DC, MC, V.*

BRAZILIAN

$–$$ ✕ **Yolie's.** If you like *rodizio* served in the fashion of a *churrascaria* (a Brazilian barbecue), then this raucous, conventioneer-filled restaurant is the place for you. For a set price of $34.95 ($16.95 at lunch) you get bread, soup, sides, and all-you-can-eat turkey, lamb, brisket, chicken, sausage, and steak, all sliced and grilled over a mesquite-fired, glass-enclosed rotisserie that you can see from the dining room. You can also order à la carte specialties, such as *feijoada* (black bean and pork stew) and garlic-marinated rack of lamb. It's a fun place to eat. ⊠*3900 Paradise Rd., Paradise Road* ☎*702/794–0700* ☐*AE, D, MC, V.*

CARIBBEAN

¢–$ ✕ **El Coqui.** Possibly the only restaurant in Nevada specializing in authentic Puerto Rican cuisine, this cheap and simple restaurant named after a singing tree frog has quickly developed a strong local following. The kitchen uses super-fresh ingredients in such dishes as roast pork with Caribbean spices, stuffed potato balls, steak sandwiches, and plantain fritters filled with ground beef. Save room for the pear flan. ⊠*2210 Paradise Rd., Paradise Road* ☎*702/737–1868* ⚠*Reservations not accepted* ☐*AE, D, MC, V.*

ECLECTIC

$-$$ ✕ **Table 34.** Run by Laurie Kendrick and Stan Carroll, two highly
★ respected Vegas chefs who trained under Wolfgang Puck, this intimate, modern restaurant with clean lines, blond-wood floors, and high ceilings looks like something you'd find in the California Wine Country. Especially good among the reasonably priced, ouststanding bistro creations are the thin-crust pizzas and fresh pastas (try the squash ravioli with sage-brown butter and toasted walnuts). Among the entrées, the herb-roasted chicken with apple-sage dressing, and all-beef meatloaf with mashed potatoes and onion gravy score high marks. The wine list, with nearly 100 selections, is impressive. It's just south of where Paradise Road intersects with I–215, just south of the airport. The constant planes overhead do contribute a bit of unpleasant noise. ⊠ *600 E. Warm Springs Rd., Paradise Road* ☎ *702/263–0034* ⊟ *AE, D, MC, V* ⊗ *Closed Sun. No lunch Sat.*

4

GERMAN

¢-$ ✕ **Hofbräuhaus Las Vegas.** Enjoy a heavy dose of kitsch at this gargantuan offshoot of Munich's most famous brewery. The interior beer garden is the perfect spot to down a brew in those notorious liter mugs, especially on too-hot Vegas evenings. Pair your beer with hearty Bavarian classics, including Wiener schnitzel, goulash, and *Schweinebraten,* or updated dishes such as Caesar salad with pretzel croutons. For dessert, try apple strudel or vanilla ice cream drenched in hot raspberry sauce. They've covered the oompah here, too: bands brought in from Germany keep things as lively as they are back in Munich. ⊠ *4510 Paradise Rd., Paradise Road* ☎ *702/853–2337* ⊟ *AE, D, DC, MC, V.*

HAWAIIAN

$-$$$ ✕ **Roy's.** A popular import from Hawaii, Roy's is plush without feeling pretentious or overdone—a good bet for a relaxed but elegant meal. You enter the restaurant along a torch-lit lane, and a highly professional, friendly staff works the bustling dining room. Chef Roy Yamaguchi has become synonymous with creative Hawaiian fusion fare, such as soft-shell-crab summer salad with ruby red grapefruit and lobster potstickers with spicy miso sauce. Among the mains, consider the slow-roasted Australian rack of lamb with a pink guava-zinfandel reduction. The food bar overlooking the action in the kitchen is perfect for those dining alone. ⊠ *620 E. Flamingo Rd., Paradise Road* ☎ *702/691–2053* ⊟ *AE, D, DC, MC, V.*

INDIAN

$-$$ ✕ **India Oven.** You have to brave a neighborhood of illicit-looking 24-hour "massage" parlors to find this surprisingly natty restaurant that serves stupendously good food. It's in a shopping center north of Sahara Casino, and the space is filled with imported antiquities. Locals make up a large part of the clientele. Tandoori meats and nan bread are prepared in the tandoor (oven), and other specialties include lamb korma with cashews, almonds, and raisins, and chicken vindaloo. ⊠ *2218 Paradise Rd., Paradise Road* ☎ *702/366–0222* ⊟ *AE, MC, V.*

JAPANESE

$$–$$$$ ✕ **Nobu.** Chef Nobu Matsuhisa has replicated the decor and menu
★   of his Manhattan Nobu in this slick restaurant with bamboo pillars,
a seaweed wall, and birch trees. Imaginative specialties include spicy
sashimi, monkfish pâté with caviar, sea-urchin tempura, and scal-
lops with spicy garlic. For dessert there's a warm chocolate soufflé.
⊠*Hard Rock Hotel and Casino, 4455 Paradise Rd., Paradise Road*
☎*702/693–5000* ⊟*AE, D, DC, MC, V* ⊘*No lunch.*

MEXICAN

¢–$ ✕ **Pink Taco.** Nothing inside the Hard Rock Hotel is boring, and that
goes for this over-the-top take on a Mexican cantina, which is fes-
tooned with old hubcaps and junkyard bric-a-brac. The Tex-Mex food
is serviceable but takes a decided backseat to the party scene, which
includes a huge four-sided bar, patio doors that open onto the hotel's
elaborate pool area, and waitresses in low-cut tops. Fill up on shred-
ded pork tacos, chiles rellenos, beer-battered rock shrimp, and baby
back ribs. Come during happy hour (weekdays from 4 to 7 at the
bar) for half-price appetizers and two-for-one beers and margaritas.
⊠*Hard Rock Hotel and Casino, 4455 Paradise Rd., Paradise Road*
☎*702/693–5000* ⊟*AE, D, DC, MC, V.*

MOROCCAN

$$ ✕ **Marrakech.** Sprawl out on soft floor cushions and feel like a pampered
★   pasha as belly dancers shake it up in a cozy Middle Eastern–style "tent"
with a fabric-covered ceiling and eye-catching mosaics. The prix-fixe
feast is a six-course affair that you eat with your hands: shrimp scampi,
vegetable salad, lentil soup, Cornish game hen, lamb shish kebab, and
the tasty dessert *pastilla*, which is baked phyllo dough layered with
apples, peaches, and pecans. Algerian wines flow freely in this upbeat
spot where servers wear Moroccan robes and patrons are invited to
join the belly dancers if they feel the urge. ⊠*3900 Paradise Rd., Paradise Road* ☎*702/737–5611* ⊟*AE, D, DC, MC, V* ⊘*No lunch.*

SEAFOOD

$–$$$ ✕ **McCormick & Schmick's.** The Portland-based spot has rustic-lodge
charm (complete with stained glass and a timber-and-stone frame)
and offers a huge menu of appetizers, oysters on the half shell, lunch
sandwiches, and imaginatively prepared fresh-fish dishes (the selection
changes daily). Popular choices are Dungeness crab and artichoke dip
with crostinis, Nantucket Bay sea scallops with *persillade* (chopped
parsley and garlic), cashew-crusted tilapia with hot rum butter, and
blackened rare Kona Hawaii ahi with wasabi cream. If the weather's
pleasant, you can dine on the patio. ⊠*335 Hughes Center Dr., Paradise
Road* ☎*702/836–9000* ⊟*AE, D, DC, MC, V* ⊘*No lunch weekends.*

STEAK

$$$$ ✕ **A.J.'s Steakhouse.** The Hard Rock Hotel offers a time-machine ride
back to Old Las Vegas with this retro-style room that's a tribute to
Hard Rock chairman Peter Morton's father, Arnie, a Chicago res-
taurateur. Behind the oxblood leather front doors lies a dining room
decorated with 1950s-style furniture and photos; there's even a piano

bar. Among the appetizers are crab cakes, a gulf shrimp cocktail, and smoked Norwegian salmon. Featured steaks include a 16-ounce New York strip sirloin and a 24-ounce prime porterhouse. Alaskan salmon and seared ahi tuna are among the nonbeef options. ⊠*Hard Rock Hotel and Casino, 4455 Paradise Rd., Paradise Road* ☎702/693–5500 ☐*AE, D, DC, MC, V* ⊘*Closed Sun. and Mon. No lunch.*

$$–$$$$ ✕ **ENVY Steakhouse.** A hip restaurant at the Rat Pack–inspired Renais-
★ sance Las Vegas, ENVY offers an updated take on the steak-house concept. The glamorous contemporary dining room is bathed in jewel tones, and the young and knowledgeable staff is quick to explain chef Richard Chamberlain's creative cuisine, or suggest wines from the 1,500-bottle repertoire. Among the starters, consider seared Kobe carpaccio or a bowl of the addictively good truffle-Reggiano french fries. Move on to the rib-eye steak with walnut-Stilton butter, or the "protein sampler" consisting of a petite filet, pork chop, and Angus beef sausage. Lunch and breakfast are served, too. ⊠*Renaissance Las Vegas, 3400 Paradise Rd., Paradise Road* ☎702/733–6533 ☐*AE, MC, V.*

GREATER LAS VEGAS

AMERICAN

$$–$$$$ ✕ **Medici Café and Terrace.** In good
★ weather, try to dine on the terrace overlooking the Florentine-inspired gardens and Lake Las Vegas at the ethereal Ritz-Carlton. The dining room is beautiful, too, and less formal than at most Ritz properties. The kitchen turns out innovative regional American fare. Start off with the classic steak tartare with black-truffle vinaigrette, or poached Hawaiian blue prawns with fennel-and-grapefruit salad and citrus oil. Among the mains, consider pan-seared diver scallops with crushed, toasted pine nuts, capers, grapes, tea-soaked raisins, and brown butter; or the dry-aged rib eye with crumbled blue cheese, sautéed spaetzle, tomato confit, and mushroom bordelaise. There's also a six-course tasting menu, available with or without wine pairings. Medici also serves a terrific breakfast, where you might sample the jumbo lump crab cakes Benedict. It's one of the best weekend brunch spreads in the city. ⊠*Ritz-Carlton, Lake Las Vegas, 1610 Lake Las Vegas Pkwy., Henderson* ☎702/567–4700 ☐*AE, D, DC, MC, V.*

> **WORD OF MOUTH**
>
> "If you will have a car, try Rosemary's Restaurant (off-strip). They have a great value prix-fixe lunch or dinner as well as excellent wines. The food is always imaginative and tasty. We always make a point of going there every time we are in Vegas."
>
> —Maggi

$$–$$$ ✕ **Rosemary's.** Husband-and-wife chefs Michael and Wendy Jordan
Fodor's Choice established their reputation in Las Vegas by opening this West Side
★ eatery with a big-city bistro vibe. It caters to locals, but its phenomenal reputation has earned it quite a following among visiting food snobs. Among the signature dishes on the American regional menu are pepper-seared sea scallops with wild mushroom orzo, prosciutto, and black-truffle emulsion. Another favorite is Creole-spiced New York

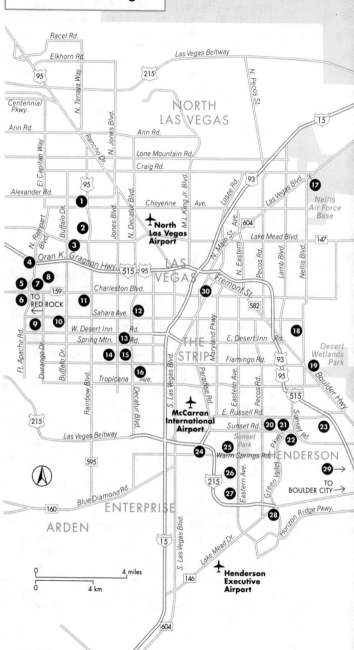

Where to Eat in Greater Las Vegas

Desert National
Wildlife Range

NORTH
LAS VEGAS

Nellis
Air Force
Base

Desert
Wetlands
Park

THE
STRIP

LAS
VEGAS

HENDERSON

TO
BOULDER CITY →

ENTERPRISE

ARDEN

North
Las Vegas
Airport

McCarran
International
Airport

Henderson
Executive
Airport

strip with garlic-roasted fingerling potatoes, capicola ham, wild mushrooms, and blue cheese. It's topped, of course, with the restaurant's trademark steak sauce. The side of white-cheddar grits is addictive. ⌂*8125 W. Sahara Ave., West Side* ☎*702/869–2251* ⌂*Reservations essential* ▤*AE, D, DC, MC, V* ⊘*No lunch weekends.*

$–$$ ✕ **Hash House A Go Go.** Come to this quirky purveyor of so-called "twisted farm food" with a gargantuan appetite and a considerable sense of humor. The spacious restaurant done up with nostalgic roadhouse accoutrements aims to please its patrons by stuffing them with heaps of savory comfort food, prepared with vaguely modern twists. A typical entrée could serve two. At breakfast, there's a savory pork tenderloin Benedict with homemade barbecue cream. Dinner faves include big o' sage-fried chicken salad, the Kokomo meat-loaf sandwich with griddled smoked mozzarella, and duck breasts with prosciutto–mashed yams, goat cheese, spicy cashews, and maple-barbecue glaze. You won't have room for the fresh-fruit cobbler, but consider maybe taking it home in a box—it's that good. ⌂*6800 W. Sahara Ave., West Side* ☎*702/804–4646* ⊕*www.hashhouseagogo.com* ▤*AE, D, MC, V* ⊘*No dinner Sun.*

BARBECUE

¢–$ ✕ **Buckingham Smokehouse Bar-B-Q.** You can smell the barbecue—actually the smoking wood that's used to cook these down-home favorites— the minute you walk in the door, at this otherwise nondescript-looking eatery in far northwest Las Vegas. It's worth the drive for exceptionally flavorful beef brisket and pork loin, which are smoked for 18 hours. The baby back ribs are Buckingham's signature piece, but less expensive choices include smoked ham, smoked salmon fillet, pulled pork, and even a hickory-smoked Philly sandwich. For a zesty change of pace, consider the horseradish coleslaw; the sweet-potato french fries are a sweet taste on the side. ⌂*2341 N. Rainbow Blvd., Northwest Las Vegas* ☎*702/638–7799* ▤*AE, D, MC, V.*

¢–$ ✕ **Memphis Championship Barbecue.** Barbecue the old-fashioned way: that's what fans are looking for, and that's what Memphis Championship Barbecue delivers. The owner–founder hails from Murphysboro, Illinois, which apparently is a well-kept secret as a barbecue stronghold, and cooks Memphis-style; hence the name. If you've got a big appetite—or a big family—try Mama Faye's Down Home Supper Dinner for four; you won't go away hungry. Other choices include smoked hot links, barbecued pork shoulder, New York strip steak, and catfish. Oh, and on the side, treat yourself to some fried dill pickles. All three locations have a down-home, road-house aesthetic. ⌂*2250 E. Warm Springs Rd., East Side* ☎*702/260–6909* ⌂*4379 Las Vegas Blvd. N, North Las Vegas* ☎*702/644–0000* ⌂*1401 S. Rainbow Blvd., Las Vegas* ☎*702/254–0520* ▤*AE, D, MC, V.*

¢–$ ✕ **The Salt Lick.** A rambling space inside the snazzy Red Rock Resort done to resemble its progenitor in Driftwood, Texas, this down-home barbecue tempts palates with delicious smoked turkey and chicken platters, chopped beef and smoked sausage sandwiches, heaping sides of slaw and baked beans, and homemade pecan pie and peach cobbler. Exposed timber beams, stone walls, and varnished-wood tables lend a country vibe, as long as you overlook the clang of slot machines in the near distance. Regardless, it's all good fun. ✉*Red Rock Casino, Resort and Spa, 11011 W. Charleston Blvd., Summerlin* ☎702/797-7576 ▭*AE, D, DC, MC, V.*

CHINESE

¢–$ ✕ **Cathay House.** Set in a strip mall of popular Asian eateries and businesses, Cathay House is a bit of a rarity in Las Vegas—a restaurant that has the feel of a mom-and-pop operation, but with a sophisticated, if rather bright, atmosphere and a menu of varied traditional Chinese favorites. It's one of the best places in town for dim sum, as well as Imperial Peking duck dinner; among other local favorites are the squid with black bean sauce; honey-glazed barbecue ribs; and strawberry chicken. ✉*5300 W. Spring Mountain Rd., West Side* ☎702/876-3838✕ *www.cathayhouse.com* ▭*AE, D, MC, V.*

ECLECTIC

$–$$ ✕ **Todd's Unique Dining.** What's really unique (for Vegas) about this intimate spot a short drive southeast of the airport is the easygoing pace and unpretentious vibe contrasted with artful, creative contemporary cooking. The dining room is stark, perhaps to show off such colorful fare as goat cheese wontons with berry-basil butter, rack of lamb with pomegranate and black peppers, and a commendably seasoned Cajun New York steak. This place used to be something of a sleeper, but it's becoming better known, so book a couple of days ahead if you want to dine Thursday through Saturday. ✉*4350 E. Sunset Rd., Las Vegas* ☎702/259-8633 ⊕*www.toddsunique.com* ▭*AE, D, MC, V* ☺*Closed Sun. No lunch.*

ENGLISH

¢–$ ✕ **Crown & Anchor British Pub.** With 24-hour service and graveyard specials, Crown & Anchor is uniquely Las Vegas (and a favorite haunt of students from nearby UNLV). Most of the food's British including the steak and kidney pie, bangers and mash, and authentic fish-and-chips. Sandwiches with American and British flavors are plenty, and nightly specials make this spot even more of a bargain proposition. There are "draught" beers from all over the world and a "shoppe" selling anglophile favorites like Branston pickle. If you still doubt the authenticity, know that the trifle is made with Bird's English custard. The decor and faux-cottage exterior are decidedly British, and special events add to the fun: on New Year's Eve the celebration starts when it's midnight in the United Kingdom, which is 4 pm in Las Vegas. ✉*1350 E. Tropicana Ave., East Side* ☎702/739-8676 ▭*AE, D, MC, V.*

FRENCH

$$$–$$$$ ✕ **Alizé.** André Rochat, who brought Vegas his two other outstanding restaurants, opened this considerably more contemporary and sleek space atop the cool Palms Hotel. You may not even notice the priceless china, crystal, and silver in the elegant dining room, given its unbeatable views of the Vegas skyline. But you may just become distracted once you sample the artful contemporary French fare. Such complex dishes as seared diver scallops with bacon confit, black truffles, sunny-

side-up quail eggs, and caviar demonstrate the kitchen's estimable skills. Pepper-crusted filet mignon with a cognac cream sauce makes for one of the better main courses. Finish your meal with a cognac from one of the world's finest collections. ⊠ *The Palms, 4321 W. Flamingo Rd., West Side* ☎702/951–7000 ▭AE, D, DC, MC, V ⊗ *No lunch.*

$$–$$$ ✕ **Pamplemousse.** The name, which is French for "grapefruit," was chosen on a whim by the late singer—and restaurant regular—Bobby Darin. The dominant color at this old-school restaurant notable for its kitschy pink-glowing sign is burgundy, orchestral music is played over the stereo system, and the food is classic French. There is no printed menu; instead, the waiter recites the daily bill of fare. Specialties include roast duckling with cranberry and Chambord sauce and Norwegian salmon with orange-curry beurre blanc. The room is small and popular, so be sure to make reservations far in advance. ⊠ *400 E. Sahara Ave., East Side* ☎702/733–2066 ⚑ *Reservations essential* ▭AE, D, DC, MC, V ⊗ *Closed Mon. No lunch.*

4

HAWAIIAN

¢ ✕ **L&L Hawaiian Barbecue.** This growing chain of zero-ambience fast-food eateries serves authentic Hawaiian-style barbecue (to the sounds of cheesy piped-in Hawaiian music). One specialty is the Loco Moco, which is two fried eggs over a hamburger patty topped with gravy and accompanied by macaroni salad and rice. The plate lunch is the thing here; it comes in many permutations, but always includes macaroni salad and rice. The chicken *katsu* (thinly cut, breaded, and fried) is crisp; the barbecue sauce is island sweet; and there's Spam on the menu. For filling food at a bargain price, L&L is it. ⊠4030 S. *Maryland Pkwy., East Side* ☎702/880–9898 ⊠2755 S. *Nellis Blvd., East Side* ☎702/597–9898 ⊠2595 S. *Maryland Pkwy., East Side* ☎702/643–9898 ⊠687 N. *Stephanie St., Henderson* ☎702/433–0240 ▭MC, V.

INDIAN

$–$$ ✕ **Gaylord.** The San Francisco original of this romantic restaurant has long been one of the best Indian restaurants in the country, and this branch at the Rio All-Suite Hotel delivers admirably. Dark wood and imported art create a refined setting for lavish, richly presented northern Indian food. Tamarind chicken; stir-fried lamb with peppers, onions, and tomatoes; and spiced lentils rank among the top entrées. Order a side of onion kulcha bread, and don't miss the starter of Bombay chicken wings tandoori. Although it's not open for lunch, Gaylord does serve a Friday–Sunday brunch buffet that's an excellent value. ⊠ *Rio All-Suite Hotel & Casino, 3700 W. Flamingo Rd., West Side* ☎702/777–7923 ▭AE, D, DC, MC, V ⊗ *No lunch Mon.–Thurs.*

IRISH

¢–$ ✕ **J.C. Wooloughan Irish Pub.** What do you get when you build a pub in ★ Ireland, dismantle it, and ship it across the ocean, to be reconstructed in the desert? An Irish pub in one of the city's most elegant off-Strip resorts that looks like a wee bit o' the Emerald Isle. J.C. Wooloughan offers Irish beers and beer blends, an extensive list of fine Irish whiskeys, and lots of Irish foods, both familiar and not-so. Cheek-by-jowl with the corned beef and cabbage, you find Irish sausage rolls, beef-and-

Guinness pie, and all-day Irish breakfast. Finish with Aunt Maura's sticky toffee pudding. ⊠*JW Marriott Las Vegas Casino Resort, 221 N. Rampart Blvd., Summerlin* ☎*702/869–7777* ⊟*AE, D, DC, MC, V.*

ITALIAN

$$–$$$$ ✕ **Nove Italiano.** Head to the Palms' new Fantasy Tower (which opened in 2006) to try out this see-and-be-seen Italian restaurant with vaulted ceilings, classical statuary, and ornately upholstered armchairs—there's an intentionally gaudy look about the place, and that's part of its allure among high rollers and poseurs. The modern Italian food, however, is seriously good and surprisingly restrained: thin-crust pizzettes topped with lobster, ricotta, and arugula; grilled octopus with lemon and rosemary; rare-seared tuna caponata in Barolo wine. The porterhouse steak topped with a lobster tail is a particularly memorable treat. ⊠*The Palms, 4321 W. Flamingo Rd., West Side* ☎*702/942–6800* ⊟*AE, D, DC, MC, V* ⊗*No lunch.*

$–$$$ ✕ **Antonio's.** Inlaid marble floors, a blue-sky dome, and murals depicting Italian scenes decorate this quiet restaurant, which has an open kitchen. The long menu offers well-prepared northern and southern Italian cuisine such as semolina-crusted fillet of salmon, veal shanks braised with vegetables and white wine, seared sea scallops with terrine of porcini mushrooms, and oven-roasted spring chicken with marinated eggplant, buffalo mozzarella, and oven-dried tomatoes. You might start with the creamy five-onion soup, served in an onion with a mascarpone and fontina crust. ⊠*Rio All-Suite Hotel & Casino, 3700 W. Flamingo Rd., West Side* ☎*702/777–7923* ⊟*AE, D, DC, MC, V* ⊗*No lunch.*

$–$$$ ✕ **Spiedini Ristorante.** Gustav Mauler, who had long been chef and restaurant developer for the former Mirage Resorts company, struck out on his own with this stylish yet affordable Italian restaurant. The menu presents a contemporary take on traditional favorites. Starters include sumptuous wild-mushroom ravioli served with a creamy white-truffle sauce. Entrées encompass handcrafted pastas, a veal chop with arugula and cherry-tomato salad, and pan-seared sea bass with shrimp, capers, grape tomatoes, and a lemon-butter sauce. Desserts often are deliciously whimsical, as in the case of the pineapple carpaccio with raspberry sorbet. ⊠*JW Marriott Las Vegas Casino Resort, 221 N. Rampart Blvd., Summerlin* ☎*702/869–8500* ⊟*AE, D, DC, MC, V* ⊗*No lunch.*

MEDITERRANEAN

$–$$ ✕ **Firefly Tapas Kitchen.** A dapper, hip bistro opened by a pair of Mon Ami Gabi alumni, Firefly occupies the same shopping center as the popular Paradise Road favorites Marrakech and Yolie's. As the name suggests, the kitchen focuses on Spanish and Mediterranean small plates, none of which cost more than $10. Order a few, and you've got a meal—try the ham-and-cheese croquettes, meatballs in a sherry-tomato sauce, marinated and grilled octopus, and ahi-tuna skewers with a mustard-ginger glaze. There are a few heartier entrées, such as steak frites and paella. For dessert, order the rich chocolate-and-cherry bread pudding with a port wine reduction. Dine in the colorful, rather compact dining room done with surrealistic designs or outside on the cheerful patio. Firefly serves until 3 am most evenings. ⊠*3900 Paradise Rd., Paradise Road* ☎*702/369–3971* ⊟*AE, D, MC, V* ⊘*No lunch weekends.*

$–$$ ✕ **Grape Street Cafe, Wine Bar & Grill.** This smart neighborhood restau-
★ rant serves food intended to coordinate nicely with the restaurant's interesting—and not stratospherically priced—wine list. There are salads, sandwiches, pizzas and the like, plus dinner specials such as grilled salmon. Desserts range from austere Stilton and port to positively deca-
dent dark-chocolate fondue. Grape Street is brick-lined, candlelighted, and cozy, and there's a patio for pleasant evenings (if you don't mind the parking-lot view). ⊠*7501 W. Lake Mead Blvd., Northwest Las Vegas* ☎*702/228–9463* ⊟*AE, D, MC, V.*

MEXICAN

$–$$ ✕ **Agave.** This cavernous nuevo Mexican place across from the Red Rock Casino, Resort and Spa has a circular hot-pink dining room with stained-glass windows and offbeat light fixtures. This is the perfect set-
ting for such whimsical creations as lobster empanadas with pineapple puree, black bean–and–smoked cheddar soup, marinated-goat tacos with avocado and cilantro, and blue-corn chicken enchiladas with fiery green chile. There's a terrific Mexican-coffee flan with cinnamon creme and fresh berries for dessert. Another big draw is the lengthy list of con-
noisseur-quality tequilas. Night owls should note that Agave is open 24 hours a day. The laid-back patio offers a refreshing contrast to the bustling dining room. ⊠*10820 W. Charleston Blvd., Summerlin* ☎*702/214–3500* ⊟*AE, MC, V.*

$ ✕ **Viva Mercado's.** The explosion of new chain restaurants in subur-
★ ban neighborhoods makes it easy to forget the charms of the first Las Vegas restaurant to bring a chef's touch to Mexican food. You can get bountiful plates of enchiladas and burritos, but more rewarding are the daily specials and fish dishes, such as orange roughy cooked four ways (including with the ultrahot *salsa de arbol*), or the *banderilla de camarones* (shrimp grilled in garlic, lemon, and spicy salsa). Stucco, fake plants, and tile awnings over rows of booths vaguely suggest an outdoor Mexican plaza, though in an endearing—if somewhat garish—
mom-and-pop way. ⊠*6182 W. Flamingo Rd., West Side* ☎*702/871–
8826* ⊟*AE, D, MC, V.*

¢–$ ✕ **Lindo Michoacán.** Javier Barajas, the congenial owner and host of this colorful cantina, named it for his home in Mexico. He presents outstanding specialties that he learned to cook while growing up in the culinary capital of Michoacán. Many menu items are named for his relatives, including *flautas Mama Chelo* (corn tortillas filled with chicken). Michoacán is known for its carnitas, so don't miss them. Or try the *cabrito birria de chivo* (roasted goat with red mole sauce). Gua-
camole is made table-side. Finish with the flan, a silken wonder. Barajas has two other similar restaurants—Bonito Michoacán and Viva Micho-
acán—on Decatur Boulevard and Sunset Road, respectively. ⊠*2655 E. Desert Inn Rd., East Side* ☎*702/735–6828* ⊠*3715 S. Decatur Blvd., West Side* ☎*702/364–9408* ⊠*2061 W. Sunset Rd., Henderson* ☎*702/492–9888* ⊟*AE, D, MC, V.*

¢–$ ✕ **SuperMex Restaurant & Cantina.** Here's a superlative case of truth in advertising: the California-based SuperMex, a dimly lit, attractive space with Old Mexico doors and slate floors, has a super-massive menu—32 combination plates, plus countless types of burritos in two sizes, salads, tostadas, appetizers, fajitas, tacos, *taquitos,* and more. You can even get a chile relleno burrito or Mexican sausage with scrambled eggs or an enchilada and a tamale or . . . you get the picture. "Extras are extra," the menu says, and you can tailor them to your tastes. There's even a "lite" menu, for those seeking, say, a whole-wheat quesadilla. It's open 24 hours daily. ⊠*3460 E. Sunset Rd., Las Vegas* ☏*702/436–5200* ⊕*www.supermexnv.com* ▭*AE, D, DC, MC, V.*

PAN-ASIAN

$$–$$$$ ✕ **Hannah's Neighborhood Bistro.** A favorite in Summerlin, this sleek Pan-Asian restaurant is accented with bamboo screens, walls of water, and a glass floor through which fish are seen swimming below. It may not be on the Strip, but it definitely has an exciting vibe, high prices, valet parking, and creative fusion fare. There's a sushi bar preparing creative rolls and sashimi plates. Popular appetizers include Dungeness crab puffs and coconut shrimp with a citrus-ginger marmalade sauce. You won't go wrong with such entrées as the grilled tiger prawns with garlic noodles. There's a popular Sunday brunch, too. ⊠*1050 S. Rampart St., Summerlin* ☏*702/932–9399* ▭*AE, D, MC, V.*

$$–$$$$ ✕ **Second Street Grill.** Although you find steaks, Chinese roast duck, and ★ Mongolian rack of lamb on the menu, Pacific Rim–inspired seafood is the specialty at this underrated insider favorite. Daily specials are flown in fresh from Hawaii. For starters try the ahi sashimi or seared sea scallops. For an entrée opt for the cedar-grilled salmon, sautéed soft-shell crab, or whole Thai snapper. The art deco–style room is dark and intimate, with oversize chairs and elegant wood paneling. The service is professional but not pretentious; and, best of all, Second Street Grill is relatively unknown in the Las Vegas fine-dining firmament, so you can usually count on same-day reservations. ⊠*Fremont Hotel and Casino, 200 E. Fremont St., Downtown* ☏*702/385–3232* ▭*AE, D, DC, MC, V* ⊗*Closed Tues. and Wed. No lunch.*

$–$$$$ ✕ **Little Buddha.** It may sound like a mixed metaphor—an Asian restaurant in Paris—but France's Buddha Bar has achieved world fame for its food and its music. The associated Little Buddha in the swanky Palms Casino continues the mystique, albeit with sometimes-iffy service. The kitchen produces such Pacific Rim wonders as Hawaiian smoked pot stickers; wok-fried salt and pepper calamari and frogs' legs; grilled lobster tail with citrus-butter sauce; spicy albacore and yellowtail rolls; and curry shrimp in banana leaf. There's also plenty of great sushi and sashimi. Finish things off with liquid-center chocolate cake with vanilla ice cream. ⊠*The Palms, 4321 W. Flamingo Rd., West Side* ☏*702/942–7777* ▭*AE, D, DC, MC, V* ⊗*No lunch.*

$–$$ ✕ **Mayflower Cuisinier.** You find creative Chinese dishes with Californian, Pan-Asian, and French accents on the menu at this attractive off-the-Strip eatery. It may not have the flashy decor of some of the better-known Asian restaurants, but it offers better food than most. Try the ginger-chicken ravioli, coconut shrimp with sweet chile sauce, grilled salmon with ginger-butter sauce, or Mongolian grilled lamb chops with cilantro-mint sauce. For dessert, consider a delectable trio of crème brûlées flavored with almond, orange, and pineapple-ginger. ✉*4750 W. Sahara Ave., West Side* ☎*702/870–8432* ⊕*www.mayflow-ercuisinier.com* ⊟*AE, D, DC, MC, V* ⊘*Closed Sun. No lunch Sat.*

RUSSIAN

$–$$ ✕ **Restaurant Eliseevsky.** Talk about an only–in–Las Vegas experience: slip into this rendition of Uncle Misha's dacha in a strip mall just a few miles from the Strip, and you may feel like an extra in *Gorky Park*. The air is thick with smoke and heavy with Russian as expatriates hunch over vodka. Shellacked log walls, piped-in Russian pop music, and doting waitresses in brightly colored costumes further the surreal ambience. The kitchen follows authentic recipes with Streletz's Plate, a colorful pastiche of grilled vegetables with garlic, and Gourmand Duck, a duck fillet with grilled oranges and cherry sauce. The familiar pierogi, borscht, blini, and Stroganoff are tasty. ✉*4825 W. Flamingo Rd., West Side* ☎*702/247–8766* ⊟*AE, D, MC, V* ⊘*Closed Mon. No lunch.*

SEAFOOD

$ ✕ **Tides Oyster Bar.** For affordable seafood, this futuristic incarnation
★ of a '50s coffee shop does the trick. The space is groovy and inviting, with blue mosaic columns soaring above the dining space, and a long counter facing the kitchen, where you can sit on a blond-wood bar stool and slurp clams and oysters on the half shell or a dinner-size bowl of gumbo. A particular specialty is the traditional crab roast, prepared in an old-timey steam kettle with tomato, herbs, butter, and brandy. ✉*Red Rock Casino, Resort and Spa, 11011 W. Charleston Blvd., Summerlin* ☎*702/797–7576* ⊟*AE, D, DC, MC, V.*

STEAK

$$–$$$$ ✕ **Billy Bob's Steak House.** Big food is the name of the game at this giddy, locally beloved steak joint at Sam's Town, known as much for its campy Old West decor as it is for its genuinely juicy chops. The 24-ounce bone-in rib eye is Texas-size, the barbecued brisket could feed a rodeo. And then there's dessert: the chocolate éclairs are a foot long, and the chocolate cake could fill up a good chunk of the Grand Canyon. Sharing is recommended. A porch area adjacent to the bar provides a great view of the Sunset Stampede, the animatronic and laser show in the resort's indoor Mystic Falls Park. ✉*Sam's Town Hotel and Gambling Hall, 5111 Boulder Hwy., Boulder Strip* ☎*702/456–7777* ⊟*AE, D, DC, MC, V* ⊘*No lunch.*

$$–$$$$ ✕ **Golden Steer.** In a town where restaurants come and go almost as quickly as visitors' cash, the longevity of this steak house, opened in 1958, is itself a recommendation. Both locals and visitors adore this San Francisco–theme restaurant with red leather chairs, polished dark wood, and stained-glass windows for the huge slabs of well-prepared meat. Steak, ribs, blackened swordfish, and such Italian classics as veal marsala and chicken parmigiana are particularly popular. Although you wouldn't know it from the outside, the Steer is cavernous. Lots of small, intimate rooms, however, break up the space. ✉*308 W. Sahara Ave., West Side* ☎*702/384–4470* ⊟*AE, D, DC, MC, V* ⊘*No lunch.*

$$-$$$$ ✕ **Hank's Fine Steaks.** Start with a martini in the classy piano bar at this
★   swish steak house that opened in 2005 at the much-loved Green Valley
Ranch. Then make your way into the ornately decorated dining room,
with its marble floors and glittering chandeliers. Start off your dinner
with the bountiful seafood jumbo jackpot: a platter of Maine lobster,
Alaskan crab, jumbo prawns, oysters, lump crab cakes, and crab claws.
Hefty 48-day-aged steaks are prepared in an 800°F mesquite charcoal
broiler—try the bone-in 20-ounce New York strip with creamy horse-
radish sauce. This is red-meat dining at its best. ⊠ *Green Valley Ranch
Resort, 2300 Paseo Verde Pkwy., Henderson* ☎702/617–7515 ⊟*AE,
D, DC, MC, V* ⊘*No lunch.*

$$-$$$$ ✕ **N9NE Steakhouse.** There's a good chance you'll spot a young Holly-
★   wood-type at this beef lover's hangout tucked in the corner of the Palms
(Leonardo DiCaprio is such a fan he once had the kitchen reopen especially for him after arriving in town after hours). N9NE serves high-quality, innovatively prepared cuts of meat in a jaunty setting of dark-walnut
and leather furniture. N9NE serves plenty of other superb entrées,
including veal osso buco with saffron risotto, pan-roasted striped sea
bass with pancetta and truffle butter, and miso-marinated black cod
with shiitake mushrooms. The pumpkin cheesecake with huckleberry
sauce makes a sweet ending. ⊠ *The Palms, 4321 W. Flamingo Rd., West
Side* ☎702/933–9900 ⊟*AE, D, MC, V* ⊘*No lunch.*

THAI

$-$$ ✕ **Lotus of Siam.** Despite being in a dreary shopping center northeast of
Fodor's Choice   the Strip, this simple Thai restaurant has attained near-fanatical cult
★   status, with some critics hailing it the best in North America. What's all
the fuss? Consider the starter of marinated prawns, which are wrapped
with bacon and rice-paper crepes, then deep-fried and served with a
tangy sweet-and-sour sauce. For a main course, try either the seared
scallops with chile-mint leaves, or the pork with stir-fried broccoli and
fried, salted fish chunks. Be warned—this is some of the spiciest food
you'll ever try. But another of Lotus's surprises is the phenomenal wine
list, on which you might find a vintage to cool your palate. ⊠*953 E.
Sahara Ave., East Side* ☎702/735–3033 ⊕*www.saipinchutima.com*
⊟*AE, D, MC, V* ⊘*No lunch.*

VEGETARIAN

¢-$ ✕ **Go Raw Cafe and Juice Bar.** The name of this all-vegan, all-organic café
refers to the fact that nothing is cooked at temperatures higher than
the 100°F-plus it takes to make flat breads and pizza dough. Devotees
of living food—as well as vegans and vegetarians—find much to like
here. You can make a healthy choice with dishes like basil, tomato,
and onion tossed in herbs, olive oil, and pine nuts; or lasagna based on
zucchini, spinach, carrots, marinara sauce, and nut "cheese." ⊠*2910
Lake East Dr., West Side* ☎702/254–5382 ⊘*Closed Sun.* ⊠*2381
Windmill La., East Side* ☎702/450–9007 ⊟*AE, D, MC, V.*

Shopping

Shopping, Mandalay Place, Mandalay Bay

WORD OF MOUTH

". . . the Venetian's shopping area is stunning, with the gondoliers and the canals running through it."

—Surfergirl

"The Forum shops are awesome! Don't miss them!"

—Ani

SHOPPING PLANNER

Getting Around

Las Vegas shopping—so demanding, yet so rewarding. With malls encompassing millions of square feet of retail space, you won't have any trouble finding ways to part with your hard-earned cash. But to make the most of your time, you should map out your shopping safari. Distances are deceiving because of the scale of the resort casinos. What looks like a quick walk might take a half hour. Due to crowd-control measures, you'll find yourself squeezing around barriers and leaping over bridges instead of just crossing a street. Grab a cab or ride the monorail ($5 a trip) and save the time for shopping. Buses, which are $2 along the Strip, are a cheaper option, but crowded at all hours.

Got a car? All resorts offer free parking and free valet service (don't worry—they'll still get your money).

Send Them Packing

Who wants to lug their packages from store to store? Most stores are happy to send your purchases back to your hotel, or even ship them back home for you.

Vegas Time

Although Las Vegas may be up all night, the people who work in the retail establishments need a little rest. Many places are open from 10 AM to 11 PM during the week, and stay open an hour later on weekends. And the shopping, like the gambling, goes on every day.

Find Out What's Going On

The city's daily newspaper, the *Las Vegas Review Journal* (⊕*www.reviewjournal.com*) has information on all the latest sales, as well as fashion shows and other events. Online you can click the site's shopping link for a guide to local malls and specialty shops and discount coupons that you can print.

From Tacky to Wacky

Set on bagging some Vegas kitsch? Visit **Bonanza** (⊠*2460 Las Vegas Blvd. S, North Strip* ☎*702/385–7359*), home of personalized shot glasses and fuzzy dice. Next, head to **Ron Lee's World of Clowns** (⊠*330 Carousel Pkwy., Henderson* ☎*702/434–1700*), where you can drop $150 on a clown sculpture entitled "Can I be Frank?" (Depending on how you look at it, it's a hot dog dressed as a clown or a clown dressed as a hot dog.) Think you've topped yourself? Oh but you haven't—at **the Liberace Museum Store** (⊠*1775 E. Tropicana Ave., East Side* ☎*702/798–5595* ⊕*www. liberace.org*) you can bag a life-size standup photo of the maestro in leather hot pants for $7. Mission accomplished.

Raves & Faves

Imperial Shopping: *Forum Shops* at Caesars
Ritziest name: *Via Bellagio*
Relive Carnavale: *Grand Canal Shoppes* at the Venetian
Best Souvenir: *A slot machine* from Gamblers General Store
Perfect Place to Wig Out: *Serge's Showgirl Wigs*

Updated by
Ryan Sarsfield

WORLD-CLASS SHOPPING IN VEGAS? Yes, among the scads of kitsch and Elvis memorabilia (looking for a piece of the King's pillowcase?), there's also the *ne plus ultra* from Cartier and Yves Saint Laurent. The square footage in the Forum Shops at Caesars alone is the most valuable retail real estate in the country; bankrolls are dropped there as readily as on the gaming tables. It's the variety of options that has pushed Las Vegas near the ranks of New York, London, or Rome: You could tote home a vintage slot machine or Lenôtre chocolates from the only place in the United States where you can buy them (at Paris Las Vegas, in case you're salivating). You might start to think those darn casinos only get in the way of your shopping safaris.

Most Strip hotels offer expensive dresses, swimsuits, jewelry, and menswear; almost all have shops offering logo merchandise for the hotel or its latest show. Inside the casinos the gifts are elegant and expensive. Outside, all the Elvis clocks and gambling-chip toilet seats you never wanted to see are available in the tacky gift shops. Beyond the Strip, Vegas shopping encompasses such extremes as a couture ball gown in a vintage store and, in a Western store, a fine pair of Tony Lamas boots left over from the town's cowboy days. Shoppers looking for more practical items can head for neighborhood malls, supermarkets, shopping centers, and specialty stores. And to avoid the stratospheric prices on the Strip, shoppers not averse to driving a bit can find the same high-ticket items at lower prices at the town's factory outlet malls.

5

MALLS ON THE STRIP

Fodor'sChoice ★ **Planet Hollywood Resort & Casino.** Miracle Mile competes easily with the Caesars Forum Shops for upscale clothing boutiques: there's Hugo/Hugo Boss, Betsey Johnson, and White House/Black Market. A bunch of upscale jewelry shops include Joli-Joli, and Gioia: The Art of Jewels. Other good shops to check out include Tommy Bahama, Z Gallerie (for home accessories), and Hilo Hattie and ABC Stores—two Hawaiian outposts for aloha wear. Many of the 170 stores are at your local mall, but you still may discover a treasure here. ⊠*3663 Las Vegas Blvd. S, Center Strip* ☎*702/866–0703 or 888/800–8284* ⊕*www.miraclemileshopslv.com.*

★ **Bellagio.** Steve Wynn spared no expense to create Bellagio, so be prepared to spare no expense shopping at its exclusive boutiques. **Via Bellagio** is a long passage lined with elegant stores such as Yves Saint Laurent Rive Gauche, Prada, Chanel, Giorgio Armani, Gucci, Hermès, and Tiffany & Co. When you're ready to cool your heels, dine on the balcony at **Olives,** right in the promenade, to snag the best seat for watching the Fountains of Bellagio (otherwise known as the dancing waters). Children, with few exceptions (such as those of hotel guests), aren't allowed anywhere in Bellagio. ⊠*Bellagio, 3600 Las Vegas Blvd. S, Center Strip* ☎*702/693–7111* ⊕*www.bellagiolasvegas.com.*

★ **Caesars Palace.** The marble halls of **Appian Way at Caesars** are centered around an exact replica of Michelangelo's *David* in Carrara marble. The upscale shops include Cartier and Cuzzens for fine menswear. If you're jazzed about the seeing Elton John show, check out the gift shop.

FodorśChoice ★   The **Forum Shops at Caesars** resemble an ancient Roman streetscape, with immense columns and arches, two central piazzas with fountains, and a cloud-filled ceiling with a sky that changes from sunrise to sunset over the course of three hours (possibly goading shoppers to step up their pace of acquisition when it looks as if time is running out?). The Festival Fountain (in the west wing of the mall) puts on its own show every hour on the hour daily starting at 10 ⊦ : a robotic, pie-eyed Bacchus hosts a party for friends Apollo, Venus, and Mars, complete with lasers, music, and sound effects; at the end, the god of wine and merriment delivers—what else?—a sales pitch for the mall. The "Atlantis" show (in the east wing) is even more amazing: Atlas, king of Atlantis, can't seem to pick between his son, Gadrius, and his daughter, Alia, to assume the throne. A struggle for control of the doomed kingdom ensues amid flame and smoke.

If you can tear yourself away from the animatronic wizardry, you find designer shops and the old standbys. For fashionistas, there are all the hard-hitters: Christian Dior, Gucci, Fendi, Pucci, Louis Vuitton, Tod's, and Valentino (whew!). Pick up your diamonds at Harry Winston, Bulgari, or Chopard, or go for a sparkling handbag at Judith Leiber. If your purse strings are a little tighter, there's always the ubiquitous Gap or Abercrombie stores. The mall is open late (until 11 Sunday through Thursday, until midnight Friday and Saturday). ⊠*Caesars Palace, 3500 Las Vegas Blvd. S, Center Strip* ☎*702/896–5599 Appian Way, 702/893–4800 Forum Shops* ⊕*www.forumshops.com.*

★ **Fashion Show Mall.** It's impossible to miss this swanky, fashion-devoted mall due to one big element: The Cloud, a futuristic steel shade structure that looms high above the mall's entrance. Ads and footage of the mall's own fashion events are continuously projected onto the eye-catching architecture (think Times Square à la Las Vegas). The inside of the mall is sleek, spacious, and airy, a nice change from some of the claustrophobic casino malls. The mall delivers on its name—fashion shows are occasionally staged in the Great Hall on an 80-foot-long catwalk that rises from the floor.

Not everything here is overpriced. Although you do find many of the same stores that are at the casino malls, such as Louis Vuitton, there's also a smattering of different fare; trendy clothes boutique Talulah G.; and the only bookstore on the Strip, Waldenbooks. Neiman Marcus, Saks Fifth Avenue, two Macy's stores, Bloomingdale's Home, Nordstrom, and Dillard's serve as the department-store anchors. Fashion Show is next to the New Frontier. ⊠*3200 Las Vegas Blvd. S, North Strip* ☎*702/369–8382* ⊕*www.thefashionshow.com.*

Hawaiian Marketplace. Modeled after the International Marketplace in Waikiki, this shopping venture re-creates a refreshing Polynesian village with indigenous Hawaiian flora under a banyan tree and a huge, shady canopy. This place is abuzz with activity. Animatronic birds chirp as you shop in the Enchanted Garden (an area festooned with tropical

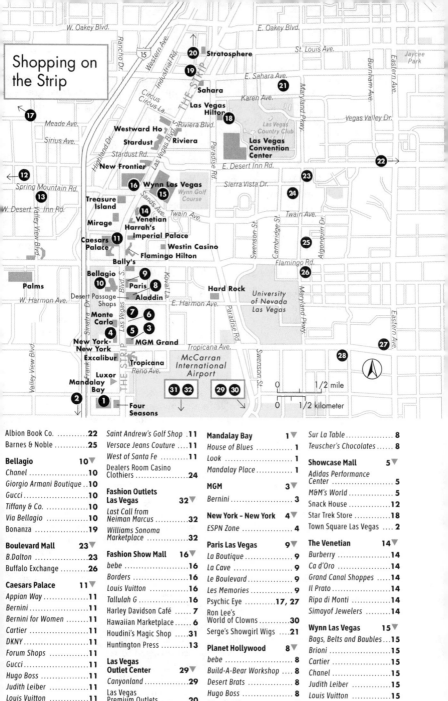

Shopping on the Strip

flora and fauna); after an hourly thunder-and-lightning storm rolls through, they warble Hawaiian songs. Las Vegas–based island-born performers entertain with traditional dancing, storytelling, and crafts. Cart retailers proffer accessories, souvenirs, and T-shirts from grass-thatch huts and kiosks. A 17-foot-tall statue of King Kamehameha (the great 1700s king who united the Hawaiian Islands) oversees the whole lively scene. If you're driving, the best place to park is behind Travelodge, adjacent to the Marketplace. ✉3743 Las Vegas Blvd. S, South Las Vegas ☎702/795-2247.

★ **Mandalay Bay.** Here's a twist on Vegas mall gimmicks: **Mandalay Place,** a sky bridge that spans the gap between Mandalay Bay and Luxor. The stores are lofty, too—you can practice your swing with Nike irons and drivers at the first-ever Nike Golf store, or pick up gold-plated or sterling-silver three-blade razors at the swanky the Art of Shaving, a high-roller "barber spa" and upscale grooming emporium. For hot, pricey brands like Juicy Couture, try the cool Look. ✉Mandalay Bay Resort & Casino, 3950 Las Vegas Blvd. S, South Strip ☎702/632-7777.

Paris Las Vegas. Petite by Vegas standards, **Le Boulevard** is a Parisian-style shopping lane chock-full of Gallic delights. This is where to go for all things French including the famous Lenôtre chocolates; the Lenôtre café is the only place in the United States where these confections are sold. And Le Journal has that jaunty French beret you know you're lusting for. ✉Paris Las Vegas, 3655 Las Vegas Blvd. S, Center Strip ☎702/946-7000 ⊕www.parislasvegas.com.

🕙 **Showcase Mall.** "Mall" is a bit of a misnomer for this place, where stores are more like highly evolved interactive marketing concepts. First off, there's M&M's World, a rollicking four-story homage to the popular candy. Head up to the fourth level to create your own custom bag of M&M's (all blue! only red! plain and peanut together!). Huge dispensers with every color and every type line one wall. If you're able to pull yourself away from all the chocolate, more sugar awaits at Everything Coca-Cola. Here, you can pony up to the old-time soda fountain and order a Coke float. All sorts of interesting collectibles, like a vintage Coke vending machine, are for sale. Need an outlet for that sugar buzz? Check out the high-tech Gameworks video arcade (Steven Spielberg had a hand in creating it), visit the Grand Canyon Experience (in case you can't make it to the real natural wonder), or suit up for your favorite sport at the Adidas Performance Center, which carries clothes, footwear, and accessories for any and every sport. Mall expansion plans are in the works at this writing. Showcase is right next to MGM Grand. ✉3785 Las Vegas Blvd. S, South Strip ☎702/597-3122.

Town Square Las Vegas. After hours spent at the craps table, head outdoors for some fresh air and spend some of those winnings. Opened in late 2007, this mall has been constructed to resemble Main Street America with open-air shopping and dining. More than 150 shops including names like Victoria's Secret, Bath & Body Works, The Body Shop, Cache, Crabtree & Evelyn, Occhiali da Sole, and Showcase Slots will help you break the bank. And, if you're tired of shopping, there's also a children's area, an outdoor concert venue, and a multiplex cinema. At this writing, a working telephone number and Web site had not been published. ☒ *Las Vegas Blvd. S, just south of Mandalay Bay, South Strip*

Fodor'sChoice
★ **The Venetian.** The **Grand Canal Shoppes** are *the* most elegant—and fun—shopping experience on the Strip. Duck into shops like Burberry or Lladró as you amble under blue skies alongside a Vegas-ified Grand Canal. Eventually, all the quaint bridges and walkways lead you to St. Mark's Square, which is full of little gift-shop carts and street performers. If you're loaded down with bags, hail a gondola— it's one of the kitschiest experiences in any of the megamalls ($15 per person).

> **NONSTOP SHOPPING**
>
> Can't wait to hit another mall? A pedestrian bridge from the Fashion Show Mall to the Esplanade at Wynn Las Vegas gives you access to millions of square feet of retail bliss. Start at the Fashion Show, which houses such heavy hitters as Neiman-Marcus and Nordstrom as well as hip boutiques like Talulah G. Head across to the Esplanade, where you can pick up high-end goodies at Jean Paul Gaultier or Shoe-In. Finish your stroll off with a cup of gelato at Sugar & Ice's gorgeous marble balcony.

Two must-see stores are Il Prato, which sells unique Venetian collectibles, including masks, stationery sets, and pen-and-inkwell sets, and Ripa de Monti, which carries luminescent Venetian glass. Also, because Arizona's famous Canyon Ranch spa has an outpost here, there's the don't-miss Canyon Ranch Living Essentials shop, full of cookbooks, body products, and spa robes. The mall is open late (until 11 Sunday through Thursday, until midnight Friday and Saturday). ☒ *Venetian Resort-Hotel-Casino, 3355 Las Vegas Blvd. S, Center Strip* ☏ *702/733–5000* ⊕ *www.venetian.com.*

OUTLET MALLS

Fodor'sChoice
★ **Fashion Outlets Las Vegas.** This outlet mall is definitely worth a shopping safari to nearby Primm, about a half hour west on I–15. Here you find many of the same superstars as on the Strip but at prices slashed by as much as 75%. And you don't often see these stores represented at an outlet mall: Burberry Factory Outlet, Williams-Sonoma Marketplace, St. John Company Store, and Versace Company Store. Last Call from Neiman Marcus stocks designer labels as well as its private labels. Besides these are the usual outlet-mall suspects: Banana Republic Factory Store, Polo Ralph Lauren Factory Store, and the Gap Outlet. If you don't want to battle the traffic, take the shuttle service that runs daily from the MGM Grand and Miracle Mile shops ($15 round-trip; 702/874–1400 for reservations). ☒ *32100 Las Vegas Blvd. S, Primm* ☏ *702/874–1400* ⊕ *www.fashionoutletlasvegas.com.*

Las Vegas Outlet Center. Immerse yourself in one of the country's largest discount malls, which is, ironically, just a few miles from the Strip's most exclusive and expensive shopping. Jones New York and Calvin

Klein are among the 130 stores selling pretty much everything at discount prices: clothing, jewelry, toys, shoes, beauty products, souvenirs, and more. The mall has two food courts and a full-size carousel. OFF 5th Saks Fifth Avenue occupies the majority of space at Las Vegas Outlet Center Annex, a small separate building on the south side. To get here, take Las Vegas Boulevard South 3 mi south from the Tropicana Avenue intersection. ⊠7400 Las Vegas Blvd. S, Las Vegas ☎702/896–5599 ⊕www.lasvegasoutletcenter.com.

Las Vegas Premium Outlets. A 2007 renovation has brought the number of stores up to 150, including rarely seen outlets of some heavy fashion hitters, such as Dolce & Gabbana, St. John Company Store, Brooks Brothers Factory Store, Catherine Malandrino, Diesel, and A/X Armani Exchange. The upscale mix at this racetrack-shape downtown outlet mall, which stands on the grounds of the old Union Pacific rail yards also includes names you can find at your own mall, but with better discounts, such as Eddie Bauer and Quiksilver. This is one of the few outdoor malls in town, and there's plenty of shade as well as misting towers to keep you cool in the hot Las Vegas desert. The mall runs a $1 shuttle from the California Hotel, the Golden Nugget, and the Downtown Transportation Center, but if you want to drive, two parking garages were recently added. ⊠875 S. Grand Central Pkwy., Downtown ☎702/474–7500 ⊕www.premiumoutlets.com.

SPECIALTY SHOPS

BOOKS

GENERAL Las Vegas has a full complement of national bookstore chains, though only the Waldenbooks at the Fashion Show Mall is directly on the Strip.

B. Dalton. ⊠Boulevard Mall, 3680 S. Maryland Pkwy., East Side ☎702/735–0008.

Barnes & Noble. ⊠2191 N. Rainbow Blvd., Las Vegas ☎702/631–1775 ⊠3860 Maryland Pkwy., East Side ☎702/734–2900 ⊠8915 W. Charleston Blvd., West Side ☎702/242–1987.

Borders Books and Music. ⊠2190 N. Rainbow Blvd., Las Vegas ☎702/638–7866 ⊠2323 S. Decatur Blvd., West Side ☎702/258–0999 ⊠3200 Las Vegas Blvd. S., North Strip ☎702/733–1049.

Used bookstores are as easy to find in Las Vegas as video-poker machines. If you venture out into the greater metro area, you inevitably find one stashed among the many strip malls and neighborhood shopping centers.

Albion Book Company. The majority of space in this voluminous bookstore, which takes in about 6,000 books a month, is devoted to hardcovers on almost every possible topic in fiction and nonfiction. First-edition books and rare finds occupy a corner in the front of the store. It's a 10-minute drive from the Strip, in the Von's shopping center

Continued on page 196

BLITZING THE STRIP

WHAT PUTS THE "FABULOUS" IN "FABULOUS LAS VEGAS"?

We think it might have something to do with the shopping. Sure, you can find your Gap or your Disney store in the malls here just like everywhere else. But in Vegas there's always the hope that someone—maybe even you—will win the jackpot, and you can bet the casinos don't want you spending that money anywhere but here. So they've brought you the best of the best—jewelry, clothes, cars, cigars, imports. The options are endless. Our favorite part? If you can't buy, you can always gawk. Window-shopping is still free.

GLITZ & GLAM

Lucky you—somehow, as if by magic, three 7's clicked into one center line on that slot machine. Now you've got some serious spending to do. Here are our most outrageous Las Vegas finds.

$325
SILK SCARF. Add instant cachet to your wardrobe with a cloud of Hermès silk. The world's most chic accessory is a must for any fashionista. *Hermès, Via Bellagio*

$105 Alternative: Silk twill pocket square. *Hermès, Via Bellagio*

$60,000
EXILE MOTORCYCLE. Blow your winnings from that hot craps table last night on this custom ride by Russell Mitchell. Let the satin black paint and old school flame job compete with the brilliantly lit Vegas Strip.
The Hard Rock Store at the Hard Rock Casino

$22.50 Alternative: Harley Davidson Black Lightning T-shirt. *Harley Davidson Café*

Photo: Jim Gianatsis

$1,600
MODERN STREAMERICA 18K WHITE GOLD CUFF LINKS. Nothing screams class and taste in the Baccarat Salon more than white cuffs fastened with Tiffany white-gold cuff links. Go on, strut your stuff.
Tiffany & Co., Via Bellagio

$1.99 Alternative: Las Vegas Dealer's Visor. *Bonanza Gifts*

$7,000
CROCODILE CIGAR HUMIDOR. Vegas is cigar heaven. High-rollers fat with cash have no qualms puffing away inside or outside the casino floor. Brioni's ultimate cigar humidor, encased in rare crocodile skin and lined in cedarwood, is the perfect match for Vegas's high quality rolled goods.
Brioni, The Esplanade at Wynn Las Vegas

$85 Alternative: Opus X fine cigar. *Cigars Du Monde, Paris Las Vegas*

$55
HOT LATHER SHAVE. Why should girls have all the fun? Gentlemen, you'll be hard-pressed to find a swankier experience than this sinfully decadent grooming session. A beautiful woman (naturally–this is Vegas) lathers your face with a warm cream and intoxicating herbs before giving you a perfectly close shave.
Art of Shaving, Mandalay Place

$15 Alternative: Hot Lather Shave. *Barber Shop Orleans Casino*

AROUND THE WORLD

Sin City's Eiffel Tower, Venetian canals, and Manhattan skyline are all kitschily faux, but these imported finds are the real deal.

$1,980

PAPER-AND-COPPER CRESCENT MOON VENETIAN MASK ADORNED WITH SWAROVSKI CRYSTALS. You'd have to hunt Venetian backstreets to find the original Il Prato, a tiny shop selling fine-crafted Carnevale masks. The journey to the Vegas branch might not be as whimsical, but that doesn't mean the finds are any less fabulous. Scoop up a Swarovski-crystal-encrusted papier-mâché mask–a quicky marriage of Venetian tradition and Vegas flash. *Il Prato, the Grand Canal Shoppes at the Venetian*

$40 Alternative: Ceramic Carnevale mask. *Il Prato, Grand Canal Shoppes, Venetian*

$295

LLADRO FIGURINE "A MOTHER'S EMBRACE." Collectors go mad for these fine porcelain sculptures hailing from the Spanish city of Valencia. An elegant mother delicately cradles a baby in this popular one. *The Grand Canal Shoppes, Venetian*

$95 Alternative: Love Ya Limited Edition clown figurine. *Ron Lee's World of Clowns*

$72

LACOSTE PIQUÉ POLO SHIRT IN AZURINE BLUE. It doesn't get much more classic than this short-sleeved French cotton polo with the signature alligator logo. *Lacoste, Fashion Show Mall*

$45 Alternative: Lacoste Essential Eau de Toilette Spray, 2.5 oz. *Lacoste, Forum Shops, Caesars*

GETTING GLOBAL

Want more exotic shopping? Head to these malls. The GRAND CANAL SHOPPES AT THE VENETIAN has **Lladró, Ca' d'Oro, Il Prato** and **Ripa di Monti**. The **Lenôtre** café at **Le Boulevard at Paris Las Vegas** is the only place in the country that sells the famous Lenôtre chocolates.

Grand Canal Shoppes at *The Venetian*

BLITZING THE STRIP 5

on the corner of Eastern Avenue and Desert Inn. ✉*2466 E. Desert Inn Rd., East Side* ☎*702/792–9554 or 800/485–1864.*

Book Magician. Science fiction and metaphysics are this shop's specialties, though you can find other genres, including a few comic books, in the mix. ✉*2202 W. Charleston Blvd., #2, West Side* ☎*702/384–5838.*

SPECIAL INTEREST **Gambler's Book Shop.** GBC is the world's largest independent bookstore specializing in books about 21, craps, poker, roulette, and all the other games of chance, as well as novels about casinos, biographies of crime figures, and anything else that relates to gambling and Las Vegas. ✉*630 S. 11th St., Downtown* ☎*702/382–7555 or 800/522–1777* ⊕*www. gamblersbook.com.*

Huntington Press. This small-press publisher produces some of the best books about gambling and Las Vegas. You can buy books, software, and handheld games at its offices, two blocks north of the Rio (less than 1 mi from the Strip). ✉*3665 S. Procyon Ave., West Side* ☎*702/252–0655* ⊕*www.huntingtonpress.com.*

Psychic Eye Book Shop. Inside the innocuous strip-mall façade are all sorts of esoteric books, lucky talismans, tarot cards, and candles. Get a psychic reading or an astrological chart on where to place your bets. ✉*6848 W. Charleston Blvd., East Side* ☎*702/255–4477* ✉*4500 E. Sunset Road, Henderson* ☎*702/451–5777* ✉*27555 Nellis Blvd., Las Vegas* ☎*702/432–4666* ⊕*www.pebooks.com.*

CHILDREN'S CLOTHING

Though the casino-hotel malls and area shopping centers have the usual children's clothing stores such as Gap Kids and Gymboree, you can find some great gifts for kids at the shops below.

Desert Brats. There's lots of styles to pick from including frothy creations with feathers and sequins that little girls will love. ✉*Miracle Mile at Planet Hollywood Resort & Casino, 3663 Las Vegas Blvd. S, Center Strip* ☎*702/892–8420.*

Harley Davidson Café. The café's retail store is the spot to outfit kids with a Harley Hog Cap, flight jacket, or Captain America T-shirt. ✉*3725 Las Vegas Blvd. S, Center Strip* ☎*702/740–4555.*

MEN'S CLOTHING

You can't walk into the shopping areas of the Strip's hotels without stumbling on high-end men's clothes shops. If the price tags on the Strip are too stratospheric, the outlet malls have brand names for less, such as Tommy Hilfiger, Eddie Bauer, and DKNY.

Bernini. This Rodeo Drive–based men's clothier purveys the very best menswear, and some branches even offer custom-made suits. The Forum Shops has a Bernini shop and a Bernini Collections, and the Appian Way has a Bernini Couture. The Bernini Collezioni at MGM Grand sells Brioni, Canali, Versace, Hugo Boss, and Zegna. ✉*Forum Shops at Caesars, 3500 Las Vegas Blvd. S, Suite L11, Center Strip* ☎*702/893–7786 for Bernini Collection, 702/870–1786 for Bernini Platinum, located inside Forum Casino* ✉*Appian Way at Caesars,*

3570 Las Vegas Blvd. S, Center Strip ☎702/731–9786 ✉*MGM Grand Hotel and Casino, 3799 Las Vegas Blvd. S, Space 6, South Strip* ☎702/798–8786.

Brioni. High rollers can have an impeccably tailored suit made to order for a cool six grand. Or splurge on a crocodile watch case for $11,000. ✉*Wynn Las Vegas, 3131 Las Vegas Blvd. S, South Strip* ☎702/770–7000.

ESPN Zone SportsCenter Studio Store. Increase your cool quotient with official ESPN and ESPN Zone merchandise, including men's sportswear. ✉*New York–New York Hotel and Casino, 3790 Las Vegas Blvd. S, South Strip* ☎702/933–3776.

Giorgio Armani Boutique. This elegant store displays the simplicity of the Armani suit as well as signature sportswear, shoes, and accessories. ✉*Via Bellagio, 3600 Las Vegas Blvd. S, Center Strip* ☎702/893–8327.

Hugo Boss. Both branches (one called Hugo/Hugo Boss and the other called Boss/Hugo Boss, for some mysterious reason) carry styles straight from European and New York runways. ✉*Forum Shops at Caesars, 3500 Las Vegas Blvd. S, Center Strip* ☎702/696–9444 ✉*Miracle Mile at Planet Hollywood Resort & Casino, 3663 Las Vegas Blvd. S, Center Strip* ☎702/732–4272.

Versace Jeans Couture. Casual and fashion-forward jeans and accessories are the objects of desire here. ✉*Forum Shops at Caesars, 3500 Las Vegas Blvd. S, Center Strip* ☎702/796–7332.

WOMEN'S CLOTHING

Vegas shopping can send the most jaded shopper into ecstasy. Prepare to find a great selection of women's wear at area hotel-casino malls and outlet centers. Name a designer, and you should find a signature shop in this town.

Bags, Belts and Baubles. Accessories suitable for high-fashion outfits can be purchased at this boutique. ✉*Wynn Las Vegas, 3131 Las Vegas Blvd. S, Central Strip* ☎702/770–3555.

bebe. Fashionistas love this boutique's stock of dresses, jeans, and separates. ✉*Fashion Show Mall, 3200 Las Vegas Blvd. S, North Strip* ☎702/892–8083 ✉*Miracle Mile at Planet Hollywood Resort & Casino, 3663 Las Vegas Blvd. S, Center Strip* ☎702/892–0406.

Bernini for Women. This Rodeo Drive–based men's clothier also has a store that caters to women where it offers its luxurious body care products and gorgeous jackets. ✉*Forum Shops at Caesars, 3500 Las Vegas Blvd. S, Suite L11, Center Strip* ☎702/893–7786.

Burberry. The luxury British brand has its famous trench coat and rain gear as well as hot fashion accessories. ✉*Grand Canal Shoppes at the Venetian, 3377 Las Vegas Blvd. S, Center Strip* ☎702/735–2600 ✉*Forum Shops at Caesars, 3500 Las Vegas Blvd. S, Center Strip* ☎702/731–0650.

Chanel. Las Vegas boasts two branches of this fine French couturier. ✉ *Wynn Las Vegas, 3131 Las Vegas Blvd. S, South Strip* ☎ *702/765–5055* ✉ *Via Bellagio, 3600 Las Vegas Blvd. S, South Strip* ☎ *702/765–5055.*

DKNY. Up-to-the-nanosecond fashion from this New York designer collection is worth a test drive. ✉ *Forum Shops at Caesars, 3500 Las Vegas Blvd. S, Center Strip* ☎ *702/650–9670.*

Gucci. If you must drop a grand on a pair of loafers, come here. Though the salespeople's noses are definitely turned up, the Gucci reputation prevails. ✉ *Forum Shops at Caesars, 3500 Las Vegas Blvd. S, Suite C1, Center Strip* ☎ *702/369–7333* ✉ *Via Bellagio, 3600 Las Vegas Blvd. S, Center Strip* ☎ *702/732–3900.*

Judith Leiber. These bejeweled handbags qualify as fine jewelry, with prices in the thousands of dollars to match. ✉ *Forum Shops at Caesars, 3500 Las Vegas Blvd. S, Suite G11, South Strip* ☎ *702/792–0661* ✉ *Wynn Las Vegas, 3131 Las Vegas Blvd. S, Center Strip* ☎ *702/770–3558.*

Last Call from Neiman Marcus. Score irresistible discounts on designer clothing as well as housewares and furnishings at this department-store outlet. ✉ *Fashion Outlets Las Vegas, 32100 Las Vegas Blvd. S, Primm* ☎ *702/874–2100.*

Look. This Las Vegas boutique stocks trendy fashions, purses, and accessories, including labels like Juicy Couture. ✉ *Mandalay Place, 3950 Las Vegas Blvd. S, South Strip* ☎ *702/632–9372.*

Louis Vuitton. Stash your winnings in a designer bag from one of three Vegas branches of this French accessory maker. ✉ *Wynn Las Vegas, 3131 Las Vegas Blvd. S, South Strip* ☎ *702/650–9007* ✉ *Fashion Show Mall, 3200 Las Vegas Blvd. S, South Strip* ☎ *702/731–9860* ✉ *Forum Shops at Caesars Palace, 3500 Las Vegas Blvd. S, South Strip* ☎ *702/732–1227.*

Oscar de la Renta. Stop here for the finest offerings of this American couturier. ✉ *Wynn Las Vegas, 3131 Las Vegas Blvd. S, South Strip* ☎ *702/770–3487.*

Talulah G. Celebrities and socialites converge at local fashionista Meital Granz's trendsetting boutique to scour her handpicked styles. ✉ *Fashion Show Mall, 3200 Las Vegas Blvd. S, North Strip* ☎ *702/737–6000.*

Versace Jeans Couture. Score trendy jeanswear and tops, including sexy Italian leather jeans. ✉ *Forum Shops at Caesars, 3500 Las Vegas Blvd. S, Center Strip* ☎ *702/796–7332.*

INDULGE YOURSELF

In Las Vegas you can indulge in luxuries rarely found in this country, including the exquisite Lenôtre chocolates in Paris Las Vegas's Le Boulevard. The Drugstore at Wynn Las Vegas carries products by Santa Maria Novella, an 800-year-old Florentine perfumery that sells elegant soaps, perfumes, and bath and body products. Instead of traveling to Italy to buy an authentic Carnevale mask, you can visit the Il Prato store at the Venetian.

★ **The Attic.** No other used-clothing store in the world compares. Thick with incense and booming with club music, the two-story building is filled with an eclectic selection of shirts, shoes, pants, hats, jewelry, halter tops, prom dresses, evening wear, and feather boas, as well as

furniture and collectors' items. Fans of 1960s and '70s styles should especially love it. ⊠*1018 S. Main St., Downtown* ☎*702/388–2848* 🖷*702/388–1047* ⊕*www.theatticlasvegas.com.*

Buffalo Exchange. This is a must-stop for the terminally hip. The very extensive collection of great vintage clothing at reasonable prices makes for satisfying shopping. You also can find great recycled discards and, since we all could use the help, lots of suggestions from the friendly staff. ⊠*4110 S. Maryland Pkwy., East Side* ☎*702/791–3960* ⊕*www. buffaloexchange.com.*

FOOD & DRINK

☺ **Ethel M Chocolates Factory and Cactus Garden.** The *M* stands for Mars, the name of the family (headed by Ethel in the early days) that brings you Snickers, Milky Way, Three Musketeers, and M&M's. Come here for two special reasons: one, to watch the candy making, and two (more importantly), to taste free samples in the adjoining shop. As for the other, not-quite-so-exciting half of this place's name, yes—there is, indeed, a cactus garden with more than 350 species of succulents and desert plants. It's at its peak during spring flowering. ⊠*2 Cactus Garden Dr., Henderson* ☎*702/458–8864* ⊕*www.ethelm.com.*

La Cave. Take your pick of decadent delights: French imported wines, pâtés, cheeses, and chocolate. ⊠*Paris Las Vegas, 3655 Las Vegas Blvd. S, Center Strip* ☎*702/946–4339.*

★ ☺ **M&M's World.** It almost sounds like something straight out of *Willy Wonka*. Colorworks, on the second floor, stocks all types and colors of M&M's; the 3-D movie *I Lost My M in Vegas* is shown on the third floor. This popular tourist attraction is usually crowded; it's not easy to maneuver strollers and wheelchairs around the displays. Be sure to catch the 3-D movies even if you're not a kid. ⊠*Showcase Mall, 3785 Las Vegas Blvd. S, South Strip* ☎*702/736–7611.*

Snack House. Asian snack foods, dried fruit, and nuts make this Chinatown Plaza shop a popular stop. ⊠*Chinatown Plaza, 4255 Spring Mountain Blvd., West Side* ☎*702/247–9688.*

Teuscher's Chocolates. The tempting Swiss chocolates and a coffee bar make for a delightful way to gather energy for more shopping. ⊠*Miracle Mile at Planet Hollywood Resort & Casino, 3663 Las Vegas Blvd. S, Center Strip* ☎*702/866–6624.*

5

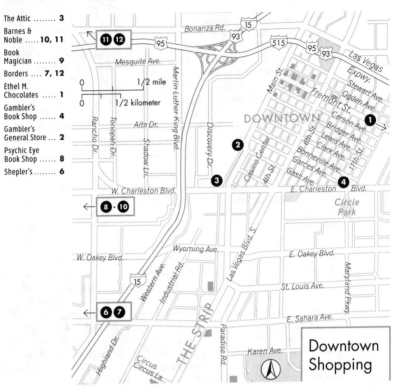

Downtown
Shopping

GIFTS & SOUVENIRS

Canyonland. A big rock fountain gives this place at Las Vegas Outlet Center an "outdoor" feel. It offers decorative items, including Southwest-style accessories, jade statues, miniature fountains, wind chimes, and cedar trinket boxes. ✉ *Las Vegas Outlet Center, 7400 Las Vegas Blvd. S, South Las Vegas* ☎ *702/361–6682.*

House of Blues. Buy music, books, hot sauce, and T-shirts at the souvenir shop in the popular bar–restaurant at Mandalay Bay. Rest for a bit in the comfortable chairs in the shop's alcove: read a book about the blues or look out the shop's windows into the restaurant. ✉ *Mandalay Bay Resort & Casino, 3950 Las Vegas Blvd. S, South Strip* ☎ *702/632–7600.*

★ **Il Prato.** Il Prato saves you a shopping foray to Venice, where the original pricey boutique stands. The Vegas outpost offers the same authentic gifts crafted by Italian artisans, such as tooled-leather journals and photo albums, glass-tip quills, wax-seal kits, miniatures, and paintings. And, just as in Venice, there's a huge collection of traditional Carnevale masks here. A back room offers a comprehensive collection of Ferrari collectibles, such as scale models and racing flags. ✉ *Grand Canal Shoppes at the Venetian, 3377 Las Vegas Blvd. S, Center Strip* ☎ *702/733–1201.*

Les Memories. A Francophile's fantasy, this shop stocks Diptyque candles, French-milled soaps, and other French delights. ⊠ *Le Boulevard at Paris Las Vegas, 3655 Las Vegas Blvd. S, Center Strip* ☎ *702/946–7000 Ext. 64329.*

★ **Ripa di Monti.** Exquisite Venetian glass creations—including smaller items like magnets and key chains, as well as the more elaborate vases and figurines—are sold at this store, one of the Grand Canal Shoppes at the Venetian. It's one of Las Vegas's must-see shops. Buy glass-bead necklaces and earrings or a bowl of glass fruit for your dining-room table. ⊠ *Grand Canal Shoppes at the Venetian, 3377 Las Vegas Blvd. S, Center Strip* ☎ *702/733–1004.*

HOME FURNISHINGS

National chains can be found in most Vegas malls, but be sure to hit Las Vegas Outlet Center for reduced prices on brand names such as Waterford Wedgwood, Springmaid, Corning-Revere, Mikasa, and more.

Sur La Table. Culinary aficionados and home chefs love the table linens, kitchen tools, and specialty foods. ⊠ *Miracle Mile at Planet Hollywood Resort & Casino, 3663 Las Vegas Blvd. S, Center Strip* ☎ *702/732–2706.*

West of Santa Fe. Find southwestern-theme items at this shop that stocks home accessories and Native American collectibles. ⊠ *Forum Shops at Caesars, 3500 Las Vegas Blvd. S, Center Strip* ☎ *702/737–1993.*

Williams-Sonoma Marketplace. All the kitchen witchery of its catalog and stores are sold here at deep discounts. ⊠ *Fashion Outlets, 32100 Las Vegas Blvd. S, Primm* ☎ *702/874–1780.*

JEWELRY

Most malls and shopping centers on and off the Strip have jewelry stores, including such national chains as Ben Bridge, Gordon's, Lundstrom, Whitehall Co., and Zales. More exclusive jewelers can be found in several of the Strip hotels, most notably Bellagio and the Venetian.

Ca' d'Oro. This is the premier jewelry shop on the Strip—perhaps in all of Las Vegas. Not surprisingly, it's one of the many unique, elegant stores in the Grand Canal Shoppes at the Venetian. The store is made up of several exclusive boutiques including the first Damiani boutique in the United States and a Charriol boutique. Oliva and Silvio Hidalgo offer jewel and enamel settings in platinum and 18-karat gold. Lovers of fine watches will find numerous brands, including Ebel, Omega, Tag Heuer, Dubey & Schaldenbrand, and Baume & Mercier. ⊠ *Grand Canal Shoppes at the Venetian, 3377 Las Vegas Blvd. S, Center Strip* ☎ *702/696–0080* ⊕ *www.cadorojewelers.com.*

Cartier. There are two outposts of this venerable jeweler in Las Vegas: at Caesars Palace on Appian Way, and at the entrance of Wynn Las Vegas. You'll find a fine collection of jewelry, watches, leather goods, accessories, and fragrances. ⊠ *Appian Way at Caesars, 3570 Las Vegas Blvd. S, South Strip* ☎ *702/733–6652* ⊠ *Wynn Las Vegas, 3131 Las Vegas Blvd. S, South Strip* ☎ *702/696–0146* ⊕ *www.cartier.com.*

Simayof Jewelers. Now you don't have to go to San Francisco to visit one of the most trusted names in the diamond business. Simayof sells loose diamonds as well as top-quality jewelry. ⊠ *Grand Canal Shoppes at the Venetian, 3355 Las Vegas Blvd. S, South Strip* ☎ *702/731–1037.*

Tiffany & Co. Browse through a full selection of Tiffany's timeless merchandise as well as the exclusive jewelry designs of Elsa Peretti, Paloma Picasso, and Jean Schlumberger. ⊠ *Via Bellagio, 3600 Las Vegas Blvd. S, Center Strip* ☎ *702/693–7111.*

ONLY IN LAS VEGAS

★ **Bonanza "World's Largest Gift Shop."** OK, so it may not, in fact, be the world's largest, but it's the town's largest—and for that matter, the town's best—souvenir store. Although it has most of the usual junk, it also stocks some unusual junk. Dying for a pair of fuzzy pink dice to hang on your car's rearview mirror? They've got 'em in spades. Can't go home without your own blinking "Welcome to Fabulous Las Vegas" sign? Or the coveted Elvis aviator sunglasses complete with black sideburns? Or how about a mechanical card shuffler, dealer's green visor, and authentic clay poker chips for poker nights back home? They're all right here. The store is so huge that you won't feel trapped, as you might in some of the smaller shops. It's open until midnight, and it's across from the Sahara. ⊠ *2460 Las Vegas Blvd. S, North Strip* ☎ *702/385–7359* ⊕ *www.worldslargestgiftshop.com.*

Dealers Room Casino Clothiers. If you've caught the gambling spirit and want to go home in a white shirt, black pants, and a big red bow tie, this place will be happy to sell you dealer's duds. ⊠ *4343 N. Rancho Dr., North Las Vegas* ☎ *702/362–7980* ⊠ *3507 S. Maryland Pkwy., East Side* ☎ *702/732–3932.*

Fodor'sChoice **Gamblers General Store.** There's a big collection of gambling books, such
★ as *Craps for the Clueless,* as well as poker chips, green-felt layouts, and slot and video-poker machines. Warning: the highly collectible vintage slots start at $2,000. They'll make sure your state allows the type of slot machine you want before you buy. You can buy used casino card decks here but only after they've been resorted and repackaged by guests of the Nevada state penal system. It's eight blocks south of the Plaza Hotel on Main Street. ⊠ *800 S. Main St., Downtown* ☎ *702/382–9903* ⊕ *www.gamblersgeneralstore.com.*

↻ **Houdini's Magic Shop.** Magicians are hot tickets in Vegas, and it's no surprise that Houdini's corporate headquarters is in town. There are also seven branches with all the tricks and gags—nearly one for every casino-mall. ⊠ *Houdini's Factory Store, 6455 Dean Martin Dr, #L, South Strip* ☎ *702/798–4789* ⊕ *www.houdini.com.*

The Liberace Museum Store. The store stocks the maestro's CDs and videos, jewelry, and, in case you're running low, his signature candelabras. ⊠ *1775 E. Tropicana Ave., East Side* ☎ *702/798–5595* ⊕ *www.liberace.org.*

↻ **Ron Lee's World of Clowns.** This store houses the world's largest collection of limited-edition clown sculptures. The figurines are even made on the

Where to Refuel

If you're on a shopping mission, keep your strength up at one of these delicious pit stops.

MALLS ON THE STRIP

Planet Hollywood Resort & Casino: Cheeseburger Las Vegas

Bellagio: Olives

Caesars Palace: Café Lago Buffet

The Forum Shops at Caesars: Il Mulino New York

Fashion Show Mall: The Capital Grille

Hawaiian Marketplace: Tanba (Indian Cuisine), China Star Buffet (Chinese), or Kapit Bahay (Philippine)

Mandalay Bay: Burger Bar

Paris Las Vegas: JJ's Boulangerie

Showcase Mall: La Salsa Cantina

The Venetian: Krispy Kreme, the Coffee Bean & Tea Leaf, or Postrio

OUTLET MALLS

Fashion Outlets Las Vegas: Hot Dog on a Stick or Vegas Burger

Las Vegas Outlet Center: Chao Praya

Las Vegas Premium Outlets: Great Steak and Potato Company

premises. ⊠*7665 Commercial Way, Suite A, Henderson* ☎*702/434–1700* ⊕*www.ronlee.com.*

★ **Serge's Showgirl Wigs.** If you always wished for the sleek tresses of those showgirls (or female impersonators), head to this Vegas institution. The largest wig store in the world can transform you into a Renaissance angel or Priscilla Presley on her wedding day. After checking out Serge's celebrity wall of fame, head for the wig outlet directly across the parking lot. ⊠*953 E. Sahara Ave., East Side* ☎*702/732–1015* ⊕*www.showgirlwigs.com.*

★ ℃ **Star Trek Store.** Inside the Star Trek Experience, Trekkies salivate over this collection of Federation merchandise: uniforms, Tribbles (Trekkies know what this is), rare artwork, and the "Original Series Communicator." There is also a large collection of Starfleet Academy Merchandise. You may come across rare props from the original series and its string of sequels. These very rare collectibles include a $5,000 life-size Borg Queen. Check out the bargains at Ferengi Liquidations. ⊠*Las Vegas Hilton, 3000 Paradise Rd., Paradise Road* ☎*888/697–8735* ⊕*www.startrekexp.com.*

SPORTING GOODS & CLOTHING

Adidas Performance Center. The coolest Adidas technology is displayed in a minimalist design at this two-story store, one of only a handful of Performance Centers in the United States. There's everything that men and women would need for any sport, all touted on interactive screens and text tickers. The black matte store is set up into three areas: preparation, competition, and recuperation. For women, don't miss British designer Stella McCartney's signature line of dance-inspired sportswear, all in muted hues. And if you like old-school style, check out the Adidas Originals collection, which includes the Original Superstar

Zoom (based on a 1969 basketball shoe). ✉ *Showcase Mall, 3791 Las Vegas Blvd. S, South Strip* ☎ *702/262–1373.*

Nike Town. This multilevel Nike theme park features booming "Just Do It" videos and giant swoosh symbols amid the latest cool technology in athletic shoes displayed in glass cases. Flashy and crowded, it's full of salespeople yelling into two-way radios. On the second floor, the swoosh info desk has the scoop on local sporting events, bike races, and hiking spots. ✉ *Forum Shops at Caesars, 3500 Las Vegas Blvd. S, Center Strip* ☎ *702/650–8888.*

Saint Andrew's Golf Shop. In the Callaway Golf Center at the south end of the Strip, this shop is part of a 45-acre state-of-the-art practice, instruction, and learning center. There's a branch at the Forum Shops at Caesars. ✉ *Callaway Golf Center, 6730 Las Vegas Blvd. S, South Strip* ☎ *702/897–9500* ✉ *Forum Shops at Caesars, 3500 Las Vegas Blvd. S, Center Strip* ☎ *702/837–1234.*

TOYS & GAMES

Build-A-Bear Workshop. The store's motto is "Where Best Friends Are Made" . . . if your best friend is a soon-to-be stuffed animal. Choose a furry friend, take it to a stuffing machine (you work the pedals!), and pick out a cloth heart to put inside. An employee sews it up, and then it's off for an air bath and brushing. If you don't want your new best friend to go out into the world naked, you can dress it in tiny clothes, shoes, and accessories. Don't forget to fill out the stats for the birth certificate; all friends go home in their own cardboard house. ✉ *Miracle Mile at Planet Hollywood Resort & Casino, 3663 Las Vegas Blvd. S, Center Strip* ☎ *702/836–0899* ⊕ *www.buildabear.com.*

WESTERN SHOPS

Shepler's. Since 1946, thousands of cowboys (and cowgirls) have bought their Wranglers and Stetsons here. ✉ *4700 W. Sahara Ave., West Side* ☎ *702/258–2000* ✉ *5111 Boulder Hwy., East Side* ☎ *702/454–5266* ✉ *3025 E. Tropicana Ave., East Side* ☎ *702/898–3000* ⊕ *www.sheplers.com.*

Shows

6

Night club, Las Vegas

WORD OF MOUTH

"Check out the Mac King and Rick Thomas afternoon shows—they are excellent. For a splurge on what can't be seen anyplace else, I suggest O. Buy 'splash' seats if available; you will be close and you won't get wet."

—lovingheart

SHOWS PLANNER

Reserved-Seat Ticketing

Most hotels offer reserved-seat show tickets, either through a "closed" in-house ticketing system or through corporate networks such as Ticketmaster. It's advisable to purchase tickets to hotter shows, such as Danny Gans and the Cirque du Soleil productions, ahead of a visit. Remember these are casinos, so ticketing isn't as democratic as it might be with a concert coming to your town.

Casinos control their inventory and make sure their big players are always taken care of. If advance tickets are no longer available, don't give up on checking for last-minute availability. Your chances of getting a seat are usually better when you're staying—and gambling—at the hotel.

If you plan on spending a fair amount of time at the tables or slots, call VIP Services or a slot host and find out what their requirements are for getting a comp, tickets that have been withheld, or a line pass (it allows you to go straight to the VIP entrance without having to wait in line with the hoi polloi).

Cirque du Soleil's risqué *Zumanity* (New York-New York).

Find Out What's Going On

Information on shows, including their reservation and seating policies, prices, suitability for children (or age restrictions), and smoking restrictions, is available by calling or visiting box offices. It's also listed in several local publications.

The *Las Vegas Advisor* (✉ 3687 S. Procyon Ave., Las Vegas ☎ 800/244–2224 ⊕ www.lasvegasadvisor.com) is available at its office for $5 per issue or $50 per year (an online membership is $37); this monthly newsletter and Web site is a bargain-focused consumer's guide to Las Vegas dining, entertainment, gambling promotions, comps, and news.

The stories tend to be of the fawning press-release variety, but two free visitor publications are filled with show listings and discount coupons: *Today in Las Vegas* (⊕ www.todayinlv.com) and *What's On, the Las Vegas Guide* (⊕ www.ilovevegas.com) are available at hotels and gift shops.

The *Las Vegas Review-Journal,* the city's morning daily newspaper, publishes a pullout section each Friday called "Neon." It provides entertainment features and reviews, and showroom and lounge listings with complete time and price information. In the tourist corridor, the daily *Review-Journal* is wrapped inside a Daily Visitor's Guide that includes show listings. The newspaper also maintains a Web site (⊕ www.reviewjournal.com), where show listings are updated each week. The *Las Vegas Sun,* once a competing daily, is now a section inside the *Review-Journal* but maintains its own editorial staff and Web site, ⊕ www.lasvegassun.com.

Two alternative weekly newspapers are distributed at retail stores and coffee shops around town and maintain comprehensive Web sites. They usually offer more details on the nightclub scene and music outside the realm of the casinos: *Las Vegas Weekly* (⊕ www.lasvegasweekly.com) and *Las Vegas City Life* (⊕ www.lasvegascitylife.com).

The colorful *Les Folies Bergere* (Tropicana) is classic Vegas.

Raves & Faves

Splashiest opening: The beginning of *O*. A regal curtain reminiscent of a European opera house is whooshed away into the backstage recesses as though it were sucked into a giant vacuum cleaner.

Best finale: The climactic scene of *LOVE* just had to be "A Day in the Life." Cirque du Soleil rises to the challenge of the famous orchestral buildup with a symbolic, moving scene featuring an angelic, floating mother figure. (Remember that both John Lennon and Paul McCartney's mothers died young.)

Best band in town: The blue baldies in the Blue Man Group never talk, so it's even more important that their silent antics be backed by a rocking soundtrack. The seven-piece band keeps the sound percussive and otherworldly, with a Spaghetti-Western influence.

Most durable drag show: *An Evening at La Cage*. It celebrated its 20th anniversary in 2005 and is still as close to alternative culture as many visitors from more staid parts of the country are likely to get.

Most deliberately provocative: Cirque du Soleil's *Zumanity*. But there was much speculation about whether a man-to-man kiss would survive previews. It did, although now it's later in the show and placed in more of a comedic context.

Best guilty pleasure: You expect to find Elvis impersonators in Las Vegas, but why stop there? *American Superstars* also gives you impressions of *both* tarnished teen angels, Britney Spears and Christina Aguilera. Can Lindsay Lohan be far behind?

Contacts & Resources

Ticketmaster. Most of the showrooms and concert venues in town are part of Ticketmaster, so you can buy tickets for many shows at any Ticketmaster outlet or on the Web site. Most Smith's Food and Drug supermarkets (⊕www.smithsfoodanddrug.com) around town are outlets. ☎ 702/474–4000 ⊕ www.ticketmaster.com.

Travelocity/ShowTickets. com. This company sells tickets to most of the casino shows. If you visit the booths in person, it's important to know the producers pay commissions for each ticket sold, which may prejudice a ticket agent's enthusiasm about a particular show. The lesser shows sometimes offer the highest commissions. Box offices are all over town, including the airport. ☎ 800/838–9383 ⊕ www.showtickets.com.

Coca-Cola Tickets2Nite and Tix4tonight. These two operations sell last-minute, discount tickets. The booths add a service charge to each ticket, deal in walk-up sales only, and agree not to advertise what shows are available or release that information over the phone.

Coca-Cola Tickets2Nite is in the Showcase Mall; Tix4tonight is on the Strip in the Fashion Show Mall and the Hawaiian Marketplace shopping center and Downtown in the Four Queens casino. ☎ 888/484–9264 *for Tickets2Nite, 877/849–4868 for Tix4tonight.*

Updated
by Mike
Weatherford

THE VERY NAME "LAS VEGAS" has been synonymous with a certain style of showbiz ever since Jimmy Durante first headlined at Bugsy Siegel's Fabulous Flamingo Hotel in 1946 and *Minsky Goes to Paris* introduced topless showgirls at the Dunes in 1957. Through the years this entertainment mecca has redefined itself a number of times, but one thing has remained consistent—doing things big, with as much attention called to the doing as possible.

The star power that made the old "supper club" days glitter with names like Frank Sinatra and Dean Martin is making a latter-day comeback in showcases by veteran concert acts Elton John, Cher, and Barry Manilow. Nationally known performers such as Penn & Teller and Carrot Top have come to roost on the Strip alongside homegrown successes such as Lance Burton. *Jubilee!* remains a shimmering example of the "feather shows" that made an icon of the showgirl, while technologically advanced shows such as *Blue Man Group* and Cirque du Soleil's *O* have modernized the spectacle. Female impersonators, "dirty" dancers, comedians—all perpetuate the original style of razzle-dazzle entertainment that Las Vegas has popularized for the world.

In the not-so-old days, the shows were loss leaders, intended to draw patrons who would eventually wind up in the casino. The casinos would write fat checks to headliners and keep admission prices dirt-cheap for audiences. Nowadays, the accounting is separate and it will cost you at least $75 to see Tom Jones and as much as $250 (before taxes and service charges) for Bette Midler. Bargain-hunters have learned to look to afternoon shows, such as the comedic magic of Mac King at Harrah's, as ways to hold ticket prices around the $20 line.

You can still find a few of the old names, such as Don Rickles or Tony Bennett, along with a new generation of resident headliners, like impressionist Danny Gans, who keep the tradition alive. The big-production spectaculars also remain a Las Vegas trademark, presenting little or no language barrier to the city's large numbers of international tourists. The same is true for the burlesque-derived revues featuring topless showgirls, whose blatant charms can be appreciated in any language. But the latest trend does tilt back toward plain English: Broadway musicals, either cloned or shortened from the New York originals, represent a corporate approach to entertainment "branding," as well as a push for something new on the ever-restless Strip.

What's next? By the time you read this, there's a good chance that the collaboration between Cirque du Soleil and magician-daredevil Criss Angel will have opened at the Luxor. The Planet Hollywood Resort & Casino planned a new show from the creators of the off-Broadway hit *Stomp.* Cher and Bette Midler were the likely divas to follow Celine Dion in the Colosseum at Caesars Palace. The sheer number of shows runs counter to concerns that as Las Vegas becomes more diverse, ticketed productions are losing ground to nightclubs, restaurants, and shopping. Those distractions do weed out some of the lesser showroom efforts. And they motivate the big players to raise the spending limit for original efforts such as the $165 million *KÀ*. If Las Vegas has proven anything over the years, it's that the house can't be easily beaten.

SHOWS

AFTERNOON SHOWS

Las Vegas has become a wider-reaching and more family-friendly destination. But at the same time, evening show prices have broken into the triple digits. These factors are sometimes at odds with one another and help explain a few afternoon shows that hold their ticket prices to around $20 or discount heavily with promotional coupons. The following are the most proven and popular.

★ ☺ ***The Illusionary Magic of Rick Thomas.*** It's rare for an afternoon show to offer big production values, but Thomas generates repeat business by offering outsize illusions at bargain prices. Once dismissed as a poor man's Siegfried & Roy for his use of white tigers, Thomas's stage is now one of the few places where you can see such creatures in action. ⊠ *The Orleans Hotel and Casino, 4500 W. Tropicana Ave. S, West Side* ☎ *702/365–7075* 💳 *$33* ☉ *Tues.–Sat. 2 and 4.*

Fodor's Choice ★ ☺ ***Mac King.*** This comic magician keeps the payroll small; the only "exotic animal" is a goldfish that pops out of his mouth at an unexpected moment. King stands apart from the other magic shows on the Strip by offering a one-man hour of low-key, self-deprecating humor and the kind of close-up magic that is baffling but doesn't take the center of attention away from King's comic persona. ⊠ *Harrah's Las Vegas Casino & Hotel, 3475 Las Vegas Blvd. S, Center Strip* ☎ *702/369–5111* 💳 *$21.95* ☉ *Tues.–Sat. 1 and 3.*

Society of Seven featuring Lani Misalucha. This old-school variety act—think matching suits and spangly jackets—built a worldwide following in Hawaii, before tackling a bigger challenge in the mainland desert. The seven performers trade instruments to give each a moment of '70s variety-TV glory. Filipina singer Lani Misalucha joins in the comic impressions, and her powerful voice adds credibility to the group's penchant for sincere Broadway tributes. ⊠ *Flamingo Las Vegas Casino & Hotel, 3555 Las Vegas Blvd. S, Center Strip* ☎ *702/733–3333* 💳 *$54.95* ☉ *Wed.–Sun. 3.*

BURLESQUE SHOWS

Dewy-eyed nostalgists would say Las Vegas is embracing its past. Cynics might argue that because no casino has dared to risk its gaming license or female patronage on a gentlemen's club of the tipping or lap-dancing variety, the overnight revival of pasties-and-tassels burlesque is the next best way to titillate outside a ticketed showroom production. Either way you explain it, the new burlesque—seminude female dancers without the baggy-pants comedians—has blossomed into the latest twist on an already competitive nightclub scene.

Ivan Kane's Forty Deuce. Las Vegas's most dedicated effort to re-create the back-alley ambience of a '50s-era bump-and-grind joint is the Vegas counterpart to Kane's celeb-laden Hollywood club of the same name. All chatter stops when the stage behind the bar comes to life with a dance number several times a night. ⊠*Mandalay Bay Resort & Casino, 3950 Las Vegas Blvd. S, South Strip* ☎*702/632–9442.*

Pussycat Dolls Lounge. Choreographer Robin Antin has popularized "21st-century burlesque" with a troupe that's less retro and more Hollywood glam than the Forty Deuce girls. After the Dolls built their cult following at Johnny Depp's Viper Room in Hollywood, Caesars Palace rolled out the animal-print carpet for the Pussycat Dolls Lounge, an adjunct to its PURE nightclub. The original troupe of LA Dolls scored success on the pop charts after the club opened. The lounge takes a free-form cabaret approach: the gals can pop up for a song-and-dance number anytime, anywhere, since the club is cheekily outfitted with prop accessories such as a swing and a giant champagne glass as well as with a conventional stage. ⊠*Caesars Palace, 3570 Las Vegas Blvd. S, Center Strip* ☎*702/731–7873.*

Tangerine at TI. This is the least committed of all new burlesque spots. For most of the night the emphasis is on the outdoor views of the casino's pirate attraction, and the '60s modern look of the interior is more *The Jetsons* than back-alley burlesque club. But several times per night the action moves indoors: a live band honks out raucous New Orleans–style versions of Led Zeppelin tunes and the like, while bartenders step back for an anachronistic bar-top burlesque number. ⊠*Treasure Island Las Vegas, 3300 Las Vegas Blvd. S, Center Strip* ☎*702/894–7580.*

COMEDY CLUBS

Even when Las Vegas wasn't the hippest place to catch a musical act, it was always up to the minute in the comedy department. From Shecky Greene to Dane Cook, virtually every famous comedian has worked a Las Vegas showroom or lounge. Although the franchised comedy club boom of the 1980s went bust in most cities, the Strip still has dependable comedy clubs with multiple-act formats featuring top names on the circuit. Cover charges are in the $25 range, but two-for-one coupons are easy to come by in freebie magazines and various coupon packages.

Comedy Stop. There are two shows each night at this 400-seat club. Three comedians perform during each show. The price of admission includes one drink. ⊠*Tropicana Resort and Casino, 3801 Las Vegas Blvd. S, South Strip* ☎*702/739–2714* ⊘*Daily 8 PM and 10:30 PM.*

The Improv. Comedy impresario Budd Friedman oversees the bookings for this 300-seat showroom on the second floor of Harrah's. It's the most expensive of the stand-up clubs but often has the most recognizable headliners. The Improv is dark on Monday night, and drinks are not included in the admission price. ⊠*Harrah's Las Vegas Casino & Hotel, 3475 Las Vegas Blvd. S, Center Strip* ☎*702/369–5111* ⊘*Tues.–Sun. 8:30 PM and 10:30 PM.*

Riviera Comedy Club. Steve Schirripa was a doorman, then manager of this long-running comedy room before he found larger fame as Bobby "Bacala" Baccalieri on *The Sopranos*. He still has a hand in booking the talent. Two shows run each night of the week in the cozy, tightly packed

Classy? You Bet Your Pinky Ring

The 1996 movie *Swingers* is about the last time anyone even acknowledged this town's past glories as a kitsch capital that self-aware hipsters could mine for irony. The remake of the film *Ocean's Eleven* and the TV show *Las Vegas* both feed the current image of a nonstop party palace. But some shows still offer camp value for those seeking the unintended laugh.

The "Samson and Delilah" segment of *Jubilee!* plays like a Mel Brooks parody (oddly enough, *The Producers* opened right next door), and its soundtrack is space-age bachelor-pad heaven: "She's got the hots for a guy named Sam. He thinks the chick is wild!" ⊠ *Bally's Las Vegas, 3645 Las Vegas Blvd. S, Center Strip* ☎ *702/739–4567.*

Barry Manilow. It's fine, he's used to it. And if you want to pay as much

as $225 to goof on the hep dance-club remix of "Copacabana" that closes the show, he's probably good with that too. ⊠ *Las Vegas Hilton, 3000 Paradise Rd., Paradise Road* ☎ *702/732–5755.*

Legends in Concert has been known to slip a Prince tribute into the mix with Tim McGraw and Liberace, even before the real Prince started working Las Vegas. ⊠ *Imperial Palace Hotel and Casino, 3535 Las Vegas Blvd. S, Center Strip* ☎ *702/794–3261.*

Why let Elvis have all the rhinestones when *America's Neil Diamond Tribute* offers Jay White as an '80s-era Neil? ⊠ *Riviera Hotel and Casino, 2901 Las Vegas Blvd. S, North Strip* ☎ *702/794–9433.*

—Mike Weatherford

375-seat club. ⊠ *Riviera Hotel and Casino, 2901 Las Vegas Blvd. S, North Strip* ☎ 702/794–9433 ☉ *Daily 8:30* PM *and 10:30* PM.

EVENING REVUES

🕐 **American Superstars.** This upstart impersonator show made *Legends in Concert* pick up its energy level by challenging it with rollicking tributes to pop stars such as Britney Spears and Christina Aguilera. Both shows were improved by the competition. ⊠ *Stratosphere Casino Hotel and Tower, 2000 Las Vegas Blvd. S, North Strip* ☎ 702/380–7711 ☎ $41.75 ☉ *Sun.–Tues. 7* PM, *Wed., Fri., and Sat. 6:30* PM *and 8:30* PM.

Fodor's Choice ★ **Blue Man Group.** The men in blue celebrated their success on the Strip by moving from the Luxor to a new, customized theater at the Venetian in fall 2005. Although it's still essentially the same show, the 1,800-seat auditorium pulls more of the audience closer to the action; in fact, the stage design is part of the action. The first half of the program still defines the troupe's quirky comic aesthetic: three silent characters in utilitarian uniforms, their heads bald and gleaming from cobalt blue greasepaint, prowl the stage committing twisted "science projects" that are alternately highbrow and juvenile. The early antics deliberately leave much of the new stage in the dark, until it comes time to reveal

Broadway West

No one ever expected Chekhov on the Strip. But who could have predicted the fate of Broadway in Las Vegas would lie in the hands of David Hasselhoff and J. Peterman?

The arrival of five Broadway musicals within three years turned a lot of heads, causing much speculation that Las Vegas would become an important component in the economic cycle of a Broadway show—and give show goers on the Strip a break from all that Cirque du Soleil. But by early 2007, it was clear that if the two most recent gambles didn't make bank—a Hasselhoff-headlined edition of *The Producers* and *Monty Python's Spamalot* with John O'Hurley of *Seinfeld* fame—then Broadway would remain on Broadway for the foreseeable future.

The arrival of *Mamma Mia!* at Mandalay Bay had casino entertainment buyers thinking established Broadway hits might be an alternative to their own creatively bankrupt ideas for production shows. The musical's instant success reversed two longstanding presumptions: that alcohol and gambling wipe out a tourist's attention span for even the most minimal storytelling and that visitors are usually here for only a compressed visit and will therefore choose a uniquely Las Vegas production over a title that might visit their own city's performing arts center.

The Strip fought the latter by making some of the musicals as exclusive as the customized Cirque du Soleil shows. Casino developer Steve Wynn rattled the theater community when he outbid national tour companies for the rights to stage *Avenue Q* at Wynn Las Vegas. Paris Las Vegas became the only place in the United States to see the Queen catalog musical *We Will Rock You.*

Las Vegas toyed with Broadway as far back as the 1950s. Theodore Bikel first played Tevye in *Fiddler on the Roof* at Caesars Palace in 1968, and Tony Randall performed *The Odd Couple* there a year earlier, well before the eponymous ABC sitcom. Then as now, most productions were cut to 90-minute "tab" versions. A 1963 ad for *South Pacific* at the Thunderbird announced "more comedy scenes added during the last month," as though the original production was a restaurant menu for songs and scenes to be chosen à la carte.

For much of the '70s through the '90s, however, a good share of high-end casino players spoke languages other than English. Casino-staged "theater" was limited to slamming-door farces such as *Natalie Needs a Nightie,* often starring over-the-hill sitcom stars such as Bob "Gilligan" Denver.

Then the floodgates opened, with results open to interpretation. *We Will Rock You,* which hasn't officially played on Broadway, did fair business, but didn't survive the corporate takeover of Paris Las Vegas by Harrah's Entertainment. *Avenue Q* operated in the black, but didn't fill a theater that was arguably too big for it. Only *Phantom: The Las Vegas Spectacular* was able to declare itself a success, but even it had trouble filling 10 shows per week. But casinos were bound to be patient with Hasselhoff and O'Hurley. No one yet knows the answer to the question, "If they don't work, what will?"

—Mike Weatherford

gorgeous high-resolution video effects and the towering set with lighting designs by Pink Floyd tour collaborator Marc Brickman. And it's all scored to a live rock band with percussion instruments made from PVC pipe. ⊠ *Venetian Resort-Hotel-Casino, 3355 Las Vegas Blvd. S, Center Strip* ☎ *702/414–7469* ⊕ *www.blueman.com* 💳 *$76–$126* ⊙ *Daily 7:30* PM, *Tues. and Sat. also 10:30* PM.

Chippendales: The Show. The Rio evened the score in a historically sexist town by building a theater dedicated to the men of Chippendales and surrounding it with a lounge and gift shop. That allows the show to have fancier staging than any G-string revue that travels on the nightclub circuit, but the bow-tied hunks have to work harder not to be upstaged by the fancy video panels and MTV-style choreography. ⊠ *Rio All-Suite Hotel & Casino, 3700 W. Flamingo Rd., West Side* ☎ *702/777–7776* 💳 *$47–$58* ⊙ *Thurs.–Tues. 8:30* PM, *Fri. and Sat. 8:30* PM *and 10:30* PM.

Crazy Girls. The Riviera staged this low-rent version of the Crazy Horse Cabaret in Paris long before the real Crazy Horse opened *La Femme* at the MGM Grand Hotel. This topless revue is considerably less demure than the French show, but the producer invested in a new production to freshen the show up in time for its 20th anniversary in October 2007; a move that was luckily timed with the closing of some competitors. ⊠ *Riviera Hotel and Casino, 2901 Las Vegas Blvd. S, North Strip* ☎ *702/794–9433* 💳 *$45–$73* ⊙ *Wed.–Mon. 9:30* PM.

Crazy Horse Paris. The MGM Grand wooed Paris's Crazy Horse Cabaret to Las Vegas by offering to remodel a lounge into a near–spitting image of the French institution. Thanks to a topless club that borrowed its name and knockoff shows such as *Crazy Girls*, the original girlie show went by the title "La Femme" for its first few years on the Strip before reclaiming its original name in early 2007. It remains a classy affair in which les femmes are symmetrically matched, naturally endowed women expertly choreographed and "painted in light" for a succession of humorous or erotically mimed vignettes. ⊠ *MGM Grand Hotel and Casino, 3799 Las Vegas Blvd. S, South Strip* ☎ *702/891– 7777* 💳 *$59* ⊙ *Wed.–Mon. 8* PM *and 10:30* PM.

Criss Angel. The star of TV's *Mindfreak* and Cirque du Soleil promise to reinvent the Las Vegas magic show with their new collaboration scheduled to arrive this summer ('08). Angel promises the show will play out like "a dream where anything is possible," with help from collaborators such as puppet designer Michael Curry (Broadway's *The Lion King*) and Eiko Ishioka, the costume designer on Francis Ford Coppola's *Bram Stoker's Dracula*. ⊠ *Luxor Resort & Casino, 3900 Las Vegas Blvd. S, South Strip* ☎ *702/262–4000*.

An Evening at La Cage. This durable female-impersonator show has been guided since 1985 by Frank Marino, whose campy take on Joan Rivers provides the live voice to introduce lip-synch musical tributes, including the likes of Jennifer Lopez, Cher, and Reba McEntire. As old as the show is, its mainstream variety approach still speaks to the understanding that it's the first, and perhaps only, drag show most conservative visitors are likely to see. ⊠ *Riviera Hotel and Casino, 2901 Las Vegas Blvd. S, North Strip* ☎ *702/794–9433* 💳 *$68–$78* ⊙ *Wed.–Mon. 7:30* PM.

Fantasy. The tamest of the midsize topless shows shortened its title from "Midnight Fantasy" and tightened up its approach by hiring music-video and concert choreographer (and former Mr. J-Lo) Cris Judd to give it an edgy new look, freshen the music, and eliminate silly recorded transitions. The new version cut a stand-up comedy spot yet still managed to preserve the show's appeal to the mainstream couples that make up the bulk of the audience. ⌧ *Luxor Resort & Casino, 3900 Las Vegas Blvd. S, South Strip* ☎ *702/262–4900* ☞ *$52–$63* ☉ *Tues. 8 PM and 10:30 PM; Sat. 11 PM; Fri., Sun., Mon., Wed. 10:30 PM.*

Jubilee! This is the last place to experience the over-the-top vision of Vegas showman Donn Arden, who produced shows on the Strip from 1952 to 1994. A cast of 80 or more performs in a theater with 1,100 seats, but the show is stolen by the gargantuan sets and props, such as the sinking of the *Titanic* and Samson destroying the temple. It's still the best vehicle for showgirls parading about in the largest spectacle of feathers and bare breasts, even if attempts to freshen some of the segments middle out between retro nostalgia and a modern reinvention of the form. Baz Luhrmann, where are you? ⌧ *Bally's Las Vegas, 3645 Las Vegas Blvd. S, Center Strip* ☎ *702/967–4567* ☞ *$65–$82* ☉ *Mon. and Tues. 7:30 PM; Sat., Sun., Wed., and Thurs. 7:30 PM and 10:30 PM.*

FodorśChoice ★ ***KÀ.*** For its fourth show on the Strip, Cirque du Soleil knew it had to swing for the fences to keep from lapsing into repetition. *KÀ* is the company's bold step into linear storytelling, an attempt to unfurl a live version of such martial-arts period fantasies as *Crouching Tiger, Hidden Dragon*. Canadian director Robert Lepage, best known in the United States for directing two Peter Gabriel tours, brings his opera–meets–music video sensibility to the adventures of two separated twins. Most show goers confess to being confused by the story, which is told without dialogue, but are blown away by the state-of-the-art stagecraft. The spectacle includes huge puppets and live-time video that responds to the movement of the performers. Even the notion of a fixed stage is replaced by an 80,000-pound deck that's maneuvered by a giant gantry arm into all sorts of positions, including vertical. Even if the show lacks an emotional knockout punch, it's still an amazing achievement. ⌧ *MGM Grand Hotel and Casino, 3805 Las Vegas Blvd. S, South Strip* ☎ *702/891–7777* ☞ *$76–$165* ☉ *Tues.–Sat. 6:30 PM and 9:30 PM.*

☾ ***Lance Burton: Master Magician.*** When Roy Horn's tiger bite suddenly put Siegfried & Roy out of business in 2003, the reigning kings of magic became David Copperfield and Burton, a nice guy from Kentucky who worked his way up the ranks from specialty act to star. Although Copperfield performs about half his annual schedule away from the Strip, Burton is a year-round attraction in an opulent 1,200-seat Victorian theater that makes a splendid long-term home. He's a charmer with the ladies and works youngsters into the show like no other act on the Strip. Unfortunately, the small magic—the sleight of hand and close-up tricks that earned him the prestigious Gold Medal from the International Brotherhood of Magicians—is lost from way up in the balcony. ⌧ *Monte Carlo Resort and Casino, 3770 Las Vegas Blvd. S, South Strip* ☎ *702/730–7160* ☞ *$66–$73* ☉ *Tues. and Sat. 7 PM and 10 PM, Wed.–Fri. 7 PM.*

Le Rêve. Though the fate of Franco Dragone's third Cirque du Soleil–style show was in limbo for a while, its purchase by casino developer Steve Wynn has given the dreamlike show new life. The newly configured aquatic theater in-the-round allows for seats to be no more than 12 rows from the stage—make sure to ask when purchasing tickets if you are seated in the "splash zone." The show features live music, elaborate special effects, and aerial acrobatics. ⊠ *Wynn Las Vegas, 3131 Las Vegas Blvd. S, North Strip* ☎ *702/770–9966* ✉ *$99–$159* ☉ *Sun.–Mon., and Thurs. 7* PM *and 9:30* PM; *Fri. 8:30* PM; *Sat. 8* PM *and 10:30* PM.

☙ **Legends in Concert.** The durable *Legends* rotates impersonations of Madonna, Liberace, Tom Jones, and others, with the Elvis Presley finale the only invariable rule. This show launched an unfortunate slew of copycats but maintains its own quality. There's no lip-synching and always a band. ⊠ *Imperial Palace Hotel and Casino, 3535 Las Vegas Blvd. S, Center Strip* ☎ *702/794–3261* ✉ *$50–$60* ☉ *Mon.–Sat. 7:30* PM *and 10* PM.

Les Folies Bergere. This piece of Vegas history has been running since 1959, but its future is uncertain. New Tropicana owner Columbia Sussex Corp. hasn't declared whether it will close the old Tiffany showroom, build around it, or move it to the new location in a two-year redevelopment of the property. What is certain though is that this revue is living history. The painted flats and dance segments show their age compared to their newer, high-tech counterparts, but the hotel preserves the show with some degree of pride. It would, perhaps, benefit from a cheekier attitude. But there's an argument for playing it straight, now that the Strip has only two classic revues complete with singers, dancers, a juggler, and, of course, showgirls in feathers. Selected early performances keep the showgirl bras on, making the revue fine for older children. ⊠ *Tropicana Resort and Casino, 3801 Las Vegas Blvd. S, South Strip* ☎ *702/739–2411* ✉ *$68–$79* ☉ *Mon., Wed., Thurs., and Sat. 7:30* PM *and 10* PM; *Tues. and Fri. 8:30* PM.

Love. Meet the Beatles again, well sort of, at this instant smash that does turnaway business and shows Cirque du Soleil isn't losing any steam in Las Vegas. Surviving members of the Beatles or their families agreed to license the group's music to Cirque du Soleil for its fifth Las Vegas production. Even if you watch the show with your eyes closed, the remixed music by producer George Martin and his son Giles is revelatory in the state-of-the-art theater, often like hearing the songs for the first time. The visuals are more of a challenge. Cirque has a tougher time coming up with something novel here, thanks to audience familiarity with the company's brand of exotically costumed acrobatics. Sometimes one's attention is split between the aerial stunt work and the more theatrical action on the ground. On the balance, director Dominic Champagne does an admirable job of blending a metaphoric band biography with a Cirque-surreal Liverpool inhabited by famous characters based on the songs. ⊠ *Mirage Hotel and Casino, 3400 Las Vegas Blvd. S, Center Strip* ☎ *702/791–7111* ✉ *$76–$165* ☉ *Thurs.–Mon. 7:30* PM *and 10* PM.

They're Here, They're Queer

CLOSE UP

The closeted gay Republican puppet in *Avenue Q* proved to be, as one of the songs in the short-lived show said, "Only For Now." But several other shows have challenged the Strip's longstanding bias toward topless girlie shows aimed at hard-drinking, dice-throwing manly men.

The durable drag show *An Evening at La Cage* is still as close to alternative culture as many a Mid-Westerner is likely to get. ⊠ *2901 Las Vegas Blvd. S, North Strip* ☎702/794–9433 ☐*$68–$78* ☼*Wed.–Mon. 7:30* PM.

The Fashionistas is a kinky, daringly original dance revue created by porn mogul John Stagliano from his four-hour hardcore video of the same name. The young ingénue is romantically entangled with both a male fashion designer and her female boss. The "fetish fashion" theme puts male dancers in fishnets and codpieces you aren't likely to see at Chippendale's. ⊠ *Empire Ballroom, 3765 Las Vegas Blvd. S, South Strip* ☎702/737–7375.

A lot of things are deliberately provocative in Cirque du Soleil's *Zumanity*, including the much talked about man-to-man kiss. ⊠ *New York–New York Hotel and Casino, 3790 Las Vegas Blvd. S, South Strip* ☎702/740–6815.

—Mike Weatherford

★ *Mamma Mia!* Introduced to the Strip in 2003, this musical phenomenon has announced it will close in late summer of 2008—most likely to make way for another Cirque du Soleil. The Las Vegas edition is presented full length, with an intermission, as it is on Broadway and in other cities. The '70s pop hits of ABBA are woven into a traditional musical comedy about a bride-to-be who uses her wedding to deduce which of her mother's past suitors is her father. The soapy sitcom plot attracts a largely female audience. ⊠ *Mandalay Bay Resort & Casino, 3950 Las Vegas Blvd. S, South Strip* ☎702/632–7580 ☐*$50–$110* ☼*Sun.–Thurs. 7* PM, *Fri. 8* PM, *Sat. 6* PM *and 10* PM.

★ *Menopause The Musical!* The Las Vegas Hilton took a risk when it booked a title that seemed the antithesis of casino entertainment: a niche musical aimed at older women who have experienced "the change." Yet the producers hit pay dirt, quickly expanding to 10 shows per week, half of them in the afternoons. It's basically a cabaret revue of song parodies running down a checklist of menopause symptoms. "We're having a heat wave," for example, becomes "I'm having a hot flash." But it's well performed by a quartet of archetypal women—who commiserate during a daylong shopping spree—and a perfect fit for the cozy Shimmer Cabaret. ⊠ *Las Vegas Hilton, 3000 Paradise Rd., Paradise Road* ☎702/732–5755 ☐*$59.45* ☼*Tues.–Fri. 7* PM, *Wed. and Thurs. 2* PM, *Sat. 4* PM, *Sun. 2* PM *and 5* PM.

Monty Python's Spamalot. *Avenue Q* struck out, but the theater was remodeled to give Broadway another shot on the Strip. Held in the aptly named Grail Theater, Eric Idle's willfully silly King Arthur spoof, derived from the cult movie *Monty Python and the Holy Grail,* is shortened from the Broadway original but staged in a thematically decorated environment complete with new precurtain antics. John O'Hurley of

Seinfeld and *Dancing with the Stars* fame opened the show as its first King Arthur. ⊠ *Wynn Las Vegas, 3131 Las Vegas Blvd. S, Center Strip* ☎702/770–9966 💻$49–$99 ⊙ *Mon., Wed., and Sun.* 8 PM; *Tues., Fri., and Sat.* 7 PM *and* 10 PM.

★ **Mystère.** Since Cirque du Soleil's new-age circus opened in 1993, it has ☺ never lost its spot as the town's top family show. *Mystère* most purely preserves the original Cirque concept, and has retained an audience amid four other sister shows by keeping the spectators close to the action and the human achievements in the spotlight. Perhaps more than at the other Cirques, you're intimately involved with this surreal wonderland. The music is rousing and haunting, and the acrobatics are thrilling. ⊠ *Treasure Island Las Vegas, 3300 Las Vegas Blvd. S, Center Strip* ☎702/894–7722 💻$66–$104 ⊙ *Wed.–Sat.* 7:30 PM *and* 10:30 PM, *Sun.* 4:30 PM *and* 7:30 PM.

Fodor's Choice **O.** More than $70 million was spent on Cirque du Soleil's theater at ★ Bellagio and the liquid stage that takes over as the real star of the show. The title is taken from the French word for water (*eau*), and water is everywhere—1.5 million gallons of it, 12 million pounds of it, contained by a "stage" that, thanks to hydraulic lifts, can change shape and turn into dry land in no time. The intense and nonstop action by the show's acrobats, aerial gymnasts, trapeze artists, synchronized swimmers, divers, and contortionists takes place above, within, and even on the surface of the water, making for a stylish spectacle that manages to have a vague theme about the wellspring of theater and imagination. Even if the deeper themes elude you, so much is going on that you may be exhausted from trying to see everything. ⊠ *Bellagio Las Vegas, 3600 Las Vegas Blvd. S, Center Strip* ☎702/693–7722 💻$102.85–$165 ⊙ *Wed.–Sun.* 7:30 PM *and* 10:30 PM.

Phantom: The Las Vegas Spectacular. This relaunch of *The Phantom of the Opera* is set in a customized "opera house" designed by popular architect David Rockwell. The audience is engulfed in period atmosphere including costumed mannequins, a chandelier that dwarfs the Broadway original, and a couple of Phantom surprises. Original Broadway director Hal Prince returned to supervise a top-notch cast and shorten the Andrew Lloyd Webber hit to 95 minutes, not much longer than the Lon Chaney silent movie that popularized the tale of the deranged "opera ghost" who coaches a young soprano. The trims are so precise that you'd have to be a "Phantom" groupie to know what's missing. Even if you are, you'll still want to see this production for the new twists. ⊠ *Venetian Resort-Hotel-Casino, 3355 Las Vegas Blvd. S, Center Strip* ☎702/414–7469 💻$82–$157 ⊙ *Thurs.* 7 PM, *Fri.–Mon.* 7 PM *and* 10 PM.

★ **The Producers.** Another Broadway condensation arrived in early 2007, ☺ with Mel Brooks personally overseeing trims to the 90-minute version of the hit musical adapted from his 1968 movie. Brooks recruited Brad Oscar, who followed Nathan Lane on Broadway in the lead role of Max Bialystock and stuck with it longer. The celebrity "stunt casting" went to a supporting role: David Hasselhoff opened the show as the flamboyant director recruited to oversee a sure-fire flop called *Springtime for Hitler,* which will allow the shifty producers to keep their investors' money. ⊠*Paris Las Vegas, 3655 Las Vegas Blvd. S, South Strip* ☎702/632–7580 ⚏*$50–$110* ☉*Sun.–Thurs. 7* PM, *Fri. 8* PM, *Sat. 6* PM *and 10* PM.

★ **The Second City.** Shoehorning itself onto a Strip filled with stand-up comedy clubs, Chicago's ensemble comedy institution is a breath of fresh air. It has the class and polish of a theatrical revue but isn't afraid to go for the cheap or lowbrow when there's a good laugh to be had. Five performers pull audience members into improvisational games that fall amid the type of rehearsed sketches popularized by *Saturday Night Live.* ⊠*Flamingo Las Vegas, 3555 Las Vegas Blvd. S, Center Strip* ☎702/733–3333 ⚏*$44* ☉*Tues., Wed., and Fri. 8* PM, *Thurs., Sat., and Sun. 8* PM *and 10:30* PM.

☺ **Stomp Out Loud.** This new show from Luke Creswell and Steve McNicholas, creators of the off-Broadway hit *Stomp,* features twice as many cast members as the original and has new sequences, choreography, and sets. And yup, still no talking. ⊠*Planet Hollywood Resort & Casino, 3667 Las Vegas Blvd. S, South Strip* ☎702/785–5000 ⚏*$50–$110* ☉*Mon. 6* PM *and 9* PM; *Tues., Thurs., Fri., and Sun. 7* PM; *Sat. 7* PM *and 10* PM.

☺ **Tournament of Kings.** One of the last vestiges of Las Vegas's "family" phase is this Arthurian stunt show in a dirt-floor arena, with the audience eating a basic dinner (warning: no utensils) and cheering on fast horses, jousting, and swordplay. It's still a great family gathering—especially for preadolescents, who get to make a lot of noise—and the realistic stunts speak to the commitment of the cast. However, corporate indecision about the show's future has kept it in limbo when it could use an overall sprucing up. ⊠*Excalibur Hotel and Casino, 3850 Las Vegas Blvd. S, South Strip* ☎702/597–7600 ⚏*$58* ☉*Wed.–Mon. 6* PM *and 8:30* PM.

Zumanity. For its third Las Vegas production, Cirque du Soleil deliberately turned away from the family market to indulge in an erotic, near-naked exploration of sexuality. The end product also followed the lead of Baz Luhrmann's movie *Moulin Rouge* by fusing Cirque acrobatics with European cabaret and English music-hall tradition. After a rocky debut, new artistic directors continued to tweak the choreography and connecting material. It seems *Zumanity* has finally hit the right balance of comedy, omnisexual titillation, and the familiar Cirque brand of acrobatics. ⊠*New York–New York Hotel and Casino, 3790 Las Vegas Blvd. S, South Strip* ☎702/740–6815 ⚏*$76–$142* ☉*Wed.–Sun. 7:30* PM *and 10:30* PM.

SHOWROOMS

RESIDENT HEADLINERS

The turn of the 21st century took Las Vegas back to one of the traditions from its past. The success of impressionist Danny Gans—not to mention the hassles of modern air travel—opened the doors to a wave of resident headliners, those who live in Las Vegas and perform on a year-round schedule comparable to the revues (as opposed to visiting

SAVE OR SPLURGE

Whether you're rollin' high or down on your luck, Vegas has a show for you. Check out the following steals and splurges:

SAVE

Mac King. The comedy magic of Mac King is worth every penny of the full $21.95 ticket price, and full-price tickets send you to the front of the line. But if you look for coupon-dispensing showgirls within the casino or check a promotions booth at the Carnaval Court lounge, you can often get in for the price of a $9.95 drink.

Fremont Street Experience. Thought the downtown Fremont Street Experience was limited to video shows on the overhead canopy covering Glitter Gulch? Not so. Every weekend live performers play free gigs on two stages; one weekend a month the acts have name recognition (past performers include early rocker Chubby Checker, country vet Pam Tillis, and classic rockers Kansas). Stages are on 1st and 3rd streets. ☎ 800/249–3559.

Discount tickets. You can get two-for-one tickets for most second-tier productions—and every so often, for some of the top-shelf fare as well—after 1 PM at Coca-Cola Tickets2Nite (in the Showcase Mall) and Tix4tonight (in the Fashion Show Mall and Hawaiian Marketplace). You have to purchase tickets in person on the day of the performance.

The Sahara's Casbar Lounge. This spot tries to live up to its famous name by offering better-than-average lounge acts—the kind who go out of their way to put on a show, including Louis Prima's daughter Lena. Better still, there's no cover and usually no drink minimum.

SPLURGE

Elton John. Ticket prices to this show can just get plain crazy, topping out at $281 for front-and-center. But *The Red Piano* is a Las Vegas exclusive, and the mesmerizing video by fashion photographer David LaChapelle that accompanies the show reenergizes the aging pop legend's performance.

KÀ. Cirque du Soleil pulled out all the stops for this operatic epic. The hard-to-follow sketch of a story is a bit easier to understand in the $150 seats, where you can see facial expressions. The $99 seats are a good bet for the bigger effects.

Love. A Beatles fan—and there are said to be a few still out there—will be in orbit over the soundtrack alone, reengineered to pump from 6,500 speakers. If that's not worth $165, the visuals carry some punch of their own.

O. Cirque's big water show has been around since 1998, but you won't ever see it go on tour. Pony up the $165 and save on your water bill when you get home.

—Mike Weatherford

headliners such as David Copperfield, Elton John, or Tom Jones, who stay anywhere from two nights to two weeks).

Rita Rudner, George Wallace, and Carrot Top all bet that audiences were ready to embrace the down-front performing tradition (not letting anything get between the performer and the audience) that put Las Vegas on the map.

★ **The Amazing Johnathan (Sahara).** The crackpot comedian and almost-magician offers the most profane and twisted comedy show to be consistently found on the Strip. The bellicose and belligerent Johnathan isn't afraid to draw a little (fake) blood as he tortures both his ding-bat stage assistant and a hapless audience volunteer who never fails to spend an inordinate amount of time onstage. ⊠ *Sahara Hotel and Casino, 2535 Las Vegas Blvd. S, North Strip* ☎ *702/737–2111* ⊡ *$54–$64* ⊙ *Fri.–Wed. 10* PM.

Barry Manilow (Las Vegas Hilton). The king of '70s piano pop isn't in residence quite as often as others on this list. But Manilow performs nowhere else in the country, making the casino feel like it hit the jackpot when his latest CD briefly hit the top of the charts in 2006. Love him or hate him, the Las Vegas showcase won't make you change your mind about him. The veteran showman structures the evening as a tribute to Las Vegas entertainers, and it feels right at home, like something that already could have been there—and very well may remain—for a long, long time. ⊠ *Las Vegas Hilton, 3555 Las Vegas Blvd. S, Center Strip* ☎ *702/732–5755* ⊡ *$110–$253* ⊙ *Weekdays 9* PM, *Sat. 7:30* PM *and 10:30* PM.

Carrot Top (Luxor). After years on the college circuit, the prop comic moved his trunks full of tricks into the Luxor, where a lot of people are discovering he is funnier than they thought he would be. The Florida native known offstage as Scott Thompson still is most unique when wielding his visual gags, but he sells them with an unrelenting manic energy and a whole running commentary on the act itself, perhaps a sly nod to his eternal lack of respect. ⊠ *Luxor Resort & Casino, 3900 Las Vegas Blvd. S, South Strip* ☎ *702/262–4900* ⊡ *$58-$69* ⊙ *Sun., Mon., and Wed.–Fri. 8* PM; *Sat. 7* PM *and 9* PM.

★ **Danny Gans (Mirage).** The impressionist (and former baseball player) pulled off a near miracle in Las Vegas, coming in from the trade-show-and-convention circuit as a no-name to become one of the hottest tickets in town. This talented impressionist leaves 'em laughing every night, after performing upward of 60 characters—everyone from Jimmy Stewart singing with Kermit the Frog to Nat and Natalie Cole's "Unforgettable" duet. With a show that plays more like a one-man theatrical revue than a nightclub act, Gans lacks spontaneity but pushes emotional buttons. ⊠ *Mirage Hotel and Casino, 3400 Las Vegas Blvd. S, Center Strip* ☎ *702/791–7111* ⊡ *$100* ⊙ *Tues., Wed., Fri., and Sat. 8* PM.

Gordie Brown (Venetian). The success of Danny Gans encouraged a big investment in another singing impressionist, who received a custom theater at the Venetian in fall 2006. Brown is looser and funnier than Gans, if not as dead-on with the impressions. His is more of a MAD-magazine approach to song parody and celebrity spoofery. ✉*3355 Las Vegas Blvd. S, Center Strip* ☎*702/414–7469* 🎫*$69–$79* 🕐*Thurs.–Tues. 7:30* PM.

★ **Penn & Teller (Rio).** After years of doing at least a third of their shows in Las Vegas, eccentric comic magicians Penn & Teller finally moved into a gorgeous 1,500-seat auditorium with opulent chandeliers and original artwork in the lobby. Penn's verbal overkill and the duo's flair for the grotesque make them an acquired taste, but what once was a fringe act has become almost mainstream. Their magic is unusual and genuinely baffling, and their comedy provocative and thoughtful, albeit blasphemous. ✉*Rio All-Suite Hotel & Casino, 3700 W. Flamingo Rd., West Side* ☎*702/777–7776* 🎫*$74–$97* 🕐*Wed.–Mon. 9* PM.

★ **Rita Rudner (Harrah's Las Vegas).** It's rare to be a female comedian in Las Vegas and rarer still to offer a "clean" act that's still insightful in its look at domestic life and female obsessions. The genteel, soft-spoken Rudner chooses not to fuel a battle of the sexes so much as poke fun at both sides and help them understand each other. ✉*Harrah's Las Vegas Casino & Hotel, 3475 Las Vegas Blvd. S, Center Strip* ☎*702/369–5111* 🎫*$62* 🕐*Mon.–Sat. 8* PM.

The Scintas (Sahara). The Buffalo, New York, quartet of three siblings and a drummer combine a warm family charm with an old-Vegas Rat Pack vibe. Their routines hearken back to the era of the "show band," where every member had double-threat comic and musical duties. The Scintas lay on the shtick and schmaltz pretty thick but have a loyal, mostly older fan base for an act that can perhaps be described as Wayne Newton meets the Smothers Brothers. ✉*Sahara Hotel and Casino, 2536 Las Vegas Blvd. S, North Strip* ☎*702/737–2111* 🎫*$39–$81* 🕐*Sat.–Thurs. 7* PM.

Toni Braxton (Flamingo). The '90s pop diva was sidelined for a few years by child-rearing and record label woes. But a Flamingo residency fit her family schedule and the comeback showcase *Toni Braxton: Revealed* finds Braxton's sex appeal and charm still intact, even if her voice seems to have lost some of the range and clarity of the recorded hits. After a rocky launch in the summer of 2006, the show has hit its groove and has settled into a comfortable reaquaintance with fans. ✉*Flamingo Las Vegas, 3555 Las Vegas Blvd. S, Center Strip* ☎*702/733–3333* 🎫*$82–$126* 🕐*Tues.–Sat. 7:30* PM.

HEADLINERS SHOWROOMS

Hilton Theater. Once famous as the home base for Elvis Presley, this 1,600-capacity showroom with a balcony has since been converted to theater seating and decked out for Barry Manilow's show for half the year. The remaining dates see everyone from Damon Wayans to Reba McEntire. ✉*Las Vegas Hilton, 3000 Paradise Rd., Paradise Road* ☎*702/732–5755.*

Hollywood Theatre. Tom Jones, David Copperfield, and Chicago are among those who make regular visits to this contemporary update of the classic showroom at the MGM Grand, which eliminated the long tables to improve sight lines but kept the booths. It's about the only part of the hotel that hasn't been remodeled, which casts doubts on its future. ⊠*MGM Grand Hotel and Casino, 3799 Las Vegas Blvd. S, South Strip* ☎*702/891–7777.*

Orleans Showroom. A super-wide stage (designed to lure TV production) highlights this 800-seat room slightly west of the Strip at the Orleans, which has proven popular with both locals and visitors. Frequent headliners include Neil Sedaka, Steven Wright, and Debbie Reynolds. ⊠*The Orleans Hotel and Casino, 4500 W. Tropicana Ave., West Side* ☎*702/365–7075.*

The Showroom at the Golden Nugget. The Golden Nugget remodeled its upstairs cabaret in 2006, turning it into a comfortable movie theater–style layout with roomy seats that expanded its capacity from 400 to 600. That left the theater ready for weekend headliners such as Don Rickles and/or a standing show, both of which were still being tested by the Nugget's new ownership in 2007. ⊠*Golden Nugget Hotel and Casino, 129 Fremont St., Downtown* ☎*702/386–8100.*

Suncoast Showroom. The Suncoast is a locals-oriented casino that is a 15 mi or so drive off the beaten path west of the tourist corridor, in the Summerlin suburb. A handsome 450-seat showroom with a classic old-Vegas feel was a risk that paid off, drawing strong local support for acts ranging from Tower of Power to Roger Williams. ⊠*Suncoast Hotel and Casino, 9090 Alta Dr., Northwest Las Vegas* ☎*702/365–7075.*

VENUES

In addition to the hotel showrooms and theaters, Las Vegas has four large multipurpose arenas for both concerts and sports, and several smaller performance venues. Check the performance schedules of the following venues to catch a great show.

Colosseum at Caesars Palace. The $95 million theater was built in 2002, mainly to house more than 150 annual performances of Celine Dion's *A New Day.* Elton John later signed on to visit in two-week stretches, a more realistic formula for most entertainers than Dion's commitment of 150-plus shows a year. The Canadian diva stepped down at the end of 2007, and Bette Midler joined the rotation in 2008. The two balconies can seem distant from the ridiculously wide 120-foot stage, but a huge video screen improves the views and the sound system is impeccable. ⊠*Caesars Palace, 3750 Las Vegas Blvd. S, Center Strip* ☎*877/427–7243.*

House of Blues at Mandalay Bay. Night in and night out, the Las Vegas branch of this chain is the busiest music venue in town, offering concerts and themed club events. As with other branches, rustic folk art covers the walls. This one is unusual, however, in having a balcony level with reserved theater seating along with the general-admission floor. ⊠*3950 Las Vegas Blvd. S, South Strip* ☎*702/632–7600.*

The Joint. This 2,000-capacity concert hall more often than not strips out all the seating for general-admission shows. It sometimes books acts that would normally play much bigger rooms—everyone from the Rolling Stones to Nine Inch Nails—just for the publicity value. (Something it will need with the opening of the Pearl at the Palms as a new rival.) For the time being, young (or young-at-heart) music fans who don't mind jostling for views of the stage will have to put up with its flaws: getting to the restrooms can be an ordeal, and the sound system is just adequate. ⊠*Hard Rock Hotel and Casino, 4466 Paradise Rd., University District* ☎888/464–2468.

Mandalay Bay Events Center. A corporate merger made this slightly smaller arena a companion rather than a competitor to the MGM Grand Garden. Each summer, **Mandalay Beach** offers weekly general-admission concerts in the hotel's lushly landscaped pool and beach area. ⊠*Mandalay Bay Resort & Casino, 3950 Las Vegas Blvd. S, South Strip* ☎702/632–7580.

MGM Grand Garden. The biggest concert names, including Madonna and the Rolling Stones, tend to headline here. The monorail stops nearby, making it easy to access without having to deal with the massive parking garage. ⊠*MGM Grand Hotel and Casino, 3799 Las Vegas Blvd. S, South Strip* ☎702/891–7777.

Orleans Arena. The Orleans Arena opened strong by luring *Disney on Ice* and the Ringling Bros. and Barnum & Bailey Circus away from the Thomas and Mack Center. The casino also signed a professional hockey team, the Las Vegas Wranglers, as the anchor tenant, but is at least third in line for concert acts. ⊠*4500 W. Tropicana Ave., West Las Vegas* ☎702/284–7777.

The Pearl. The Palms set out to make its 2,500-capacity music hall better than both The Joint at the Hard Rock and the House of Blues at Mandalay Bay: better sightlines, luxury boxes for high rollers, and a stage big enough for big tours to squeeze in their arena staging. It has a flat floor for general admission and two decks of reserved seating. ⊠*The Palms, 4321 W. Flamingo Rd., West Las Vegas* ☎702/942–7777.

Planet Hollywood Theatre for the Performing Arts. Since Las Vegas is just now building its own municipal theater, this theater often hosts touring companies for Broadway musicals such as *Les Misèrables* along with an array of concert acts. The 7,000-seat concert hall was the only part of the original Aladdin to survive the "implosion" of the resort. ⊠*Planet Hollywood Resort & Casino, 3667 Las Vegas Blvd. S, South Strip* ☎702/785–5000.

Sam's Town Live! This smartly designed concert and convention hall has retractable seating, but is unfortunately underutilized and used more for casino events than ticketed concerts these days. ⊠*Sam's Town Casino, 5111 Boulder Hwy., Boulder Strip* ☎888/464–2468.

Thomas and Mack Center. Since the MGM Grand and Mandalay Bay both built their own concert and sporting arenas, this venue, on the campus of UNLV, has come to rely on such sporting events as the National Finals Rodeo and, of course, Runnin' Rebels basketball. ⊠*Tropicana Ave. at Swenson St., University District* ☎702/739–3267.

FINE ARTS

Although it's known more for theatrical spectacles than serious theater, Las Vegas does have a lively cultural scene. The groups listed below offer full seasons of productions each year.

BALLET

Nevada Ballet Theatre. The city's longest-running fine-arts organization (this being Las Vegas, it only dates from 1973) stages three to five productions each year, anchored by an annual December presentation of *The Nutcracker*. Bruce Steivel is artistic director for the troupe, and most performances are held in UNLV's Judy Bayley Theatre. ✉*4505 S. Maryland Pkwy., University District* ☎*702/243–2623, 702/895–2787 for tickets* ⊕*www.nevadaballet.com.*

CLASSICAL MUSIC

Las Vegas Philharmonic. Formed in 1998, the Philharmonic performs at Artemus Ham Hall on the UNLV campus, as well as in the Penn & Teller Theatre at the Rio. ✉*4505 S. Maryland Pkwy., University District* ☎*702/258–5438 for schedule information, 702/895–2787 for tickets* ⊕*www.lasvegasphilharmonic.com.*

THEATER

Away from the Strip, a booming community theater scene caters to the area's many new residents, retirees in particular, who are looking for a low-cost alternative to the pricey shows. With the exception of Las Vegas Little Theatre, most don't have their own performance spaces and instead rent municipal auditoriums for their productions.

Jade Productions. This senior-citizen-oriented group focuses on Broadway musicals and revues themed around Broadway composers or stars. ☎*702/263–6385* ⊕*www.jadepro.com.*

Las Vegas Little Theatre. Las Vegas's oldest community theater has branched out from its base of Neil Simon comedies to more wide-ranging productions such as *A Few Good Men* and *What the Butler Saw*. ✉*3920 Schiff Dr., West Side* ☎*702/362–7996* ⊕*www.lvlt.org.*

University of Nevada–Las Vegas Theater Department. UNLV brings in outside professionals and holds community-wide auditions for a full season of productions each academic year. Most performances are held in the Judy Bayley Theatre on campus. ✉*4505 S. Maryland Pkwy., University District* ☎*702/985–2787.*

After Dark

Zuri Bar, MGM Grand

WORD OF MOUTH

"We always begin a night out in Vegas at Red Square. You can get a Key Lime Pie Martini, with graham cracker crust on the rim, or a Chernobyl (guaranteed to cause a meltdown!) for under $10."

—Here_today_gone2Maui

"Ghost Bar is pretty overrated in my opinion. The view from outside is great, but the drinks are super expensive."

—jcolem2

AFTER DARK PLANNER

Raves & Faves	Finding Out What's Going On

Raves & Faves

Best place to channel the Rat Pack: Peppermill's Fireside Lounge, with its lethal Scorpion cocktail.

Best outdoor patio: With Strip views, cabanas, private tables, a deejay, and a dance floor, **PURE** at Caesars Palace is the perfect way to spend a night under the stars. Those without a fear of heights might also try **Mix** at Mandalay Bay's THEhotel and **Moon** at the Palms.

Best antidote to the Strip: For an alternative scene, the no-frills rocker pub **Double Down Saloon** rules, although up-and-comers like **Art Bar**, **Beauty Bar**, and the **Artisan Lounge** are giving it a run for its money.

Best burlesque joint: A sultry three-piece jazz combo provides the jams for sexy burlesque performances at **Ivan Kane's Forty Deuce**.

Best legal high: The "hookahs" at **Paymon's Mediterranean Café and Hookah Lounge**.

Best happy hour noshing: The affordable tapas and sangria at **Firefly on Paradise**.

Best nonstop party: Seamless turns on a dime from elegant strip club to all-night dance party, especially on the weekends and at Monday's Industry Night at **Forty Deuce**.

Finding Out What's Going On

With the number of nightlife options in Las Vegas, it's not hard to be overwhelmed. These local publications can steer you in the right direction and help you plan your ultimate Vegas night out. Remember that party schedules—as well as the popularity of any one spot—can change overnight, so the best way of keeping current is to consult these publications.

The *Las Vegas Advisor* (✉ *3687 S. Procyon Ave., Las Vegas89103* ☎ *800/244–2224*) is available at its office for $5 per issue or $50 per year; this monthly newsletter is invaluable for its information on Las Vegas dining, entertainment, gambling promotions, comps, and news. If you're here for a short visit, pick up free copies of *Today in Las Vegas* and *What's On in Las Vegas* at hotels and gift shops.

The *Las Vegas Review-Journal,* the city's daily newspaper, publishes a tabloid pullout section each Friday called "Neon." It provides entertainment features and reviews, and showroom and lounge listings with complete time and price information. The "Neon" section is sold separately for a quarter in some news boxes along the resort corridor. The *Review-Journal* maintains a Web site (⊕ *www.reviewjournal.com*) where show listings are updated each week. The *Las Vegas Sun,* once a competing daily, is now a section inside the *Review-Journal* but maintains its own editorial staff and Web site, ⊕ *www.lasvegassun.com*.

Two excellent alternative weekly newspapers are distributed at retail stores and coffee shops around town and maintain comprehensive Web sites. *Las Vegas Weekly* (⊕ *www.lasvegasweekly.com*) and *Las Vegas City Life* (⊕ *www.lasvegascitylife.com*) offer some timely and incisive reflections on the nightclub scene and music outside the realm of the casinos.

How to Get In

Nobody comes to Las Vegas to wait in line. So how exactly do you get past those velvet ropes? Short of personally knowing the brutal-looking bouncers and serious-looking women holding clipboards that guard the doors, here are a few pointers.

First, know that even though this is a 24-hour town, lines start forming around 10. If you're not on a list, get there early and dress the part—which is to say, don't expect to go straight from the pool to the club. Vegas bars and clubs have pretty strict dress codes, so leave those T-shirts, baseball caps, and ripped jeans in your hotel room (unless you're headed to the Art Bar or some other hipster haven). Arguing that your sneakers were made by Hugo Boss probably won't help, either. At most of the trendier spots, skin is in—this *is* Vegas, after all. And needless to say, the universal rule of big-city nightlife also applies in Vegas: groups of guys almost always have a harder time getting in without a few women in the mix. If your group is gender impaired, consider politely asking some unaccompanied women to temporarily join you, perhaps in exchange for some drinks once you're all inside. Too shy, you say? If there was ever a place to check your shyness at the airport, it's Vegas.

Most spots have two lines: a VIP line and a regular line. You can usually get in the VIP line if you're on the guest list or have reserved a table with bottle service. You can either ask your hotel concierge for help contacting a club to get on a guest list, or contact the club directly. Some Web sites such as ⊕ *www.vegas.com* sell passes they guarantee will get you past the crush, but save your money for the door—better to slip the bouncer $20 per person than hope they'll acknowledge the Internet ticket you've bought for the same amount. If you have a few people in your group, it might be worth it to splurge on a table reservation: without one, a group of five could easily spend $20 each getting in good with the bouncers, plus $20 each for the cover charge, and then there's always the expensive drinks.

Avoiding the Scams

There are a couple of scams to keep in mind. First, nearly every tourist—and even many locals—uses taxis to get around at night. (Forget the perils of driving after knocking back a few drinks—just finding parking can make your head spin.) Some cabbies enjoy a sort of symbiotic relationship with club owners. If you ask your driver to take you to "the hottest club in town," chances are you'll end up at a club where the manager will pay the driver a kickback. The place might be hot, but chances are better that it will be not. This system seems to be especially true with nude strip clubs, where the lack of a liquor license makes managers even more anxious to pack the place.

Another scam involves the "celebrity buzz" around certain hotspots—for example, "Last weekend Paris Hilton was making out with a busboy at Jet!" Although this might cause a stampede to the club in question, a celebrity's presence there—or anywhere, for that matter—is very likely thanks to the cool fifty grand (or upward) that clubs are said to pay for such visitations.

Even if you're not staying at a given club's resort, ask the concierge for a VIP admission pass. If you do it right, you have a better chance of scoring free or VIP entry.

Updated by
Gary Lippman

LAS VEGAS'S NIGHTLIFE HAS NEVER been hotter, spicier, or, for that matter, more competitive. Fueled by the "What happens in Vegas, stays in Vegas" advertisements (read: "All your sins here expunged completely once you pay your credit card bill"), nightlife impresarios on the Strip are dipping into their vast pockets in order to create over-the-top experiences where party-mad Visigoths—plus, well, you and me—can live out some wild fantasies. The number of high-profile nightclubs, trendy lounges, and sizzling strip bars continues to grow, each attempting to trump the other in order to attract not just high rollers, but A-list celebrities and the publicity that surrounds them. Gambling? Why bother when you can lounge beside the pool by day and bellow at the moon by night while dancing half-clad at a club until noon the following day (when it's back into the pool you go)?

In the late 1990s, once the Vegas mandarins decided that the "family experience" just wasn't happening, Sin City nightlife got truly sinful again, drawing raves from clubbers worldwide. A wave of large dance clubs, such as the Luxor's Ra, opened their doors, followed by a trendy batch of cozier ultralounges—lounges with dance floors—like the MGM Grand's Tabú.

The game of one-upmanship has continued—recent additions that have kept the city hopping include the would-be-amazing-even-without-the-nudity Men's Club and the Palms' sensational two-fer of Moon and the Playboy Lounge. What's more, bawdy '50s-era burlesque lounges are continuing their comeback with a gaggle of clubs, including Ivan Kane's bump-and-grind Forty Deuce at Mandalay Bay and the ultra-popular Pussycat Dolls Lounge at Caesars, now dedicated to the art of striptease.

Few cities on earth match Vegas in its dedication to upping the nightlife ante. So with all these choices, no one—not even the Visigoths—have an excuse for not having fun, whether it's at a chic lounge, a dance club, or even a strip joint.

BARS & LOUNGES

CASINO-RESORT HOT SPOTS

The lounges of the Las Vegas casino-hotels were once places where such headliners as Frank, Dean, and the gang would go after their shows, taking a seat in the audience to laugh at the comedy antics of Shecky Greene or Don Rickles. Now the lounges have been mostly reduced to small bars within the casino where bands play Top 40 hits in front of people pie-eyed from the slots. Virtually every casino has such a spot; all you need to do is buy a drink or two, and you can listen to the music all night long. A few lounges—the Las Vegas Hilton and Boardwalk among them—have computerized lighting and larger dance floors, making them as much a small dance club as a live music club. Some of the nicest are at the Stratosphere, Mandalay Bay, the Mirage, the Wynn, and the Orleans.

Out at 4 AM

Vegas is a 24-hour town, and when the party starts to wind down in some places, the doors to others are just opening. The following are our picks for after-hours hot spots. Remember, even after 4 AM, expect lines—sometimes very long ones—to get in. And bring your sunglasses to protect those bleary eyes from the morning rays when you finally stumble out.

The dimly lighted **Drai's** has long been the after-hours king. Although others have tried to take the title away from the subterranean nightclub, it still stands high above the competition. Deejays spin house and hip-hop until well after the sun rises. ☎ 702/737–7801.

The **Empire Ballroom**, the stiffest competition to Drai's for after-hours party of choice, usually boasts extra-long lines, so get there as early as possible for its roaring large-scale naughtiness. ☎ 702/737–7111.

Ivan Kane's Forty Deuce gets going at 4 AM Thursday through Saturday when the dancers take the stage for a late performance. ☎ 702/632–9442.

Singles flirt among the plush environment at **OBA at House of Blues**, a sleek and narrow ultralounge. The deep red lighting creates a sensual yet calming mood. ☎ 702/632–7600.

It's 4 AM—do you know where your mojo is? If Drai's is too small and the Empire too big, you may find **Seamless** just right. The dancers have covered up and gone home, but the hipsters are probably pouring in by the dozens. ☎ 702/227–5200.

If you're looking for a more chill atmosphere instead of a club, check out the Hard Rock's **Circle Bar** for nonstop action, or grab a late (or early) bite at the casino's coffee shop, **Mr. Lucky's 24/7**. ☎ 800/473–7625.

—Gary Lippman

The turn of the 21st century, however, brought an explosion of hybrid nightspots aiming for the middle ground between dance club and conventional lounge.

Fodor'sChoice ★ **The Artisan Lounge.** This not-yet-well-known favorite of ours is in the slightly out-of-the-way Artisan Hotel and is sort of an upscale version of the Peppermill. The vibe is relatively chill even on weekends, so it can serve as a tonic to the usual Vegas lunacy. The interior is filled with gilt-framed paintings (and sometimes frames without the paintings), which are even on the ceiling. Ordinarily, a crazy ceiling stunt like this one would seem stupid, but the muted romantic ambience here (candlelight, soft music, dark wood, comfy leather couches) makes it work, and then some. ⊠ *The Artisan Hotel, 1501 W. Sahara Ave., West Side* ☎ *702/214–4000* ⊕ *www.theartisanhotel.com.*

The Bar at Times Square. Dueling pianos pack 'em in like sardines at this high-energy sing-along spot. Want to hear "New York, New York" or another favorite tune? The pianists take requests. And though the crowd skews toward an older demographic, it's still fun. ⊠ *New York–New York Hotel and Casino, 3790 Las Vegas Blvd. S, South Strip* ☎ *702/740–6969.*

★ **The Beatles Revolution Ultra-Lounge.** Designed for synergy with Cirque du Soleil's Beatles-theme *Love* next door, the "Rev," as it's known locally, is already wowing tourists and locals alike with its private alcoves, hippie-outfitted sexy servers, ubiquitous beanbag chairs, and eye-popping, ever-shifting psychedelic fractal projections on every bit of wall space available, and earning its place among the very best nightspots in Vegas. The low lighting and high volume deemphasize the "lounge" aspect of "ultralounge" here, but late at night, when the inevitable Fab Four tunes give way to pumping dance music, it's rightly all about the "ultra," as in "ultrafun." Try to drop by late on Monday nights for Cirque du Soleil's "Family Nights," when the performers from all the Cirque shows citywide gather here to dance like the adrenaline fiends they are, were, and always will be. ⊠*Mirage Hotel and Casino, 3400 Las Vegas Blvd. S, South Strip* ☎702/891–7777 ⊕*http://thebeatles-revolutionlounge.com.*

Caramel. The owners of Bellagio's dance club, Light, opened Caramel as a warm-up, wind-down alternative to the larger club. The sweet name is backed up by martinis served in signature chocolate and caramel-coated chilled glasses. ⊠*Bellagio Las Vegas, 3600 Las Vegas Blvd. S, Center Strip* ☎702/693–8300 ⊕*www.caramelbar.com.*

Carnaval Court. Harrah's has the rare outdoor lounge to take advantage of the Strip's endless parade. Expect kitsch, kitsch, and more kitsch, with bartenders juggling bottles to the awe of customers who down margaritas in huge plastic containers. ⊠*Harrah's Las Vegas Casino & Hotel, 3475 Las Vegas Blvd. S, Center Strip* ☎702/369–5000.

Centrifuge. Choreographed dancers doing corny routines and live music make this small-yet-cozy bar the center of the action at the MGM Grand. Across from Studio 54, it has a gorgeous circular setting, with moving sails above you. ⊠*MGM Grand Hotel and Casino, 3799 Las Vegas Blvd. S, South Strip* ☎702/891–7777.

Coyote Ugly. Barmaids in tight clothes break into choreographed bar-top dances intended to make Hooter's look like a church picnic at this noisy tourist trap. Patrons line up to savor this reincarnation of the 2000 movie's title nightspot. It's the poor person's Pussycat Dolls Lounge, but if you want to gaze at galvanized aluminum siding, old license plates, and an impressive bra collection, who are we to stop you? ⊠*New York–New York Hotel and Casino, 3790 Las Vegas Blvd. S, South Strip* ☎702/740–6330 ⊕*www.coyoteuglysaloon.com.*

Drai's. Once the tony restaurant's tables are cleared away after evening dining hours, the wild scene inside the modestly sized Drai's—named for nightlife impresario Victor Drai—is closer to a dance club or a rave than to a lounge. Some folks whisper about the decadence being practiced inside, but it wouldn't be a hot after-hours spot if people weren't talking about it, right? ⊠*Bill's Gamblin' Hall & Saloon, 3595 Las Vegas Blvd. S, Center Strip* ☎702/737–0505 ⊕*www.draislasvegas.com.*

Flirt. They say it's "designed for women by women," which apparently makes reference to the gentle curves of the furniture, the subtlety of the lighting, and the indulgent, beefcakey bartenders. A fun place—not only for its target audience but also for men who might want to sniff around, pretending to be "sensitive." Climb into the "gossip pit" and let it rip. There's a special early entry for Chippendale's ticket holders.

✉ *Rio All-Suite Hotel & Casino, 3700 W. Flamingo Rd., West Side* ☎ *702/777–7777* ⊕ *www.riovegasnights.com.*

Ghostbar. Perched on the penthouse level of the Palms, this apex of ultralounges has rock music, glamorous patrons, glowing lights, and a glassed-in view of the city. Step outside and you'll find that the nice outdoor deck is cantilevered over the side of the building, with a Plexiglas platform that allows revelers to look down 450 feet below. Because of the laughably complicated process to get in the door, some might find this spot frustrating (although, with the right blend of patience and good humor, getting inside can be highly entertaining). ✉ *The Palms, 4321 W. Flamingo Rd., West Side* ☎ *702/938–2666 or 702/492–3960* ⊕ *www.n9negroup.com.*

★ **Ivan Kane's Forty Deuce.** This old-school burlesque club, imported from L.A., has the friendliest doormen in Vegas and a live three-piece bump-and-grind combo that pumps up the energy level while dancers writhe on stage. In a small but perfectly shaped room (with a "What the hell?" diorama on one wall showing two beavers murdering each other), the Deuce shows are on nightly, but Monday—"Industry Night," when local nightlife employees get off their leashes to play—are an especially good bet. ✉ *Mandalay Bay Resort & Casino, 3590 Las Vegas Blvd. S, South Strip* ☎ *702/632–9442* ⊕ *www.fortydeuce.com.*

Lucky Bar. Its stupendous circular bar, relaxed yet lively atmosphere, sexier-than-usual staff, and abundant chandeliers, make this newcomer on the hotel bar scene one of the best, despite its far-flung location at the impressive Red Rock complex. What's more, it's a mere 30-second walk to the nearby Rocks Lounge, an otherwise undistinguishable bar that features some top-notch Thursday-through-Saturday entertainment that includes the blondly beautiful band Zowie Bowie, which somehow yokes together Sinatra and Eminem and kicks some serious 21st-century keyster in the process. ✉ *Red Rock Casino, Resort & Spa, 11011 W. Charleston Blvd., Summerlin* ☎ *702/797–7777.*

★ **Lure.** The rajah of Vegas nightlife, Victor Drai, has done it again with this Barbarella-style fever-dream of an ultralounge. The interior is as glossy and gorgeous as the drop-dead clientele, especially during the Wednesday night parties. Diaphanous curtains billow around glass-legged divans as sequined servers approach with come-hither smiles— you get the point. When you factor in the outdoor garden, this is probably the best ultralounge we know. ✉ *Wynn Las Vegas, 3131 Las Vegas Blvd. S, Center Strip* ☎ *702/770–3350.*

Mist. The partners behind Bellagio's Caramel room opened a similarly casual but elegant room off the casino floor of Treasure Island. The crowd leans toward skateboard-toting refugees from L.A., especially at the Wednesday party, while the "Munchie Menu" includes the Pooh Bear, a peanut-butter-and-jelly sandwich on banana nut bread. ✉ *Treasure Island Las Vegas (TI), 3300 Las Vegas Blvd. S, Center Strip* ☎ *702/894–7330* ⊕ *www.mistbar.com.*

Fodor'sChoice ★ **Mix at THEhotel.** Floor-to-ceiling windows, an appealing curved bar, an equally appealing staff—what could top all that? An outdoor deck that offers stunning views of the Strip, that's what. At this spot atop THEhotel at Mandalay, even the glass-walled restrooms give you a window onto the city. Black leather accented by red lighting creates a hipper-than-thou vibe. ⊠*Mandalay Bay Resort & Casino, 3590 Las Vegas Blvd. S, South Strip* ☎877/632–9500.

★ **Parasol Up and Parasol Down.** Two exquisite-looking—and exquisitely tranquil—settings ensure you can indulge in the most-endangered-of-all-pleasures: a good conversation. These umbrella-shape bars each have their own personality. Upstairs stays open all night, so it tends to be livelier; downstairs, with its outdoor terrace giving you a prime view of the light show and waterfall, is, if anything, even more romantic. ⊠*Wynn Las Vegas, 3131 Las Vegas Blvd. S, Center Strip* ☎702/770–7000.

★ **Paymon's Mediterranean Café and Hookah Lounge.** Centerpiece of one of the most decadent crazes to hit Sin City in recent memory, the hookah is an elaborate Middle Eastern water pipe that is used to smoke exotic tobaccos (and yes, we just mean *tobacco*). Thanks to a helpful "Hookah Man" and some available samples, no prior experience with water pipes is required. But the hookah is only one part of the appeal here: designed by local entrepreneur Paymon Raouf for the ultimate chill-out experience, this red velvet–laden, exquisitely carpeted, incense-filled environment redefines "Vegas plush," thereby making Paymon's place one of the most romantic spots in town. And its young, somewhat bohemian crowd and those sexy paintings on the wall don't hurt the romance, either. Trust us—one visit and you'll get "hookah-ed." ⊠*511 Main St., Downtown* ☎702/437–2787 ⊕*www.paymons.com.*

★ **The Playboy Club.** "The Bunny is back!" So said Hugh Hefner at the recent grand opening of this phoenix-rising-from-the-ashes 1960s nightlife legend, now rocking the 52nd floor of the Palms' new Fantasy Tower. A few of the old fixings are absent: the constantly changing vintage Playboy photos projected on LCD screens everywhere include no nudity, for example. (This isn't a topless joint, mind you—it's as upscale as ultralounges get.) Still, all the servers and croupiers wear the classic Bunny outfits, and the plush dark bachelor-pad-on-a-grand-scale feel here, complete with fireplace and a multitude of couches, proves that everything old can be new again. When you're ready to dance, take the escalator up to Moon. It's connected to the Playboy and is included in your cover charge—$20 on weeknights, $40 on weekends. ⊠*The Palms, 4321 W. Flamingo Rd., West Side* ☎702/942-7777 ⊕*www.playboyclub.com.*

Pussycat Dolls Lounge. Tied with Forty Deuce for the best cabaret show in the city, this little gem of a burlesque house—next to PURE—makes up for what it lacks in size with pizzazz. Gasp as the entertainers (from the famed song-and-dance Hollywood troupe) perform and tease the bejeezus out of audiences by dropping in on swings or popping out of gigantic champagne glasses. ⊠*Caesars Palace, 3570 Las Vegas Blvd. S, Center Strip* ☎702/212-8806 ⊕*www.pussycatdolls.com.*

Red Square. It's easy to forget there's a Russian restaurant behind

> **WORD OF MOUTH**
>
> "Red Square in Mandalay Bay makes 'the best' martinis. We go every visit. The bar has a 'cool' ice strip to set your drink on."
>
> —KVR

this gorgeous and creatively designed lounge that functions as a virtually self-sufficient nightspot. Soviet-era propaganda posters and an enormous statue of Lenin set the mood. There's a seemingly limitless vodka selection, a homegrown "Cuban Missile Crisis" cocktail (its contents, appropriately enough, are top-secret), and a bar made of a flat panel of ice that keeps your drink at a sipping temperature. ⊠*Mandalay Bay Resort & Casino, 3950 Las Vegas Blvd. S, South Strip* ☎*702/632–7407.*

Risqué. The distinction between ultralounge and dance club blurs at this sizable second-floor room. Views from the six individual balconies take in both the Strip and Bellagio's fountain show across the street, but if you're not a VIP, your best chance of scoring one is on a weeknight. Famous faces such as Bill Gates have been known to charter the separate Salon Privé, which includes its own deejay setup and big round furniture fixtures that look like beds, but its glory days seem to have slipped by. ⊠*Paris Las Vegas, 3655 Las Vegas Blvd. S, Center Strip* ☎*702/946–4589.*

Romance Lounge. The Stratosphere might be downscale compared to other Vegas hotels, but there ain't nothing "down" about the high-in-the-sky experience to be had here. From this sleek, attractively streamlined room, the view of Sin City is truly, truly amazing (if slightly remote). Couldn't they have thought of a zestier name, though? ⊠*Stratosphere Casino Hotel and Tower, 2000 Las Vegas Blvd. S, South Strip* ☎*702/380–7777.*

Rouge. Guess what color the interior of this place is? After one or two drinks here, we guarantee you'll be "seeing red," even at night's end while brushing your teeth … As far as the MGM Grand bars go, this newbie (formerly Teatro) is slicker than Zuri (dig those backlit projections by design wunderkind Adam Tihany!), less frenetic than Tabu and more intimate than Centrifuge. ⊠*MGM Grand Hotel and Casino, 3799 Las Vegas Blvd. S, South Strip* ☎*702/891–1111.*

Shadow. Caesars Palace converted one of its lounges into Shadow, thus named because of the silhouettes of seemingly naked women dancing behind scrims. This small lounge often draws an older crowd, which of course is either good or bad, depending on your own age (and taste). ⊠*Caesars Palace, 3570 Las Vegas Blvd. S, Center Strip* ☎*702/731–7990.*

Stack. Yes, we *know* it's primarily a steak house—but the front bar gets so much of "the three J's" (jukin', jivin' and jrinkin') that we have to mention it as a hotspot. It's especially fine for anyone stumbling out of the phantasmagorical nearby *Love* show (the best single entertainment in Vegas). Despite the gently undulating walls and warm wood-covered decor, Stack is a little loud for our tastes, but fun for carnivores and herbivores alike. ⊠*Mirage Hotel and Casino, 3400 Las Vegas Blvd. S, South Strip* ☎*702/792–7800.*

Tabú. Here you'll find the high-tech touches of a big dance club, with square tables that double as "canvases" for projected images and "murals" of light that change depending on the perspective of the viewer. But the peach-color banquettes and mirrored columns lend it the coziness of a lounge. The fine deejays actually understand the music they play. Not exactly cutting-edge, but it's still worth a pop-in. ✉ *MGM Grand Hotel and Casino, 3799 Las Vegas Blvd. S, South Strip* ☎ *702/891–7183* ⊕ *www.mgmgrandnightlife.com.*

Tangerine. This is another cabaret, although the feel here is much more like a dance club—and an overcrowded, overripe one at that. Wednesday night's ultrapopular "Moonshine" party is particularly packed, with burlesque dancers gyrating on the bar in this teeny, orange-tinted lounge. The large outdoor deck opens onto Sirens Cove, giving you courtside seats to the campy *Sirens of TI* show. ✉ *Treasure Island Las Vegas (TI), 3300 Las Vegas Blvd. S, Center Strip* ☎ *702/894–7111.*

VooDoo Lounge. Take in great views of the city at this spot with an outdoor deck high atop the Rio. Deejays, great dance bands, and faux-primitive voodoo paintings adorn the walls as bartenders mix concoctions such as the rum-packed "Witch Doctor." Except for the fun Sunday night party, the crowd tends to be slightly older and less shall-we-say sophisticated than at similar clubs. ✉ *Rio All-Suite Hotel & Casino, 3700 W. Flamingo Rd., West Side* ☎ *702/992–7970* ⊕ *www. riovegasnights.com.*

The Whiskey. Rande Gerber, the entrepreneur better known to some as Mr. Cindy Crawford, banked on the popularity of his "Whiskey"-named clubs in other cities to lure celebrities and club-hoppers to Green Valley Ranch, a suburban casino several miles from the Strip. For the most part, this ploy has worked here. The sleek main room opens out onto a comfortable landscaped pool area. It's as much a dance club as a bar, but unless you're already in Green Valley, you might not find the Whiskey worth the long trip. ✉ *Green Valley Ranch Resort, Casino & Spa, 2197 Paseo Verde Pkwy., Henderson* ☎ *702/614–5283* ⊕ *www. midnightoilbars.com.*

DIVE BARS & LOCAL HANGOUTS

Outside the realm of the big casinos, the Las Vegas bar scene is dominated by so-called video-poker taverns, named for the 15 video-poker machines they are legally allowed to have. Most are generic, but there are exceptions—in some cases, glorious exceptions. Hot tip: combine a visit to some of the downtown bars with a stroll around the area. Despite the touristy "Fremont Street Experience," downtown is the real deal, and essential to see if you want to claim you "know Vegas."

Art Bar. Sort of a downtown Double Down, this sensational hipster joint compensates for its slightly out-of-the-way location with bizarre (sometimes spicy) paintings on the walls, rockabilly deejays, hot bands, and a funky local crowd. The place is much wilder on weekends and at their monthly art openings. ✉ *511 Main St., Downtown* ☎ *702/437–2787.*

★ **Beauty Bar.** This charming little downtown joint, spun off from a popular New York watering hole, is laid out like an old-fashioned hair salon (complete with hair-dryer chairs acquired from a defunct New Jersey salon), so you can pretend to be your mother (ironically or not) while you listen to local bands (primarily of the rocking type), sip away at creative cocktails with names like "Shampoo" and "Conditioner," and ogle the hipster crowd. The first Friday of each month features the *uber*-popular "Get Back" party, and on warm nights, a patio is opened with a second bar. ✉ *517 Fremont St., Downtown* ☎ *702/598–1965* ⊕ *www.beautybar.com.*

Crown & Anchor Pub. Not far from the Strip, this friendly British-style pub caters to the university crowd. Grab a Guinness, Newcastle, or Blackthorn Cider from the very, very, very extensive drinks menu, play a game of darts, or settle in and grab some grub. ✉ *1350 E. Tropicana Ave., University District* ☎ *702/739–8676* ⊕ *www.crownandanchorlv.com.*

Double Down Saloon. The grand poobah of Vegas dive bars, the Double D is a short walk from the Hard Rock Hotel and a long, long way from Paradise (although a sign above the door proclaims it to be "The Happiest Place On Earth"). Delicious decadence prevails here. For the boho crowd, this deliberately downscale bar has everything from live bands to a jukebox that blasts everything from Patsy Cline to Frank Sinatra, rockabilly to bluegrass, and classic punk to classic funk. Fans of the place include filmmaker Tim Burton. Don't miss the clever yet often obscene graffiti. Wear black and don't bother checking this place out before the witching hour. ✉ *4640 Paradise Rd., Paradise Road* ☎ *702/791–5775* ⊕ *http://doubledownsaloon.com.*

Firefly on Paradise. This low-lit, understated restaurant is the epitome of the "local hang" and is especially popular with the artsy after-work crowd. Most come for the cheap ($3 to $10) and delicious variety of Spanish-style *tapas,* but the red and white sangrias, which are said to marinate for several days before being served, are even better. ✉ *3900 Paradise Rd., Paradise Road* ☎ *702/437–2787* ⊕ *www.fireflylv.com.*

Gordon Biersch Brewing Co. A brewery as well as a restaurant, this place caters to Las Vegas's new breed of white-collar workers and becomes a local singles' haven for the after-work crowd. Try one of the house brews, which include seasonal beers, as well as the popular marzen (lager), blonde bock, pilsner, and hefeweizen. ✉ *3987 Paradise Rd., Paradise Road* ☎ *702/312–5247* ⊕ *www.gordonbiersch.com.*

Fodor's Choice
★ **Peppermill's Fireside Lounge.** Many visitors to Sin City looking for a bit of ring-a-ding-ding leave disappointed, finding the frequently swinging wrecking ball has left behind little but massive movie-set-like resort-casinos to dominate the landscape. But benign neglect has preserved this shagadelic lounge, one of the town's truly essential nightspots. Near the old Stardust Hotel, this evergreen ironic-romantic getaway serves food, but what you're really here for is the must-see-to-believe firepit, the crazy waitress outfits, and the lethally alcoholic Scorpion cocktail. The Pep showed up in the Martin Scorsese film *Casino.* ✉ *2985 Las Vegas Blvd. S, Center Strip* ☎ *702/735–7635* ⊕ *www.peppermilllasvegas.com.*

Rainbow Bar & Grill. We hate to break it to the anti-franchise crowd, but this nightspot is an outpost of a Hollywood hangout—and it's right across the street from the Hard Rock. Similar to the Hard Rock's club Body English in look—think dark wood walls and red banquettes—the Rainbow is far friendlier. There's amazing rock memorabilia everywhere, a stage on which local bands let it blow, two dining rooms serving good grub, celebrity customers like Quentin Tarantino, an outdoor patio, a rocker crowd, and an open-all-night-long policy. All this, plus a free "designated driver" public telephone. ✉ *4480 Paradise Rd., Paradise Road* ☎ *702/898–3525* ⊕ *www.rainbowbarandgrill.com.*

The Lounge Evolution

Trends are fickle in Vegas. Take lounges: once the hub of the hip, they plummeted to the dregs of popular culture, then resurged with a vengeance, even spawning upscale spin-offs. Now the word *lounge* encompasses both the old cliché—an open casino hangout where a trio in matching sequined vests warbles Top 40 covers—and the newer meaning of a trendy spot where everyone lines up to pay $8 a drink and rubberneck for a glimpse of a celebrity.

The lounge came into its own as an all-night party in the early 1950s, when stars like Louis Prima, the Treniers, and the Mary Kaye Trio kept gamblers energized until dawn. Casino employees—showgirls, pit bosses—wired from their late-night shifts joined the mix, packing out the 5 AM shows. The hot ticket was Chinese food at the Sands, a far cry from the chic nightclubs and busy sports bars lining the Strip today.

The '70s were a rough time for lounge lovers. On the casino front, slot machines became all the rage, and casino managers cut down the size of the free lounges in order to create more floor space for the lucrative machines. Pop culture turned to rock and roll, and suddenly the Vegas music scene, former home to legends like the Rat Pack, was the punch line of the music industry. "Lounge singer" became synonymous with Bill Murray's cheesy character, Nick the Lounge Lizard, who crooned the theme to *Star Wars* on *Saturday Night Live*.

But Vegas is a town that reinvents itself, and lounges are no exception. Movies like *Swingers* spun the city back around to its '50s cool image, and for people in the know, lounges

became ironically hip spots to hang out. Even that reviled lounge music made a comeback on the Strip as tribal casinos and legalized pockets of gaming around the country made casino gambling by itself less unique. People missed the tinselly Vegas. Once again, like the old days, hipsters are wisely descending on places like **Peppermill's Fireside Lounge** (☎ 702/369–5000), **Paymon's Mediterranean Café** (☎ 702/437–2787), **Firefly on Paradise** (☎ 702/437–2787), and the **Artisan Lounge** (☎ 702/214–4000), which adds candles and chill music and fine art to class up the cheese-vibe.

The latest lounge makeover is the wave of so-called ultralounges, which combine aspects of a cocktail lounge and a larger dance club. Cool Gen-Xers looking for an alternative to the confetti-falling-from-the-ceiling megaclub scene drop their cash on pricey drinks at places like **Tabú** (☎ 702/891–7183) at the MGM or **Lure** (☎ 702/770–3350) at the Wynn. Tables at these posh cribs often come with a hefty "bottle service" price tag: you can reserve a seat if you dish out anywhere from $100 to $250 for a bottle of wine or liquor. Other superb ultralounge experiences include the splashy psychedelia of **Revolution** (☎ 702/891–7777) at the Mirage, **Rouge** (☎ 702/891–1111), and **Mix at THEHotel** (☎ 877/632–9500).

—Gary Lippman

DANCE CLUBS

The usual Catch-22 of nightlife applies: the more "in" the place, the harder it is to get in, and the more oppressively crowded and noisy it will be once you do. Cover charges have correspondingly crept into the $10 to $20 range—and don't be surprised to find that, even in these "enlightened" times, men will pay higher cover charges than women. Although the level of capital investment gives these clubs a longevity their New York counterparts don't enjoy, dance clubs are still by nature a fickle, fleeting enterprise, so check with more updated sources to ensure that they are still hot.

FodorsChoice **Body English.** An increasingly competitive nightclub environment sent
★ Hard Rock reps scouring Europe's hottest nightspots in search of a winning design to replace the previous dance emporium. The chosen theme seems to be "1970s decadent English rock aristocracy's living room," and it works. As wallflowers swill brandy, very sexy singles gyrate on the dance floor under a huge crystal chandelier said to be valued at $250,000. Meanwhile, you'll find celebs (and there tend to be a lot of them, depending on the event—one time we were there, Jenna Jameson and Jenny McCarthy were purring at each other) hang out in VIP areas that overlook the action. Sunday night is when the grooviness soars for the weekly party night. ⊠*Hard Rock Hotel and Casino, 4455 Paradise Rd., Paradise Road* ☎*702/693–5000.*

Cherry. Nightlife impresario Rande Gerber has done it again, sending the glorious-looking Red Rock Casino into the stratosphere with this equally glorious-looking new dance club, located just yards away from the wonderful Lucky Bar. Guests enter through a futuristic silver-painted tunnel and are hit with the most vibrant shade of red that bathes the entire elegant and intimate circular room. There are smoke machines, an especially beautiful red glass bar, a towering sculpture of cherries, and enormous curtained VIP rooms, some more deluxe than others. Best of all, there's a private but rather large pool just outside—with its own bar, of course (though not a swim-upper)—so that the fiesta can include stargazing, swimming, and topless sunbathing—maybe even topless stargazing. ⊠*Red Rock Casino, Resort & Spa, 11011 W. Charleston Rd., Summerlin* ☎*702/797–7777.*

Empire Ballroom. The decadence of Drai's is writ large in this cavernous old ballroom. Three bikini-clad women on the stage are always doing the Jerk while psychedelic lights blind you, techno and trance sounds make you deaf, and multiracial, mostly beautiful local hardcore-types—for "hardcore," read "piercings and tattoos on the inside as well as the outside of their bodies"—dance themselves into a frenzy. This is as over-the-top as after-hours gets, though Seamless seems to be stealing some of its thunder lately. Sunday nights go Latin for a party called "Latin Empire." ⊠*3665 Las Vegas Blvd. S, South Strip* ☎*702/415–5283* ⊕*www.latenightempire.com.*

Foundation Room. Given the Mandalay's seemingly bottomless big pockets, it's no surprise that this club takes aesthetic appeal to an unprecedented level. A members-only club six nights a week, the Foundation Room—actually a series of different rooms, each with its own set of design themes and type of music (disco, house, etc.)—opens its doors to the ultrahip (and no one but—these doors are tough to get through) on Monday nights for its "Godspeed" party. Feel like dancing your booty off while surrounded by ancient statues, tapestry-covered walls, pirated Mississippi road signs, and windows that look out on all of Vegas? So do we! ⊠*Mandalay Bay Resort & Casino, 3590 Las Vegas Blvd. S, South Strip* ☎702/632–7777.

Jet. Though it's not as elegant as Tao or Body English, and doesn't have the view to match PURE, Jet is bigger, darker, and louder than just about any other dance club in Vegas. And on a good night—Monday, for example, which is when the party really gets going—the sexy revelers are packed in and pumping like you wouldn't believe. Gawk at the cryogenic effects system from either the long dance floor or the equally long bar (one of the world's lengthiest, we hear). A series of side rooms are for chilling out or for different dance music variations, so don't be shy about exploring. As for the stripper pole at the center of everything: don't expect it to be unused for long. ⊠*Mirage Hotel and Casino, 3400 Las Vegas Blvd. S, South Strip* ☎702/792–7900.

Light. This club at Bellagio once emphasized the exclusivity of its 30 reserved tables and expensive bottle service, but its focus has changed to satisfying the tastes of those with more limited means. Hence its elegant though decidedly uncreative decor and lackluster hip-hop and dance music repertoire. Sunday is currently the big party night, though in our humble opinion, the joint is waning slightly in its appeal. ⊠*Bellagio Las Vegas, 3600 Las Vegas Blvd. S, Center Strip* ☎702/693–8300 ⊕*www.lightlv.com.*

Fodor's Choice
★
Moon. Picture this: Writhing ladies in two-piece space suits atop noise-blaring monoliths that surround you. Suddenly, the roof opens and starlight comes pouring in. Now, this could either be a seizure or you're partying at Moon, quite simply the best new nightclub in Vegas. Packing in more futuristic technology than a space station, this spacious-but-not-overwhelmingly-so megalopolis of cool has multiple dance floors, two ample outdoor balconies, banquettes seating 20, stripper poles galore, and some of the best views in town (including a few without glass—it's just you and the vista). And what would a hot new scene be without its celebrity enthusiasts? Justin Timberlake and Lindsay Lohan are among those who've gotten hedonistic here, even seizing control of the turntables on occasion. Oh, and if you'd like to take a breather from the space suits (and look at Bunny outfits instead), simply take the escalator to the Playboy Club. (It's included in your ticket price–$20 on weeknights, $40 on weekends.) ⊠*The Palms, 4321 W. Flamingo Rd., West Side* ☎702/942–7777 ⊕*www.n9negroup.com.*

Fodor's Choice
★
PURE. Although Jet is newer, Tao more sublimely appointed, and Rain more filled with special effects, PURE still takes the cake for best all-around shake appeal. In addition to its super-cool Tuesday night party and alluring crowd, it's got a secret weapon in its outdoor terrace, one complete with waterfalls, private cabanas, dance floor, and a view that places you not high above but right in the middle of the action on the Strip. Indoor types party in a cream-color main room or in the smaller Red Room, which is a special VIP area. For the deejay mavens out

CLOSE UP

Specialty Bars

Since the desires of many visitors run far beyond the standard sinful troika of "sex, alcohol, and gambling," the powers-that-be have been kind enough to provide certain settings for the more exotically inclined.

All You Need is Love: If you believe that good music stopped with the Beatles, ride your Yellow Submarine to Cirque du Soleil's wonderful new show *Love* at the Mirage and then step inside the **Revolution Lounge** next door, where Beatles-inspired decor and music give way to general dancemania. ✉ *Mirage Hotel and Casino, 3400 Las Vegas Blvd. S, South Strip* ☎ *702/891–7777.*

Cigar Bar: There are plenty of fine stogies—and the dreaded hookah pipe—at **Cuba Libre.** ✉ *Hard Rock Hotel and Casino, 4455 Paradise Rd., Paradise Road* ☎ *702/693–5000.*

Country-Song-Tie-In Bar: The guitar-shape bar at **Toby Keith's I Love This Bar and Grill** is just one of the attractions. There's also the possibility that Mr. Keith will appear and sign autographs for you, even if you've never heard of him or his mediocre "I Love This Bar" ditty. ✉ *Harrah's Las Vegas Casino & Hotel, 3475 Las Vegas Blvd. S, Center Strip* ☎ *702/693–6111.*

… And Speaking of Tie-Ins: Jimmy Buffett's Margaritaville brings some of Key West's wacky good-time tropical ambience to Vegas, with guess whose music and lifestyle ethos coming to the fore? ✉ *Flamingo Las Vegas, 3555 Las Vegas Blvd. S, Center Strip* ☎ *702/733–3302* ⊕ *www.margaritavillelasvegas.com.*

Futuristic Bar: With cocktails like "Klingon Blood Draft," you can only imagine what kind of food is served

at **Quark's Bar.** It's in "Star Trek: The Experience." ✉ *Las Vegas Hilton, 3000 Paradise Rd., Paradise Road* ☎ *702/697–8725.*

Irish in Green Valley: Should you find yourself at the somewhat far-flung Green Valley Resort, no need to fret, because in our humble opinion, the Irish tavern **Fado** is the best-appointed and fun Irish bar in the whole damn state of Nevada. ✉ *Green Valley Ranch Resort, Casino & Spa, 32300 Paseo Verde Pkwy., Henderson* ☎ *702/407–8691.*

Shaken, Not Stirred: If James Bond became an architect after hanging up his "license to kill," he'd probably design something like the fun, out-of-the-way **Drop Bar.** The go-go-booted servers will certainly indulge your 007 fantasies here—but only up to a point, of course. ✉ *Green Valley Ranch Resort, Casino & Spa, 32300 Paseo Verde Pkwy., Henderson* ☎ *702/221–6560.*

Sports Bar: Jumbo video screens on the walls and a smaller one at every table are found at **The Sports Book.** ✉ *Caesars Palace, 3570 Las Vegas Blvd. S, Center Strip* ☎ *702/731–7110.*

A Tequila Sunrise: Latin music, a Southwestern setup, Mexican meals—all these are found at the simply named **Tequila Bar.** ✉ *Bally's, 3645 Las Vegas Blvd. S, Center Strip* ☎ *702/739–4111.*

Wine Bar: It's actually a wine store, but **55 Degrees** has a cool design, a drinking area in the back, and hundreds of vintages. It's named for the temperature at which wine is best stored. You knew that, of course. ✉ *Mandalay Bay Resort & Casino, 3590 Las Vegas Blvd. S, South Strip* ☎ *702/632–9355.*

7

there, red-hot spinmeister (and former Nicole Richie beau) DJ AM is in residence. It connects to the fabulous Pussycat Dolls Lounge if you need a breather. ⊠ *Caesars Palace, 3500 Las Vegas Blvd. S, Center Strip* ☎ *702/731–7873.*

Rain in the Desert. This vast round nightclub and concert house got tons of free publicity in 2002 and 2003 as a major setting for MTV's *The Real World.* It's still equipped with dancing waters (trust us, they dance), video projections on a 40-foot-high water curtain (trust us, it looks like a curtain), and occasional blasts of fire. Perhaps because the Palms shares ownership with the Sacramento Kings, the club even includes "skyboxes" that go for exorbitant fees. Thursday is the signature night, known as Drenched. In summer the action expands to the adjacent pool area for Skin, a pool lounge with the same management. ⊠ *The Palms, 4321 W. Flamingo Rd., West Side* ☎ *702/940–7246* ⊕ *www.rainatthepalms.com.*

rumjungle. Disney-style lines trailed from this Mandalay Bay version of a Brazilian paradise since the day it opened, but these have grown shorter as the novelty and the hype have waned. The "fire wall" out front beckons club goers into a wild room with waterfalls, dancing girls on platforms, percussionists banging on giant conga drums, and aerialists soaring above you while attached to trapezelike harnesses. For some, it's way too much—sort of like a very rich kid's bar mitzvah. For others, who just dig the nonstop house, hip-hop, and Latin music, it's as in as ever. Our recommendation: start the evening at the nearby Red Square, then come here to check out the scene. ⊠ *Mandalay Bay Resort & Casino, 3950 Las Vegas Blvd. S, South Strip* ☎ *702/632–7408.*

Studio 54. This three-level, four-dance-floor club inside the MGM Grand tries to channel the 1970s club of the same name—in case you miss the connection, they've got plenty of photos on the walls to remind you. Still, why settle for a carbon copy of the real thing? Although the crowd is young, the music is loud, and the go-go dancers and acrobats are somewhat fetching, the room is one big, impersonal, charmless hangar, and no famous name can change that. Tuesday is its signature night called EDEN, which stands for "Erotically Delicious Entertainers Night." ⊠ *MGM Grand Hotel and Casino, 3799 Las Vegas Blvd. S, South Strip* ☎ *702/891–7254.*

★ **Tao.** Nowhere else in Vegas furnishes you with "the four D's"—dining, drinking, dancing, and drooling—in quite as alluring a mix as this multilevel (and multimillion-dollar) playground. The ground floor and mezzanine levels are exquisite enough (you almost tumble into rosewater baths before you're in the door), but once you get off the elevator at the top floor, where an army of dramatically lighted stone deities greet you, the party truly begins. Chinese antiques, crimson chandeliers, and a so-called "Opium Room" set the mood. This is also a voyeur's paradise of hallways where fashion models in lingerie sit meditating. Don't be offended if they don't answer your entreaties or remarks—they have taken a temporary vow of silence. ⊠ *Venetian Resort-Hotel-Casino, 3355 Las Vegas Blvd. S, Center Strip* ☎ *702/388–8588* ⊕ *www.taolasvegas.com.*

Continued on page 245

BRIDAL PARTIES GONE WILD

New York may be the city that never sleeps, but Las Vegas makes the Big Apple look positively somnolent. Activities aren't merely available to you at all hours of the day and night; they practically follow you around, demanding you to take part in Vegas's fun and games.

The best man and maid-of-honor know that Vegas is the only place in the world to sate the needs of the partiers for one brief, hot-burning, 48-hour flame of a weekend.

So take a peek at a sample bachelorette party. Go to the places they go, do what they do, giggle like they do. Then check out the bachelor party. Watch the boys be boys. Hey, just because they grew up doesn't mean they grew out of it.

STAY WHERE YOU PLAY

DON'T SKIMP ON THE HOTEL Things aren't as close as they appear, and cabs can be a hassle. The best plan is to stay where you play. If your party has a certain scene in mind, whether it's a casino, bar, club, or pool, your best bet is to stay where you plan to play.

FRIDAY

The hunks from *Thunder from Down Under*

Girls

Eight girls fly in and head to the Strip. There are hugs all around and mischief in the air as they gather in the lobby.

Timeline

CHECK-IN & COCKTAILS: First stop—the lavish rooms at the Bellagio for freshening up before gathering downstairs at **Caramel**. The girls sip funky martinis and catch up before presenting the bride-to-be with her veil, not to be removed until beyond Nevada state lines.

DINNER: Surrounded by glass walls and flowing waterfalls at Bellagio's **Sensi**, the girls opt for ahi tuna ceviche, wood-fired foccaccia, and more conversation.

MALE REVUE: The shoulder devil wins the first major scuffle of the trip as the group heads to *Thunder from Down Under*, (Excalibur) where, as the men of the Aussie all-male revue gyrate, the bride-to-be has just enough to drink to do things she won't tell her fiancé about.

LATE-NIGHT: The girls get down at **Studio 54** (MGM Grand) in a sea of navel-piercings and biceps. The music fades from BeeGees into GoGo's and finally into more contemporary techno-house. The guy break dancing in the corner? That's Mr. Freeze from the Rock Steady Crew.

Boys

For Bachelor Parties, there's only one way to go: off-Strip.

Timeline

CHECK-IN & COCKTAILS: Our boys are kicking it at the **Hard Rock Hotel**. The Circle Bar in the middle of the casino provides the perfect meet-up location for the bachelor, the best man, and the groomsmen (one of whom is already down two large at the Blackjack tables).

DINNER: The guys head over to **Emeril's** (MGM Grand) for some oysters and Cajun specialties.

CLUBBING: After a gut-busting dinner, it's off to **Body English** (Hard Rock), the ultimate guys' nightclub. Some say it has a Playboy Mansion feel, and with the number of bunnies wandering around, who could argue? With DJ Dig Dug spinning, the cozy club gets packed fast. It's a good thing our boys headed out around 10—they managed to skip the two-hour line.

EVEN LATER: We all know that every red-blooded American male has one need at 2 AM on Saturday: a pedicure. The boys sip Cristal by candlelight as the lingerie-clad technicians of **AMP Salon** (Palms) tend to their toes.

SATURDAY

Girls

The Maid-of-Honor brings out the bottle of ibuprofen she bought for this trip.

Timeline

SHOPPING: After everyone's recovered from the night before, they're off to the **Forum Shops** (Caesars Palace) for therapeutic shopping.

LUNCH: The girls settle on patio-seating at **Spago** (Caesars Palace) for unrivaled people-watching and Wolfgang Puck creations.

SPA: The group hits the rock-climbing wall at **Canyon Ranch SpaClub** (Venetian) and then indulges in seaweed wraps and watsu pool massages.

DINNER: The girls clean up and head to **Aureole** (Mandalay Bay) for celebrity chef Charlie Palmer's multicourse taster menus.

CLUBBING: It's time for **Tryst** (Wynn Las Vegas): the Blue Lagoon setting, a 90-foot waterfall, the most beautiful people, and the sounds of some of the city's most talented DJs.

LATER: The girls move on to **Tao** (Venetian) for plenty of groove-thing shaking and celebrity sightings (was that Michael Jordan?). In the taxi back to the hotel, the glimmers of dawn are just beginning to appear over the mountains to the east.

Boys

The sun tortures their eyes, but the cab ride to the Hilton is oh so worth it . . .

Timeline

BREAKFAST: The guys are channeling Elvis, who made his big live comeback here decades ago, and James Bond, who climbed down from the roof in *Diamonds Are Forever*. The focus is the hearty and endless chow at the **Hilton's The Buffet**.

GOLF: The boys tee off at **TPC the Canyons**, a championship-level course designed by Raymond Floyd.

DINNER: After a day on the links, the evening kicks off with a steak dinner at the unassuming **Gordon Biersch Brewery**. The atmosphere is the perfect prep for another night on the town.

CLUBS: The starting point is **Pure** (Caesars Palace), the hottest all-around club in Vegas (and a Fodor's Choice): its mix of hip-hop, house, and rock is split into 3 sub-clubs within the 36,000 square-foot space.

STRIP CLUB: This is a bachelor party, so a strip-club visit is de rigeur. **Spearmint Rhino's** clubby setting gives it a classy feel (well, as classy as classy gets at a strip club).

AFTER-HOURS CLUB: The boys hit **Seamless**, an ultralounge/afterhours/topless club (could you ask for anything more?). After 4 AM the performers don eveningwear and join the party.

SUNDAY

Girls

Last on the weekend's agenda is an exotic pole-dancing class at **Studio Ohm** (☎ 702/810-4156 ⊕ www.studiohmlv.com). Then it's back to the pool for an hour or two of the equatorial desert sun before the girls start making their way to the airport. For the bachelorette, it's a weekend she'll never forget—although she may want to when the maid of honor pulls out the pictures at the wedding reception.

Boys

Manly-man hugs abound as the guys begin to make their way to the airport. For those with late flights, there's time to squeeze in a few Hold'em or Omaha hands at the Venetian's newly remodeled poker room. The bachelor's going to need to work up some cover stories on what to tell the fiancée about what happened. Of course, she's probably working on her own.

The Game Plan

No matter what the nature of your bachelor or bachelorette party is, here are some tips:

YOU CAN'T EXPECT EVERYONE TO STICK TOGETHER all the time. Build anchor events into the trip that everyone will be expected to attend, like a fancy dinner or club outing for a Saturday night so that those who have to arrive late or leave early can attend.

WANT TO GET INTO THE CLUBS? So do a trillion other people. Above all else, dress the part. Clubs want well-put-together patrons who look like they belong with the beautiful people.

DISNEYLAND FIGURED IT OUT A FEW YEARS AGO: position in line is a product that can be sold just like anything else, so higher-budget parties can buy Front-of-the-Line passes that give you license to cut. Sounds good, right? The thing is, it doesn't actually work. Front-of-Line passes just move you to the front of one line but to the back of another. Don't waste your money. Instead, to secure a reservation, call ahead and book a table with bottle service.

PLAN AHEAD. That means dinner and show reservations, golf and other outdoor excursions, and especially night-time activities. The further ahead you plan, the more likely you are to get seats for the shows and meals you want, and the more likely you are to gain entrance to the hottest clubs. Even though Vegas has a lot of places to play, start building an itinerary at least a month before your trip.

Studio 54

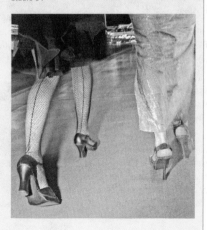

Fodor's Choice **Tryst.** Rising from the ashes of a not-quite-compelling-enough club is
★ Victor Drai's latest wonder, a dance emporium that bests most competitors by playing a wider variety of music—even rock. There's also
a friendlier staff (a sharper and sexier-dressed staff, too). It may lack
the spectacular views of Ghostbar or Mix, but it does have a waterfall to gape at. And dig that eerie red lighting, the gorgeous stairway
at the entrance, and the cleverly curtained VIP section. If you're in
for the weekend, make sure you stick around for the Sunday night
extravaganza—you won't be sorry. ✉ *Wynn Las Vegas, 3131 Las
Vegas Blvd. S, Center Strip* ☎ *702/770–3375.*

GAY & LESBIAN NIGHTLIFE

Las Vegas was never really known for gay tourism, but things have
changed rapidly in the past few years. Now a number of bars and
nightclubs cater to different segments of the community, and the all-gay
Blue Moon Resort (⊕ *www.bluemoonlv.com*) has 45 rooms near Sahara
Avenue and I–15.

Most gay and lesbian nightlife is concentrated into two areas of town.
The most prominent is near the intersection of Naples Drive and Paradise Road, just north of the airport and near the Hard Rock Hotel and
Casino. The other is the area in and around Commercial Center, one of
the city's oldest shopping centers, on East Sahara Avenue, just west of
Maryland Parkway. Expect cover charges to be around $10 for dance
clubs on weekends.

For a more complete list pick up a copy of *Q Vegas,* the city's gay
monthly, or visit its Web site ⊕ *www.qvegas.com.*

Badlands Saloon. For anyone who loved *Brokeback Mountain,* this gay
cowboy haven is a must. Not only is it decorated with a mocklog-cabin
façade, there are Western trappings everywhere, and even more cow
images than the Western trappings. There's also a jukebox crammed
to the coin slot with Country-and-Western hits. Plus, the Nevada Gay
Rodeo Association hosts its fundraisers here every fourth Saturday of
the month. Oh, in case you *really* want to get kinky, the Green Door
swingers club is just a few (nongreen) doors down. ✉ *953 E. Sahara
Dr. (inside Commercial Center), East Side* ☎ *702/792–9262.*

Buffalo. One of Vegas's more popular "Levi bars" (read: wear blue
jeans, the tighter the better), this understated tavern has pool tables,
gaming, and an especially fun happy hour from 4 to 7. ✉ *4640 S. Paradise Rd., East Side* ☎ *702/733–8355.*

8 ½ Ultra-Lounge and Piranha Nightclub. As the sister—no, make that
brother—establishment to the ever-popular Gipsy, this gorgeous
new-and-already-scorchingly-hot two-in-one spot has been packing
them in like mad. It's across the street from Gipsy, too, on Vegas's
famed "Fruit Loop" (which wins our award for cleverest gay zone
name). ✉ *4633 Paradise Rd., East Side* ☎ *702/491–0100* ⊕ *www.
piranhalasvegas.com.*

Flex. A smaller, more neighborhood-oriented club for men, this place
sometimes has floor shows, contests, and entertainment, with Wednes-

day being their big night. ✉*4371 W. Charleston Ave., West Side* ☎*702/385–3539.*

★ **Freezone.** An egalitarian mix of men and women congregate at this bar with a dance floor, pool tables, and video-poker machines. There's a lesbian joint next door (guys can enter with a female "date"), which features near-topless female dancers. Each night brings a different theme: "Ladies' Night" is Tuesday, the "Boy'z Night" male revue is on Thursday, and the "What a Drag!" show is Friday and Saturday. ✉*610 E. Naples Dr., Paradise Road* ☎*702/794–2300* ⊕*www. freezonelv.com.*

Gipsy. The oldest, largest, and most famous alternative dance club in Las Vegas is within walking distance of the Hard Rock Hotel and Casino. Predominantly a male club, it has always welcomed the open-minded regardless of sexual preference. Competition from newer mainstream nightclubs has taken a little of the edge off its crossover appeal, but the Gip manages to stay busy. There are nightly drink specials, a "Crush Tuesday," which brings a younger crowd, and go-go boys on Saturday. ✉*4605 Paradise Rd., Paradise Road* ☎*702/731–1919* ⊕*www.gipsylv.net.*

Goodtimes. The location of this bar and dance club will appeal to anyone with a refined sense of camp: it's in the same strip mall as the Liberace Museum. Though this used to be the place to go on Monday, it seems to be on the downward slide in terms of popularity. ✉*1775 E. Tropicana Ave., East Side* ☎*702/736–9494.*

Krave. Live entertainers and go-go dancers put a mixed crowd in motion at this club. The erotic dance revue *Fashionistas,* which uses video screens to tell a love story between a woman, her female boss, and a male designer, is surprisingly good. The show runs Tuesday through Saturday at 9:30 PM. ✉*3667 Las Vegas Blvd. S, Center Strip* ☎*702/836–0833* ⊕*www.kravelasvegas.com.*

Las Vegas Lounge. If you want to see something really different, catch the nightly shows (except Sunday) in this offbeat room billed as the city's premier transvestite and transgender bar. Be ready for a very lively evening out. ✉*900 E. Karen Ave., East Las Vegas* ☎*702/737–9350* ⊕*www.lasvegaslounge.com.*

Suede Restaurant and Lounge. The food isn't fancy here, but the lounge is slick, slick, slick and splendidly appointed. There's karaoke on Tuesday, Wednesday, and Thursday and Kenny Kerr channels Barbra Streisand on Friday and does double duty on Saturday, playing both La Barbra *and* his own fabulously fabulous creation, Ms. Loretta Lieberman. ✉*4640 S. Paradise Rd., East Side* ☎*702/791–3463.*

LIVE MUSIC

BLUES

Sand Dollar Blues Lounge. This is a classic Vegas joint, and no other word but "joint" will do. After shutting down for a spell, this local institution is again alive and kicking. It's a bit of a hike from the Strip, but well worth the trip. Throw your arm around the nearest biker and do the hucklebuck to a song by the Moanin' Blacksnakes or whatever other blues band is currently blowing down the house. ✉*3355 W. Spring Mountain Rd., Center Strip* ☎*702/871–6651* ⊕*www.sanddollarblues.com.*

COUNTRY & WESTERN

Dylan's Dance Hall & Saloon. This Boulder Highway honky-tonk is the spiritual heart of Las Vegas country music, and far more "down-home" than the bombastic though more centrally located Gilley's. It's open Friday and Saturday from 7 PM. ✉*4660 Boulder Hwy., Boulder Strip* ☎*702/451–4006.*

★ **Gilley's Dancehall Saloon & Barbecue.** This cavernous yet extremely colorful institution, which hails from Texas, has less live music than line dancing, but it's country's one and only home on the Strip. It's now the chief claim to fame for the faded New Frontier Hotel (which still has the best billboard in town). Specials include daily all-you-can-drink drafts for $15, bikini bull riding Thursday through Saturday, and Wednesday "dirty girl" mud wrestling. ✉*New Frontier Hotel and Gambling Hall, 3120 Las Vegas Blvd. S, South Strip* ☎*702/794–8434* ⊕*www.gilleyslv.com.*

JAZZ

Jazzed Cafe and Vinoteca. One of your best bets away from the Strip is this fun room that's decorated as a bold piece of living pop art. It seats about 40 for dinner but stays open past the dinner hour as a cozy spot for live music. ✉*8615 W. Sahara Ave., West Las Vegas* ☎*702/233–2859.*

ROCK

Club Madrid. Sunset Station was built after sister property Boulder Station enjoyed success with concert acts, and Club Madrid was designed as a lounge and concert venue with room to seat 500 people. ✉*1301 E. Sunset Rd., Henderson* ☎*702/547–7777.*

★ **House of Blues.** This nightclub–concert hall hybrid at Mandalay Bay is the seventh entry in this chain of successful intimate music clubs. As if the electric roster of performers taking the stage almost nightly wasn't enough (past acts include Al Green, Bo Diddley, Bob Weir, Sarah Silverman, the Dropkick Murphys, and Seal), the decor is lusciously imaginative. (Our favorite decoration isn't inside, though—it's the Voodoo Mama statue greeting you outside.) And touristically cheesy as it is (you'll hear "Everybody get up and clap your hands!" quite a bit), the Gospel Brunch on Sundays has great live music and is well worth one visit. ✉*3950 Las Vegas Blvd. S, South Strip* ☎*702/632–7600* ⊕*www. hob.com.*

The Joint. Big-ticket attractions usually found in arenas—the Rolling Stones, the Eagles, and Sting—as well as smaller acts more often matched to an intimate club play this venue inside the Hard Rock Hotel and Casino. ✉*4455 Paradise Rd., Paradise Road* ☎*702/693–5000.*

Monte Carlo Pub and Brewery. One of the largest microbreweries in the country features one of the most smoking-fierce rock bands. The six members of ONX have had stints with Keith Richards, Stone Temple Pilots, Robert Plant, and Al Green. Don't forget to try some Winner's Wheat and High Roller Red (the in-house special brews) while rocking out. ✉*3770 Las Vegas Blvd. S, Center Strip* ☎*702/730–7423.*

The Railhead. This comfortable venue in Boulder Station started as an open casino and lounge that occasionally hosted ticketed concerts. It has since become an enclosed club, nearly perfect for a diverse range of local and midlevel concerts. ✉ *4111 Boulder Hwy., Boulder Strip* ☎ *702/432–7777.*

STRIP CLUBS

It's not called Sin City for nothing. Strip clubs are a major industry here, but they do have some quirks. Zoning laws restrict most clubs to industrial areas not far off the Strip. You've got to make a choice: alcohol or nudity—clubs can have one or the other, but not both. (The Palomino Club, in North Las Vegas, is the one exception.) Needless to say, the joints with liquor licenses have the sharper designs, the bigger spaces, the more savory customers, and the better-looking dancers. (Oops—the correct term is "entertainers.") Interestingly enough, however, most newer places are opting to get rid of the drinks and the G-strings.

Be prepared to shell out your cash. Most places have instituted cover charges of $20 or more (most or all of which goes into your cabbie's pocket), but that's just the beginning. The real money is made on the table dances continuously solicited inside, with most going for $20 per song (and three dances for a C-note).

Cheetah's. The good news: this is the topless gentlemen's club at which the hilariously (though unintentionally) campy movie *Showgirls* was filmed. More good news: a lap-dance happy hour daily 7 PM–7 AM, drink specials 6 PM–2 AM (including $1 beers), and a free lunch weekdays 10–4. The bad news: for a gentlemen's club, where zing is the thing, it's looking a bit tired. But it's still worth a peek. ✉ *2112 Western Ave., West Side* ☎ *702/384–0074* ⊕ *www.cheetahsnv.com.*

Club Paradise. Its location—directly across from the Hard Rock Hotel and Casino—has been a plus for this place. It was also one of the first local clubs to embrace the "gentlemen's club" boom of the 1990s. Beyond those geographical and historical advantages—well, let's say that its time has come and gone. A better bet is the next-door Rainbow, though that place substitutes "rock'n'roll" for "sex." Alas—not even hedonists get to have it all. ✉ *4416 Paradise Rd., Paradise Road* ☎ *702/734–7990* ⊕ *www.clubparadise.net.*

Crazy Horse Too. A standard top-of-the-line gentlemen's club, this place has a lived-in atmosphere, friendly gals swirling everywhere, lots of dark pockets for privacy, and three theme rooms: Cleopatra's Lounge, the Emperor's Room, and Circus Maximus. ✉ *2476 Dean Martin Dr./Industrial Rd., West Side* ☎ *702/382–8003* ⊕ *www.crazyhorsetoo.com.*

★ **Déjà Vu Showgirls.** No city in the free world can boast of more breast implants *per capita* than Las Vegas, and few all-nude clubs in Vegas can boast of *less* artificial pulchritude than this lovable little joint. There's lots of "natural beauty" here amid the silicone and saline, not to mention red velvet curtains, tasteful PLPs (that's "private lapdance pods" for the uninitiated), Country-and-Western music, a more-roomy-than-usual bachelor party area, and a shower show in which two naked women demonstrate ways to use soap and water that Mommy and Daddy never taught you. ✉*3247 Industrial Rd./Dean Martin Ave, West Side* ☎*702/894–4167* ⊕*www.dejavu.com.*

Fodor's Choice ★ **Men's Club.** Ever get the urge for foie gras or caviar while watching naked women sashay around a strange place at 3 AM? If so, follow us to this ridiculously gorgeous and sublimely comfortable Moroccan-theme newbie, which is easily one of Vegas's most attractive nightspots, topless or otherwise. The decorating scheme is like an oil sheik's dream, with two levels of plush banquettes, VIP rooms, and skyboxes, plus a 10,000-bottle wine cellar, the Alchemy Kitchen, which serves practically nonstop, *and* a raw bar. Best of all, the dancers fully match the surrounding classiness. Given how stunning the Men's Club's sights are, be careful not to spill any foie gras in your lap. ✉*4575 S. Polaris Ave., West Side* ☎*702/889–6367* ⊕*www.mensclublv.com.*

★ **Minxx.** Not only is this the only Vegas strip joint owned and operated by a Princeton grad (finally, someone does something *useful* with that degree!), but it's a red-hot new kid on the block whose intimate scale and amiable vibe have Minxx beating out the quality of most old standbys on the scene as well. The second floor is where the appeal really soars, with six private dance rooms whose decor themes include Virgin (all white), Raiders (silver and black), Snake (as in snakeskin), and Dirty (see for yourselves). ✉*4636 Wynn Rd., West Side* ☎*702/220–9416.*

Olympic Garden. Yes, it's the granddaddy of Vegas strip clubs, and the first to install several smaller stages to take the place of the single stage found in older clubs. But the OG has hit hard times, and is worthwhile only if you find yourself on the northern edge of the Strip with nothing else to do. A separate room has male revues for the ladies, where the publicity line is "More Than You Can Imagine." ✉*1531 Las Vegas Blvd. S, Downtown* ☎*702/385–9361* ⊕*www.ogvegas.com.*

Palomino Club. This is one of the oldest strip clubs in the area (the Rat Pack used to hang out here) as well as the most notorious; two separate owners have been accused of murders, and it was also owned briefly by a noted and nonhomicidal heart surgeon. Because the Pal was grandfathered into the North Las Vegas zoning codes, it's allowed to have both a full bar *and* full nudity—Now *that* makes for a party, huh? And the Pal stays multigenerational by keeping its old-time burlesque-style stage downstairs while having the dancers upstairs perform on tiny platforms and solicit private dances. ✉*1848 Las Vegas Blvd. N, North Las Vegas* ☎*702/642–2984.*

Sapphire. The owners claim to have spent $26 million for the bragging rights of proclaiming their club the "largest adult entertainment complex in the world." Formerly a gym, this place boasts 40,000 square feet of topless dancing, complete with 13 second-floor "skyboxes." The entertainers descend a ramp to a clear, elevated main stage that towers over the floor. ✉*3025 S. Industrial Rd/ Dean Martin Dr, West Side* ☎*702/796–6000* ⊕*www.sapphirelasvegas.com.*

Fodor's Choice ★ **Scores.** On the ever-changing, ever-competitive topless club scene, this young lion—an outpost of the New York/Chicago/Miami empire—is an out-and-out winner. Though it lacks the worn-in feel of the other joints, it's pretty much our favorite for its neat balance between classiness, fun, and creativity. The entertainers are friendlier than at most other clubs, the decor is beyond tasteful (check out the "Library Room" for private parties—even parties of one if you've got the greenbacks!), and—in a bid to compete with the town's burlesque shows—the hourly performances are top-drawer: topless twins on a trapeze, anyone? The new after-hours party is called Sky. ✉ *3355 S. Procyon St., West Side* ☎ *702/367–4000* ⊕ *www.scoreslasvegas.com.*

Seamless. This isn't just a topless bar—it's also an ultralounge and a super-popular after-hours dance club, where you don't have to be a stripper or stripperphile to get your groove on. Could such three-in-one spots be the next wave of Vegas nightlife? Come see for yourself. Forget the girl in the gigantic martini glass at the entrance (you've seen that already at the Pussycat Dolls Lounge)—the real action takes place at the plush, vaguely futurist lounge complete with a catwalk that descends from the ceiling. And tell Page, the very hospitable manager, that we sent you. ✉ *4740 S. Arville St., West Side* ☎ *702/227–5200* ⊕ *www.seamlessclub.com.*

Sheri's Cabaret. This enormous new club—complete with a frank slogan ("Other clubs only give you half the view")—has friskier-than-usual entertainers and state-of-the-art lights and sound. For all-nude shows, this place is pretty much the ticket. If your date for any reason rebels at your having brought her (or him) here, take them to the romantic Artisan, right across the street, to pacify their outrage. ✉ *2580 S. Highland Dr., West Side* ☎ *702/792–1400* ⊕ *www.sheriscabaret.com.*

Fodor'sChoice
★ **Spearmint Rhino.** Now *this* is a strip club—one of the town's two or three best. What it lacks in grittiness it makes up for in over-the-topness. The national chain got a late start in Vegas, but it grew fast, expanding its original space to 18,000 square feet. It's also the rare topless club that offers lunch, including pizza, burgers, and steak sandwiches. ✉ *3340 S. Highland Dr., West Las Vegas* ☎ *702/796–3600* ⊕ *www.spearmintrhino.com.*

Best Side Trips

Horseback riding, Red Rock Canyon

8

WORD OF MOUTH

"Valley of Fire is great and so close that you can do it in ½ a day including some hikes. . . ."

—Mincepie

"A helicopter over the Grand Canyon is money well spent . . . what a panoramic view!"

—rxtennis

Updated by
Swain Scheps

A FAVORED BUMPER STICKER IN rural Nevada reads: "Eat Nevada lamb—10,000 coyotes can't be wrong." The same goes for adventuring into the incredibly diverse Southwest region surrounding the bright city bauble of Las Vegas: tens of millions of adventurers can't be wrong. They dutifully drive to the Grand Canyon to peer over the edge and discover a vast record of time in the colorful rock layers. They drive north, only wanting to escape the city for a spell, and end up sitting in a sun-flooded diner talking to a crusty cowpoke.

The only trick is knowing when to get out of the city, and how. In general, go north, or high into the mountains, in summer; and stay low in the deserts in winter. As for leaving Las Vegas, it's pretty easy once you get onto the freeways, especially if you're heading north or south. But be aware that weekend traffic, especially on I–15, can imitate a parking lot both leaving and entering the city. Leave extra early, or travel midweek, if possible. Conversely, weekday traffic within the city can be murderously slow during morning, noon, and late-afternoon rush hours. Because the city continues to grow, roads are constantly being improved or built; your best bet is to ask locals for new travel options and tips on construction delays.

Dining and lodging price ranges in this chapter refer to the charts in chapters 2 and 4.

MT. CHARLESTON AREA

45 mi northwest of Las Vegas on U.S. 95.

In winter Las Vegans crowd the upper elevations of the Spring Mountains to throw snowballs, sled, cross-country ski, and even slide downhill at a little ski area. In summer they return to wander the high trails and escape the valley's 115°F heat (temperatures are at least 20°F cooler
★   than in the city), and maybe even make the difficult hike to **Mt. Charleston,** the range's high point. Easier trails lead to seasonal waterfalls or rare, dripping springs where dainty columbine and stunted aspens spill down ravines and hummingbirds zoom. Or they might lead onto high, dry ridges where ancient bristlecone trees have become twisted and burnished with age. For camping information contact the **U.S. Forest Service** (☎702/515–5400). For recorded snow reports and winter road conditions call the **Las Vegas Ski and Snowboard Resort** (☎702/593–9500).

At the intersection of U.S. 95 and Route 157, turn left to Kyle Canyon. The first stop on Kyle Canyon Road (about 17 mi up) is the **Mt. Charleston Hotel,** which was extensively renovated in 2005. The large, lodgelike lobby has a big hearth, bar, and Mt. Charleston Steakhouse, a spacious restaurant with a mountain view and an excellent chef. ⊠*2 Kyle Canyon Rd.* ☎*702/872–5500 or 800/794–3456* ⊕*www.mtcharlestonhotel.com.*

If you take Route 157 to its end, you reach the **Mt. Charleston Lodge.** At 7,717 feet above sea level, the lodge overlooks Kyle Canyon; it has a fireside cocktail lounge and log cabin rentals and is close to hik-

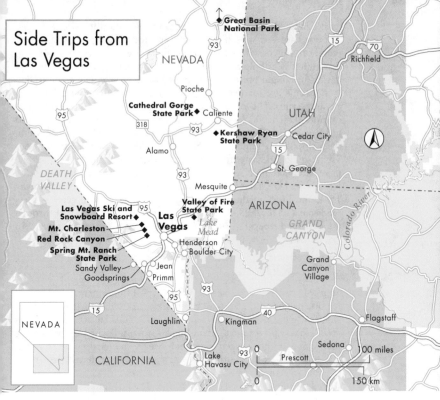

Great Basin
National Park

93

NEVADA

Pioche

95

Cathedral Gorge
State Park ◆ Caliente

318

93

Kershaw Ryan
State Park

Alamo

93

DEATH
VALLEY

Mesquite

Valley of Fire
State Park

Las Vegas Ski and
Snowboard Resort ◆

95

Las
Vegas

Lake
Mead

Mt. Charleston
Red Rock Canyon

Spring Mt. Ranch
State Park

Sandy Valley
Goodsprings

Jean
Primm

Henderson
Boulder City

UTAH

Richfield

70

15

Cedar City

15

St. George

ARIZONA

GRAND
CANYON

Grand
Canyon
Village

Colorado River

95

NEVADA

15

Laughlin

95

93

Kingman

40

Flagstaff

Sedona

0

100 miles

CALIFORNIA

Lake
Havasu City

93

0

Prescott

150 km

ing trails. ✉ *1200 Old Park Rd.* ☎ *702/872–5408 or 800/955–1314*
⊕ *www.mtcharlestonlodge.com.*

SPORTS & THE OUTDOORS

HIKING

Fodor's Choice

★

Mt. Charleston. In summer, hikers escape the heat by traveling 45 minutes up to the Spring Mountains National Recreation Area, known
informally as Mt. Charleston, where the U.S. Forest Service maintains
more than 50 mi of marked hiking trails for all abilities. Trails vary
from the ¼-mi (one-way) Robber's Roost trail to the 6-mi Bristlecone
Loop trail to the extremely strenuous 10-mi (one-way) North Loop
Trail, which reaches the Mt. Charleston summit at 11,918 feet; the
elevation gain is 4,213 feet. There are also plenty of intermediate trails,
along with marathon two-, three-, four-, and five-peak routes only for
hikers who are highly advanced (and in peak physical condition). The
Mt. Charleston Wilderness is part of the Humboldt–Toiyabe National
Forest; for information, contact the U.S. Forest Service *4701 N. Torrey
Pines Dr., Las Vegas, NV 89130* ☎ *702/515–5400* ⊕ *www.fs.fed.us.*

SKIING &
SNOWBOARDING

★ ☾

Las Vegas Ski and Snowboard Resort. Southern Nevada's skiing headquarters is a mere 47 mi northwest of downtown Las Vegas. Depending
on traffic and weather conditions, it can take as little as an hour to go
from a 70°F February afternoon on the Strip to the top of a chairlift at
an elevation of 9,500 feet. "Ski Lee," as it's affectionately known (for

its site in Lee Canyon), is equipped with four chairlifts—three double and one triple—a ski school, a half pipe and terrain park, a ski shop, rental equipment, and a day lodge with a coffee shop, espresso station, and lounge. Clothing rentals are even available for those who left their parkas in Poughkeepsie. There are 40 acres of groomed slopes: 20% of the trails are for beginners, 60% are intermediate, and 20% are advanced runs. The longest run is 3,000 feet, and there's a vertical drop of more than 1,000 feet. You know you're at the closest ski resort to Las Vegas when you see the slope names: Blackjack, High Roller, Keno, the Strip, Bimbo 1 and 2, and Slot Alley. The lifts are open from about Thanksgiving to Easter for skiing. Lift tickets are normally $45, but the price can fluctuate if some of the trails are closed due to limited snowfall. To get here, take U.S. 95 north to the Lee Canyon exit (Highway 156), and head up the mountain. A telephone call will get you **snow conditions** (☎702/593–9500); driving conditions can be had through the **local road report** (☎702/486–3116). ⊠*Mt. Charleston, Hwy. 156* ☎702/645–2754 ⊕*www.skilasvegas.com.*

LAKE MEAD AREA

Southeast of Las Vegas sits Boulder City—prim, languid, and full of historic neighborhoods, small businesses, parks, greenbelts—and not a single casino. Over the hill from town, enormous Hoover Dam blocks the Colorado River as it enters Black Canyon. Backed up behind the dam is incongruous, deep-blue Lake Mead, the focal point of water-based recreation for southern Nevada and northwestern Arizona and the major water supplier to seven Southwestern states. The lake is ringed by miles of rugged desert country. The breathtaking wonderland known as Valley of Fire, with its red sandstone outcroppings, petrified logs, petroglyphs, and hiking trails, is along the northern reach of the lake. And all of this is an hour or less from Vegas.

EN
ROUTE

In the city of Henderson you can stop at the **Clark County Heritage Museum** (⊠*1830 S. Boulder Hwy., Henderson* ☎702/455–7955 ⊠*$1.50* ☉*Daily 9–4:30*). A chronological history of southern Nevada includes exhibits on settler life, early gambling, and nuclear testing. Other attractions include a restored bungalow from the 1920s, built by a pioneer Las Vegas merchant; a replica of a 19th-century frontier print shop; and buildings and machinery dating from the turn of the 20th century.

More than 200 bird species have been spotted among the system of 13 ponds at the 140-acre **Henderson Bird Viewing Preserve** (⊠*2400 B Moser Dr., Henderson* ☎702/267–4180 ⊠*Free* ☉*Daily 6–3*). The ponds are a stop along the Pacific flyway for migratory waterbirds, and the best viewing times are spring and fall. The ponds also harbor hummingbirds, golden eagles, peregrine falcons, tundra swans, cormorants, ducks, hawks, and herons. The office will loan out a pair of binoculars if you ask.

Numbers in the margin correspond to numbers on the Lake Mead Area map.

BOULDER CITY

❶ *25 mi southeast of Las Vegas via U.S. 93.*

In the early 1930s Boulder City was built by the federal government to house 5,000 construction workers on the Hoover Dam project. A strict moral code was enforced to ensure timely completion of the dam, and to this day, the model city is the only community in Nevada in which gambling is illegal. Note that the two casinos at either end of Boulder City are just outside the city limits. After the dam was completed, the town shrank but was kept alive by the management and maintenance crews of the dam and Lake Mead. Today it's a vibrant little Southwestern town.

★ Be sure to stop at the historic **Boulder Dam Hotel,** built in 1933. On the National Register of Historic Places, the 21-room bed-and-breakfast once was a favorite getaway for notables, including the man who became Pope Pius XII and actors Will Rogers, Bette Davis, and Shirley Temple. The **Boulder City/Hoover Dam Museum** (☎*702/294–1988* ⊕*www.bcmha.org* 🖅*$2* ✆*Mon.–Sat. 10–5, Sun. noon–5*) occupies the second floor of the hotel. The museum has artifacts relating to the workers and construction of Boulder City and Hoover Dam. ✉*1305 Arizona St.* ☎*702/293–3510* ⊕*www.boulderdamhotel.com.*

The **Boulder City Chamber of Commerce** is a good place to gather information on the Hoover Dam and sights around town. ✉*465 Nevada Way* ☎*702/293–2034* ⊕*www.bouldercitychamber.com* ✆*Weekdays 9–5.*

HOOVER DAM

8 mi northeast from Boulder City via U.S. 93.

❷ In 1928 Congress authorized $175 million for construction of a dam on the Colorado River to control destructive floods, supply a steady water supply to seven Colorado River Basin states, and generate electricity. Considered one of the seven wonders of the industrial world, the art deco **Hoover Dam** is 726 feet high and 660 feet thick at the base.

Fodor'sChoice

★ Construction required 4.4 million cubic yards of concrete—enough to build a two-lane highway from San Francisco to New York. Originally referred to as Boulder Dam, the structure was later officially named Hoover Dam in recognition of President Herbert Hoover's role in the project. Look for artist Oskar Hansen's plaza sculptures, which include the 30-foot-tall *Winged Figures of the Republic.* ◾TIP➔**Don't miss Hansen's most intriguing work: the plaza's terrazzo floor, inlaid with a celestial map.**

Ⓒ The **Discovery Tour** allows you to see the power plant generators and other features. Guide staffers give talks every 15 minutes at each stopping point from 9 to 4:15 (early tours are less crowded). Cameras, pagers, tote bags, and cell phones are subject to X-ray screening. The top of the dam is open to pedestrians during daylight hours only; approved vehicles can cross the dam 24/7. ✉*U.S. 93 east of Boulder City* ☎*702/494–2517* ⊕*www.usbr.gov/lc/hooverdam* 🖅*Discovery*

8

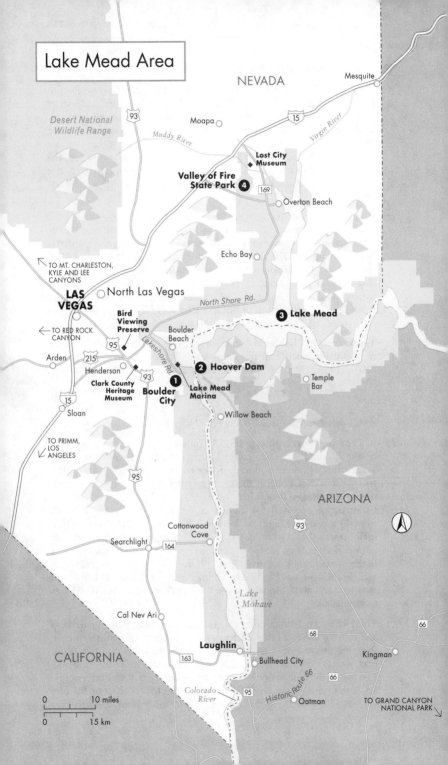

Lake Mead Area

NEVADA

Mesquite

Desert National
Wildlife Range

93

Moapa

15

Muddy River

Virgin River

Lost City
Museum

Valley of Fire
State Park ❹

169

Overton Beach

Echo Bay

← TO MT. CHARLESTON,
KYLE AND LEE
CANYONS

LAS
VEGAS

North Las Vegas

North Shore Rd.

❸ Lake Mead

Bird
Viewing
Preserve

Boulder
Beach

← TO RED ROCK
CANYON

95

Arden

215

Henderson

Clark County
Heritage
Museum

93

❷ Hoover Dam

❶

Lake Mead
Marina

Temple
Bar

Boulder
City

Lakeshore Rd.

15

Sloan

Willow Beach

TO PRIMM,
LOS
ANGELES ↙

95

ARIZONA

93

Cottonwood
Cove

Searchlight

164

Lake
Mohave

Cal Nev Ari

66

Laughlin

68

Kingman

CALIFORNIA

163

Bullhead City

66

66

95

Historic Route 66

TO GRAND CANYON
NATIONAL PARK

Colorado
River

Oatman

0		10 miles
0		15 km

Tour $11, parking $7 ⊙ Daily 9–5 ☞ Security, road, and Hoover Dam crossing information: 888/248–1259.

SPORTS & THE OUTDOORS

RAFTING Black Canyon, just below Hoover Dam, is the place for river running near Las Vegas. You can launch a raft here on the Colorado River year-round. On the Arizona side, the 11-mi run to Willow Beach, with its vertical canyon walls, bighorn sheep on the slopes, and feeder streams and waterfalls coming off the bluffs, is reminiscent of rafting the Grand Canyon. The water flows at roughly 5 mph, but some rapids, eddies, and whirlpools can cause difficulties, as can head winds, especially for inexperienced rafters.

If you want to go paddling in Black Canyon on your own, you need to make mandatory arrangements with one of the registered outfitters. They provide permits ($10) and launch and retrieval services. You can get a list of outfitters at ☎702/494–2204, or go to the paddle craft and rafting tours section on the Web site ⊕ www.usbr.gov/lc/hooverdam/.

If you're interested in seeing the canyon on large motor-assisted rafts, **Black Canyon/Willow Beach River Adventures** launches every morning at 10. ✉ Box 60130, Boulder City, NV 89006 ☎800/455–3490 ⊕ blackcanyonadventures.com.

LAKE MEAD

❸ **Lake Mead,** which is actually the Colorado River backed up behind the Hoover Dam, is the nation's largest man-made reservoir: it covers 229 square mi, is 110 mi long, and has an irregular shoreline that extends for 550 mi. You can get information about the lake's history, ecology, recreational opportunities, and the accommodations available along its shore at the **Alan Bible Visitors Center** (☎702/293–8990 ⊕ www. nps.gov/lame/visitorcenter/ ⊙ Daily 8:30–4:30). People come to Lake Mead to swim: **Boulder Beach** is the closest to Las Vegas, only a mile or so from the visitor center.

Angling and houseboating are favorite pastimes; marinas strung along the Nevada shore rent houseboats, personal watercraft, and ski boats. The lake is regularly stocked with a half-million rainbow trout, and at least a million fish are harvested every year. You can fish here 24 hours a day, year-round (except for posted closings). You must have a fishing license (details are on the National Park Service Web site), and if you plan to catch and keep trout, a separate trout stamp is required. Divers can explore the murk beneath, including the usually submerged foundations of St. Thomas, a farming community that was inundated in 1938. ⊕ www.nps.gov/lame ᠍$5 per vehicle, good for 5 days; lake-use fees $10 first vessel, $5 additional vessel, good for 1–5 days.

⟲ At **Lake Mead Cruises** you can board the 300-passenger Desert Princess, a paddle-wheeler that plies a portion of the lake; breakfast, cocktail, and dinner-and-dancing cruises are available. Ninety-minute sightseeing cruises occur daily, and dinner cruises are scheduled on weekends. ✉*Hemenway Harbor* ☎*702/293–6180* ⊕*www.lake-meadcruises.com* 📧*$22–$58; reservations strongly recommended for dinner cruises* ☉*Tours Nov.–Mar., daily noon and 2; Apr.–Oct., daily noon, 2, and 4.*

Lake Mead Resort Marina has boat rentals, a beach, a gift shop, and a floating restaurant. ✉*322 Lakeshore Rd.* ☎*702/293–3484 or 800/752–9669* ⊕*www.sevencrown.com.*

A drive of about an hour will take you along the north side of the lake, where there are three more marinas. When you reach the upper arm of the lake, about a mile past Overton Beach, look for the sign announcing the Valley of Fire. Turn left here and go about 3 mi to reach the Valley of Fire Visitors Center. ■TIP➔At this juncture it may also be possible to see some of the remnants of St. Thomas, as drought conditions have lowered lake levels dramatically.

SPORTS & THE OUTDOORS

SCUBA DIVING & SNORKELING The creation of Lake Mead flooded a huge expanse of land, and, as a result, sights of the deep abound for scuba divers. The old Mormon town of St. Thomas, inundated by the lake in 1938, has many a watery story to tell. Wishing Well Cove has steep canyon drop-offs, caves, and clear water. Ringbolt Rapids, an exhilarating drift dive, is for the advanced only, and the Tennis Shoe Graveyard, near Las Vegas Wash, is one of many footholds of watery treasures. The yacht *Tortuga,* doomed and said to be haunted, rests at 50 feet near the Boulder Islands, and Hoover Dam's asphalt factory sits on the canyon floor nearby. The boat *Cold Duck,* in 35 feet of water, is an excellent training dive. In summer Lake Mead is like a bathtub, reaching 85°F on the surface and staying at about 80°F down to 50 feet below the surface. Divers can actually wear bathing suits rather than wet suits to do some of the shallower dives. But visibility—which averages 30 feet to 35 feet overall—is much better in the winter months before the late-spring surface-algae bloom obscures some of the deeper attractions from snorkelers. The National Park Service has designated an underwater trail at Boulder Beach, near the Pyramid Island Causeway; just follow the buoys. Be aware that Lake Mead's level has dropped because of low snowfall in the Rockies. This has had some effect on diving conditions; St. Thomas, for example, is now only partially submerged.

Outfitters & Information **American Cactus Divers.** If you have the time to take the two-week course, American Cactus offers scuba-diving classes and issues certificates. ✉*3985 E. Sunset Rd., East Side* ☎*702/433–3483.*

Desert Divers Supply. Snorkelers and divers can rent masks, fins, boots, wet suits, tanks, and regulators. ✉*5720 E. Charleston Blvd., East Side* ☎*702/438–1000.*

AAI Neptune Divers. Neptune Divers rents scuba equipment and offers lessons. ✉*5831 E. Lake Mead Blvd., East Side* ☎*702/452–5723.*

VALLEY OF FIRE

❹ *50 mi northeast of Las Vegas; take I–15 north about 35 mi to Exit 75–Rte. 169 and continue 15 mi.*

The 56,000-acre **Valley of Fire State Park** was dedicated in 1935 as Nevada's first state park. Valley of Fire takes its name from its distinctive coloration, which ranges from lavender to tangerine to bright red, giving the vistas along the park road an otherworldly appearance. The jumbled rock formations are remnants of hardened sand dunes more than 150 million years old. You find petrified logs and the park's most photographed feature—Elephant Rock—just steps off the main road. Mysterious petroglyphs (carvings etched into the rocks) and pictographs (pictures drawn or painted on the rock's surface) are believed to be the work of the Basketmaker and ancestral Puebloan people who lived along the nearby Muddy River between 300 "# and !$ 1150.

☾ The **Valley of Fire Visitors Center** has displays on the park's history, ecology, archaeology, and recreation, as well as slide shows and films, an art gallery, and information about the 51 campsites within the park. The park is open year-round; the best times to visit, especially during the heat of summer, are sunrise and sunset, when the light is truly spectacular. ⌂ *Rte. 169, Box 515, Overton 89040* ☎ *702/397–2088* ⊕ *www.parks.nv.gov* ▧ *$6 per vehicle or $14 per night for a campsite* ☉ *Daily 8:30–4:30.*

OFF THE BEATEN PATH

Lost City Museum. The Moapa Valley has one of the finest collections of ancestral Puebloan artifacts in the American Southwest. Lost City was a major outpost of the ancient culture. The museum's artifacts include baskets, weapons, a restored Basketmaker pit house, and black-and-white photographs of the 1924 excavation of Lost City. To get to the Lost City Museum from Valley of Fire, turn around on the park road and head back to the T intersection at the entrance to the Valley of Fire. Turn left and drive roughly 8 mi into Overton. Turn left at the sign for the museum. Kids get in free. ✉ *721 S. Moapa Valley Blvd., Overton* ☎ *702/397–2193* ⊕ *www.comnett.net/~kolson* ▧ *$3* ☉ *Daily 8:30–4:30.*

GRAND CANYON NATIONAL PARK

240 mi east of Las Vegas; south on U.S. 93 to Kingman, east on I–40 to Williams, north on Rte. 64.

★ If you only make one side trip from Las Vegas, make it to **Grand Canyon National Park.** The Colorado River has carved through colorful and often contorted layers of rock, in some places more than 1 mi down, to expose a geologic profile spanning a time between 1.7 billion and 2.5 billion years ago—one-third of the planet's life. There's nothing like standing on the rim and looking down and across at layers of distance, color, and shifting light. Add the music of a canyon wren's merry, descending call echoing off the cliffs and springwater tinkling from the rocks along a trail, and you may sink into a reverie as deep and beautiful as the canyon.

There are two main access points to the canyon: the **South Rim** and the **North Rim**, both within the national park, but the hordes of visitors converge mostly on the South Rim in summer, for good reason. Grand Canyon Village is here, with most of the lodging and camping, restaurants and stores, and museums in the park, along with the airport, railroad depot, rim roads, scenic overlooks, and trailheads into the canyon. The East or North rims, which are less accessible and have fewer, though comparable, tourist services, are less crowded. The geology and vistas of the East Rim closely resemble what you see from the South Rim, and the entrance is accessible from

> ### THE GREATEST VIEW ON EARTH
>
> Most visitors to the Grand Canyon expect awesome views, but the 720-degree vistas from the **Grand Canyon Skywalk** (☎877/716–9378 ⊕ www.destinationgrand-canyon.com) are likely to give new meaning to the word "awe." The Skywalk is a glass, U-shape structure that juts out over the western rim at Eagle Point, 4,000 feet above the canyon floor. Chicago's Sears Tower (1,450 feet) and the Taipei 101 Tower (1,671 feet) could easily stand end to end in that space, with room to spare. It extends 70 feet out over the canyon. Children under 4 years of age are not allowed.

both the South Rim and Flagstaff. The North Rim, by contrast, stands 1,000 feet higher than the South Rim and has a more alpine climate, with twice as much annual precipitation. Here, in the deep forests of the Kaibab Plateau, the crowds are thinner, the facilities fewer, and the views even more spectacular. ☎928/638–7888, 928/638–7875 *campground reservations* ⊕*www.nps.gov/grca* ☎*$25 per car, $12 per individual; $18 per night/campsite at Mather Campground, $12 per night/campsite at Desert View Campground* ⊙*North Rim, daily mid-May–mid-Oct.*

Numbers in the margin correspond to numbers on the Grand Canyon National Park map.

SOUTH RIM

❺ Mather Point, approximately 4 mi north from the south entrance, gives you the first glimpse of the canyon from one of the most impressive and accessible vista points on the rim; from it you can see nearly a fourth of the Grand Canyon.

The **Canyon View Information Plaza,** in Grand Canyon Village at Mather Point, orients you to many facets of the site, and it's an excellent place for gathering information, whether you're interested in escapist treks or group tours. If you'd like a little exercise and great overlooks of the canyon, it's an easy hike from the back of the visitor center to the El Tovar Hotel. Walk through a pretty wooded area for about ½ mi; from there the path runs along the rim for another ½ mi or so.

Grand Canyon National Park

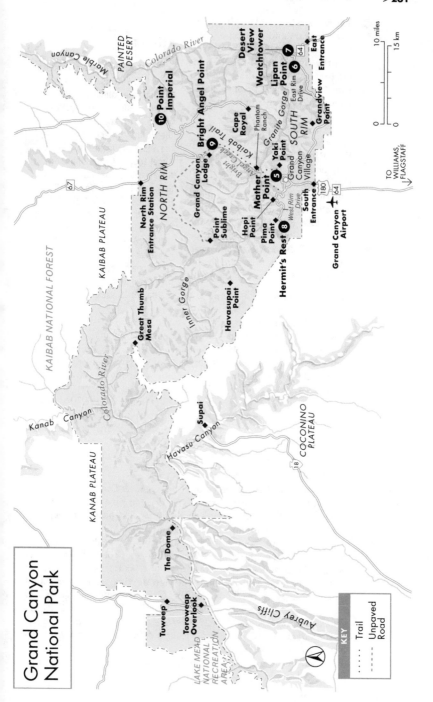

Marble Canyon

Colorado River

Desert View Watchtower ⑦

Lipan Point ⑥

East Entrance

10 **Point Imperial**

Bright Angel Point ⑨

Cape Royal

Phantom Ranch

Granite Gorge

SOUTH RIM

East Rim Drive

Grandview Point

North Rim Entrance Station

NORTH RIM

KAIBAB PLATEAU

67

Grand Canyon Lodge

Bright Angel Trail

North Kaibab Trail

Yaki Point

5 **Mather Point**

Grand Canyon Village

South Entrance

180

64

TO WILLIAMS, FLAGSTAFF

KAIBAB NATIONAL FOREST

Point Sublime

Hopi Point

Pima Point

West Rim Drive

8 **Hermit's Rest**

Grand Canyon Airport

Inner Gorge

Great Thumb Mesa

Havasupai Point

Colorado River

Kanab Canyon

Supai

Havasu Canyon

18

COCONINO PLATEAU

KANAB PLATEAU

The Dome

Tuweep

Toroweap Overlook

Aubrey Cliffs

LAKE MEAD NATIONAL RECREATION AREA

KEY

⋯⋯ Trail

--- Unpaved Road

10 miles

15 km

0

6 The **East Rim Drive,** relatively unclut-
tered by cars and tour buses, also
has beautiful views of the canyon
and the river. The 23-mi, 45-min-
ute (one-way) drive along the East
Rim takes you past **Lipan Point,** the
widest and perhaps most spectacular part of the canyon, and continues to where you see partially
intact ancient rock dwellings. On
East Rim Drive you find **Tusayan
Ruin and Museum** (☉*Daily 9–5*),
which has exhibits about Native
American tribes that have inhabited the region in the past 2,000
years. East Rim Drive ends at the
East Rim Entrance Station and the
7 70-foot-tall **Desert View Watchtower,**
which clings precariously to the lip
of the chasm.

8 The **West Rim Drive** runs 8 mi west
Fodor'sChoice from Grand Canyon Village. Along
★

KNOW BEFORE YOU STAY

A master concessionaire, Xanterra Parks and Resorts, handles all lodging reservations for all Grand Canyon National Park facilities on the North and South rims: the North's Grand Canyon Lodge, the South's El Tovar Hotel, Bright Angel Lodge, the Kachina Lodge, the Maswik Lodge, Yavapai Lodge, and Thunderbird Lodge. A toll-free number (☎888/297–2757) is available for reservations, and Xanterra uses a local number (☎928/638–2631) to reach hotel guests at any of the properties. Occasionally, reservations can be made at individual properties on the day of arrival.

this tree-lined, two-lane drive are scenic overlooks with panoramic views of the inner canyon—all popular sunset destinations.The West Rim Drive terminates at **Hermit's Rest.** Canyon views from here include Hermit's Rapids and the towering cliffs of the Supai and Redwall formations. From March through November only the free shuttle bus is allowed on West Rim Drive. You can catch it at the West Rim Interchange near Bright Angel Lodge every 30 minutes 4:30–7:30 AM, every 10 to 15 minutes 7:30 AM–sunset, and every 30 minutes from sunset to an hour after sunset. The shuttle stops at all eight canyon overlooks on the 8-mi trip out to Hermit's Rest, but only stops at Mojave and Hopi Points on the inbound leg. A round-trip takes 75 minutes.

WHERE TO STAY & EAT

$$–$$$$ ✕▦ **El Tovar Hotel.** A registered national Historic Landmark, El Tovar
Fodor'sChoice was built in 1905 of native stone and Oregon pine logs. The hotel's
★ proximity to all of the canyon's facilities, its European hunting-lodge atmosphere, and its renowned dining room ($–$$$) make it the best place to stay on the South Rim. It's usually booked well in advance (up to 13 months ahead), though it's easier to get a room during winter months. Three suites and several rooms have canyon views (these are booked early), but you can enjoy the view anytime from the cocktail-lounge back porch. ⊠ *West Rim Dr., Grand Canyon Village* ⊅*PO 699, Grand Canyon, AZ 86023* ☎*888/297–2757 reservations via Xanterra Resorts, 928/638–2631 Xanterra switchboard* ⊕*www.grand-canyonlodges.com* ⊅*70 rooms, 12 suites* ♿*In-hotel: restaurant, room service, bar, no-smoking rooms* ☐*AE, D, MC, V.*

¢–$$$ ✕▦ **Bright Angel Lodge.** Famed architect Mary Jane Colter designed
♺ this 1935 log-and-stone structure, which sits within a few yards of

the canyon rim and blends superbly with the canyon walls. It offers a similar location to El Tovar for about half the price. Accommodations are in motel-style rooms or cabins. Lodge rooms don't have TVs, and some rooms do not have private bathrooms. Scattered among the pines, 50 cabins, some with fireplaces, have TVs and private baths. Expect historic charm but not luxury. The Bright Angel Dining Room serves family-style meals all day and a Warm Apple Grunt dessert large enough to share. The Arizona Room serves dinner only. Adding to the experience are an ice-cream parlor, gift shop, a small history museum with exhibits on restaurateur Fred Harvey and Mary Jane Colter, an Internet room, and a coffee shop. ⊠ *West Rim Dr., Grand Canyon Village* ⌂ *Grand Canyon Village, Box 699, Grand Canyon, AZ 86023* ☎ *888/297–2757 reservations via Xanterra Resorts, 928/638–2631 Xanterra switchboard* ⊕ *www.grandcanyonlodges.com* ⬅ *39 rooms, 6 with shared toilet and shower, 13 with shared shower; 50 cabins* ⌂ *In-room: no a/c, no TV (some). In-hotel: restaurant, bar* ☰ *AE, D, MC, V.*

$ ✕ 🏠 **Phantom Ranch.** Popular with hikers and mule riders going to the
★ bottom of the canyon, Phantom Ranch is the only lodging below the canyon's rim. These primitive quarters, built in 1922 along Bright Angel Creek, consist of cabins and dorm spaces. Cabins are included with the two-day mule trips (run only November through March), while gender-segregated dormitory-style lodging is available to backpackers. The Canteen has breakfast, sack lunches, and dinners served at two seatings. The early seating serves steak and vegetarian meals, while the second seating serves hiker's stew. The rooms don't have TVs—there's plenty to see outside. ⊠ *On canyon floor, at intersection of Bright Angel and Kaibab trails, AZ* ☎ *888/297–2757 reservations via Xanterra Resorts, 928/638–2631 Xanterra switchboard* ⬅ *4 dormitories and 2 cabins for hikers, 7 cabins with outside showers for mule riders* ⌂ *In-room: no a/c, no TV, no elevator* ☰ *AE, D, MC, V.*

OFF THE BEATEN PATH

Historic Route 66. If you're driving to the Grand Canyon from Las Vegas, an easterly diversion at the Andy Devine turnoff in Kingman puts you on the "old highway," known as U.S. Route 66—the longest remaining uninterrupted stretch of the "Main Street of America." Before taking off from Kingman, though, you'll want to start your adventure by exploring the Route 66 Museum and the Mohave Museum of History and Arts—two cultural centers that put into perspective the area's history, including the life of gravelly voiced actor Andy Devine, who grew up in Kingman. Taking I–40 may be 18 mi shorter and 15 minutes quicker, but you'll miss the road made famous by John Steinbeck's novel *The Grapes of Wrath* and the old Hackberry store with an exterior reminiscent of the 1950s and an interior filled with nostalgic goodies, not to mention snacks, pop, and water. Farther down the road are the Peach Springs headquarters for the Hualapai Tribe, one of several Native American tribes living in northern Arizona, and the Grand Canyon Caverns, limestone caves found more than 200 feet below. Visit the **Powerhouse Visitor Center and Route 66 Museum** (⊠ *120 W. Andy Devine Ave., Kingman, AZ 86401* ☎ *928/753–6106 visitor cen-*

8

ter, 928/753–9889 museum ⬜*$4* ⏱*Mar.–Nov., daily 9–6; Dec.–Feb., daily 9–5* ⬛*No credit cards*) and the **Mohave Museum of History and Arts** (✉*400 W. Beale St., Kingman, AZ 86401* ☎*928/753–3195* ⊕*www. citlink.net/~mocohist/museum/* ⬜*$4* ⏱*Weekdays 9–5, Saturday 1–5*). Admission to one museum is good for the other museum as well.

NORTH RIM

❾ **Bright Angel Point,** on the North Rim, is one of the most awe-inspiring overlooks on either rim. The trail leading to it begins on the grounds of the Grand Canyon Lodge and proceeds along the crest of a point of rocks that juts into the canyon for several hundred yards. The walk is only 1 mi round-trip, but it's an exciting trek because there are sheer drops just a few feet away on each side of the trail.

❿ For spectacular sunrise views of the eastern canyon and Painted Desert, head to **Point Imperial.** The road to Point Imperial and Cape Royal intersects Route 67 about 3 mi north of Grand Canyon Lodge. The picture-perfect road winds 8 mi through stands of quaking aspen into a forest of conifers. When the road forks, continue 3 mi north to the overlook.

WHERE TO STAY & EAT

$–$$ ✕▦ **Grand Canyon Lodge.** This historic property, constructed mainly in
Fodor's Choice the 1920s and '30s, is the premier lodging facility in the North Rim
★ area. The main building has limestone walls and timbered ceilings. Lodging options include small, rustic cabins; larger cabins (some with a canyon view and some with two bedrooms); and newer, traditional motel rooms. You might find marinated pork kebabs or linguine with cilantro on the dining room's dinner menu ($–$$$). Dining room reservations are essential and should be made as far in advance as possible. ✉*Hwy. 67, North Rim, Grand Canyon National Park, AZ 86052* ☎*888/297–2757 reservations via Xanterra Resorts, 928/638–2631 Xanterra switchboard* ⊕*www.grandcanyonnorthrim.com* ⬐*44 rooms, 157 cabins* ♿*In-room: no a/c, no TV. In-hotel: restaurant, bar, laundry facilities, no-smoking rooms, no elevator* ⬛*AE, D, MC, V.*

$–$$ ▦ **Kaibab Lodge.** Rustic cabins with simple furnishings are in a wooded area 5 mi from the park's entrance. When you're not lolling in the fine, big meadow outside, you can sit around the lodge's stone fireplace (it can be chilly up here even in summer because it sits at a 9,000-foot elevation). The 1920s-era, pine-beam-supported lodge is open year-round, but access during the winter months is only for those with 4x4 vehicles, a snowmobile, or cross-country skis. Shuttle service from the lodge to the rim is available for $20 a person. ⌂*HC 64 Box 30, Fredonia, AZ 86022* ☎*928/638–2389* ⊕*www.kaibablodge.com* ⬐*28 cabin-style units* ♿*In-room: no a/c, no phone, no TV. In-hotel: restaurant, bar* ⬛*D, MC, V.*

Freebies at the Canyon

While you're here, be sure to take advantage of the many freebies offered at Grand Canyon National Park. The most useful of these services is the system of free shuttle buses at the South Rim; it caters to the road-weary, with three routes winding through the park—Hermits Rest Route, Village Route, and Kaibab Trail Route. Of the bus routes, the Hermits Rest Route runs only from March through November; the other two run year-round, and the Kaibab Trail Route provides the only access to Yaki Point. Hikers coming or going from the Kaibab Trailhead can catch the Hikers Express, which departs three times each morning from the Bright Angel Lodge, makes a quick stop at the Backcountry Office, and then heads out to the South Kaibab Trailhead.

Ranger-led programs are always free and offered year-round, though more are scheduled during the busy spring and summer seasons. These programs might include activities such as stargazing and topics such as geology and the cultural history of prehistoric peoples. Some of the more in-depth programs may include a fossil walk or a condor talk. Check with the visitor center for seasonal programs including wildflower walks and fire ecology.

Kids ages 4 to 14 can get involved with the park's Junior Ranger program, with ever-changing activities including hikes and hands-on experiments.

Despite all of these options, rangers will tell you that the best free activity in the canyon is watching the magnificent splashes of color on the canyon walls during sunrise and sunset.

GRAND CANYON ESSENTIALS

8

To research prices, get advice from other travelers, and book travel arrangements, visit www.fodors.com.

TRANSPORTATION

BY CAR

It's a little less than 300 mi to the South Rim from Las Vegas. Take U.S. 93 to Kingman, Arizona; I–40 east from Kingman to Williams; then Route 64 and U.S. 180 to the edge of the abyss. The North Rim is about 282 mi from Las Vegas. Take I–15 east to Hurricane, Utah; Routes 59 and 389 to Fredonia; and U.S. 89 and Route 67 to the North Rim. The North Rim is closed to automobiles after the first heavy snowfall of the season (usually in late October or early November) through mid-May. All North Rim facilities close between October 15 and May 15, though the park itself stays open for day use from October 15 through December 1, if heavy snows don't close the roads before then.

Contacts North Rim road conditions and other general park information ☎ *928/638–7888.*

CONTACTS & RESOURCES

TIME

Hours of operation listed for the Grand Canyon use Arizona time.

The state of Nevada is in the Pacific Time Zone, while Arizona is in the Mountain Time Zone. Arizona does not use daylight saving time, however, and as a result, during the summer Nevada and Arizona observe the same hours.

TOURS

Ground tours to the Grand Canyon can be had from the Grand Canyon Tour Company, but if you're short on time (and can check your fear of heights at the bell desk) consider winging your way there on a small plane or helicopter. A host of air-tour companies will give you the bird's-eye view of the Strip, Hoover Dam, and Lake Mead on the way to the Grand Canyon rim and even down to the Colorado River bed itself on tours as brief as two hours and as inexpensive as $200 per person. Helicopter tours are usually more expensive than those in a small fixed-wing plane. All possible permutations of flight plans and amenities are available, from lunch, to river rafting, to overnight accommodations. Most tours include pick-up and drop-off service from your hotel (sorry Hotshot, you get picked up in a van or limo, not by a chopper). Weekday tours actually fill up faster than weekends; it can't hurt to book a few days in advance. The scenery is spectacular, but the ride can be bumpy and cold, even in summertime.

Air Tours **Air Vegas** (☎ *702/501–8470 or 800/940–2550* ⊕ *www.airvegas.com*). **Grand Canyon Tour Company** (☎ *702/655–6060 or 800/222–6966* ⊕ *www.grandcanyontourcompany.com*). **HeliUSA** (☎ *702/736–8787 or 800/359–8727* ⊕ *www.heliusa.com*). **Maverick Helicopter Tours** (☎ *702/261–0007 or 888/261–4414* ⊕ *www.maverickhelicopter.com*). **Papillon** (☎ *702/736–7243 or 888/635–7272* ⊕ *www.papillon.com*). **Scenic Airlines** (☎ *702/638–3300 or 800/634–6801* ⊕ *www.scenic.com*). **Sundance Helicopters** (☎ *702/736–0606 or 800/653–1881* ⊕ *www.sundancehelicopters.com*).

VISITOR INFORMATION

Contacts **Grand Canyon Chamber of Commerce and Visitors Bureau** (✉ *Box 3007, Grand Canyon, AZ 86023* ☎ *928/638–2901* ⊕ *www.grandcanyonchamber.com* ⊙ *Weekdays 8–5*).

Grand Canyon National Park Visitors Services (✉ *Box 129, Grand Canyon, AZ 86023* ☎ *928/638–7888 recorded information* ⊕ *www.nps.gov/grca*). **Kane County Office of Tourism** (✉ *78 S. 100 E, Kanab, UT 84741* ☎ *435/644–5033 or 800/733–5263* ⊕ *www.kaneutah.com*).

LAUGHLIN, NEVADA

90 mi south of Las Vegas.

Laughlin is a unique state-line city separated from Arizona by the Colorado River. Its founder, Don Laughlin, bought an eight-room motel here in 1966 and basically built the town from scratch. By the early

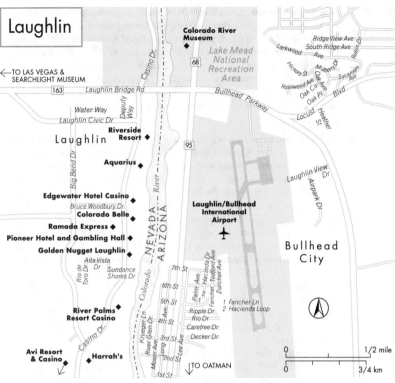

Laughlin

Colorado River Museum

Lake Mead National Recreation Area

68

←TO LAS VEGAS & SEARCHLIGHT MUSEUM
163
Laughlin Bridge Rd

Bullhead Parkway

Water Way
Laughlin Civic Dr
Deputy Way

L a u g h l i n   Riverside Resort ◆

95

Aquarius ◆

Big Bend Dr

Edgewater Hotel Casino ◆
Bruce Woodbury Dr.
Colorado Belle ◆
Ramada Express ◆
Pioneer Hotel and Gambling Hall ◆
Golden Nugget Laughlin ◆

Laughlin/Bullhead International Airport

Laughlin View Dr
Airpark Dr

Ridge View Ave
South Ridge Ave
Larkwood Ave
Hickory St   Mulberry Ave
Rosewood Ave   Oak Cir   Oak Ave
Oak Pl
Locust
Heather St
Sycamore Ave
Robin Dr
Blvd

B u l l h e a d   C i t y

NEVADA
ARIZONA
Alta Vista Dr
Rio de Toro Dr   Sundance Shores Dr

7th St
6th St
5th St
4th St
3rd St
2nd St
1st St

Palm Ave
Hacinda Dr
Fancher
Tedford Ave
Zurcher Ave

1 Fancher Ln
2 Hacienda Loop

Ripple Dr
Rio Dr
Carefree Dr
Decker Dr

Colorado

River Palms Resort Casino ◆

Krueger Ln
River Glen Dr.
Moser Ave.
Long Ave.
Lee Ave.

Casino Dr.

Avi Resort & Casino ◆   ◆ Harrah's

↓TO OATMAN

0   1/2 mile
0   3/4 km

8

1980s Laughlin's Riverside Hotel-Casino was drawing gamblers and river rats from northwestern Arizona, southeastern California, and even southern Nevada, and his success attracted other casino operators. Today Laughlin is the state's third major resort area, attracting more than 5 million visitors annually. The city fills up, especially in winter, with both retired travelers who spend at least part of the winter in Arizona and a younger resort-loving crowd. The big picture windows overlooking the Colorado River lend a bright, airy, and open feeling particular to Laughlin casinos. Take a stroll along the river walk, then make the return trip by water taxi ($3 round-trip, $2 one-way). Boating, Jet Skis, fishing, and plain old wading are other options for enjoying the water.

Across the Laughlin Bridge, ¼ mi to the north, the **Colorado River Museum** displays the rich past of the tri-state region where Nevada, Arizona, and California converge. There are artifacts from the Mojave Indian tribe, models and photographs of steamboats that once plied the river, rock and fossil specimens, and the first telephone switchboard used in neighboring Bullhead City. A military memorabilia collection formerly housed in the Ramada Casino is now housed at the museum. ✉ *2201 Rte. 68* ☎*928/754–3399* ⊕*www.bullheadcity.com/tourism/ Hismuseum.asp* 🖾*$2* ⊗ *Sept.–June, Tues.–Sat. 10–4, Sun. 1–4.*

Searchlight Museum. Searchlight was once the biggest boomtown in southern Nevada, and this modern, one-room exhibit inside the town hall details the area's rich mining and railroad history. It also exposes the lives of its most famous couple, legendary silent screen stars Rex Bell and Clara Bow. On the way to Laughlin from Las Vegas on U.S. 95, turn off at Cottonwood Cove Road, drive almost a mile to the end of town and turn left on Michael Wendell Way. ⊠ *200 Michael Wendell Way* 🕾 *702/297–1682* 🎫 *Free* ⊙ *Weekdays 1–5, Sat. 9–1.*

WHERE TO STAY & EAT

¢–$$ ✕🏨 **Colorado Belle.** This is a Nevada anomaly—a riverboat casino that's actually on a river. The 608-foot replica of a Mississippi paddle wheeler has nautical-theme rooms with views of the Colorado River. No-smoking gamblers will appreciate the smoke-free section in the slot machine area. The **Boiler Room Brew Pub** ($), the only microbrewery in Laughlin, pumps out 155,000 gallons of beer each year. ⊠ *2100 S. Casino Dr., 89029* 🕾 *702/298–4000 or 866/352–3553* ⊕ *www.coloradobelle. com* ➥ *1,119 rooms, 49 suites* ⚷ *In-hotel: 6 restaurants, pools, laundry service, Wi-Fi, no-smoking rooms* ⊟ *AE, D, DC, MC, V.*

¢–$ ✕🏨 **Golden Nugget Laughlin.** A tropical atrium in this miniversion of the Las Vegas Golden Nugget has two cascading waterfalls and more than 300 types of plants from around the world. **Joe's Crab Shack** ($$–$$$) offers the only riverfront dining in town. ⊠ *2300 S. Casino Dr., 89029* 🕾 *702/298–7111 or 800/950–7700* ⊕ *www.goldennugget.com* ➥ *300 rooms* ⚷ *In-hotel: 4 restaurants, bar, pool, no-smoking rooms* ⊟ *AE, DC, MC, V.*

¢–$ ✕🏨 **Harrah's.** Completely remodeled in 2006, this is the classiest joint in Laughlin, and it even comes with a private sand beach. It also has two casinos (one is no-smoking), and big-name entertainers perform in the Fiesta Showroom and at the 3,000-seat Rio Vista Outdoor Amphitheater. The **Range Steakhouse** ($–$$$) serves Continental fare. ⊠ *2900 S. Casino Dr., 89029* 🕾 *702/298–4600 or 800/427–7247* ⊕ *www.harrahs.com* ➥ *1,561 rooms* ⚷ *In-hotel: 5 restaurants, bars, pools, gym, spa, beachfront, no-smoking rooms, public Wi-Fi* ⊟ *AE, D, DC, MC, V.*

¢–$ ✕🏨 **Riverside Resort.** Town founder Don Laughlin still runs this north-
★ ernmost joint himself. Check out the Loser's Lounge, with its graphic homage to famous losers, such as the *Hindenburg,* the *Titanic,* and the like. And don't pass up Don's two free classic-car showrooms, with more than 80 rods, roadsters, and tin lizzies. The **Gourmet Room** restaurant serves Continental and American cuisine. The Riverside is one of only two bingo parlors in Laughlin; the other is the River Palms Resort Casino. ⊠ *1650 S. Casino Dr., 89029* 🕾 *702/298–2535 or 800/227–3849* ⊕ *www.riversideresort.com* ➥ *1,440 rooms* ⚷ *In-hotel: 6 restaurants, bar, pools, children's programs (ages 3 months–12 yrs), no-smoking rooms, public Wi-Fi* ⊟ *AE, D, DC, MC, V.*

¢ ✕🏨 **Avi Resort & Casino.** The only tribally owned casino in Nevada is
★ run by the Fort Mojave tribe. The 25,000-square-foot casino houses nearly 1,000 slot and video-poker machines; a 156-room tower with river views was opened in late 2003. The biggest draw, however, is

the private white-sand beach where you can lounge or rent a watercraft from April through September. The tribe operates an eight-screen Brenden movie theater nearby. Be sure to visit the **Moonshadow Grille,** preferably for the finest Sunday champagne brunch in the tri-state area. ⊠*10000 Aha Macav Pkwy., 89029* ☎*702/535–5555 or 800/284–2946* ⊕*www.avicasino.com* ⬩*455 rooms, 29 spa suites* ⚴*In-hotel: 5 restaurants, bar, golf course, pool, gym, beachfront, children's programs (ages 6 wks–12 yrs), no-smoking rooms, Internet* ⊟*AE, D, DC, MC, V.*

¢ ✕⌂ **Pioneer Hotel and Gambling Hall.** You can spot this small (by casino standards) motel by looking for the neon mascot, River Rick—he's Vegas Vic's brother. Although other casinos stress the new, the Pioneer retains its laid-back Western theme with checkered tablecloths and wagon-wheel light fixtures. **Granny's Gourmet Room** ($–$$$) serves Continental and American cuisine. ⊠*2200 S. Casino Dr., 89028* ☎*702/298–2442 or 800/634–3469* ⊕*www.pioneerlaughlin. com* ⬩*416 rooms* ⚴*In-hotel: 2 restaurants, bar, pool, beachfront, no-smoking rooms, no elevator* ⊟*AE, D, DC, MC, V.*

¢–$ ⌂ **Ramada Express.** Reserved for adults only, the newly renovated Casino Tower in this Victorian-theme hotel and casino is a perfect refuge for those seeking a child-free escape. There are also adults-only hours at the train-shape pool. The casino has state-of-the-art slots and a sports book. Kids are welcome in the Promenade Tower and they'll enjoy the free miniature train that chugs around the resort's 27 landscaped acres. ⊠*2121 S. Casino Dr., 89029* ☎*702/298–4200 or 800/243–6846* ⊕*www.ramadaexpress.com* ⬩*1,500 rooms* ⚴*In-hotel: 5 restaurants, bar, pool, no-smoking rooms, Ethernet* ⊟*AE, D, DC, MC, V.*

¢–$ ⌂ **River Palms Resort Casino.** A large balcony overlooks the table games in the 65,000-square-foot casino. The hotel's south wing, adjacent to the outdoor pool and hot tub, offers a quiet refuge away from the casino. The River Palms is one of only two bingo parlors in Laughlin; the other is Riverside Resort. ⊠*2700 S. Casino Dr., 89029* ☎*702/298–2242 or 800/835–7904* ⊕*www.river-palms.com* ⬩*1,001 rooms* ⚴*In-hotel: 4 restaurants, bars, pool, gym, spa, airport shuttle, no-smoking rooms, Wi-Fi* ⊟*AE, D, MC, V.*

¢ ⌂ **Aquarius.** The Flamingo Laughlin was renamed in late 2006 after an ownership change. Along with the new moniker, Aquarius boasts a fully renovated guest lobby and casino, featuring 1,500 slot and video-poker machines, a poker room, and a sports book. The 3,000-seat outdoor amphitheater, on the bank of the Colorado River, hosts big-name entertainers. Standard rooms have two double beds or a queen-size bed. Suites are larger (650–1,000 square feet) and equipped with coffeemakers, minibars, irons, and ironing boards. ⊠*1900 S. Casino Dr., 89029* ☎*702/298–5111 or 800/352–6464* ⊕*www.flamingolaughlin. com* ⬩*1,907 rooms, 82 suites* ⚴*In-hotel: 6 restaurants, bars, tennis courts, pool, gym, no-smoking rooms* ⊟*AE, D, DC, MC, V.*

¢ ⌂ **Edgewater Hotel Casino.** This 26-story hotel has a large casino with over 1,000 machines. ⊠*2020 S. Casino Dr., 89029* ☎*702/298–2453 or 800/677–4837* ⊕*www.edgewater-casino.com* ⬩*1,356 rooms*

8

CLOSE UP

Tips for Avoiding Canyon Crowds

"I find that in contemplating the natural world, my pleasure is greater if there are not too many others contemplating it with me, at the same time."—Edward Abbey

It's hard to commune with nature while you're searching for a parking place, dodging video cams, and stepping away from strollers. However, this scenario is likely to occur only during the very peak months of mid-May through mid-October. One option is to bypass Grand Canyon National Park altogether and head to the West Rim of the canyon, tribal land of the Hualapai and Havasupai. If only the park itself will do, the following tips will help you to keep your distance and your cool.

TAKE ANOTHER ROUTE

Avoid road rage by choosing a different route to the South Rim, foregoing the traditional highways 64 and U.S. 180 from Flagstaff. Take U.S. 89 north from Flagstaff instead, passing near Sunset Crater and Wupatki national monuments. When you reach the Cameron Trading Post at the junction with Highway 64, take a break—or stay overnight. This is a good place to shop for Native American artifacts, souvenirs, and the usual postcards, dream-catchers, recordings, and T-shirts. There are also high-quality Navajo rugs, jewelry, and other authentic handicrafts, and you can sample Navajo tacos. U.S. 64 to the west takes you directly to the park's east entrance; the scenery along the Little Colorado River Gorge en route is eye-popping. It's 25 mi from the Grand Canyon east entrance to the visitor center at Canyon View Information Plaza.

BYPASS THE SOUTH RIM ALTOGETHER

Although the North Rim is just 10 mi across from the South Rim, the trip to get there by car is a five-hour drive of 215 mi. At first it might not sound like the trip would be worth it, but the payoff is huge. Along the way, you will travel through some of the prettiest parts of the state and be granted even more stunning views than those on the more easily accessible South Rim. Those who make the North Rim trip often insist it offers the canyon's most beautiful views and best hiking. To get to the North Rim from Flagstaff, take U.S. 89 north past Cameron, turning left onto U.S. 89A at Bitter Springs. En route you'll pass the area known as Vermilion Cliffs. At Jacob Lake, take Hwy. 67 directly to the Grand Canyon North Rim. The road to the North Rim closes from around mid-October through mid-May because of heavy snow, but in summer months and early fall, it's a wonderful way to beat the crowds at the South Rim.

RIDE THE RAILS

There is no need to deal with all of the other drivers racing to the South Rim. Forget the hassle of the twisting rim roads, jaywalking pedestrians, and jammed parking lots and sit back and relax in the comfy train cars of the Grand Canyon Railway. Live music and storytelling enliven the trip as you journey past the breathtaking landscape. The train departs from the depot every morning between 8:30 and 10:30am, depending on the season, and makes the 65-mi journey in 2 hours. You can do the round-trip in a single day; however, you may choose to stay overnight at the South Rim and return to Williams the following afternoon.

⚘In-hotel: 3 restaurants, pool, no-smoking rooms, Wi-Fi ▤AE, D, DC, MC, V.

OFF THE BEATEN PATH

Oatman. Wild burros, descendants of animals employed during the area's gold-mining era, freely roam the streets of modern-day Oatman. The main street is right out of the Old West, and the town served as a backdrop for several films, including *How the West Was Won*. While visiting the gift shops and munching on churros (sticks of deep-fried dough), visit the **Oatman Hotel** (⊠*U.S. 66*) where Hollywood's Clark Gable and Carole Lombard spent their honeymoon night. Though it's no longer an operating hotel, you can still climb up the steep, squeaking staircase that leads to their famous room, still adorned with frilly lace. The building is on historic Route 66, the "Main Street of America." From the Laughlin Bridge, take Arizona Route 95 south about 15 mi to Boundary Cone Road. Turn left and go toward the mountains about 11 mi to reach Oatman.

☼ **Gold Road Mine.** Two miles east of Oatman is the Gold Road Mine, an active operation that dates to 1900. A one-hour tour takes modern-day prospectors underground for a demonstration of drilling equipment and a visit to the "Glory Hole," where the vein structures in the rock are highlighted with a black light to show the gold. Tours leave every 30 minutes until 4 ⊙ . ⊠*U.S. 66* ☎*928/768–1600* ⊕*www.goldroad-mine.com* ☜*$12.50* ⊙*Daily 10–5.*

LAUGHLIN ESSENTIALS

To research prices, get advice from other travelers, and book travel arrangements, visit www.fodors.com.

8

TRANSPORTATION

AIRPORTS

Contacts **Laughlin/Bullhead International Airport** (☎*928/754–2134*).

BY AIR

Sun Country flies from 35 cities in 11 states, including Seattle, Denver, Minneapolis–St. Paul, San Francisco, Phoenix, and Dallas–Ft. Worth. Several hotel-casinos, like Harrah's, also sponsor charter flights.

Airlines **Sun Country Airlines** (☎*800/359–6786* ⊕*www.suncountry.com*).

BY BUS

Greyhound buses stop at the Airport Sunridge Chevron Mini-Mart at 2996 Highway 68 in Bullhead City, Arizona. Individual hotel-casinos also sponsor bus trips from Las Vegas, Los Angeles, and other destinations.

Contacts **Greyhound** (☎*800/231–2222* ⊕*www.greyhound.com*).

BY CAR

To get to Laughlin from Las Vegas, take U.S. 95–93 south (I–515 east), then exit where U.S. 95 veers to the southwest. Drive for an hour, almost to the California border. A left turn onto Route 163 takes you east into Laughlin.

CAR RENTAL   Avis, Enterprise, and Hertz vehicles are available at the Laughlin/Bullhead International Airport. Other agencies can be found in Bullhead City; some companies have separate locations in some of the Laughlin hotels. Fuel up in Arizona—all grades of gasoline can be as much as 30¢–50¢ per gallon less in Bullhead City than in Laughlin.

Contacts **Avis-Airport** (☎ 928/754–4686 ⊕ www.avis.com). **Enterprise-Airport** (☎ 928/754–2700 ⊕ www.enterprise.com). **Hertz-Airport** (☎ 928/754–4111 ⊕ www.hertz.com).

CONTACTS & RESOURCES

TIME
The state of Nevada is in the Pacific time zone, while Arizona is in the mountain time zone. Arizona does not use daylight saving time, however. As a result, in summer Nevada and Arizona observe the same hours.

TRAIN TRAVEL
Amtrak's *Southwest Chief* stops at Needles, California, which is 25 mi south of Laughlin, and at Kingman, Arizona, which is about 30 mi east of Laughlin. Amtrak provides bus service from Kingman to the Ramada Express in Laughlin.

Contacts **Amtrak** (☎ 800/872–7245 ⊕ www.amtrak.com).

VISITOR INFORMATION
Contacts **Laughlin Chamber of Commerce** (⊠ 1585 S. Casino Dr., 89029 ☎ 702/298–2214 or 800/227–5245 ⊕ www.laughlinchamber.com). **Laughlin Visitors Bureau** (⊠ 1555 Casino Dr., 89029 ☎ 702/298–3321 or 800/452–8445 ⊕ www.visitlaughlin.com ☉ Weekdays 8–5, Weekends 8:30–5).

LINCOLN COUNTY: PARKS & GHOST TOWNS

Lincoln County, with U.S. 93–Great Basin Highway as its transportation spine, has been long overlooked as a Vegas getaway. No glaring neon or rush-hour freeway traffic here; rather, an occasional dim streetlight in one of the county's five tiny communities breaks up the vast star-studded sky or a sputtering hay baler negotiates the lonely asphalt ribbon.

Lincoln County encompasses ghost towns and near-ghost towns, national wildlife refuges, large ranches, and abundant water. The five state parks in the area are ideal destinations for just plain relaxing or for more strenuous activities like boating, fishing, hiking, and mountain biking.

Plan your trip and make reservations well in advance; the entire county is "tourist challenged," meaning that it has fewer than 100 hotel–motel rooms and fewer than a half-dozen restaurants. Contact the Bureau of Land Management for a map of off-highway travel. ■ TIP➔ **Be sure to bring a coat or sweater; it can get chilly because the elevation varies from 3,200 to 6,200 feet.**

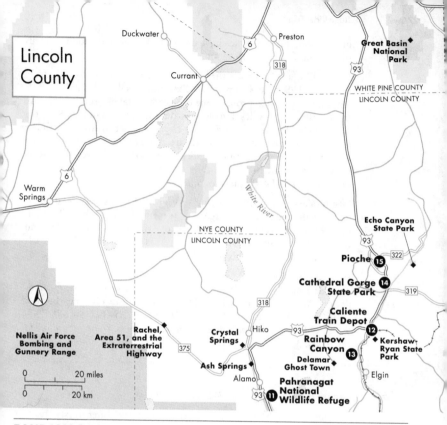

PAHRANAGAT VALLEY

92 mi from Las Vegas via I–15 to U.S. 93.

Desert vistas of creosote bushes and towering mountain ranges line the first 65 mi of this drive out of Las Vegas. But after cruising through a narrow volcanic rock pass, the world changes. Underground aquifers turn the landscape from stark to lush.

11 The 5,380-acre **Pahranagat National Wildlife Refuge** is a chain of three lakes, marshes, and meadows that provides a convenient stop on the Pacific Flyway for ducks, herons, egrets, eagles, and other species. The Upper Lake is the most accessible, with campsites, picnic tables, and observation points. *Box 510, Alamo 89001* ☏ *775/725–3417* ✉ *Free.*

OFF THE BEATEN PATH

Area 51. Known as Dreamland, this is a tiny nub in the northeastern corner of the vast 3.5-million-acre Nellis Air Force Base. According to sketchy and unconfirmed media reports, Area 51 is a supersecret military installation where the Air Force has tested top-secret aircraft (such as the U-2 spy plane and the Stealth bomber). Some people also believe the government stores and conducts research on UFOs and even collects and studies extraterrestrial beings here. It's illegal to approach the installation; military police have complete authority (including deadly force, if necessary) to prevent intrusions.

Route 375, a 98-mi road that runs through southeast Nevada from U.S. 93 to U.S. 6, was named the "Extraterrestrial Highway" in 1995. Signs along the road promote the eye-catching label—though they are frequently stolen. A desolate 36 mi from the junction of U.S. 93 is the tiny town of Rachel, about as close as you can get to Area 51. Today, thanks to its proximity to the secret area (and to the mysterious "black box" where the installation's mail was supposedly delivered), Rachel is a pilgrimage site for UFO enthusiasts from around the world. ⊠*143 mi northeast of Las Vegas, west on Rte. 375.*

Little A'Le'Inn. The main gathering spot in Rachel has photos of UFOs on the walls and an Alien Burger on the menu. Its rooms have TVs, but there's no TV reception; you can borrow videos, including UFO and Area 51 documentaries, from the inn's library. *⌂Rte. 375, HCR 61, Box 45, Rachel 89001* ☎*775/729–2515* ⊕*www.littlealeinn.com.*

WHERE TO STAY

¢–$ Alamo Meadow Lane Motel. You get basic prices for basic ground-floor rooms here. There's a handful of places to grab a bite nearby, too. ⊠*300 N. U.S. Hwy. 93, Alamo 89001* ☎*775/725–3371 or 888/740–8009* ⟲*15 rooms* ♿*In-hotel: no-smoking rooms, some pets allowed* ▭*AE, D, MC, V.*

CALIENTE

149 mi from Las Vegas via I–15 to U.S. 93.

Caliente used to be an important layover stop for water-thirsty steam locomotives making the trek through the steep, narrow canyons surrounding the town. Today Lincoln County's largest community has 1,100 residents and serves as a hub for visitors striking off in all directions to see the five nearby state parks, the county seat of Pioche, or the ghost town of Delamar. And, as the name implies, it's hot here—not because of oppressive temperatures, but from the hot springs, where townsfolk can relax.

⑫ The **Caliente Train Depot,** built in 1923, is a classic mission-style station. Having outlived its usefulness as a depot, it now houses the Caliente Chamber of Commerce, the library, and an art gallery. ⊠*100 Depot Ave.* ⊕*www.lincolncountynevada.com.*

Head north on Spring Street to **Company Row.** The railroad company built these 18 homes in 1905 for workers manning this major refueling site for steam locomotives. The historic buildings are still in use today as privately owned homes.

⑬ On the south side of town, Route 317 leads to the magnificent **Rainbow Canyon.** You pass between towering cliffs of red and orange, gold, and even deep green, where spring water drips from cracks in some places. Ancient petroglyphs have been pecked into some of the rocks. The bank-robbing duo of Butch Cassidy and the Sundance Kid hid out from the law deep inside some of the side canyons. You might also catch a close-up glimpse of a long diesel train winding its way through the chasm on the railroad's main line. **Kershaw-Ryan State Park**, which is part of Rainbow Canyon, is a destination for picnickers and hikers. ✒️*HC 64 Box 3, Caliente89008* ☎️*775/726–3564* 🌐*www.parks. nv.gov* 💲*$4 per vehicle.*

⓮ Erosion has shaped the bentonite clay of **Cathedral Gorge State Park** into odd formations, with twisting, tall, damp corridors of solidified mud leading to caves, more passageways, and sudden high perches. Step inside one of the curtains of wavy mud to escape the hot sun. Campsites are first-come, first-serve and have firepits, grills, and hot showers within walking distance. **Miller Point Overlook** is about 2 mi north of the park's entrance. The overlook reveals part of the ancient lake bed. Eagle View Trail, which starts at the overlook, is one of several park trails leading hikers closer to the formations. The visitor center for Cathedral Gorge is the regional center for all state parks in Lincoln County. ✒️*Box 176, Panaca 89042* ☎️*775/728–4460* 🌐*www.parks. nv.gov* 💲*$4 per vehicle, $14 per night for a campsite.*

OFF THE BEATEN PATH

Delamar Ghost Town. Some dilapidated buildings and rusted-out equipment are all that remain of this former silver-mining town that had a population of 3,000 around 1900. The so-called "Delamar Dust" inhaled by miners was actually silica dust, and the town earned a reputation as the "maker of widows" from the resulting deaths. Four-wheel-drive vehicles are recommended for the 16-mi jaunt over the bumpy gravel-and-rock road that's chopped with several dry washes along the way. ✉️*South off U.S. 93, 16 mi west of Caliente* 🌐*www. ghosttowns.com/states/nv/delamar.html* ☞*No services.*

WHERE TO STAY & EAT

¢–$ ✕ **Brandin' Iron Restaurant.** Two rooms are separated by an island bar in this rustic downtown café on the south side of the railroad tracks. It opens at 6 AM for breakfast, but go at dinner, when you can have twice-baked potatoes. ✉️*190 Clover St., Caliente* ☎️*775/726–3164* 🍽️*AE, D, MC, V.*

¢–$ ✕ **Knotty Pine Restaurant.** The walls are done in tongue-and-groove knotty pine at this eatery on the north side of the tracks. It's a good place to eat breakfast (try the excellent pancakes) and watch the train chug by, cutting the town in half. ✉️*690 Front St., Caliente* ☎️*775/726– 3767* 🍽️*AE, D, MC, V.*

¢–$ 🛏️ **Caliente Hot Springs Motel.** The rooms may be the usual, but what's unusual is the bathhouse with natural hot springs to soothe tight, car-cramped muscles. The bathhouse is open daily from 8 AM to 10 PM. For those willing to spend a little extra, five rooms have mineral baths inside. Access to the motel is off a side street (look for the directional sign); the motel is set back a distance from the highway and nestled against the mountain to the rear. ✉️*451 N. Spring St., Caliente 89008* ☎️*775/726–3777* 🛏️*17 rooms* ♿*In-hotel: some pets allowed, no elevator* 🍽️*AE, D, MC, V.*

¢ 🛏️ **Shady Motel.** The newest, largest, and tallest motel in Lincoln County has twin two-story buildings on a modern-looking complex. They face each other and not the highway, giving visitors peace and quiet throughout the night. ⊠*450 Front St., Caliente 89008* ☎*775/726–3107* ⮜*28 rooms* ⚇*In-hotel: no-smoking rooms, some pets allowed, no elevator* ▤*AE, D, DC, MC, V.*

PIOCHE

⑮   *174 mi from Las Vegas via I–15 to U.S. 93.*

Fodor's Choice
★

A mining town dating to the 1870s, Pioche once had the reputation of being more recklessly lawless than the notorious Western towns of Tombstone, Bodie, and Dodge City. According to legend, more than 70 gunfight victims were buried in Boot Hill Cemetery before anyone who had died of natural causes found a place there. Relics of the boom-and-bust mining periods—from silver mining in the late 1800s to zinc and lead mining in the 1940s—are more prevalent on the streets today than gunplay, however. At 6,064 feet, walking around hilly Pioche can take your breath away—literally. Walk slowly and enjoy the sights.

The **Lincoln County Museum,** on Main Street, houses thousands of rock specimens, photos, and artifacts. The antique X-ray machine, with its long, pointy "arm," looks like something out of a Ray Bradbury novel. ⊠*69 Main St., Pioche* ☎*775/962–5207* ☒*Free* ⊙*Daily 10–3.*

The **Million Dollar Courthouse** is so named because that's how much it costs to pay off the building's debt of $16,400 over the course of 66 years. The first floor has restored offices, and the second floor is the original courtroom with fancy old light fixtures, ornate woodwork, and a molded-tin ceiling. The only ones holding court these days are life-size dummies dressed in old-time garb representing the judge, jury, attorneys for the prosecution and defense, and, of course, the suspect. Outside the courtroom is the jail, with tiny holding cells made of stone and iron. ⊠*Lacour St.* ☎*775/962–5182 mid-Apr.–mid-Oct.* ☒*By donation* ⊙*Mid-Apr.–mid-Oct., daily 11–4.*

There are several old buildings along Main Street that you can view from the outside. The **Mountain View Hotel** is a three-story wooden structure built in 1895. Former president Herbert Hoover, himself a mining engineer, stayed here on a visit to the town. Other buildings include the **Old Commercial Building and Fire Hall, Thompson Opera House,** and the **Gem Theater.** On the outskirts of town are the **Glory Holes and Pioche Aerial Tramway,** which hauled ore by gravity from the Treasure Hill mine to the mill in the valley below, and **Boot Hill,** where graves and carved wooden headstones recall the past.

The 65-acre reservoir at **Echo Canyon State Park** is a favorite for fishing and boating. The park has a campground and picnic area. Jackrabbits, bobcats, coyotes, hawks, eagles, and even, on occasion, tundra swans call this lake-centered haven of Great Basin scrub, piñon, and juniper home. ⊠*12 mi east of Pioche via Rtes. 322 and 323* ☎*775/962–5103* ⊕*www.parks.nv.gov* ☒*$4 per vehicle.*

**OFF THE
BEATEN
PATH**

Great Basin National Park. The state's last remaining glacier is in a scooped-out rock bowl just below the tip of the second-highest peak in Nevada, the 13,063-foot Wheeler Peak in White Pine County. Underground, water dripping through limestone over the ages has created the fantastic and lovely configurations that make up **Lehman Caves** (☎775/234–7331 Ext. 242 ✍*Guided tours: $10 1½ hr, $8 1 hr* ☉*Tours at 9* AM *and 3* PM). It's one of the most remote and diverse national parks in the nation, taking you from sagebrush steppes up into cool forests with creeks, and on up through the high groves of 5,000-year-old bristlecone pine trees until you ascend beyond the tree line. ■**TIP→A jacket and treaded walking shoes are recommended for all adventures here—it can snow in July—and inside the caves, the "weather" is a constant 50°F with 90% humidity.** Take U.S. 93 81 mi north to the U.S. 6–50 junction, turn right (east) and go 28 mi to the Route 487 turnoff. Turn right (south) and go 5 mi to Baker, where you turn right (west) on Route 488 into the park. ✉*Rte. 488, Baker* ☎775/234–7331 ⊕*www.nps.gov/grba* ✍*Free* ☉*Visitor center June–Aug., daily 7:30–6; Sept.–May, daily 8:30–5.*

WHERE TO STAY & EAT

¢–$ ✕ **Silver Cafe.** The building dates to 1907, and the restaurant has been in operation for nearly as long. Owner Barbi Cammarano serves hearty and plentiful meals at skinny prices. It's pure Lincoln County here: there's a cozy stove, historic photos on the wall, a tin bucket on the counter with issues of the local newspaper (just drop a quarter in), and cowboys murmuring at nearby tables. ✉*97 Main St., 89043* ☎775/962–5124 ⊟*AE, D, DC, MC, V.*

¢–$ ☷ **Overland Hotel & Saloon.** This relic from Pioche's past was rebuilt in the 1940s after the original building was destroyed in one of the town's numerous fires. The rooms are quaint, not fancy. You have to climb a long set of creaky stairs to get to them. ✉*85 Main St., 89043* ☎775/962–5895 ⟿*13 rooms* ⚐*In-hotel: no-smoking rooms, some pets allowed, no elevator* ⊟*AE, D, MC, V.*

8

LINCOLN COUNTY ESSENTIALS

To research prices, get advice from other travelers, and book travel arrangements, visit www.fodors.com.

TRANSPORTATION

BY CAR

Take I–15 north 22 mi from downtown Las Vegas to the U.S. 93 turn-off. Most of the Lincoln County sights, including Caliente and Pioche, are along 93.

Given the remoteness of the area and the lack of services, make sure that you have plenty of fuel, water, food, and supplies before leaving any town. A good rule is to keep your gas tank at least half full at all times. Also, the weather can be tricky in eastern Nevada. Monitor weather reports frequently and check road conditions, even in July, especially before leaving U.S. 93.

The Bureau of Land Management office sells detailed maps of Lincoln County that are useful for off-highway travel.

Contacts **BLM Caliente Field Station** ⊠ *1440 S. Front St., Caliente* ☎ *775/726–8100* ⊕ *www.nv.blm.gov/ely* ⊙ *Weekdays 7:30–4:30* ▭ *AE, D, DC, MC, V.*

CONTACTS & RESOURCES

LODGING

Most Lincoln County motels observe a strict, no-nonsense no-smoking policy that can result in heavy fines ($50–$100 is common) and immediate eviction, no questions asked, if the smell of smoke is detectable or lingers in no-smoking rooms.

VISITOR INFORMATION

For rural communities, a quick call or Web visit to the local Chambers of Commerce can be a good starting place for planning an off-Strip itinerary. They list local businesses, places of interest, and often offer maps—just like a tourism office.

Contacts **Caliente Chamber of Commerce** (⊠ *Caliente Train Depot, 89008* ⊙ *Weekdays 10–2).* **Greater Lincoln County Chamber of Commerce** (⌀ *Box 915, Panaca, 89042* ⊕ *www.lincolncountynevada.com).* **Pahranagat Valley Chamber of Commerce** (⌀ *Box 421, Alamo, 89001).* **Pioche Chamber of Commerce** (⊠ *55 Main St., 89043* ☎ *775/962–5544* ⊕ *www.piochenevada.com* ⊙ *May–early Sept., Mon.–Thurs. 11–3).*

UNDERSTANDING
LAS VEGAS

Las Vegas at a Glance

Glitter, Gambling,
Growth

LAS VEGAS AT A GLANCE

DID YOU KNOW?

- Nine of the 10 largest hotels in the United States are in Las Vegas. They are the MGM Grand, Luxor, Mandalay Bay, Venetian, Excalibur, Bellagio, Circus Circus, Flamingo, and Caesars Palace.

- The cities of Las Vegas, Henderson, and North Las Vegas were among the 10 fastest-growing incorporated places (with populations of 100,000 or more), according to the 2000 U.S. Census.

- Clark County's gaming revenue was $9.7 billion in 2005, of which $7.6 billion was accumulated in the city of Las Vegas.

- Famous natives and residents of Las Vegas include Andre Agassi, Benjamin "Bugsy" Siegel, and Orson Welles.

- In Nevada it is required that video slot machines pay a minimum of 75% on average.

- Las Vegas casinos never use dice with round corners.

- Vegas Vic, the massive neon cowboy that guards Fremont Street, is the world's largest mechanical neon sign.

- The pyramid-shape Luxor Hotel is covered by 13 acres of glass. A specially designed window-washing device takes 64 hours to clean the four slanted walls.

- Boulder City is the only community in the state of Nevada where gambling is illegal.

FAST FACTS

Nickname: Sin City

Type of government: The Las Vegas Valley metropolitan area has four cities: Las Vegas, Henderson, North Las Vegas, and Boulder City. Each has a council-manager form of government, with an elected mayor. The rest of Clark County is governed by the county commission, with an appointed county manager.

Population: City 591,536, Clark County 1.91 million

Population density: 174 people per square mi in Clark County

Median age: Female 34, male 35

Crime rate: 738 violent crimes and 4,642 property crimes per 100,000 people in Metro Las Vegas

Infant mortality rate: 6.0 per 1,000 live births

Ethnic groups (Clark County): Caucasian 60.2%; Hispanic 22.0%; African American 9.1%; Asian–Pacific Islander 5.3%

Religion: Unaffiliated 65%; Catholic 16%; other Christian 8%; Mormon 6%; Jewish 5%

"Las Vegas has become, just as Bugsy Siegel dreamed, the American Monte Carlo . . ."

—Tom Wolfe, Kandy-Kolored Tangerine-Flake Streamline Baby

GEOGRAPHY & ENVIRONMENT

Latitude: 36°N (close to those of Algiers, Algeria; Athens, Greece; and Gibraltar)

Longitude: 115°W (close to those of Calgary, Alberta; San Diego, CA; and Tucson, AZ)

Elevation: 2,030 feet

Land area: City 81 square mi; Las Vegas Valley urban area 516 square mi; Clark County 8,060 square mi

Terrain: Desert, mountain

Natural hazards: Earthquakes

Environmental issues: The level of Lake Mead, which supplies about 90% of Southern Nevada's water, has dropped more than 70 feet since 1999. The decline is expected to continue due to low snowpack on the western slope of the Rocky Mountains. When the snowpack melts, the runoff feeds the Colorado River, which in turn supplies Lake Mead.

"Breasts are more than a body part here. They're entertainment."

—Comedian Rita Rudner

ECONOMY

Per capita income (county): $21,785

Unemployment (city): 3.5%

Work force: 688,917; service industries 79%; construction 11.2%; manufacturing 9.5%

Major industries: Gaming, tourism, construction, military

"We are never one thing. We are whatever we need to be next to get people here."

—Hal Rothman, chairman of the history department at the University of Nevada, Las Vegas

GLITTER, GAMBLING, GROWTH

The Las Vegas of the Strip and downtown is Wayne Newton, the Blue Man Group, and Cirque du Soleil. It's cards, dice, roulette wheels, and slots. It's harried keno runners and leggy cocktail waitresses, grizzled pit bosses and nervous break-in dealers. It's cab and limo drivers, valet attendants, and bellmen. Las Vegas is showgirls with smiles as white as spotlights and head wear as big and bright as fireworks. It's a place where thousands of people earn their livings counting billions in chips, change, bills, checks, and markers.

Gimmicks, glitz, and gigawatts of electrical power are what keep Las Vegas humming day and night—as do the more than 36 million casino-bound visitors who arrive every year and bed down in some of the world's largest, showiest hotels (the city has 18 of the 21 biggest in the world). Vegas Vic, the 50-foot-tall ambassador of Glitter Gulch, is forever duded up in high Western style to give gamblers a flashy welcome.

While the Strip and downtown are the best known and principal tourist areas of the city, nearly 2 million people live—and lead "normal" lives—within 10 mi of them. Endless subdivisions enclose rows and rows of pink-stucco and red-tile, three-bedroom-two-bath houses, most of them less than 10 years old and occupied by transplants hoping to cash in on the boom. "Lost Wages" is a city of dreamers: gamblers hoping to beat the odds and get rich; dancers, singers, magicians, acrobats, and comedians praying to make it in the Entertainment Capital of the World; and increasingly real estate agents, supermarket cashiers, computer techs, credit-card accounting clerks, shoe salespeople, and librarians seeking a better way of life.

For all the local talk about Las Vegas citizens being average people who just happen to live and work in an unusual city,

living here is undeniably different. The town is full of people whose jobs involve catering to strangers 24 hours a day, 365 days a year. Las Vegas probably has the largest graveyard shift in the world. And the notion that locals never gamble and rarely see a show or eat at a buffet is also largely a myth—residents are a large and active part of the total market that relishes 99¢ breakfasts and $5 prime ribs, slot clubs, casino paycheck-cashing promotions, and free lounge entertainment. Indeed, the casinos that cater primarily to locals (Palace Station, Boulder Station, Texas Station, the Rio, Gold Coast, Orleans, Santa Fe, Green Valley Ranch, Cannery, Arizona Charlie's, and Fiesta) are among the most successful in town. Surprisingly, Las Vegas is also a religious town—about a third of the 450 congregations here are Mormon—which adds a somewhat incongruous conservative dimension to local politics and morals.

Gambling and tourism are not the only games in town. Nellis Air Force Base employs thousands of people. The construction industry is huge. Large corporations and small manufacturing firms frequently relocate to southern Nevada, which offers tax incentives as well as a lower cost of living. But local life is merely a curiosity to the 36 million tourists whose primary concern is choosing among more than 65 major hotel-casinos, dozens of shows, a mind-boggling list of gambling options, limitless dining, and spectacular day trips.

Las Vegas is the largest city in Nevada and one of the most remote large cities in the country: the nearest major population center to the west is Barstow, California, 2½ hours away; St. George, Utah, is two hours to the east. Through the years Las Vegas has wrested the political and economic power of Nevada away from Reno, 448 mi to the northwest, the city where legalized gambling first became popular and where the early casinos were built.

Las Vegas is surrounded by the Mojave Desert, and Las Vegas Valley is flanked by mountain ranges. Among them are the Spring Mountains, including Mount Charleston (11,918 feet), which has skiing and snowboarding, and Red Rock Canyon, characterized by stunning Southwest sandstone. The Las Vegas Wash drains the valley to the southeast into Lake Mead and the Colorado River system.

Average high temperatures in Las Vegas rise to 105°F in July and August; lows drop to 30°F in January and February. The heat is saunalike throughout the summer, except during electrical storms that can dump an inch of rain an hour and cause dangerous flash floods. Heavy rains any time of year exacerbate two of Las Vegas's major problems: a lack of water drainage and a surplus of traffic. The summer blaze often makes it very uncomfortable to be outside for any length of time. Winters can be surprisingly chilly during the day and especially cold after the sun goes down. But in September and October and April and May it doesn't get any better.

Las Vegas is the largest U.S. city founded in the 20th century—1905 to be exact. Some might argue that the significant year was 1946, when Bugsy Siegel's Fabulous Flamingo opened for business. But the beginnings of modern Las Vegas can be traced back to 1829, when Antonio Armijo led a party of 60 on the Old Spanish Trail between Santa Fe and Los Angeles. While his caravan camped about 100 mi northeast of the present site of Las Vegas, an advance party set out to look for water. Rafael Rivera, a young Mexican scout, left the main party, headed due west over the unexplored desert, and discovered an oasis. The abundance of artesian spring water here shortened the Spanish Trail to Los Angeles by allowing travelers to go directly through, rather than around, the desert and eased the rigors of travel for the Spanish traders who used the route. They named the oasis Las Vegas, Spanish for "the meadows."

The next major visitor to the Las Vegas Springs was John C. Fremont, who in 1844 led one of his many explorations of the Far West. Today he is remembered in the name of the principal downtown thoroughfare—Fremont Street.

Ten years later a group of Mormon settlers were sent by Brigham Young from Salt Lake City to colonize the valley. They built a large stockade; a small remnant of it—a 150-square-foot, adobe-brick fort—still stands. The fort is the oldest building in Las Vegas. The Mormons spent two years growing crops, mining lead, and converting the indigenous Paiutes, but the climate and isolation defeated their ambitions and by 1857 the fort was abandoned.

Things didn't start hopping here until 1904, when the San Pedro, Los Angeles, and Salt Lake Railroad laid its tracks through Las Vegas Valley, purchased the prime land and water rights from the handful of homesteaders, and surveyed a town site for its railroad servicing and repair facilities. In May 1905 the railroad held an auction and sold 700 lots. Las Vegas became a dusty railroad watering stop with a few downtown hotels and stores, a saloon and red-light district known as Block 16, and a few thousand residents. It remained just that until 1928, when the Boulder Canyon Project Act was signed into law, in which $165 million was appropriated for the building of the world's largest antigravity dam, 40 mi from Las Vegas.

Construction of Hoover Dam began in 1931, a historic year for Nevada. In that year Governor Fred Balzar approved the "wide-open" gambling bill that had been introduced by a Winnemucca rancher, Assemblyman Phil Tobin. Gambling had been outlawed several times since Nevada became a state in 1864, but it had never been completely eliminated. Tobin maintained that controlled gaming would be good for tourism and the state's economy; people were going to gamble anyway, so why shouldn't the state tax the profits? Thus, he was able to convince lawmakers to make gambling permanently legal. Also in 1931, the legislature reduced the residency requirement for divorce to a scandalous six weeks, immediately turning Nevada into a "divorce colony."

The early 1930s marked the height of the Great Depression and Prohibition. The construction of the dam on the Colorado River (bridging the gap between Arizona and Nevada) brought thousands of job seekers to southern Nevada. Because the federal government didn't want dam workers to be distracted by the temptations of Las Vegas, it created a separate government town, Boulder City—still the only community in the state where gambling is illegal.

At this time Nevada's political and economic power resided in the northern part of the state: the capital in Carson City and the major casinos (notably Harold's Club and Harrah's) in Reno. But the completion of the dam in 1935 turned southern Nevada into a magnet for federal appropriations, thousands of tourists and new residents, and a seemingly inexhaustible supply of electricity and water. In addition, as the country mobilized for World War II, tens of thousands of pilots and gunners trained at the Las Vegas Aerial Gunnery School, opened by the federal government on 3 million acres north of town. Today this property is Nellis Air Force Base and the Nevada Test Site.

By the early 1940s downtown Las Vegas boasted several luxury hotels and a dozen small but successful gambling clubs. In 1941 Thomas Hull, who owned a chain of California motor inns, decided to build a place in the desert just outside the city limits on Highway 91, the road from Los Angeles. El Rancho Vegas opened with 100 motel rooms, a Western-motif casino, and, right off the highway, a large parking lot with an inviting swimming pool in the middle. El Rancho's quick success led to the opening a year later of the Last Frontier Hotel, a mile down the road. Thus, the Las Vegas Strip was established.

Benjamin "Bugsy" Siegel, who ran the New York mob's activities on the West Coast, began to see the incredible potential of a remote oasis where land was cheap and gambling was legal. He struggled for two years to build the Flamingo, managing to alienate his local partners and silent investors with his lavish overspending. He opened the joint prematurely, on a rainy night, the day after Christmas 1946 with fanfare and a who's who guest list. But the Flamingo flopped—the casino paid out more money than it took in, and six months later Bugsy was dead. Ironically, Bugsy's murder made the Flamingo infamous, and suddenly the big pink hotel was hopping.

The success of the Flamingo paved the way for gamblers and gangsters from all over the country to invest in Las Vegas hotel-casinos, one after another. The Desert Inn, Horseshoe, Sands, Sahara, Riviera, Dunes, Fremont, Tropicana, and Stardust were all built in the 1950s, financed with mob money. Every new hotel came on like a theme park opening for the summer with a new ride. Each was bigger, better, more unusual than the last. The Sahara had the tallest freestanding neon sign. The Riviera was the first high-rise building in town. The Stardust had 1,000 rooms and the world's largest swimming pool.

That the underworld owned and ran the big joints only added to the allure of Las Vegas. And the town's great boom in the 1950s couldn't have happened without the mob's access to millions of dollars in cash. Under the circumstances, no bank, corporation, or legitimate investor would have touched the gambling business.

In time, however, the state began to take steps to weed out the most visible undesirables. The federal government assisted in the crackdown, using its considerable resources to hound the gangsters out of business. And, finally, an eccentric man arrived on a train and soon revolutionized the nation's image of Las Vegas.

Howard Hughes had just sold Trans World Airlines for $546 million, and he either had to spend half the money or turn it in as taxes. During a three-year stay in Las Vegas he bought the Desert Inn, Frontier, Sands, Landmark, and Silver Slipper hotels, a television station, an airfield, and millions of dollars' worth of real estate. His presence in Las Vegas gave gambling its first positive image: as a former pilot and aviation pioneer, Hollywood mogul, and American folk hero, Hughes could in no way be connected with gangsters.

Hughes's presence also opened the door to corporate ownership of hotel-casinos. In 1971 Hilton Corporation purchased the International (now the Las Vegas Hilton) and the Flamingo, becoming the first major publicly traded hotel chain to step onto the Las Vegas playing field. Ramada, Holiday Inn, Hyatt, Sheraton, and others have since followed suit.

Las Vegas felt the effects of both the legalization of gambling in Atlantic City in the late 1970s and of the national recession of the early 1980s—but not for very long. Through the years the city has carved a secure niche for itself as a destination for national and international tourists; a winter sojourn for snowbirds from the north; a weekend getaway for gamblers and families from California, Arizona, and Utah; and convention central. Las Vegas has expanded at a ferocious pace since the 1990s: more than 65,000 hotel rooms have been added and more than a half million people have moved to the area, many of them fleeing California.

And why not? Though inching up, room rates are lower than in any other major U.S. city. There are lavish gourmet spots, but the inexpensive restaurants and buffet dining here can be cheaper than preparing a meal at home. Entertainment is abundant and reasonably priced. Las Vegas is possibly the easiest place in the world to receive freebies—the ubiquitous "comps." And best of all, gambling promotions such as coupons, slot clubs, paycheck bonuses, and drawings provide a fighting chance to win in the casino. In the back of everyone's mind is the idea that a trip to Las Vegas can be free or even a money-making vacation. That kind of thinking keeps the corporations smiling as they add a few more finishing touches to their $2-billion hotels.

Las Vegas in Print

History & Biography. *Learning from Las Vegas–The Forgotten Symbolism of Architectural Forms,* by Robert Venturi et al., and *Viva Las Vegas—After Hours Architecture,* by Alan Hess, are readable analyses of the shapes, sizes, and placement of Las Vegas's signs, casinos, parking lots, and false fronts. *Literary Las Vegas,* edited by Mike Tronnes, is a superb collection of work by well-known writers—Tom Wolfe, Joan Didion, Michael Herr, Hunter S. Thompson, among them—about the neon jungle. Of course, Hunter S. Thompson's *Fear and Loathing in Las Vegas* is the famous psychedelic account of the gonzo journalist's late-1960s trip to Las Vegas. For the most savage indictment of Las Vegas and its mobsters, payoffs, cheating, corruption, and prostitution, read *Green Felt Jungle,* by Ovid Demaris and Ed Reid. The book that Reid and Demaris used as their model to expose the seamy underside of Las Vegas was *The Great Las Vegas Fraud* by Sid Meyers, published in 1958, the first—and most vicious—in a long series of books that came to be called the Las Vegas Diatribe.

For the antidote to *Green Felt Jungle* and *The Great Las Vegas Fraud,* try to find *Playtown, U.S.A.,* by Katherine Best and Katherine Hillyer, a snapshot of Las Vegas written in 1955—one of the most insightful and colorful portraits of Sin City ever written. *Las Vegas—As It Began, As It Grew,* by Stanley Paher, covers in detail the popular early history of Las Vegas, from the Old Spanish Trail up through the building of Hoover Dam. *Resort City in the Sunbelt,* by Eugene Moehring, is a comprehensive, academic, and heavily footnoted history of Las Vegas's development since the 1930s. A more recent history of Las Vegas is *The Money and the Power: The Making of Las Vegas and Its Hold on America* by Sally Denton and Roger Morris. *Fly on the Wall—Recollections of Las Vegas' Good Old, Bad Old Days,* by Dick Odessky, is the personal account of a newspaper-reporter-turned-casino-publicist who lived through the transition from mob-run to corporate-owned Las Vegas. *Las Vegas—A Desert Paradise,* by Ralph Roske, is a large-format pictorial that covers Las Vegas's historical highlights. *Cult Vegas,* by *Las Vegas Review-Journal* entertainment columnist Mike Weatherford (a contributor to this book), delves into the offbeat entertainment history of the Entertainment Capital of the World. *Howard Hughes in Las Vegas,* by Omar Garrison, concerns the four years the enigmatic billionaire spent sequestered on the ninth floor of the Desert Inn. *No Limit—The Rise and Fall of Bob Stupak and the Stratosphere Tower,* by John L. Smith, is the fascinating biography of Las Vegas's most flamboyant modern casino operator. *Easy Street* is the sad and gripping autobiography of Susan Berman, only child of David Berman, one of the earliest mobsters to relocate in Las Vegas.

The 2005 Centennial Celebration brought a host of Las Vegas history and picture books. One worth checking out is *Las Vegas: A Centennial History,* by local historians Eugene P. Moehring and Michael S. Green. On the less conventional side, William L. Fox's *In the Desert of Desire* meditates on the nature of culture and the culture of nature in Las Vegas.

Fiction. Most of Mario Puzo's novels contain an enormous amount of inside dirt on Las Vegas, but *Fools Die* is centered on the city and contains some excellent descriptions of casino color and scams. *The Death of Frank Sinatra,* by L.A. novelist Michael Ventura, is a dark and disturbing but brilliant fictional look at the meaning of Las Vegas. Larry McMurtry's *Desert Rose,* conversely, is an affectionate and poignant character study of an aging showgirl and her ties to Las Vegas. *Last Call,* by Tim Powers, is a strange, suspenseful, violent tale about chaos and randomness, the patron saints of Las Vegas. *Devil's Hole,* by Las Vegas novelist Bill Branon, concerns a hit man hired by a Las Vegas casino to take out a wildly successful sports bettor. *Neon Mirage,* by Max Allan Collins, is a novel about Bugsy Siegel, as is *Las Vegas Strip,* by Morris Renek. *The Big Night* is a story about a notorious gambler who assembles a team of five women to beat Las Vegas out of a million bucks, by Ian Andersen, one of the world's most successful high-stakes blackjack players. Andersen's book is one of a long list of pulp fiction titles based on "the great Las Vegas heist" theme: *The Vegas Trap,* by Hal Kantor; *Fortune Machine,* by Sam Ross; *Snake Eyes,* by Edwin Silberstang; and *Murder in Las Vegas,* by renaissance man Steve Allen, are other examples. If you want to bet on a sure thing, it would have to be *Murder in Vegas: New Crime Tales of Gambling and Desperation,* a collection of stories gathered by the International Association of Crime Writers and author Michael Connelly.

Gambling. *Comp City—A Guide To Free Las Vegas Vacations,* by Max Rubin, exposes the guarded world of the casino complimentary system. *Knock-Out*

Blackjack, by Olaf Vancura and Ken Fuchs, is the easiest card-counting system ever devised. Ian Andersen, who's made his living at high-stakes blackjack for nearly three decades, tells all in two books, *Turning the Tables on Las Vegas* and *Burning the Tables in Las Vegas. The Man with the $100,000 Breasts and Other Gambling Stories,* by Michael Konik, takes readers deep inside the world of high rollers, hustlers, card counters, and poker champions. The best low-roller guide to gambling ever written is *The Frugal Gambler,* by Jean Scott. *Casino Secrets,* by Barney Vinson, is a gambling primer and Las Vegas guide.

Las Vegas on Film

Frank Sinatra made his feature-film debut in the 1941 picture *Las Vegas Nights.* Barbara Stanwyck loses house and husband after becoming a gambling addict in the melodrama *The Lady Gambles* (1949). Sinatra gangs up with the rest of the Rat Pack for a heist in the cornball *Ocean's Eleven* (1960). Elvis Presley plays a race-car driver on the loose in Las Vegas, meeting up with Ann-Margret, in the famous *Viva Las Vegas* (1964).

The James Bond film *Diamonds Are Forever* (1971) mixes footage of real-life casinos with shots from a fictional, studio-built casino. The main action in *The Electric Horseman* (1979) centers on Caesars Palace. *Melvin and Howard* (1980) tells the tale of Melvin Dummar, who presented for probate a will supposedly written by Howard Hughes. Much of the Albert Brooks comedy *Lost in America* (1985) takes place at the Desert Inn. Burt Reynolds stars as a Vegas private investigator in *Heat* (1987). On their way across the country in *Rain Man* (1988), Tom Cruise and Dustin Hoffman make a stop in Vegas to count cards.

Flying Elvises drop from the sky in the light comedy *Honeymoon in Las Vegas* (1992), part of which is set at Bally's casino. Robert Redford makes the titular *Indecent Proposal* (1993) to married couple Demi Moore and Woody Harrelson; some footage of the Las Vegas Hilton is included. Much of the campy, schlocky *Showgirls* (1995) takes place at the Stardust. Nicolas Cage plays an unrepentant drunk in the bleak but moving *Leaving Las Vegas* (1995). Two of the better films about the role of organized crime in Las Vegas are *Bugsy* (1991), which traces the early days of mob involvement, and the Martin Scorsese movie *Casino* (1995), a look at how greed in the 1970s killed the goose that laid the Mafia's golden egg.

For scenes of present-day Las Vegas, check out *The Great White Hope* (1996), a satire about boxing that was shot at the MGM Grand; *Mars Attacks!* (1996), which incorporates real-life footage of the implosion of the Landmark Hotel-Casino (and also includes shots of the Luxor); *Swingers* (1996), which immortalizes the L.A.-to-Vegas road trip; *Con Air* (1997), whose closing action is set at the Sands Hotel; and *Austin Powers: International Man of Mystery* (1997), with Mike Myers as a swingin' secret agent from the 1960s who is cryogenically frozen and then defrosted decades later, in 1997, shagging his way through Las Vegas. The fountains of Bellagio mesmerize George Clooney and his gang of thieves in Steven Soderbergh's 2001 remake of *Ocean's Eleven.* Ben Stiller and Vince Vaughn enter a dodgeball tournament held in Vegas in *Dodge Ball* (2004), and Sandra Bullock breezes through Sin City in *Miss Congeniality 2* (2005). The adaptation of Capcom's game series "Resident Evil" was made into a movie called *Resident Evil: Extinction* (2007), which starred Mila Jovovich and was filmed in and around Vegas. *Lucky You* (2007), starring Drew Barrymore and Eric Bana, takes a look at life and love in the risky world of Las Vegas.

Las Vegas Essentials

PLANNING TOOLS, EXPERT INSIGHT, GREAT CONTACTS

There are planners and there are those who, excuse the pun, fly by the seat of their pants. We happily place ourselves among the planners. Our writers and editors try to anticipate all the issues you may face before and during any journey, and then they do their research. This section is the product of their efforts. Use it to get excited about your trip to Las Vegas, to inform your travel planning, or to guide you on the road should the seat of your pants start to feel threadbare.

GETTING STARTED

We're really proud of our Web site: Fodors.com is a great place to begin any journey. Scan Travel Wire for suggested itineraries, travel deals, restaurant and hotel openings, and other up-to-the-minute info. Check out Booking to research prices and book plane tickets, hotel rooms, rental cars, and vacation packages. Head to Talk for on-the-ground pointers from travelers who frequent our message boards. You can also link to loads of other travel-related resources.

▮ RESOURCES

ONLINE TRAVEL TOOLS

LasVegas.com (⊕ *www.lasvegas.com*) has a partnership with the *Las Vegas Review-Journal,* and it offers travel information and reservations, as does the *Review-Journal*'s site, ⊕ *www.review-journal.com.*

VEGAS.com (⊕ *www.vegas.com*) advertises that in Las Vegas, "it's who you know." Part of the Greenspun Media Group, which also publishes the *Las Vegas Sun,* VEGAS.com offers information about and instant booking capabilities for everything from hotels to shows.

About.com This *New York Times*–owned site has an excellent online "Las Vegas for Visitors" guide (⊕ *www.govegas.about. com*), which includes dozens of original articles and reviews as well as links to many other Vegas resources.

One of the oldest sites is the **Las Vegas Leisure Guide** (⊕ *www.pcap.com*), full of hotel, restaurant, and nightlife info. **Las Vegas Online Entertainment Guide** (⊕ *www.lvol.com*) has listings for hotels and an online reservations system, plus local history, restaurants, a business directory, and even some gambling instruction.

Only Vegas (⊕ *www.visitlasvegas.com*), the official Las Vegas tourism Web site,

has a little bit of everything going on in Sin City. Find out about events, book hotels, get special deals, and find out other vital travel info.

The **City of Las Vegas** has its own Web site, ⊕ *www.lasvegasnevada.gov*, which is a great resource for service-related information, including how to pay a ticket or citation. Remember, what happens in Vegas, stays in Vegas.

Marriage Licenses If you plan on getting hitched during your Vegas stay, you might want to check out the **Clark County** Web site (⊕ www.accessclarkcounty.com) for necessary marriage license information.

Safety Transportation Security Administration (TSA ⊕ www.tsa.gov).

Time Zones Timeanddate.com (⊕ www.timeanddate.com/worldclock) can help you figure out the correct time anywhere.

Weather Accuweather.com (⊕ www.accuweather.com) is an independent weather-forecasting service with good coverage of hurricanes. **Weather.com** (⊕ www.weather.com) is the Web site for the Weather Channel.

Other Resources CIA World Factbook (⊕ www.odci.gov/cia/publications/factbook/index.html) has profiles of every country in the world. It's a good source if you need some quick facts and figures.

VISITOR INFORMATION

Before you go, contact the city and state tourism offices for general information. When you get there, you might want to visit the Las Vegas Convention and Visitors Authority (3150 Paradise Road), next door to the Las Vegas Hilton, for brochures and general information. Hotels and gift shops on the Strip have maps, brochures, pamphlets, and free-events magazines—*What's On in Las Vegas, Showbiz,* and *Las Vegas Today*—that list shows and buffets and offer discounts to area attractions.

The *Las Vegas Advisor,* a monthly print newsletter and online Web site, keeps up-to-the-minute track of the constantly changing Las Vegas landscapes of gambling, accommodations, dining, entertainment, Top Ten Values (a monthly list of the city's best deals), complimentary offerings, coupons, and more and is an indispensable resource for any Las Vegas visitor. Send $5 for a sample issue, or buy a 72-hour membership to the *Advisor's* online version by logging on to ⊕*www. lasvegasadvisor.com.* Annual print memberships cost $50, and online memberships cost $37 per year.

Contacts **Las Vegas Advisor** (☎702/252–0655 ⊕www.lasvegasadvisor.com). **Las Vegas Convention and Visitors Authority** (☎702/892–0711 or 877/847–4858 ⊕www.visitlasvegas.com). **Nevada Commission on Tourism** (☎775/687–4322 or 800/638–2328 ⊕www.travelnevada.com).

▋ THINGS TO CONSIDER

GEAR

Ever since the original Frontier Casino opened on the Los Angeles Highway (now the Strip), visitors to Las Vegas have been invited to "come as you are." The warm weather and informal character of Las Vegas render casual clothing appropriate day and night. However, there are some exceptions. A small number of restaurants require jackets for men, and some of the city's increasingly exclusive and overhyped "ultralounges" and high-profile dance clubs have specific requirements such as no sneakers or jeans or that you must wear dark shoes or collared shirts. At a minimum, even if there's no set dress code, you're going to fit in with the scene

if you make some effort to dress stylishly when heading out either to the hipper nightclubs or even trendier restaurants (i.e., those helmed by celeb chefs or with trendy followings and cool decor). Just as an example, where jeans and T-shirts might be technically allowed at some establishments, try to wear plain, fitted T-shirts versus those with logos and designs, and choose jeans that are appropriate for a venue (crisp and clean for a nice restaurant, designer labels for a top club). It's always good to pack a few stylish outfits for the evening, and when you're making dinner reservations at an upscale spot or considering a visit to a nightclub, ask for the dress-code specifics.

Although the desert sun keeps temperatures scorching outside in warmer months, the casinos are ice-cold. Your best insurance is to dress in layers. The blasting air-conditioning may feel good at first, but if you plan on spending some time inside, bring a light sweater or jacket in case you feel chilly.

Always wear comfortable shoes; no matter what your intentions, you cover a lot of ground on foot.

Trip Insurance Resources

INSURANCE COMPARISON SITES		
Insure My Trip.com	800/487–4722	www.insuremytrip.com
Square Mouth.com	800/240–0369	www.quotetravelinsurance.com
COMPREHENSIVE TRAVEL INSURERS		
Access America	866/807–3982	www.accessamerica.com
CSA Travel Protection	800/873–9855	www.csatravelprotection.com
HTH Worldwide	610/254–8700 or 888/243–2358	www.hthworldwide.com
Travelex Insurance	888/457–4602	www.travelex-insurance.com
Travel Guard International	715/345–0505 or 800/826–4919	www.travelguard.com
Travel Insured International	800/243–3174	www.travelinsured.com
MEDICAL-ONLY INSURERS		
International Medical Group	800/628–4664	www.imglobal.com
International SOS	215/942–8000 or 713/521–7611	www.internationalsos.com
Wallach & Company	800/237–6615 or 504/687–3166	www.wallach.com

TRIP INSURANCE

What kind of coverage do you honestly need? Do you even need trip insurance at all? Take a deep breath and read on.

We believe that comprehensive trip insurance is especially valuable if you're booking a very expensive or complicated trip (particularly to an isolated region) or if you're booking far in advance. Who knows what could happen six months down the road? But whether you get insurance has more to do with how comfortable you are assuming all that risk yourself.

Comprehensive travel policies typically cover trip-cancellation and interruption, letting you cancel or cut your trip short because of a personal emergency, illness, or, in some cases, acts of terrorism in your destination. Such policies also cover evacuation and medical care. Some also cover you for trip delays because of bad weather or mechanical problems as well as for lost or delayed baggage. Another type of coverage to look for is financial default—that is, when your trip is disrupted because a tour operator, airline, or cruise line goes out of business. Generally you must buy this when you book your trip or shortly thereafter, and it's only available to you if your operator isn't on a list of excluded companies.

Expect comprehensive travel insurance policies to cost about 4% to 7% of the total price of your trip (it's more like 12% if you're over age 70). A medical-only policy may or may not be cheaper than a comprehensive policy. Always read the fine print of your policy to make sure that you are covered for the risks that are of most concern to you. Compare several policies to make sure you're getting the best price and range of coverage available.

BOOKING YOUR TRIP

Unless your cousin is a travel agent, you're probably among the millions of people who make most of their travel arrangements online.

But have you ever wondered just what the differences are between an online travel agent (a Web site through which you make reservations instead of going directly to the airline, hotel, or car-rental company), a discounter (a firm that does a high volume of business with a hotel chain or airline and accordingly gets good prices), a wholesaler (one that makes cheap reservations in bulk and then re-sells them to people like you), and an aggregator (one that compares all the offerings so you don't have to)?

Is it truly better to book directly on an airline or hotel Web site? And when does a real live travel agent come in handy?

▌ ONLINE

You really have to shop around. A travel wholesaler such as Hotels.com or Hotel-Club.net can be a source of good rates, as can discounters such as Hotwire or Priceline, particularly if you can bid for your hotel room or airfare. Indeed, such sites sometimes have deals that are unavailable elsewhere. They do, however, tend to work only with hotel chains (which makes them just plain useless for getting hotel reservations outside of major cities) or big airlines (so that often leaves out upstarts like jetBlue and some foreign carriers like Air India).

Also, with discounters and wholesalers you must generally prepay, and every-thing is nonrefundable. And before you fork over the dough, be sure to check the terms and conditions, so you know what a given company will do for you if there's a problem and what you'll deal with on your own.

▌TIP→ To be absolutely sure everything was processed correctly, confirm reservations made through online travel agents, discounters, and wholesalers directly with your hotel before leaving home.

Booking engines like Expedia, Trav-elocity, and Orbitz are actually travel agents, albeit high-volume, online ones. And airline travel packagers like Ameri-can Airlines Vacations and Virgin Vaca-tions—well, they're travel agents, too. But they may still not work with all the world's hotels.

An aggregator site will search many sites and pull the best prices for airfares, hotels, and rental cars from them. Most aggre-gators compare the major travel-booking sites such as Expedia, Travelocity, and Orbitz; some also look at airline Web sites, though rarely the sites of smaller budget airlines. Some aggregators also compare other travel products, including complex packages—a good thing, as you can sometimes get the best overall deal by booking an air-and-hotel package.

▌ WITH A TRAVEL AGENT

If you use an agent—brick-and-mortar or virtual—you'll pay a fee for the service. And know that the service you get from some online agents isn't comprehensive. For example Expedia and Travelocity don't search for prices on budget airlines like jetBlue, Southwest, or small foreign carriers. That said, some agents (online or not) *do* have access to fares that are diffi-cult to find otherwise, and the savings can more than make up for any surcharge.

A knowledgeable brick-and-mortar travel agent can be a godsend if you're booking a cruise, a package trip that's not available to you directly, an air pass, or a complicated itinerary including sev-eral overseas flights. What's more, travel agents that specialize in a destination

Online Booking Resources

AGGREGATORS		
Kayak	www.kayak.com;	also looks at cruises and vacation packages.
Mobissimo	www.mobissimo.com	
Qixo	www.qixo.com	also compares cruises, vacation packages, and even travel insurance.
Sidestep	www.sidestep.com	also compares vacation packages and lists travel deals.
Travelgrove	www.travelgrove.com	also compares cruises and packages.
BOOKING ENGINES		
Cheap Tickets	www.cheaptickets.com	a discounter.
Expedia	www.expedia.com	a large online agency that charges a booking fee for airline tickets.
Hotwire	www.hotwire.com	a discounter.
lastminute.com	www.lastminute.com	specializes in last-minute travel the main site is for the U.K., but it has a link to a U.S. site.
Luxury Link	www.luxurylink.com	has auctions (surprisingly good deals) as well as offers on the high-end side of travel.
Onetravel.com	www.onetravel.com	a discounter for hotels, car rentals, airfares, and packages.
Orbitz	www.orbitz.com	charges a booking fee for airline tickets, but gives a clear breakdown of fees and taxes before you book.
Priceline.com	www.priceline.com	a discounter that also allows bidding.
Travel.com	www.travel.com	allows you to compare its rates with those of other booking engines.
Travelocity	www.travelocity.com	charges a booking fee for airline tickets, but promises good problem resolution.
ONLINE ACCOMMODATIONS		
Hotelbook.com	www.hotelbook.com	focuses on independent hotels worldwide.
Hotel Club	www.hotelclub.net	good for major cities worldwide.
Hotels.com	www.hotels.com	a big Expedia-owned wholesaler that offers rooms in hotels all over the world.
Quikbook	www.quikbook.com	offers "pay when you stay" reservations that let you settle your bill at checkout, not when you book.
OTHER RESOURCES		
Bidding For Travel	www.biddingfortravel.com	a good place to figure out what you can get and for how much before you start bidding on, say, Priceline.

10 WAYS TO SAVE

1. Nonrefundable is best. If saving money is more important than flexibility, then nonrefundable tickets work. Just remember that you'll pay dearly (as much as $200) if you change your plans.

2. Comparison shop. Web sites and travel agents can have different arrangements with the airlines and offer different prices for exactly the same flights.

3. Beware the listed prices. Many airline Web sites—and most ads—show prices *without* taxes and surcharges. Don't buy until you know the full price.

4. Stay loyal. Stick with one or two frequent-flier programs. You'll rack up free trips faster and you'll accumulate the perks more quickly. On some airlines these include a special reservations number, early boarding, and more roomy economy-class seating.

5. Watch those ticketing fees. Surcharges are usually added when you buy your ticket anywhere but on an airline Web site.

6. Check early and often. Start looking for cheap fares up to three months in advance. Keep looking until you find a price you like.

7. Don't work alone. Some Web sites have tracking features that will e-mail you immediately when good deals are posted.

8. Jump on the good deals. Waiting even a few minutes might mean paying more.

9. Be flexible. Look for departures on Tuesday, Wednesday, and Saturday, typically the cheapest days to travel. And check on prices for departures at different times and to and from alternative airports.

10. Weigh your options. What you get can be as important as what you save. A cheaper flight might have a long layover, or it might land at a secondary airport, where your ground transportation costs might be higher.

may have exclusive access to certain deals and insider information on things such as charter flights. Agents who specialize in types of travelers (senior citizens, gays and lesbians, naturists) or types of trips (cruises, luxury travel, safaris) can also be invaluable.

■ TIP → Remember that Expedia, Travelocity, and Orbitz are travel agents, not just booking engines. To resolve any problems with a reservation made through these companies, contact them first.

Because Las Vegas is a city essentially built to attract leisure travelers, and it's incredibly easy to book rooms, shows, air tickets, and package vacations yourself online, it's quite easy to forego a travel agent when planning a visit here. By the same token, travel agents can more easily search among the many packages and deals available out there, but for the most part, the services of travel agents are far from necessary for Vegas trips.

Agent Resources American Society of Travel Agents (☎ 703/739–2782 ⊕ www.travelsense.org).

▌ AIRLINE TICKETS

Most domestic airline tickets are electronic; international tickets may be either electronic or paper. With an e-ticket the only thing you receive is an e-mailed receipt citing your itinerary and reservation and ticket numbers.

The greatest advantage of an e-ticket is that if you lose your receipt, you can simply print out another copy or ask the airline to do it for you at check-in. You usually pay a surcharge (up to $50) to get a paper ticket, if you can get one at all.

The sole advantage of a paper ticket is that it may be easier to endorse over to another airline if your flight is canceled and the airline with which you booked can't accommodate you on another flight.

■TIP➡ Discount air passes that let you travel economically in a country or region must often be purchased before you leave home. In some cases you can only get them through a travel agent.

Just remember that you'll pay dearly (often as much as $100) if you must change your travel plans (with Southwest Airlines, which charges no fee for changes other than the potential price difference in the fare, a notable exception).

Always ask about package rates, as these tend to be the best bargains to Las Vegas—in addition to round-trip air, the rates include hotel room and sometimes car rental.

▌ RENTAL CARS

When you reserve a car, ask about cancellation penalties, taxes, drop-off charges (if you're planning to pick up the car in one city and leave it in another), and surcharges (for being under or over a certain age, for additional drivers, or for driving across state or country borders or beyond a specific distance from your point of rental). All these things can add substantially to your costs. Request car seats and extras such as GPS when you book.

Rates are sometimes—but not always—better if you book in advance or reserve through a rental agency's Web site. There are other reasons to book ahead, though: for popular destinations, during busy times of the year, or to ensure that you get certain types of cars (vans, SUVs, exotic sports cars).

■TIP➡ Make sure that a confirmed reservation guarantees you a car. Agencies sometimes overbook, particularly for busy weekends and holiday periods.

Rates in Las Vegas average anywhere from $18 to $60 a day for intermediate to full-size cars—usually you can find a car for under $30 a day, but during very busy times expect sky-high rates, especially at the last minute. Las Vegas has among the highest car-rental taxes and surcharges in the country, however, so be sure to factor in the 7.5% (in Clark County) sales tax, a 6% license tag fee, and a 4% recovery fee. If you rent your car at the airport, an additional 10% tax applies.

Owing to the high demand for rental cars and significant competition, there are many deals to be had at the airport for car rentals. During special events and conventions, rates frequently go up as supply dwindles, but at other times you can find bargains. For the best deals, check with the various online services, or contact a representative of the hotel where you'll be staying, as many hotels have business relationships with car-rental companies.

Although there are several local car-rental companies along the Strip itself, they tend to be more expensive than those at the airport or elsewhere in the city.

In Nevada you must be 21 to rent a car, and some major car-rental agencies have a minimum age of 25. Those agencies that do rent to people under 25 often assess surcharges to those drivers. There's no upper age limit for renting a car. Non-U.S. residents will need a reservation voucher, a passport, a driver's license, and a travel policy that covers each driver when picking up a car.

CAR-RENTAL INSURANCE

Everyone who rents a car wonders whether the insurance that the rental companies offer is worth the expense. No one—including us—has a simple answer. It all depends on how much regular insurance you have, how comfortable you are with risk, and whether or not money is an issue.

If you own a car and carry comprehensive car insurance for both collision and liability, your personal auto insurance will probably cover a rental, but read your policy's fine print to be sure. If you don't have auto insurance, then you should probably buy the collision- or loss-damage waiver (CDW or LDW) from the

10 WAYS TO SAVE

1. Beware of cheap rates. Those great rates aren't so great when you add in taxes, surcharges, and insurance. Such extras can double the initial quote.

2. Rent weekly. Weekly rates are usually better than daily ones. Even if you only want to rent for five or six days, ask for the weekly rate; it may be cheaper than the daily rate for the same period of time.

3. Don't forget the locals. Price local companies as well as the majors.

4. Airport rentals can cost more. Airports often add surcharges, which you can avoid by renting from an agency whose office is just off airport property.

5. Wholesalers can help. Investigate wholesalers, which don't own fleets but rent in bulk from firms that do, and which frequently offer better rates.

6. Look for rate guarantees. With your rate locked in, you won't pay more, even if the price goes up in the local currency.

7. Fill up farther away. Avoid hefty refueling fees by filling the tank at a station well away from where you plan to turn in the car.

8. Pump it yourself. Don't buy the tank of gas that's in the car when you rent it unless you plan to do a lot of driving.

9. Get all your discounts. Find out whether a credit card you carry or organization or frequent-renter program to which you belong has a discount program. And confirm that such discounts really are a deal. You can often do better with special weekend or weekly rates offered by a rental agency.

10. Check out packages. Adding a car rental onto your air/hotel vacation package may be cheaper than renting a car separately.

rental company. This eliminates your liability for damage to the car.

Some credit cards offer CDW coverage, but it's usually supplemental to your own insurance and rarely covers SUVs, minivans, or luxury models. If your coverage is secondary, you may still be liable for loss-of-use costs from the car-rental company. But no credit-card insurance is valid unless you use that card for *all* transactions, from reserving to paying the final bill.

■TIP→Diners Club offers primary CDW coverage on all rentals reserved and paid for with the card. This means that Diners Club's company—not your own car insurance—pays in case of an accident. It *doesn't* mean that your car-insurance company won't raise your rates once it discovers you had an accident.

You may also be offered supplemental liability coverage; the car-rental company is required to carry a minimal level of liability coverage insuring all renters, but it's rarely enough to cover claims in a serious accident if you're at fault. Your own auto-insurance policy will protect you if you own a car; if you don't, you have to decide whether you are willing to take the risk.

U.S. rental companies sell CDWs and LDWs for about $15 to $25 a day; supplemental liability is usually more than $10 a day. The car-rental company may offer you all sorts of other policies, but they're rarely worth it. Personal accident insurance, which is basic hospitalization coverage, is an especially egregious rip-off if you already have health insurance.

■TIP→You can decline the insurance from the rental company and purchase it through a third-party provider such as Travel Guard (www.travelguard.com)—$9 per day for $35,000 of coverage. That's sometimes just under half the price of the CDW offered by some car-rental companies.

Car Rental Resources

AUTOMOBILE ASSOCIATIONS		
American Automobile Association	315/797–5000	www.aaa.com;
		most contact with the organization is through state and regional members.
National Automobile Club	650/294–7000	www.thenac.com; membership open to CA residents only.
MAJOR AGENCIES		
Alamo	800/462–5266	www.alamo.com
Avis	00/230–4898 or 0870/606–0100 in U.K.	www.avis.com
Budget	00/527–0700	www.budget.com
Hertz	800/654–3131 or 0870/844–8844 in U.K.	www.hertz.com
National Car Rental	800/227–7368	www.nationalcar.com

∎ VACATION PACKAGES

Packages *are not* guided excursions. Packages combine airfare, accommodations, and perhaps a rental car or other extras (theater tickets, guided excursions, boat trips, reserved entry to popular museums, transit passes), but they let you do your own thing. During busy periods packages may be your only option, as flights and rooms may be sold out otherwise.

Packages will definitely save you time. They can also save you money, particularly in peak seasons, but—and this is a really big "but"—you should price each part of the package separately to be sure. And be aware that prices advertised on Web sites and in newspapers rarely include service charges or taxes, which can up your costs by hundreds of dollars.

First, always pay with a credit card; if you have a problem, your credit-card company may help you resolve it. Second, buy trip insurance that covers default. Third, choose a company that belongs to the United States Tour Operators Association, whose members must set aside funds to cover defaults. Finally, choose a company that also participates in the Tour Operator Program of the American

Society of Travel Agents (ASTA), which will act as mediator in any disputes.

You can also check on the tour operator's reputation among travelers by posting an inquiry on Fodors.com.

Package tours are highly popular in Las Vegas because they offer great value on air tickets and hotels (and sometimes car rental), and often you can find packages that include admission to shows or other deals. Also, it's nice having your airport transfers arranged for you. If you're visiting the city on a tight budget, this can be a great way to get here and spend very little on where you stay. On the other hand, this is an easy city to navigate on your own and the logistics of purchasing separate airfare, hotels, car rentals, and shows here is not especially daunting if you're even a modest traveler. You may be able to find nearly comparable deals by purchasing these items separately on your own; you'll have more choices and more control over your trip than if you book a package deal.

Organizations **American Society of Travel Agents** (ASTA ☎703/739–2782 or 800/965–2782 ⊕www.astanet.com). **United States Tour Operators Association** (USTOA ☎212/599–6599 ⊕www.ustoa.com).

TRANSPORTATION

Most visitors to Las Vegas focus their time on or near the Strip, where you can get everywhere by walking, taking cabs, or hopping on the city's monorail, which provides access to several Strip and Paradise Road casinos and hotels (as well as the convention center). Outside the Strip, the city sprawls in all directions, and renting a car is the best way to get around, especially if you're staying in Lake Las Vegas, Summerlin, or another area more than a few miles from the Strip. Vegas is served by buses, but it's impractical for visitors to rely on them.

▌ BY AIR

Flying times to Las Vegas: from New York, five hours; from Dallas, two hours; from Chicago, four hours; from Los Angeles, one hour; from San Francisco, one-and-a-half hours.

▌TIP→ **If you travel frequently, look into the TSA's Registered Traveler program. The program, which is still being tested in several U.S. airports, is designed to cut down on gridlock at security checkpoints by allowing prescreened travelers to pass quickly through kiosks that scan an iris and/or a fingerprint.**

A handful of Vegas hotels offer off-site baggage check-in, which allows hotel guests to obtain boarding passes and check their luggage directly at the hotel. Venetian and Luxor were the first properties to offer this, and it's expected that others will eventually follow. Of course, even where off-site luggage check-in is not available, you can always save time by checking in online and printing out your boarding pass before you depart for the airport.

Airlines & Airports **Airline and Airport Links.com** (⊕www.airlineandairportlinks.com) has links to many of the world's airlines and airports.

NAVIGATING LAS VEGAS

The modern, sprawling Western city of Las Vegas is fairly easy to get around by car, as it's laid out largely in a grid and crisscrossed by freeways. The only pitfall is traffic. Public transportation is of relatively little use to visitors.

■ Fortunately, the Vegas skyline is defined by perhaps the most distinctive grouping of high-rise buildings in the world, from the pointy Luxor pyramid to the elegant Wynn Hotel and Casino. From just about anywhere in town, you can see the Strip in the distance and use it to guide your way around.

■ Although the city's layout isn't confusing, traffic along the Strip and intersecting roads, as well as parallel I–15, can be horrendous. It's especially challenging on weekend evenings and when there are conventions in town, but traffic jams can spring up virtually any time of day or night. Give yourself plenty of time when you're traveling to or from the Strip. On the plus side, parking is free at virtually every resort on the Strip (although downtown garages and lots usually charge a fee, the rate is often free if you get your ticket stamped by the casino cashier).

■ Although Vegas is served by an extensive bus system, most visitors will find it impractical to learn local bus routes and schedules. If you're planning to travel much beyond the Strip, rent a car.

FLYING 101

Flying may not be as carefree as it once was, but there are some things you can do to make your trip smoother.

Minimize the time spent standing in line. Buy an e-ticket, check in at an electronic kiosk, or—even better—check in on your airline's Web site before leaving home. Pack light and limit carry-on items to only the essentials.

Arrive when you need to. Research your airline's policy. It's usually at least an hour before domestic flights and two to three hours before international flights. But airlines at some busy airports have more stringent requirements. Check the TSA Web site for estimated security waiting times at major airports.

Get to the gate. If you aren't at the gate at least 10 minutes before your flight is scheduled to take off (sometimes earlier), you won't be allowed to board.

Double-check your flight times. Do this especially if you reserved far in advance. Schedules change, and alerts may not reach you.

Don't go hungry. Ask whether your airline offers anything to eat; even when it does, be prepared to pay.

Get the seat you want. Often, you can pick a seat when you buy your ticket on an airline Web site. But it's not guaranteed; the airline could change the plane after you book, so double-check. You can also select a seat if you check in electronically. Avoid seats on the aisle directly across from the lavatories. Frequent fliers say those are even worse than back-row seats that don't recline.

Got kids? Get info. Ask the airline about its children's menus, activities, and fares. Sometimes infants and toddlers fly free if they sit on a parent's lap, and older children fly for half price in their own seats. Also inquire about policies involving car seats; having one may limit seating options. Also ask about seat-belt extenders for car seats. And note that you can't count on a flight attendant to produce an extender; you may have to ask for one when you board.

Check your scheduling. Don't buy a ticket if there's less than an hour between connecting flights. Although schedules are padded, if anything goes wrong you might miss your connection. If you're traveling to an important function, depart a day early.

Bring paper. Even when using an e-ticket, always carry a hard copy of your receipt; you may need it to get your boarding pass, which most airports require to get past security.

Complain at the airport. If your baggage goes astray or your flight goes awry, complain before leaving the airport. Most carriers require this.

Beware of overbooked flights. If a flight is oversold, the gate agent will usually ask for volunteers and offer some sort of compensation for taking a different flight. If you're bumped from a flight *involuntarily*, the airline must give you some kind of compensation if an alternate flight can't be found within one hour.

Know your rights. If your flight is delayed because of something within the airline's control (bad weather doesn't count), the airline must get you to your destination on the same day, even if they have to book you on another airline and in an upgraded class. Read the Contract of Carriage, which is usually buried on the airline's Web site.

Be prepared. The Boy Scout motto is especially important if you're traveling during a stormy season. To quickly adjust your plans, program a few numbers into your cell: your airline, an airport hotel or two, your destination hotel, your car service, and/or your travel agent.

Airline Security Issues Transportation Security Administration (⊕www.tsa.gov) has answers for almost every question that might come up.

AIRPORTS

The gateway to Las Vegas is McCarran International Airport (LAS), 5 mi south of the business district and immediately east of the southern end of the Strip.

McCarran International Airport (LAS), which is just a few minutes' drive from the Strip, is well served by nonstop and direct flights from all around the country and a handful of international destinations. It's also consistently rated among the most passenger-friendly airports in the United States.

■TIP→ Long layovers don't have to be only about sitting around or shopping. These days they can be about burning off vacation calories. Check out www.airportgyms. com for lists of health clubs that are in or near many U.S. and Canadian airports. In Las Vegas, McCarran Airport has a 24-Hour Fitness in the terminal that's open 5 AM–11 PM weekdays and 6 AM–9 PM on weekends. Guest day passes cost $10–$15.

Also, McCarran is close enough to the Strip that if you ever find yourself with more than an hour on your hands, you can easily catch a 5- to 15-minute cab ride to one of the South Strip casinos, such as Mandalay Bay or MGM Grand, and while away some time. Additionally, as you might expect, McCarran has scads of slot machines to keep you busy.

Airport Information McCarran International Airport (LAS) (☎702/261–5211 ⊕www.mccarran.com).

GROUND TRANSPORTATION

By shuttle van: this is the cheapest way from McCarran to your hotel. The service is shared with other riders, and costs $4.50 to $5.50 per person to the Strip, $6 to $7.50 to downtown, and $6 to $21 to outlying locals' casinos. The vans wait for passengers outside the terminal

in a marked area. Because the vans make numerous stops at different hotels, it's not the best means of transportation if you're in a hurry.

By taxi: the metered cabs awaiting your arrival at McCarran are the quickest way of getting to your destination. The fare is $3.20 on the meter when you get in and $2 for every mile (plus 25¢ per every 41 seconds of standing in traffic), plus an airport surcharge of $1.20. The trip to most hotels on the south end of the Strip should cost $10 to $12, to the north end of the Strip should cost $13 to $18, and to downtown should cost $18 to $23. Beware of drivers who suggest taking the quickest route. They may take you through the airport tunnel and up I-15, which may be a few minutes faster but will cost considerably more because taxis charge by the mile. Drivers who take passengers through the airport tunnel without asking are committing an illegal practice known as "long-hauling." Ask a hotel employee to contact the Taxi Cab Authority if you need to report a driver, or you can call the Authority yourself at 702/486–6532.

Contacts Bell Trans (☎702/739–7990 ⊕www.bell-trans.com). Checker/Yellow/ Star Cab (☎702/873–2000). CLS shuttle (☎702/740–4050). Gray Line (☎702/739–5700 or 800/559–9522 ⊕www.grayline.com).

FLIGHTS

All the major airlines operate frequent service from their hub cities and, as a whole, offer one-stop connecting flights from virtually every city in the country. In addition to nonstop service from the usual hub cities (e.g., Atlanta, Chicago, Cincinnati, Dallas, Denver, Houston, Minneapolis, Newark, Phoenix, Salt Lake City, San Francisco), nonstop service is offered to many other destinations, sometimes by smaller airlines. Southwest remains the dominant airline (carrying nearly double the number of passengers as its closest competitor, US Airways, thanks to its 2006 merger with America West), and it offers frequent flights to many cities in the South and West, including San Diego, Los Angeles, Oakland, Seattle, Salt Lake, Albuquerque, and Phoenix. Southwest service to San Francisco is expected to be added at some point in 2007. Be sure to check the rates of the other discount airlines that serve Las Vegas, such as AirTran, jetBlue, Midwest Airlines, Spirit Airlines, and Ted.

Airline Contacts Alaska Air (☎800/426–0333 ⊕www.alaskaair.com). **American Airlines** (☎800/433–7300 ⊕www.aa.com). **ATA** (☎800/435–9282 or 317/282–8308 ⊕www.ata.com). **Continental Airlines** (☎800/523–3273 for U.S. and Mexico reservations, 800/231–0856 for international reservations ⊕www.continental.com). **Delta Airlines** (☎800/221–1212 for U.S. reservations, 800/241–4141 for international reservations ⊕www.delta.com). **jetBlue** (☎800/538–2583 ⊕www.jetblue.com). **Northwest Airlines** (☎800/225–2525 ⊕www.nwa.com). **Southwest Airlines** (☎800/435–9792 ⊕www.southwest.com). **Spirit Airlines** (☎800/772–7117 or 586/791–7300 ⊕www.spiritair.com). **United Airlines** (☎800/864–8331 for U.S. reservations, 800/538–2929 for international reservations ⊕www.united.com). **USAirways** (☎800/428–4322 for U.S. and Canada reservations, 800/622–1015 for international reservations ⊕www.usairways.com).

Smaller Airlines AirTran Airways (☎800/247–8726 ⊕www.airtran.com). **Allegiant Air** (☎877/202–6444 ⊕www.allegiantair.com). **Aloha** (☎800/367–5250 ⊕www.alohaairlines.com). **Frontier Airlines** (☎800/432–1359 ⊕www.flyfrontier.com). **Harmony Airways** (☎866/248–6789 ⊕www.hmyairways.com). **Hawaiian Airlines** (☎800/367–5320 ⊕www.hawaiianair.com). **Midwest Airlines** (☎800/452–2022 ⊕www.midwestexpress.com). **Sun Country Air** (☎800/359–6786 ⊕www.suncountryairlines.com). **Ted** (☎800/225–5833 ⊕www.flyted.com).

▌BY BUS

Greyhound provides regular Las Vegas service; the bus terminal is downtown. Visit its Web site for fare and schedule information. Cash, traveler's checks, and credit cards are accepted, but reservations are not. Seating is on a first-come, first-served basis. The most frequently plowed route out of Las Vegas is the one to Los Angeles, with departures a few times a day; the trip takes five to seven hours, depending on stops. The fare is about $45 one-way. Arriving at the bus station 30 to 45 minutes before your bus departs nearly always ensures you a seat. On Sunday evening and Monday morning, arriving an hour or more before departure is recommended.

The county-operated Citizens Area Transit (CAT) runs local buses throughout the city and to most corners of sprawling Las Vegas Valley. The overall quality of bus service along the main thoroughfares is good. Nonlocals typically only ride CAT buses up and down the Strip, between Mandalay Bay and the Stratosphere. Some continue on to the Downtown Transportation Center. If you're heading to outlying areas, you may need to change buses downtown. Mornings and afternoons the buses are frequently crowded, with standing-room only. The fare for CAT buses on the Strip is $2 (exact change required; $1 bills are accepted); $5 24-hour passes are also available. The buses stop on the street in front of all the major hotels every 10 minutes (in a perfect world) between 5:30 AM and 1:30 AM and every 15 minutes between 1:30 AM and 5:30 AM. Because traffic is quite heavy along the Strip, however, delays are frequent. Other routes serve the Meadows and Boulevard shopping malls and Sam's Town Hotel and Casino, on Boulder Highway. The operating hours for most buses, other than those along the Strip, are 5 AM–1:30 AM daily; the fare is $1.25 and must be paid with exact change or with tokens, which are available at the Downtown Transportation Center.

The Las Vegas Strip Trolleys are a bit more charming with their old-fashioned appearance, and they deliver you right to the door of most major casinos on the Strip and downtown. Bear in mind, however, that providing door-to-door delivery makes them a little slower, as they have to fight the knots of cabs, limos, airport shuttles, and private vehicles that collect at every casino at any hour of the day. From 9:30 AM to 1:30 AM, the Trolleys travel every 15 to 20 minutes among Strip hotels, with stops at the Fashion Show Mall (service is every 30 minutes or so along the southern end of the Strip and downtown). Look for the Trolley signs. The exact fare of $2.50 is required when you board, and all-day passes cost $6.50.

Bus Information **Downtown Transportation Center** (☎702/228–7433).

Greyhound (☎800/231–2222 ⊕www.greyhound.com).

Citizens Area Transit (☎702/228–7433 or 800/228–3911 ⊕www.rtcsouthern-nevada.com/cat/). **Las Vegas Strip Trolley** (☎702/382–1404).

▌ BY CAR

Though you can get around Las Vegas fine without a car, the best way to experience the city can be to drive it. A car gives you easy access to all the casinos and attractions; lets you make excursions to Lake Mead, Hoover Dam, and elsewhere at your leisure; and gives you the chance to cruise the Strip and bask in its neon glow. If you plan to spend most of your time on the Strip, a car may not be worth the trouble, but otherwise, especially given the relatively high costs of taxis, renting or bringing a car is a good idea.

Parking on and around the Strip, although free, can require a bit of work. You'll have to brave some rather immense parking structures. Valet parking is available but can take a while at busy times and requires that you tip the valets ($1 to $2). Still, it's usually less expensive to rent a

car and drive around Vegas, or to use the monorail, than to cab it everywhere.

Las Vegas is an easy city to navigate. The principal north–south artery is Las Vegas Boulevard (I–15 runs roughly parallel to it, less than a mile to the west). A 4-mi stretch of Las Vegas Boulevard South is known as the Strip, where a majority of the city's hotels and casinos are clustered. Many major streets running east–west (Tropicana Avenue, Flamingo Road, Desert Inn Road, Sahara Avenue) are named for the casinos built at their intersections with the Strip. Highway 215 and I–15 circumnavigate the city, and the I–515 freeway connects Henderson to Las Vegas. Because the capacity of the streets of Las Vegas has not kept pace with the city's incredible growth, traffic can be slow at virtually any time, especially on the Strip, and particularly in the late afternoon, in the evening, and on weekends. At those times drive the streets parallel to Las Vegas Boulevard: Paradise Road, to the east, and Industrial Road/Dean Martin Drive, to the west. The Industrial Road shortcut (from Tropicana Avenue almost all the way to downtown) can save you an enormous amount of time. You can enter the parking lots at Caesars Palace, the Mirage, Treasure Island, Fashion Show Mall, the Stardust, the New Frontier, and Circus Circus from Industrial Road. Exit Frank Sinatra Drive off I–15 North, and you can access the hotels from Mandalay Bay to Bellagio.

Visitors from Southern California should at all costs try to avoid traveling to Las Vegas on a Friday afternoon and returning home on a Sunday afternoon. During these traditional weekend-visit hours, driving times can be more than twice as long as during other, nonpeak periods.

GASOLINE

It's easy to find gas stations, most of which are open 24 hours, all over town. There aren't any gas stations along the main stretch of the Strip, but you will find them within a mile of the Strip in either direction, along the main east–west cross streets. Gas is relatively expensive in Las Vegas, generally 30¢ to 40¢ per gallon above the national average. There's no one part of town with especially cheap or pricey gas, although the stations nearest the airport tend to charge a few cents more per gallon—it's prudent to fill up your car rental before returning it a few miles away from the airport.

PARKING

You can't park anywhere on the Strip itself, and Fremont Street in the casino district downtown is a pedestrian mall closed to traffic. Street parking regulations are strictly enforced in Las Vegas, and meters are continuously monitored, so whenever possible it's a good idea to leave your car in a parking lot or garage. Free self-parking is available in the massive garages and lots adjacent to virtually every hotel, although you may have to hunt for a space, and you can wind up in the far reaches of immense facilities. You can avoid this challenge by paying for valet parking (charges vary greatly from property to property). Parking in the high-rise structures downtown is generally free or inexpensive, as long as you validate your parking ticket with the casino cashier.

ROAD CONDITIONS

It might seem as if every road in Las Vegas is in a continuous state of expansion or repair. Orange highway cones, road-building equipment, and detours are ubiquitous. But once the roads are widened and repaved, they're efficient and comfortable. The city's traffic-light system is state of the art, and you can often drive for miles on major thoroughfares, hitting green lights all the way. Signage is excellent, both on surface arteries and on freeways. The local driving style is fast and can be less than courteous. Watch out for unsignaled lane changes and turns.

For information on weather conditions, highway construction, and road clo-sures, visit the Web site of the Nevada Department of Transportation (⊕*www. nevadadot.com/traveler*) or call the department by dialing 511 in Nevada or 800/427–7623 from outside the state.

ROADSIDE EMERGENCIES

You can call 911 from most locations in Nevada to reach police, fire, or ambulance assistance. Otherwise, dial the operator. If you have a cellular or digital phone, dial *647 to reach the Nevada Highway Patrol.

RULES OF THE ROAD

Always strap children under age five or under 40 pounds into approved child-safety seats. In Nevada children must wear seat belts regardless of where they're seated.

The speed limit on residential streets is 25 mph. On major thoroughfares it's 45 mph, though drivers often get impatient with people who obey the speed limit and pass on either side—in part because radar detectors are legal and widely used. On the interstate and other divided highways within the city, the speed limit is a fast 65 mph; outside the city the speed limit is 70 or 75 mph. Police officers are highly vigilant about speeding laws within Las Vegas, especially in school zones, but enforcement in rural areas is fairly rare. Similarly, the Las Vegas police are extremely aggressive about catching drunk drivers—you are considered legally impaired if your blood-alcohol level is .08% or higher (this is also the law in neighboring states). California's speed limit is 70 mph. Right turns are permitted on red lights after coming to a full stop. Nevada requires seat-belt use in the front and back seats of vehicles. Chains are required on Mt. Charleston and in other mountainous regions when snow is fresh and heavy; signs indicate conditions. Nevada has no restrictions on handheld cellular phones.

304 <   **Transportation**

▌ BY MONORAIL

The monorail, which was begun in 1995 and greatly expanded in 2004, gives Las Vegas an even more Disney-esque look. The monorail stretches from MGM Grand, on the south, to the Sahara, to the north, with several stops in between, and makes the 4-mi trip in about 14 minutes. To head farther south to Mandalay Bay, walk across the Strip and pick up the small, free monorail at the Excalibur. To the north, a downtown monorail extension is in the planning stages but completion is several years away. Also, although it's a fairly short walk (10 minutes tops) between the Mirage and Treasure Island casinos, you can also get between them on the free tram that runs roughly every 10 to 15 minutes, 9 AM–1 AM.

The monorail runs Monday–Thursday 7 AM–2 AM, Friday–Sunday 7 AM–3 AM. Fares are $5 for one ride, $9 for two rides, $35 for 10 rides, $15 for a one-day pass, and $40 for a three-day pass. You can purchase tickets at station vending machines or in advance online.

Contacts **Las Vegas Monorail Company** (☎ 702/699–8200 ⊕ www.lvmonorail.com).

▌ BY TAXI

Las Vegas is heavily covered by 16 taxi companies. You can find cabs waiting at the airport and at every hotel in town. If you dine at a restaurant off the Strip, the restaurant will call a cab to take you home. ▌TIP➔ **Cabs aren't allowed to pick up passengers on the street, so you can't hail a cab New York–style. You have to wait in a hotel taxi line or call a cab company.**

The fare is $3.20 on the meter when you get in, plus $2 for every mile. Also, in slow traffic, a $0.25 charge may be incurred every 41 seconds. Taxis are limited by law to carrying a maximum of four passengers, and there's no additional charge per person. No fees are assessed for luggage, but taxis leaving the airport are allowed

to add an airport surcharge of $1.20. Drivers should be tipped around 15% for good service (⇨ *Tipping*). Drivers cannot accept credit cards and carry only nominal change with them.

If it's busy on the Strip (and most often, it is), ask your driver to take the Industrial Road shortcut. It runs parallel to the Strip and can cut your fare substantially. Some drivers may advise you to take I–15 instead, but this is almost always more expensive than Industrial Road. ▌TIP➔ **Be sure to specify to your driver that you do not want to take I–15 or the airport tunnel on your way to or from the airport. This is always the longer route distance-wise, which means it's the most expensive, but it can sometimes save you 5 to 10 minutes on the trip, if traffic is heavy on the Strip.** You have every right to ask your driver about the routes he or she is using; don't be afraid to speak up. If you have trouble with your cab driver, be sure to get his or her name and license number and call the Taxi Cab Authority to report the incident.

Taxi Companies **Checker/Yellow/Star** (☎ 702/873–2000). **Desert Cab** (☎ 702/386–9102). **Taxi Cab Authority** (☎ 702/668–4000 ⊕ www.taxi.state.nv.us). **Whittlesea/Henderson Cab** (☎ 702/384–6111).

ON THE GROUND

▌BUSINESS SERVICES & FACILITIES

Las Vegas is one of the nation's leading convention destinations, and all of the major hotels in town have comprehensive convention and meeting-planning space and services. The best business centers in town are run by the chain FedEx Kinko's, which has about a dozen locations throughout the area, with the Hughes Center Drive outpost (open 24 hours) being the closest one to the Strip.

Contacts FedEx Kinko's (✉ 395 Hughes Center Dr. ☎ 702/951–2400 ⊕ www.fedex. kinkos.com).

▌COMMUNICATIONS

INTERNET

As is the case in all major U.S. cities, high-speed and Wi-Fi are ubiquitous throughout Las Vegas, at virtually every major hotel in town (sometimes for a fee of anywhere from $5 to $15 per 24-hour period, sometimes for free) as well as at numerous cafés, restaurants, and other shops and businesses throughout the city.

Contacts Cybercafes (⊕ www.cybercafes. com) lists more than 4,000 Internet cafés worldwide.

▌DAY TOURS & GUIDES

BOAT TOURS

The *Desert Princess,* a 300-passenger Mississippi River–style stern-wheeler, and *Desert Princess Too,* a 149-passenger Mississippi River–style paddle wheeler, cruise Lake Mead. Tours include 90-minute sightseeing cruises, two-hour pizza party cruises, two-hour dinner and champagne brunch cruises, and three-hour dinner-and-dancing excursions.

CON OR CONCIERGE?

Good hotel concierges are invaluable—for arranging transportation, getting reservations at the hottest restaurant, and scoring tickets for a sold-out show or entrée to an exclusive nightclub. They're in the know and well connected. That said, sometimes you have to take their advice with a grain of salt.

It's not uncommon for restaurants to ply concierges with free food and drink in exchange for steering diners their way. Indeed, European concierges often receive referral *fees.* Hotel chains usually have guidelines about what their concierges can accept. The best concierges, however, are above reproach. This is particularly true of those who belong to the prestigious international society of Les Clefs d'Or.

What can you expect of a concierge? At a typical tourist-class hotel you can expect him or her to give you the basics: to show you something on a map, make a standard restaurant reservation (particularly if you don't speak the language), or help you book a tour or airport transportation. In Asia concierges perform the vital service ...riting out the name or address of your ...nation for you to give to a cab driver.

Savvy concierges at the finest hotels and resorts, can arrange for just about any good or service imaginable—and do so quickly. You should compensate them appropriately. A $10 tip is enough to show appreciation for a table at a hot restaurant. But the reward should really be much greater for tickets to that U2 concert that's been sold out for months or for those last-minute sixth-row-center seats for *The Lion King.*

Tour Operators Lake Mead Cruises (✉Lake
Mead marina ☎702/293–6180 ⊕www.lake-
meadcruises.com).

BUS TOURS

Gray Line and several other companies
offer Las Vegas city and neon-light tours;
trips to Red Rock Canyon, Lake Mead,
Colorado River rafting, Hoover Dam,
and Valley of Fire; and longer trips to different sections of the Grand Canyon.

Tour Operators **Gray Line Tours**
(☎702/384–1234 or 800/634–6579 ⊕www.
graylinelasvegas.com).

HELICOPTER TOURS

Helicopters do two basic tours in and
around Las Vegas: a brief flyover of the
Strip and a several-hour trip out to the
Grand Canyon and back.

Tour Operators **Maverick Helicopters Tours**
(☎702/261–0007 or 888/261–4414 ⊕www.
maverickhelicopter.com). **Papillon Grand
Canyon Helicopters** (☎702/736–7243 or
888/635–7272 ⊕www.papillon.com). **Sundance Helicopters** (☎702/736–0606 or
800/653–1881 ⊕www.helicoptour.com).

▮ HEALTH

The dry desert air in Las Vegas means
that your body will need extra fluids,
especially during the punishing summer
months. Always drink lots of water even
if you're not outside very much. When
you're outdoors, wear sunscreen and
always carry water with you if you plan
a long walk.

▮ HOURS OF OPERATION

Las Vegas is a 24-hour city 365 days a
year. Casinos, bars, supermarkets, almost
all gas stations, even some health clubs
and video stores cater to customers at all
hours of the day and night (many people
work odd hours here).

Most museums and attractions are open
seven days a week.

Most pharmacies are open seven days a
week from 9 to 7. Many, though, including local outposts of Walgreens, Rite Aid,
and CVS pharmacy, several of them on
the Las Vegas Strip, offer 24-hour and
drive-through services.

Shopping hours vary greatly around
town, but many stores are open weekdays and Saturday from 9 or 10 until
9 or 10 and Sunday 10 or 11 until 5 or
6. The souvenir shops on the Strip and
downtown often remain open until midnight, and some are open 24 hours. Quite
a few grocery stores are open around
the clock.

▮ MONEY

The prices of typical items in Las Vegas
can be gratis or outrageous. For example, you can get a deli sandwich at one of
the rock-bottom casino snack bars (Riviera, Four Queens) for $3–$4, or you can
spend $15 for a "George Foreman" at the
Stage Deli in the Forum Shops at Caesars.
A cup of coffee in a casino coffee shop
or Starbucks will set you back $2 to $5,
while that same cup is free if you happen
to be sitting at a nickel slot machine when
the cocktail waitress comes by. A taxi
from the airport to the MGM Grand goes
as low as $10 if you tell the driver to take
Tropicana Avenue and there's no traffic
or runs as high as $25 if you take the Air-
port Connector and there's a wreck on
the freeway. The more you know about
Las Vegas, the less it'll cost you.

ATMs are widely available in Las Vegas;
they're at every bank and at virtually all
casinos, hotels, convenience stores, and
gas stations. In addition, all casinos have
cash-advance machines, which take credit
cards. You just indicate how large a cash
advance you want, and when the transaction is approved, you pick up the cash at
the casino cashier. But beware: you pay
up to a 12% fee in addition to the usual
cash-advance charges and interest rate
for this "convenience"; in most cases,
the credit-card company begins charging

interest the moment the advance is taken, so you will not have the usual grace period to pay your balance in full before interest begins to accrue. To put it another way, don't obtain cash this way.

ITEM	AVERAGE COST
Cup of Coffee	$2.50
Glass of Wine	$6
Glass of Beer	$5
Sandwich	$6
One-Mile Taxi Ride in Capital City	$5
Museum Admission	$10

Prices throughout this guide are given for adults. Substantially reduced fees are almost always available for children, students, and senior citizens.

CREDIT CARDS
Throughout this guide, the following abbreviations are used: **AE**, American Express; **D**, Discover; **DC**, Diners Club; **MC**, MasterCard; and **V**, Visa.

It's a good idea to inform your credit-card company before you travel, especially if you're going abroad and don't travel internationally very often. Otherwise, the credit-card company might put a hold on your card owing to unusual activity—not a good thing halfway through your trip. Record all your credit-card numbers—as well as the phone numbers to call if your cards are lost or stolen—in a safe place, so you're prepared should something go wrong. Both MasterCard and Visa have general numbers you can call (collect if you're abroad) if your card is lost, but you're better off calling the number of your issuing bank, since MasterCard and Visa usually just transfer you to your bank; your bank's number is usually printed on your card.

Reporting Lost Cards **American Express** (☎800/992-3404 in U.S., 336/393-1111 collect from abroad ⊕www.americanexpress. com). **Diners Club** (☎800/234-6377 in U.S.,

303/799-1504 collect from abroad ⊕www. dinersclub.com). **Discover** (☎800/347-2683 in U.S., 801/902-3100 collect from abroad ⊕www.discovercard.com). **MasterCard** (☎800/622-7747 in U.S., 636/722-7111 collect from abroad ⊕www.mastercard.com). **Visa** (☎800/847-2911 in U.S., 410/581-9994 collect from abroad ⊕www.visa.com).

TRAVELER'S CHECKS & CARDS
Some consider this the currency of the cave man, and it's true that fewer establishments accept traveler's checks these days. Nevertheless, they're a cheap and secure way to carry extra money, particularly on trips to urban areas. Both Citibank (under the Visa brand) and American Express issue traveler's checks in the United States, but Amex is better known and more widely accepted; you can also avoid hefty surcharges by cashing Amex checks at Amex offices. Whatever you do, keep track of all the serial numbers in case the checks are lost or stolen.

ATM machines in Vegas are ubiquitous, and it's the very rare business that does not accept credit cards, so it's hard to think of a good reason to use traveler's checks in this city. If you do plan on using them, ask before checking into a hotel room or sitting down to a meal to make sure the property accepts them, as not all Vegas businesses do.

American Express now offers a stored-value card called a Travelers Cheque Card, which you can use wherever American Express credit cards are accepted, including ATMs. The card can carry a minimum of $300 and a maximum of $2,700, and it's a very safe way to carry your funds. Although you can get replacement funds in 24 hours if your card is lost or stolen, it doesn't really strike us as a very good deal. In addition to a high initial cost ($14.95 to set up the card, plus $5 each time you "reload"), you still have to pay a 2% fee for each purchase in a foreign currency (similar to that of any credit card). Further, each time you use the card in an ATM you pay a transaction

FOR INTERNATIONAL TRAVELERS

CURRENCY

The dollar is the basic unit of U.S. currency. It has 100 cents. Coins are the penny (1¢); the nickel (5¢), dime (10¢), quarter (25¢), half-dollar (50¢), and the very rare golden $1 coin and even rarer silver $1. Bills are denominated $1, $5, $10, $20, $50, and $100, all mostly green and identical in size; designs and background tints vary. You may come across a $2 bill, but the chances are slim.

The exchange rates at this writing are as follows: US$1.95 per British pound, $1.31 per Euro, 86¢ per Canadian dollar, 78¢ per Australian dollar, and 70¢ per New Zealand dollar.

CUSTOMS

Information **U.S. Customs and Border Protection** (⊕ www.cbp.gov).

DRIVING

Driving in the United States is on the right. Speed limits are posted in miles per hour (usually between 55 mph and 70 mph). Watch for lower limits in small towns and on back roads (usually 30 mph to 40 mph). Most states require front-seat passengers to wear seat belts; many states require children to sit in the back seat and to wear seat belts. In major cities rush hour is between 7 and 10 AM; afternoon rush hour is between 4 and 7 PM. To encourage carpooling, some freeways have special lanes, ordinarily marked with a diamond, for high-occupancy vehicles (HOV)—cars carrying two people or more.

Highways are well paved. Interstates—limited-access, multilane highways designated with an "I–" before the number—are fastest. Interstates with three-digit numbers circle urban areas, which may also have other limited-access expressways, freeways, and parkways. Tolls may be levied on limited-access highways. U.S. and state highways aren't necessarily limited-access, but may have several lanes.

Gas stations are plentiful. Most stay open late (24 hours along major highways and in big cities) except in rural areas, where Sunday hours are limited and where you may drive for long stretches without a refueling opportunity. Along larger highways, roadside stops with restrooms, fast-food restaurants, and sundries stores are well spaced. State police and tow trucks patrol major highways. If your car breaks down on an interstate, pull onto the shoulder and wait for help, or have your passengers wait while you walk to an emergency phone (available in most states). If you carry a cell phone, dial *55, noting your location on the small green roadside mileage marker.

ELECTRICITY

The U.S. standard is AC, 110 volts/60 cycles. Plugs have two flat pins parallel to each other.

EMERGENCIES

For police, fire, or ambulance, dial 911 (0 in rural areas).

EMBASSIES

Contacts **Australia** (☎ 202/797–3000 ⊕ www.austemb.org). **Canada** (☎ 202/682–1740 ⊕ www.canadianembassy.org). **United Kingdom** (☎ 202/588–7800 ⊕ www.britainusa.com).

HOLIDAYS

New Year's Day (Jan. 1); Martin Luther King Day (3rd Mon. in Jan.); Presidents' Day (3rd Mon. in Feb.); Memorial Day (last Mon. in May); Independence Day (July 4); Labor Day (1st Mon. in Sept.); Columbus Day (2nd Mon. in Oct.); Thanksgiving Day (4th Thurs. in Nov.); Christmas Eve and Christmas Day (Dec. 24 and 25); and New Year's Eve (Dec. 31).

MAIL

You can buy stamps and aerograms and send letters and parcels in post offices. Stamp-dispensing machines can occasionally be found in airports, bus and train stations, office buildings, drugstores, and convenience stores. U.S. mail boxes are stout, dark blue steel bins; pickup schedules are posted inside the bin (pull down the handle to see them). Parcels weighing more than a pound must be mailed at a post office or at a private mailing center.

Within the United States a first-class letter weighing 1 ounce or less costs 39¢; each additional ounce costs 24¢. Postcards cost 24¢. A 1-ounce airmail letter to most countries costs 84¢, an airmail postcard costs 75¢; a 1-ounce letter to Canada or Mexico costs 63¢, a postcard 55¢.

To receive mail on the road, have it sent c/o General Delivery at your destination's main post office (use the correct five-digit ZIP code). You must pick up mail in person within 30 days, with a driver's license or passport for identification.

There are post offices throughout Las Vegas, with the closest one to the Strip at 3100 Industrial Road, and the closest one to downtown at 201 Las Vegas Boulevard South. Most are open 8:30 until 5 on weekdays, and some are open Saturday (but with shorter hours). There is one branch, at 4801 Spring Mountain Road, that's open daily. There are drop boxes for overnight delivery services all over town as well as at UPS Stores in nearly every strip mall.

Contacts DHL (☎800/225–5345 ⊕www.dhl.com). **Federal Express** (☎800/463–3339 ⊕www.fedex.com). **Mail Boxes, Etc./ The UPS Store** (☎800/789–4623 ⊕www.mbe.com). **United States Postal Service** (⊕www.usps.com).

PASSPORTS & VISAS

Visitor visas aren't necessary for citizens of Australia, Canada, the United Kingdom, or most citizens of European Union countries coming for tourism and staying for fewer than 90 days. If you require a visa, the cost is $100, and waiting time can be substantial, depending on where you live. Apply for a visa at the U.S. consulate in your place of residence; check the U.S. State Department's special Visa Web site for further information.

Visa Information Destination USA (⊕www.unitedstatesvisas.gov).

PHONES

Numbers consist of a three-digit area code (702 in the Las Vegas region) and a seven-digit local number. Within many local calling areas you dial only the seven digits; in others you dial "1" first and all 10 digits—just as you would for calls between area-code regions. The same is true for calls to numbers prefixed by "800," "888," "866," and "877"—all toll free. For calls to numbers prefixed by "900" you must pay—usually dearly.

For international calls, dial "011" followed by the country code and the local number. For help, dial "0" and ask for an overseas operator. Most phone books list country codes and U.S. area codes. The country code for Australia is 61, for New Zealand 64, for the United Kingdom 44. Calling Canada is the same as calling within the United States, whose country code, by the way, is 1.

For operator assistance, dial "0." For directory assistance, call 555–1212 or occasionally 411 (free at many public phones). You can reverse long-distance charges by calling "collect"; dial "0" instead of "1" before the 10-digit number.

Instructions are generally posted on pay phones. Usually you insert coins in a slot (usually 25¢–50¢ for local calls) and wait for a steady tone before dialing. On long-distance calls the operator tells you how much to insert; prepaid phone cards, widely available in various denominations, can be used from any phone. Follow the directions to activate the card (there's usually an access number, then an activation code), then dial your number.

CELL PHONES

The United States has several GSM (Global System for Mobile Communications) networks, so multiband mobiles from most countries (except for Japan) work here. Unfortunately, it's almost impossible to buy a pay-as-you-go mobile SIM card in the U.S. without also buying a phone. That said, cell phones with pay-as-you-go plans are available for well under $100. The cheapest ones with decent national coverage are the GoPhone from Cingular and Virgin Mobile, which only offers pay-as-you-go service.

Contacts Cingular (☎888/333–6651 ⊕www.cingular.com). **Virgin Mobile** (☎No phone ⊕www.virginmobileusa.com).

fee of $2.50 on top of the 2% transaction fee for the conversion—add it all up and it can be considerably more than you would pay when simply using your own ATM card. Regular traveler's checks are just as secure and cost less.

Contacts **American Express** (☎888/412–6945 in U.S., 801/945–9450 collect outside of U.S. to add value or speak to customer service ⊕www.americanexpress.com).

▌ RESTROOMS

Free restrooms can be found in every casino.

Find a Loo **The Bathroom Diaries** (⊕www. thebathroomdiaries.com) is flush with unsanitized info on restrooms the world over—each one located, reviewed, and rated.

▌ SAFETY

The well-known areas of Las Vegas are among the safest places for visitors in the world. With so many people carrying so much cash, security is tight inside and out. The casinos have visitors under constant surveillance, and hotel security guards are never more than a few seconds away. Outside, police are highly visible, on foot and bicycles and in cruisers. But this doesn't mean you can throw all safety consciousness to the wind. You should take the same precautions you would in any city—be aware of what's going on around you, stick to well-lighted areas, and quickly move away from any situation or people that might be threatening—especially if you're carrying some gambling cash. When downtown, it's wise not to stray too far off the three main streets: Fremont, Ogden, and Carson between Main and Las Vegas Boulevard.

Be especially careful with your purse and change buckets around slot machines. Grab-and-run thieves are always looking for easy pickings, especially downtown.

Apart from their everyday vulnerability to aggressive men, women should have

---

WORST-CASE SCENARIO

All your money and credit cards have just been stolen. In these days of real-time transactions, this isn't a predicament that should destroy your vacation. First, report the theft of the credit cards. Then get any traveler's checks you were carrying replaced. This can usually be done almost immediately, provided that you kept a record of the serial numbers separate from the checks themselves. If you bank at a large international bank like Citibank or HSBC, go to the closest branch; if you know your account number, chances are you can get a new ATM card and withdraw money right away. **Western Union** (☎800/325–6000 ⊕www.westernunion.com) sends money almost anywhere. Have someone back home order a transfer online, over the phone, or at one of the company's offices, which is the cheapest option.

---

few problems with unwanted attention in Las Vegas. If something does happen inside a casino, simply go to any pit and ask a boss to call security. The problem will disappear in seconds. Outside, crowds are almost always thick on the Strip and downtown, and there's safety in numbers.

Men in Las Vegas need to be on guard against predatory women. "Trick roller" is the name of a particularly nasty breed of female con artist. These women are expert at meeting single men by "chance." After getting friendly in the casino, the woman joins the man in his hotel room, where she slips powerful knockout drugs into his drink and robs him blind. Some men don't wake up. Prostitution is illegal in Clark County.

▌TIP→ **Distribute your cash, credit cards, IDs, and other valuables between a deep front pocket, an inside jacket or vest pocket, and a hidden money pouch. Don't reach for the money pouch once you're in public.**

▌TAXES

The Las Vegas and Reno-Tahoe international airports assess a $6 departure tax, or passenger facility charge. The hotel room tax is 9% in Las Vegas.

The sales tax rates for the areas covered in this guide are: Las Vegas, 7.5%; Arizona, 5.85%; and California, 7.25%.

▌TIME

The states of Nevada and California are in the Pacific time zone. Arizona is in the mountain time zone. Arizona does not observe daylight saving time.

▌TIPPING

Just as in other U.S. destinations, workers in Las Vegas are paid a minimal wage and rely on tips to make up the primary part of their income. A $1 tip per drink is appropriate for cocktail waitresses, even when they bring you a free drink at a slot machine or casino table. On package tours, conductors and drivers usually get $10 per day from the group as a whole; check whether this has already been figured into your cost. For local sightseeing tours, you may individually tip the driver-guide $5 if he or she has been helpful or informative. Tip dealers with the equivalent of your average bet once or twice an hour if you're winning; slot-machine change personnel and keno runners are accustomed to a buck or two. Ushers in showrooms may be able to get you better seats for performances for a gratuity of $5 or more. Tip the concierge 10%–20% of the cost of a ticket to a hot show. Tip $5–$10 for making dinner reservations or arrangements for other attractions.

TIPPING GUIDELINES FOR LAS VEGAS	
Bartender	$1 to $5 per round of drinks, depending on the number of drinks.
Bellhop	$1 to $5 per bag, depending on the level of the hotel
Coat Check Personnel	$1 to $2 per item checked; if there's a fee, nothing.
Hotel Concierge	$5 or more, if he or she performs a service for you
Hotel Doorman	$1 to $2 if he helps you get a cab
Hotel Maid	$1 to $3 a day (either daily or at the end of your stay, in cash)
Hotel Room-Service Waiter	$1 to $2 per delivery, even if a service charge has been added
Porter at Airport or Train Station	$1 per bag
Restroom Attendants	$1 or small change
Skycap at Airport	$1 to $3 per bag checked
Taxi Driver	15% to 20%, but round up the fare to the next dollar amount
Valet Parking Attendant	$1 to $2, but only when you get your car
Waiter	15% to 20%, with 20% being the norm at high-end restaurants; nothing additional if a service charge is added to the bill

INDEX

PHOTO CREDITS

Cover Photo (Slot machine in casino): *Sean Murphy/Stone/Getty Images*. 5, *Michelle Chaplow/Alamy*. **Chapter 1: Experience Las Vegas:** 7, *Ken Ross/viestiphoto.com*. 8 (top), *Darius Koehli/age fotostock*. 8 (bottom), *Las Vegas News Bureau/LVCVA*. 9 (top), *Corbis*. 9 (bottom), *Ken Ross/viestiphoto.com*. 10, *Bob Brye/LVCVB*. 14 (left), *Tomasz Rossa*. 14 (right), *Hervè Donnezan/age fotostock*. 15 (left), *David Zanzinger/Alamy*. 15 (top center), *Bob Brye/LVCVB*. 15 (bottom center), *JTB Photo/Alamy*. 15 (top and bottom right), *MGM Mirage*. 16 (left), *Richard Cummins/viestiphoto.com*. 16 (top right), *Brent Bergherm/age fotostock*. 16 (bottom right), *Ken Ross/viestiphoto.com*. 17, *Liane Cary/age fotostock*. 18, *Buzz Pictures/Alamy*. 19, *Richard Cummins/viestiphoto.com*. 21 (left), *Brian Jones/LVCVB*. 21 (right), *Kerrick James/Alamy*. 22, *Angelo Cavalli/Marka*. 23 (left), *Palms Casino Resort*. 23 (top right), *Michelle Chaplow/Alamy*. 23 (bottom right), *Green Valley Ranch Resort, Spa and Casino*. 24 (top left), *Digital Vision*. 24 (top right), *Harrah's Entertainment, Inc*. 24 (bottom left), *Ian O'Leary/Mode Images Limited*. 24 (bottom right), *Four Seasons Las Vegas*. 25 (top left and bottom left), *Digital Vision*. 25 (top right), *Hard Rock Hotel and Casino*. 25 (bottom right), *MGM Mirage*. 26 (top left), *Corey Weiner/Hyatt Lake Las Vegas*. 26 (top right), *MGM Mirage*. 26 (bottom), *Tropicana Resort and Casino*. 27 (top left), *Palms Casino Resort*. 27 (top right and bottom), *Green Valley Ranch Resort, Spa and Casino*. 28, *David Sanger Photography/Alamy*. 29, *Ron Niebrugge/Alamy*. 30, *Atomic Testing Museum*. 31, *Richard Faverty/Beckett Studios*. 32, *Pictorial Press Ltd/Alamy*. 33 (left), *Kevin Foy/Alamy*. 33 (right), *Brian Jones/LVCVB*. 34, *(c) 2006 Ansel Adams Publishing Rights Trust Courtesy Center for Creative Photography, University of Arizona/Bellagio Gallery of Fine Art*. 36, *José María Riola/age fotostock*. 38, *Richard Cummins/viestiphoto.com*. **Chapter 2: Where to Stay and Play:** 41, *Stuart Pearce/World Pictures/age fotostock*. 42 (top), *Richard Cummins/viestiphoto.com*. 42 (center), *Hank Delespinasse/age fotostock*. 42 (bottom), *Ian Dagnall/Alamy*. 44, *Palms Casino Resort*. 46–47, *MGM Mirage*. 49, *LOOK Die Bildagentur der Fotografen GmbH/Alamy*. 50, *Stuart Pearce/World Pictures/age fotostock*. 52, *Harrah's Entertainment, Inc.*. 53–55, *Hard Rock Hotel & Casino*. 56, *SuperStock/age fotostock*. 58–59, *MGM Mirage*. 62, *Brad Mitchell/Alamy*. 64, *MGM Mirage*. 65, *LVCVB*. 67, *MGM Mirage*. 68, *Joe Viesti/viestiphoto.com*. 70, *Ken Ross/viestiphoto.com*. 71–73, *Palms*. 74, *Emmanuel Coupe/Alamy*. 76, *Stuart Pearce/World Pictures/age fotostock*. 77–79, *MGM Mirage*. 80, *Las Vegas Sands Corp*. 82, *Brent Bergherm/age fotostock*. 83, *LVCVB*. 85, *PCL/Alamy*. 86, *Starwood Hotels and Resorts*. 87, *MGM Mirage*. 88 (top), *Wynn Las Vegas*. 88 (bottom), *Las Vegas Sands Corporation*. 89 (top and bottom), *MGM Mirage*. 90 (top and bottom), *Ritz-Carlton Las Vegas*. 91 (top and bottom), *MGM Mirage*. 92, *Four Seasons Hotel Las Vegas*. **Chapter 3: Gamble:** 103, *Rex Argent/Alamy*. 109, *Harrah's Entertainment, Inc*. 112, *Greg Vaughn/Alamy*. 117, *imagesource.com/Punchstock*. 124, *Photo Network/Alamy*. 129, *Ken Ross/Alamy*. 132, *Javier Larrea/age fotostock*. 134, *M. Timothy O'Keefe/Alamy*. 138, *Mark Harmel/Alamy*. **Chapter 4: Where to Eat:** 141–42, *MGM Mirage*. 149 (top), *Station Casinos*. 149 (bottom left), *Marie-Louise Avery/Alamy*. 149 (bottom right), *Harrah's Entertainmment, Inc*. 150 (top), *Wynn Las Vegas*. 150 (bottom), *Profimedia/Alamy*. 151 (top), *Darrin Bush/LVCVB*. 151 (bottom), *Rough Guides/Alamy*. 152 (top left), *Bill Sitzmann/Alamy*. 152 (top right), *Claver Carroll/age fotostock*. 152 (bottom), *José María Riola/age fotostock*. **Chapter 5: Shopping:** 185, *Ken Ross/viestiphoto.com*. 193 (left), *Ken Ross/viestiphoto.com*. 193 (top right), *Dooney & Bourke*. 193 (bottom right), *Agence Images/Alamy*. 194 (top left), *Jim Gianatsis*. 194 (top right), *Hermès Paris*. 194 (bottom left), *Tiffany & Co*. 194 (bottom right), *Mandalay Place*. 195 (left), *Alan King/Alamy*. 195 (top right), *Lladro*. 195 (right center), *Lacoste*. 195 (right bottom), *Las Vegas Sands Corporation*. **Chapter 6: Shows:** 205, *Ricardo Funari/age fotostock*. 206, *Tomasz Rossa*. 207, *Tropicana Resort and Casino*. **Chapter 7: After Dark:** 225, *Douglas Peebles Photography/Alamy*. 241 (left), *Trinette Reed/Brand X Pictures/Jupiter Images*. 241 (top right), *Adam Taplin*. 241 (bottom right), *Pedro Coll/age fotostock*. 242 (top left), *Nick Leary*. 242 (top right), *foodfolio/Alamy*. 242 (bottom left), *Chloe Johnson/Alamy*. 242 (bottom right), *Stuart Pearce/age fotostock*. 243 (top left), *Trinette Reed/Brand X Pictures/Jupiter Images*. 243 (top right), *foodfolio/Alamy*. 243 (center), *Mode Images Limited/Alamy*. 243 (bottom), *Pierre D'Alancaisez/Alamy*. 244 (top), *MGM Mirage*. 244 (bottom), *Thinkstock/Jupiter Images*. **Chapter 8: Best Side Trips:** 251, *LVCVB*.

ABOUT OUR WRITERS

Former Fodor's staff editor Andrew Collins lives in Albuquerque, New Mexico, but has been regularly road-tripping to Vegas for years (the drive, if you go the back way past the Grand Canyon and Zion national parks, is amazing). He updated the Where to Eat , and Smart Travel Tips chapters, as well as the lodging portion of the Where to Stay and Play chapter, and he wrote our illustrated features The Pool Scene and Best Buffets, largely by sneaking anonymously around casinos, restaurants, and museums and trying not to look suspicious. He's the author of Fodor's *Gay Guide to the USA* and has written or contributed to dozens of other guidebooks. He's the expert "guide" on gay travel for About.com, and he writes for a variety of publications (including *Travel + Leisure, Sherman's Travel, Sunset, Out Traveler,* and *New Mexico Magazine*).

Born and raised in that most exotic of all travel destinations, New Jersey, Gary Lippman has previously written on travel for a number of publications. Lippman entered the savage jungle of modern Las Vegas nightlife prepared for anything. Armed with emergency flares, an elephant gun, a pith helmet, mosquito netting, plenty of insect repellent, and gifts for the natives, he took down names, took no prisoners, and emerged bloodied but unbowed, ready to share his tales with Fodor's readers.

Swain Scheps became hooked on Las Vegas while at The University of Texas after he and three friends piled into a compact car and drove 25 hours through a blizzard just to spend a few hours on the Strip. Since then he's returned to Nevada countless times and has written or ghost-written on the topic of gambling in a variety of formats, most recently contributing to Kevin Blackwood's *Casino Gambling for Dummies.* For this edition, Swain updated the Gambling chapter and wrote the Bachelor/Bachelorette party piece. He lives in Dallas, Texas, with his wife, Nancy, and four dogs.

Mike Weatherford came to us well prepared for the task of revising the Shows and Where to Stay & Play chapters of this book. He's lived in Las Vegas since 1987, is the author of *Cult Vegas—The Weirdest! The Wildest! The Swingin'est Town on Earth,* and, because he's the entertainment reporter for the *Las Vegas Review-Journal,* sees all the shows.